FRONTIER CAVALRYMAN

LIEUTENANT JOHN BIGELOW WITH THE BUFFALO SOLDIERS IN TEXAS

SECOND LIEUTENANT JOHN BIGELOW, JR.

FRONTIER CAVALRYMAN

LIEUTENANT JOHN BIGELOW WITH THE BUFFALO SOLDIERS IN TEXAS

Marcos E. Kinevan
Brigadier General, USAF (Ret.)
Professor Emeritus of Law, USAF Academy

Texas
Western
Press
1998

The University of Texas at El Paso
El Paso, Texas 79968-0633

First Edition
Library of Congress Catalog No. 96-61728
ISBN 0-87404-243-7

∞ Texas Western Press books are printed on acid-free paper, meeting the guidelines for permanence and durability of the Committee on Production Guidelines for Book Longevity of the Council on Library Resources.

For

Bobby

Contents

Illustrations

Photographs and Drawings

Maps

Acknowledgments

No work of this nature would be possible, of course, but for the assistance of many people. Among those to whom I am indebted are Lt. Gen. Winfield W. Scott, former Air Force Academy superintendent, and Lt. Gen. Erwin J. Rokke, former dean of faculty, who made possible my preliminary research concerning the nineteenth-century military justice system. I am grateful as well to my dedicated secretary, the late Julia Volosin, for her patience and assistance, and to my former deputy department head, Prof. Edward Hume, recently of West Point's Law Department, for his help in obtaining follow-up information there.

I appreciate the recommendations of Robert M. Utley that enabled this project to get under way most effectively, and the suggestions of Paul A. Hutton that led down some highly productive avenues. I am also beholden to Marie Capps, former manuscript librarian at West Point, for introducing me to the journals of John Bigelow, Jr., and to her capable successors, Judith A. Sibley and Susan Lintelmann, for their continuing assistance. Similarly, Director of Libraries Barbara Jones, Archivist Ellen H. Fladger, and Assistant Archivist Betty Allen at the Schaffer Library of Union College graciously furnished essential assistance in locating and granting access to long-lost portions of Bigelow's journals.

Numerous others also contributed to this effort, including Dr. Richard J. Sommers and Edward J. Drea of the Army's Military History Institute at Carlisle Barracks; Howard Wedmann of the Navy and Old Army Division and Maida Loescher of the Military Service Branch of the National Archives; Eric Bittner of the Rocky Mountain Region Branch of NARA; James Hutson, chief of the Manuscript Division at the Library of Congress; Julia Eddy and Diane Stevens of The Colorado College Library; and the specialists at several university libraries throughout the Southwest and as far away as Yale, as well as at the Colorado State Historical Society, Arizona State Historical Society, Wyoming Historical Research Division, and elsewhere.

In addition, I am grateful for the help of the archivists, historians, and rangers at national parks and historical sites, including Mary L. Williams of Fort Davis, John Neilson of Fort Concho, and Neil Mangum, formerly of the Custer Battlefield, as well as Fort Stockton Historical Society's Leanna Biles, Richard Roome, and Mary Kay Shannon, and the Menger Hotel's Anita Younes. And a special tip of the hat to all those at my "home" library, including Donald J. Barrett, archivist Duane J. Reed, government documents expert Betty Fogler, technician Bob Jennings, and especially Sharon Johnson and Kelly Merriam, directors of interlibrary loan. Further, my profound thanks to Associate Director Marcia Daudistel, and to Lisa Miller, Bobbi Gonzales, Nancy Hamilton, Mary Anne Maier, and the entire staff at Texas Western Press. They represent the quintessence of ability and professionalism in the realm of university pressdom, and any author who works with them is indeed fortunate.

Throughout this undertaking my wife, Bobby, has been indispensable not only for her ideas, proofing, other support, and encouragement, but also for the long hours spent with me in musty archives and in tramping over many parts of the former frontier to locate long-abandoned (and at times forgotten) sites that still faintly echo from the hardships of those who helped forge a civilization out of the wilderness.

Marcos E. Kinevan
Colorado Springs, Colorado
1998

Prologue

After graduating from the United States Military Academy in 1877, John Bigelow, Jr., chronicled his activities, observations, ideas, and musings as a new second lieutenant assigned to a company of African American cavalry soldiers in Texas. This book is based primarily on his journals from the fall of 1877 until the end of 1879, augmented by letters and memoirs of his associates and friends as well as other records and accounts.[1] Pieced together, they provide a better understanding of the events and conditions he describes and the issues then facing the army and the nation.

Bigelow was the son of a prominent New York family whose father—a lawyer, author, editor, publisher, and diplomat—was one of the nation's leading citizens.[2] Bigelow, Jr., an astute and perceptive young man characterized as an "aristocratic intellectual" by Edward Coffman and "remarkable" by Russell Weigley, was far more worldly than most of his contemporaries.[3] As a child he lived in Paris for five years and in Germany from ages sixteen to nineteen. At seventeen he enrolled at the University of Berlin, a year later transferred to the School of Mines in Freiburg, Saxony, and the following year accepted an appointment to West Point.[4]

Photographs portray an alert, slender individual of above-medium height with a mildly intense demeanor that belied his casual friendliness and wit. He clearly was a product of his time and breeding: a consummate gentleman, a sophisticate, and also an elitist. As a cadet he conscientiously performed his duties, but personal interests appear to have been more important to him than high rank, which might explain why he finished only forty-seven among the seventy-six members of his class.[5]

Because an awareness of West Point's impact on its graduates is necessary to understand their values, attitudes, and conduct, the book commences with a brief description of the Military Academy, its purposes and programs, the characteristics of appointees, and the experiences as cadets of the Class of '77. Next, the challenges confronting the army in the late 1870s are considered, followed by an explanation of how the assignments of graduates were determined and what significance they had. Bigelow became a member of the 10th Cavalry, one of only four regiments composed of black troops. The controversy surrounding the creation of these organizations in 1866 and their remarkable performances are examined, commencing with the 10th's initial years in Kansas at such transitory encampments as Mud Creek, Tar Creek, and Camp Buggy from which it protected settlers and railroad workers from bands of Cheyennes, Comanches, and Kiowas. The regiment later moved south into Indian Territory, and by the mid-1870s its companies were scattered across West Texas.

After the Class of 1877 graduated, a dispute erupted between Congress and the new president, Rutherford B. Hayes, which delayed appropriations for the army and resulted in six months of idleness before the new lieutenants reported for duty. Once the impasse was resolved, Bigelow commenced his trip by railroad from New York to San Antonio and by stage from there to the Rio Grande. His experiences and those of several classmates (some of whom became victims of "road agents") are related, and the conditions they found at their posts are described.

The focus then shifts to how Bigelow adjusted to his duties and life at Fort Duncan, a small garrison on the Rio Grande, where he promptly became commander of its only cavalry company. Although lacking experience or much training in handling his myriad duties, he explains how, with the help of capable sergeants, he was able to create a highly effective organization. He also discusses the problems he encountered, how he resolved them, and the enormous amounts of time he and most officers were required to devote to courts-martial. This leads to an analysis of the army's lumbering, antiquated criminal law system and its frequent abuse, especially by a few high-ranking officers who resorted to charges and counter-charges against each other over frivolous disputes.

By early 1878 a flare-up of Indian raids led to the transfer of Bigelow's company to Fort Stockton, requiring a two-week, multi-hundred-mile trek north that he narrates day by day. A few weeks later his principal and almost continuous duties became leading scouting parties of "Buffalo Soldiers" in search of "hostile" Indians over hundreds of miles throughout the vast and mostly uninhabited regions of West Texas. Then for three months his company, accompanied by "Comanche Jack" Stilwell, one of the army's most colorful civilian scouts, bivouacked at a remote subpost called Peña Blanca from which they patrolled the rugged Big Bend country. During this time the egregious misconduct of the company commander resulted in a court-martial that took Bigelow to San Antonio for several weeks as a witness.

Shortly after returning to Stockton he again became enmeshed as a witness in the trial of another officer for indecent behavior involving the eighteen-year-old daughter of a first lieutenant. Once more an extended stay in San Antonio was required. With virtually no responsibilities, the young bachelor led an active social life involving a number of prominent young ladies. The enforced idleness also enabled him to record the life and customs of that era, something usually found only in distaff accounts. Orders to rejoin his company finally rescued him from the overabundance of feminine companionship in which he had been submerged.

Leaving broken hearts behind, Bigelow returned to Stockton only long enough to set forth to command a small encampment from which he and his troops explored the White Sand Hills and adjacent regions frequented by Mescalero marauders from the Fort Stanton Reservation. While he searched for routes of travel, sources of water, and raiding parties, the first of two major Indian uprisings in 1879 occurred (one by Apaches in the Southwest and the other by Utes in Colorado). Several classmates were involved in the fighting, with three emerging with Medals of Honor. Bigelow's company soon joined in the conflicts, but before it did so he was unexpectedly ordered to West Point to teach French and tactics, leaving the frontier strife behind him for the next few years.

A primary purpose of this book is to provide an awareness not just of what young army officers did to help secure the frontier during the late 1870s, but of who they were and why they did it. For most of them a rigid code of duty, honor, and country was the cornerstone of their lives. Not all of their attitudes and actions were noble, of course. Egalitarian they were not, and the low repute in which many of them held African Americans, Indians, Mexicans, foreigners, and persons of different religious beliefs would now be considered blatantly racist or bigoted. Nevertheless, while some people today might ridicule the values held by these young men, none can successfully denigrate the importance of what they helped achieve. Bigelow's accounts and the supplemental materials also provide a springboard to a greater awareness of:

- how and why West Point educated, trained, and developed members of the thin blue line of young men sent forth to police the frontier—yet failed to prepare them for the type of fighting they found there;
- some of the major problems and issues then confronting the army and the country, which in addition to implementing national policies on the frontier included preparing for another war with Mexico;
- the discord surrounding the use of Negroes as soldiers in peacetime and the creation of "colored regiments" after the Civil War; the significant achievements of the mostly illiterate and widely scorned black troops during their long years on the frontier; why they were stationed in areas of searing summer heat while most white troops were in cooler places; and most importantly, their performances in combat that helped blur, if not erase, the color line and ultimately helped lead the armed forces to the forefront in racial integration and equality of opportunity;
- life on scouts and marches, at isolated subposts, and in army garrisons as viewed by the men who were there, with glimpses of such wide-ranging matters as the role of religion and why chaplains were often resented by many officers; the problems with scurvy; why desertion was a major problem among white (but not black) troops; and the consequences of requiring heavy woolen uniforms to be worn even during a West Texas summer, and of subsisting on substandard rations;

- how the obsolete military justice system functioned, and why its inordinate demands adversely affected the army's ability to perform its missions;
- the Victorian values and customs of community leaders, army officers, and their wives that helped shape manners, morals, and mores in the trans-Mississippi West;
- the negative views Bigelow formed about some military luminaries, but his high regard for others.

With limited exceptions the structure, punctuation, and spelling found in Bigelow's journal are intact. As few changes as possible have been made, and only when required to avoid confusion or distraction. (For example, "to day" and "can not" have become respectively "today" and "cannot.") Similarly, an occasional misspelling of a word or name might be noted by a [*sic*] the first time it appears but usually not thereafter. What Bigelow and his friends observed, experienced, and thought deserve to be read with minimal diversions.

CHAPTER 1

WEST POINT IN THE 1870s

> Education at a service academy is the...most crucial experience of a professional soldier.... (T)he academies set the standards of behavior...(and)...are the source of the pervasive "like-mindedness" about military honor and the sense of fraternity....[1]

Although fewer than 40 percent of the army's officers in the late 1870s were graduates of the Military Academy, the values inculcated in them not only permeated their lives but also set the standards for virtually all others.[2] What has been called the "Mystique of West Point"[3] was achieved in large part because of the military, academic, and personal demands relentlessly imposed on cadets in their monastic-like environment over a span of four years, and the severe consequences of even minor transgressions. The adversities shared by those who survived fused them into cohesive classes with coherent views on matters ranging from the military tradition of public service to gentlemanly behavior, group loyalty, allegiance, and personal valor.[4] A prerequisite to understanding these young men is an awareness of their academy experience.

WEST POINT: THE EARLY YEARS

After a controversial and rocky beginning in 1802 as little more than a training school for engineering and artillery officers, the fledgling United States Military Academy had floundered until 1817 when Sylvanus Thayer, a thirty-two-year-old brevet major, was appointed superintendent.[5] The bold innovations that he introduced during his sixteen-year tenure soon transformed West Point into the primary source of professional officers for all branches of the army, as well as the nation's first and for decades leading school of engineering.[6]

To prepare cadets for whatever might be required of them as officers, the "Thayer System" demanded successful completion of four years of academic and military programs within a harsh disciplinary environment that was designed to test their commitments to military life and develop self-control, confidence, and obedience to authority.[7] Thayer insisted that all cadets, even the new ones, be treated equally; established a uniform system of punishments for each violation of regulations; and dismissed anyone who exceeded a specified number of demerits. Except for the summer between the second and third year, annual vacations were rescinded in favor of a year-round schedule, cadets were prohibited from leaving the post without permission, and any practice that might imply favoritism or partiality was abolished.[8]

Thayer's totally prescribed curriculum concentrated on mathematics, science, engineering, and French while (contrary to most educational practices at that time) eschewing Greek, Latin, and other classical studies. The academic year extended from early September to late May, during which cadets marched to classes every day but Sunday when a short respite might be available after mandatory religious services;[9] preparation of lessons and graded recitations were required in every course every day;[10] grades were posted weekly to show each cadet how he compared to his classmates and to encourage competition; students were assigned to small sections based on their demonstrated abilities; Socratic instructional methods were used instead of lectures; comprehensive examinations were administered at the end of each semester; graduation occurred only once a year; and every student was ranked by an order of merit that determined the cadet rank he might attain and more importantly the branch of the army to which he might be assigned.

Military training, which had a secondary role to academics, took place in the summer and in late afternoon during the academic year. Most of the time was spent on drill, target practice, weaponry, fortifications, tactics; "practical instruction" in infantry, artillery, and cavalry; and exercises in ordnance, gunnery, signaling, and military engineering.[11] Cadets also became active in testing new weapons and the tactics needed to employ them most effectively.[12]

And superimposed on all else was developing the sine qua non of every officer: an unflinching sense of veracity, integrity, and personal honor.[13]

THE POST–CIVIL WAR ACADEMY

Thayer's concepts and policies remained essentially unchanged for more than a century. Although the affiliation between the academy and the Corps of Engineers diminished after the Civil War,[14] the intransigence of senior faculty members, many of whom were former students and disciples of Thayer, prevented much change, hence contributing to West Point's loss of its former preeminence in engineering.[15] In addition, contrary to Thayer's beliefs and despite disapproval by academy authorities, a severe and on occasion odious system of hazing developed among cadets.[16]

Military training in the latter third of the century continued to center on waging "civilized" war despite the recurring clashes on the distant frontier. The primary reason that little effort was devoted to teaching cadets how to either pacify or fight primitively armed Indians engaging in a guerrilla type of resistance was the widespread belief that the greatest threat to the nation's survival was a possible coastal or border attack by a formidable European power (most likely England). Hence, as a matter of priorities, scant effort was devoted to the small unit tactics employed on the Plains, so "nothing [cadets] learned at the academy prepared them to deal with such an elusive and tricky foe as the Indian."[17] Additionally, the academy persisted in cramming far too much into four years, leaving no room for more. With all but a minor portion of a cadet's time committed to the demanding academic curriculum, choices had to be made among other competing interests. In hindsight, of course, more effort could have been channeled into better preparation for what would immediately confront most graduates, but popular perceptions to the contrary, the academy's purpose was not simply to produce second lieutenants. Instead it was to develop the knowledge and character required for graduates to progress into positions of high responsibility and leadership. In other words, the goal was to turn out prospective generals, not just proficient junior officers, or as Sherman explained:

> The education imparted at West Point always has been and must continue to be preliminary, that is...calculated to prepare them for the work of life...so that a

cadet may graduate...and yet not be familiar with the knowledge indispensable to feed, clothe, manage, and fight a company or a regiment.[18]

But if West Point did not purport to be a training ground in "how to" be a second lieutenant, where was such skill to be acquired? One approach to this long-smoldering issue was a five-year program adopted in 1854 but abandoned in 1861 because of exigencies of the Civil War.[19] Another was the creation in 1881 of "schools of application" that had long been advocated by Lee, Sherman, and others, but for several years they too concentrated primarily on conventional warfare.[20] Consequently, throughout the Indian wars young graduates had to rely primarily on personal experience supplemented, if available, by the guidance of more experienced officers when dealing with unorthodox opponents who had never heard of Jomini, Clausewitz, or Mahan, nor seen a siege gun.[21] Nevertheless, having emerged from the Civil War with an enhanced reputation because of the battlefield achievements of its graduates,[22] West Point continued to attract some of the nation's best and brightest prospects.

HOW ASPIRANTS BECAME CADETS

A young man who wanted to be a cadet first had to obtain a nomination, most of which were made by congressmen or senators.[23] In early summer those who were successful reported to West Point, about sixty miles north of New York City, where they were subjected to a traumatic introduction to military discipline as well as lengthy qualifying examinations to determine whether they would be admitted or rejected. A few days later the nominees lined up to hear the results. As the names of the unlucky (or as one candidate in 1873 wrote, "many of us then thought the lucky")[24] were read, they stepped forward two paces, then gathered up their meager possessions to return to their homes or go their separate ways.[25]

In 1873 almost all of the 150 nominees for the Class of 1877, then the largest number in the academy's history, had reported by May 24. Officials first verified that each was unmarried, between the ages of seventeen and twenty-two, at least five feet tall, and free of any "infectious or immoral disorder" or any deformity, disease, or infirmity that might make him unfit for military service.[26] Several days later when the academic examinations and initial ordeals were concluded, eighty-six (about

57 percent) of the nominees were found qualified for appointment as cadets. They were later augmented by three "turnbacks," and before classes started an additional thirty-two nominees replaced some of those previously rejected.[27]

The group admitted to West Point that summer was dissimilar in several respects from the young men entering colleges and universities. Not only were all of them pursuing the same goal of becoming army officers, but the statutorily mandated nomination system assured a geographic diversity not then found on civilian campuses. Hence, clipped New England accents blended with the soft, slurred sounds of the Old South, the flat, nasal speech of the Midwest, and the twangy drawls of the Southwest. Additionally, as a group they were somewhat older than most of their civilian counterparts since a large number had already graduated from college or completed one or more years. Despite previous academic achievements, however, they were required to start over as the equivalent of freshmen.

Although many of the appointees (derisively known as "plebes") were products of "upper-middle-class" families (as were most college students at that time), some were there for the "free" education or to escape what they regarded as the ennui of farming or small-town life.[28] Regardless, sharply different backgrounds and attitudes were represented. At the highest end of the social and economic spectra, for example, was John Bigelow, Jr., whose journal is the gist of this book. Another member of an affluent family was Harry Hammond, the only appointee whose father, a railroad president and head of San Francisco's board of police commissioners, had graduated from West Point. Conversely, Henry Flipper, the seventeen-year-old son of former slaves, learned to read in a woodshed and with parental encouragement had striven to complete four years of study at Atlanta University. Although Flipper, who was to become the first African American graduate of West Point, was ostracized by most cadets, a few (including Bigelow, whose father had been a staunch abolitionist) covertly offered him encouragement.[29]

None of the new cadets had been old enough to serve in the Civil War, but almost one-fourth were from places where as children they witnessed some of the agony of that conflict. In addition to Flipper these included Henry Kirby, a Davidson College student born and raised on his father's South Carolina plantation; Charles Gatewood, a courtly young

JOHN BIGELOW, JR.
(Courtesy USMA Library)

HENRY OSSIAN FLIPPER
The son of slaves, he became West Point's first African American graduate. His potential for military greatness ended five years later with his dismissal from the army. (Courtesy USMA Library)

gentleman from Virginia; and John Haden, the son of a former Confederate officer. In contrast, Calvin Esterly's father had maintained an underground station in Ohio for escaping slaves, and as a boy Calvin often drove a wagon to the next station with an escapee hidden underneath a load of farm produce. Similarly, Albert Todd's father had moved his family from Connecticut to the new Kansas Territory in the mid-1850s to help prevent slavery from spreading there.

In addition to Todd a few other new cadets, such as Jacob Galbraith, also were acquainted with some of the hardships of the trans-Mississippi frontier. Galbraith was the son of the Indian agent at the Yellow Medicine, Minnesota, trading post. When the 1862 Santee Sioux Uprising broke out, he, his mother, and sixty other pioneers had been saved by John Other Day, a "converted" Indian who for days led them from the slaughtering sites to the safety of distant white settlements.

Charles Crane, one of the three turnbacks in the class, also was from the then-rawer regions of the country. He grew up near Independence, Texas, where his father, a less-than-prosperous Baptist clergyman, was president of Baylor University, from which Charles graduated at seventeen in the two-member Class of 1869. Because money was so scarce, he and a few friends organized a cattle drive to the terminus of the AT&SF railroad at Newton, Kansas, some 650 miles north. Swollen rivers and creeks, stampedes caused by lightning, Indian perils, and other obstacles (including several thousands of buffalo, part of the southern herd, that passed nearby) were encountered during the journey, which required almost five months. After hearing about West Point from another drover, Charles obtained a nomination, and with the few dollars he had saved from the cattle drive he purchased a coach ticket to New York. That winter, however, he succumbed to a severe case of rheumatism that resulted in his temporary disenrollment.[30] Another turnback was Louis Wilhelmi, a native of Prussia whose family had migrated to Pennsylvania. Similar to Crane, he had to leave in 1872 because of illness, but after rejoining the Corps of Cadets he lasted only a semester before a recurrence caused his discharge.[31]

More typical of the other appointees, Millard Eggleston had been raised on an Indiana farm and graduated from Wabash College. George Baxter, the son of a federal judge, had finished one year at the University of Tennessee and another at the University of the South. William

CHARLES CRANE

The son of an impoverished Baptist clergyman who was president of Baylor University, he could not have afforded to travel to West Point except for what remained of the $100 he earned on a five-month cattle drive to Kansas. (Courtesy USMA Library)

JOHN J. BRERETON

After studying law, he pursued a more adventuresome career in the army. He might have lived longer if he had stayed in New Jersey. (Courtesy USMA Library)

Galbraith had received a degree from the State College of Pennsylvania, then farmed for two years. Solon Massey, the son of a Sandusky, Ohio, physician, was an accomplished pianist and organist who had graduated from the University of Michigan in 1872, after which he "read medicine" for a year. Robert Emmet, whose great-granduncle was the Irish patriot of the same name, had grown up on a small estate near Pelham, New York, where he developed skills as a horseman and yachtsman while attending school in Westchester. James Paddock from Illinois and John McMartin from New York, both barely seventeen, were among those who had left home for the first time. Matthias Day, almost twenty, was a rambunctious and highly popular young man from Oberlin, Ohio. John Brereton had "read law" with a lawyer in Paterson, New Jersey, prior to deciding that he preferred a more adventuresome career. After teaching school in Pennsylvania for two years, Alexander Patch was appointed to West Point where he and Charles Crane roomed together for the next four years. In 1865, when he was thirteen, Francis Patten had left his Maine home for the University of Bonn, and while there he met Bigelow who was two years younger than he; after returning in 1869 Patten enrolled at Cornell but withdrew in his last year to attend the academy. And as a prelude to cadet life, Edwin Glenn, a fun-loving but somewhat lethargic son of a Greensboro, North Carolina, physician, had attended a preparatory school appropriately located in Sing Sing, New York, near another type of confinement facility.

WEST POINT, NEW YORK, JUNE 1873 TO JUNE 1877

During the next four years the experiences of the new cadets (then fourthclassmen or plebes) were generally similar to those of other classes at that time. They were initially assigned to one of the four cadet companies (which determined where and with whom they roomed and attended classes) on the basis of height, with the taller cadets such as Bigelow in either "A" or "D" (the "flank" companies) and the shorter ones in the interior (or "runt") companies.[32] A few weeks after their arrival the graduating Class of 1873 (firstclassmen or seniors) departed, much to the relief of the newcomers who had suffered through the first phase of "Beast Barracks" under their less-than-compassionate tutelage. Two weeks later the young appointees were marched to plebe camp, which they found "infinitely worse" than the earlier hazing they had endured.[33] Finally, in late August after many weary days of "boning gun" (learning to use firearms), sweeping tent floors for upperclassmen as well as themselves, carrying water, and being constantly tormented by their keepers, they returned to the relative comfort of the Spartan-like barracks for the start of the fall semester.[34]

Less than a month into the academic regimen, the collapse of the leading financial house of Jay Cooke and Company triggered the Panic of 1873 and the ensuing multi-year economic depression. During that fall twenty-two members of the class were separated (voluntarily or otherwise). After Christmas, which was spent far from families and friends on the bleak, cold banks of the Hudson, the next few months passed routinely. On May 20 the first of the 1874 nominees arrived, marking the long-awaited day of emancipation of the Class of 1877 from their lowly status as plebes. Ten classmates were lost because of spring examinations and one turnback was added. Until late June the new thirdclass (sophomore or "yearling") cadets were busy training the new appointees, after which the balance of the summer was devoted to target practice and other military activities.

Academics began again in September and in November riding instruction commenced, much to the pleasure of many cadets but to some city dwellers "the *bête noir* of their existence."[35] That fall twelve more members of the class were eliminated. In mid-June 1875 their long-awaited furlough began; then, after a summer of freedom, all but one cadet assembled in New York "ready, if not willing, to return to West Point" for their secondclass (junior or "cow") year.[36]

During the summer of 1875 disorderliness of the then-senior class during training camp resulted in all but four of the eighteen cadet officers being demoted to the ranks, and others being placed in arrest for sixty days.[37] The positions vacated were filled by members of '77, which was generally well behaved the rest of the year except for Richard Wilson, who attempted to amuse himself one dark October night by borrowing a sword from Matthias Day and prowling around after taps disguised as a "tactical officer" (a commissioned officer assigned to each cadet company) to terrify any plebe he might catch out of his room. After severely castigating the first person he met, he discovered that the suspect was himself a real, unamused "tac," a mistake that cost Wilson many dreary days of confinement and Day his rank as a cadet officer.[38]

CADET ROOM

During the day bedding had to be arranged as shown, shoes and clothing precisely aligned, and the room cleaned for daily inspection. Each occupant had a small table and chair as well as his own waterbucket, risking demerits for such infractions as "dust on water." (Courtesy USMA Library)

ARTILLERY DRILL

In summer and in late afternoon during the academic year cadets received military training. This shows a pause in drill at "Siege Battery." (Courtesy USMA Library)

BIGELOW AND FRIENDS, SUMMER CAMP 1876

Bigelow is third from left, looking to his left. (Courtesy USMA Library)

CADET OFFICERS, CLASS OF 1877

The person with three chevrons (a cadet captain) seated right of center is Albert Todd, and the lieutenant (two chevrons) on his left is John Bigelow. (Courtesy USMA Library)

For the first and only time in four years, the cadet battalion left the academy to take part in the Centennial Celebration, traveling by steamer to Jersey City and by train to Philadelphia where on the Fourth of July, 1876, they joined in the "grand procession." What revelry there was soon ended, however, as news reached the East of the disaster on the Little Big Horn and the death there of young Jim Sturgis, who had graduated just a year before.

The final year passed uneventfully except for the newly initiated hops (dances) in the fall and winter, and the customary New Year's Eve war dance around the gaslight in the center of the barracks area, during which some humorless tactical officers (a description cadets, then as now, would regard as redundant) appeared to disperse the mob.[39] On Hundredth Night a traditional show was presented by the firstclass, and for the remaining weeks preparations for graduation and departure were superimposed on academic and other duties. As the date for replacing cadet grey with army blue approached, merchants from New York made their perennial treks upriver to sell goods. Even though the massive depression of 1873 was nearing its fourth anniversary, the soon-to-be officers "were ready to purchase anything and everything," which even included a strange garment known as a "pajama" that one prodigal cadet bought.[40] After final examinations there was little to do until Graduation Ball on the night of June 13. At its end the members of '77 wearily trudged back for a final night of rest in the small and austere rooms that had been their homes for the past four years.

Chapter 2

The Challenges Awaiting '77

> I welcome you to the hardships and perils of a soldier's life in time of peace. The noise and the necessities of war drive men in upon themselves and keep their faculties awake and alert; but the seductive influence of peace, when a soldier must spend his time in preparation for the active duties of his profession rather than in their practice, is indeed a peril to which the horrors of warfare are subordinate. It is so much easier for men to fight other men than themselves.

So said Prof. Charles Oliver Thompson, newly appointed chairman of West Point's Board of Visitors, at the Military Academy's graduation ceremony on June 14, 1877.[1] He was one of four speakers on that warm and partly cloudy day when the graduating cadets, underclassmen, faculty, staff, dignitaries, families, and friends assembled in the grove of maple trees near the Library on the Plain above the Hudson River.

The professor was accurate enough about the risk of tedium in a peacetime army, even though he had never experienced military life in either peace or war.[2] In any event, the suggestion that warfare was preferable to peacetime service must have especially bemused that irascible warrior, William Tecumseh Sherman, commanding general of the army, who sat through the proceedings (patiently or otherwise), as well as Major Generals John M. Schofield and Winfield Scott Hancock who shared the podium. Veterans such as they and others present must have also found it strange that Professor Thompson was either uninformed about or failed to understand the continuing challenges that would confront the graduates as they helped accommodate the nation's relentless push westward.

Foremost, military service then involved the threat of another armed conflict with Mexico, which many people viewed as imminent.[3] Also, much remained to be done in many regions of the largely inhospitable West: areas were yet to be explored and tamed; safe travel by stagecoach and wagon train assured; roads and telegraph lines constructed and guarded; railroads forged and shielded; posts built or renovated; laws enforced; order maintained; government policy implemented; settlers protected; and friendly Indians safeguarded from the cupidity of some whites. Most of these tasks fell on the "peacetime" army that would soon be augmented by seventy-six new second lieutenants.

Furthermore, with the Custer disaster less than a year old, scattered and sporadic skirmishes and battles still lay ahead to embroil the fewer than 20,000 officers and men (about 80 percent of the army) garrisoned between the Missouri River and the Pacific.[4] In terms of the numbers of participants, the massive casualties, and the widespread suffering of the Civil War, the encounters between troops and those Indians resisting further encroachments were, of course, minuscule. Consequently most people not directly affected might have been only dimly aware of what was happening on the remote frontier and what its impact would be on the future of the nation. These apparently included the professor, whose views of army life seem to have been shaped in some idyllic place such as the shores of Walden Pond. Notwithstanding such obliviousness, however, casualties are casualties, and as Lt. Gen. Philip H. Sheridan reported from the Division of the Missouri in 1877:

> During the last two years the ratio of loss of officers and men in proportion to the number engaged in this Division in the Indian wars has been equal to or greater than the ratio of loss on either side in the present Russo-Turkish campaign or in the late Civil War in this country.[5]

In addition to Professor Thompson, the graduates also were addressed by General Hancock, whose corps had held the line on Cemetery Ridge against Pickett's charge, and who in 1867 led a major expedition against Indians. At least his experience lent credibility to his remarks.[6] He counseled them that:

> The lessons of hard service are salutary and necessary to give the soldier a practical understanding of the world and its ways as he will encounter them in war. I advise

> you to go when young to the Plains—to the wilderness—seek active service there, put off the days of indulgence and of ease...and by no means leave your books behind you.... There are many "extreme Western" posts today.... And if any of you wish to seek that service, your taste will not be difficult to gratify, for the hardest lessons will certainly be avoided by many.[7]

The general was correct: in 1877 a new lieutenant's taste for the wilderness was not difficult to gratify.

THE ASSIGNMENTS OF CADETS TO BRANCHES

The army's "Troops of the Line" then consisted of only five regiments of artillery, ten of cavalry, and twenty-five of infantry.[8] Except for three batteries at San Antonio, four of the five artillery regiments were garrisoned along the East Coast, while the fifth guarded the West Coast. Conversely, nine of the ten cavalry regiments were scattered over more than fifty posts from Canada to the Rio Grande and from Kansas to California, as were twenty of the twenty-five infantry regiments.

The number of officers and men policing the frontier was pitifully small because of successive reductions by Congress that had decreased the army to "an impotent state" of just 25,000 soldiers.[9] In 1876, partly in reaction to the events on the Little Big Horn, a temporary increase of 2,500 men in Indian-fighting cavalry units was authorized, and each company was permitted to have up to 100 men (a goal seldom reached) instead of the 87 previously specified.[10] In total numbers of officers on active duty in 1877, the infantry led with 877, followed by 566 on the General Staff, 439 in cavalry, 284 in artillery, and 199 in the Corps of Engineers.[11] About one-tenth of all officers were of foreign extraction, led by the Irish.[12]

In the post–Civil War era many line (combat) officers, most of whom were isolated in desolate western posts far from families and friends, enviously viewed staff officers as not only living comfortably in or near established cities, but also as having greater opportunities for promotion. To a lesser extent officers in the artillery as well as the Corps of Engineers and the non-line components (such as the Ordnance, Pay, and Quartermaster Departments) were also considered privileged. The advantages of such assignments undoubtedly influenced many of the top graduates in their choices of branches, and induced others who had been relegated to the hardships in the West to later seek staff positions. In addition, families and wives sometimes used whatever political influence they might have had in attempts to effect transfers of officers to "gilt-edged" details in the East, but not always with the results desired.[13] For example, when the secretary of interior asked that the senior captain of the 15th Infantry be detailed to his department "to do some clerical work," General Sherman's trenchant response was:

> When peace has so far corrupted the military service that a captain will leave his company to do clerical work in Washington, the time has come for disbandment.[14]

Similarly, when Robert Temple Emmet, Bigelow's classmate and close friend, was stricken with dysentery at Fort Union, New Mexico, in 1880, his worried mother agitated for a sick leave for him so she could provide maternal care.[15] The blunt but compassionate Sherman replied:

> There is no government on earth which provides its fighting Army with so good a corps of Surgeons and Physicians as the U. S., and the moment I received your letter I saw that you were "stampeded." New Mexico is extremely healthy, and [your son is] where they had to shoot a man to inaugurate the graveyard. I was there two years ago and the hospital was empty, and had been for five months. Any old soldier would laugh at the idea of bringing a man from New Mexico to New York for health....
>
> The Love which subsists between the Mother and her Child is too holy to be spoken of lightly. If the Catholics had not introduced the Virgin Mary into their Religion I doubt if it could have existed this long.... But boys, and young officers are boys,...will make fun of sacred things. Even old men do sometimes and I heard General Grant once exclaim...that he would never again appoint a boy to the Army who had a Mother.[16]

Apart from the Corps of Engineers and on occasion the Ordnance Department, all graduates of the Military Academy were commissioned in the artillery, cavalry or infantry and assigned to regiments based on their class standings and preferences, the army's needs, and the vacancies that existed.[17] A graduate's initial assignment held considerable importance since most officers remained in their branches and with their regiments for many years, some throughout their entire careers; additionally, the first few promotions usually depended on regimental vacancies, not armywide or branchwide competition.

Whatever the reasons, and in disregard of Hancock's advice and contrary to Sherman's unequivocal view that "every cadet of spirit wants to go to the Cavalry,"[18] the few vacancies—only three that year—in the

GENERAL WILLIAM TECUMSEH SHERMAN

Officers who preferred staff assignments to frontier service so infuriated him that he declared, "When peace has so corrupted the military service that a captain will leave his company to do clerical work in Washington, the time has come for disbandment." (Courtesy USMA Library)

engineers were taken by the top three graduates. Twelve of the next thirteen chose artillery, which left the remaining sixty-one lieutenants to be spread among the nine cavalry and seventeen infantry regiments with openings.[19] As General Hancock predicted, many had avoided the hardest lessons.

After graduation all three engineers were stationed at Willet's Point in New York Harbor, and none participated in the Frontier Indian Wars. Most of the artillery lieutenants were scattered along the East Coast from Fort Preble near Portland to Fort Barrancas near Pensacola, at such serene and relatively pleasant posts as Charleston, Fort McHenry, Fort Hamilton, and Boston Harbor. One was sent to Madison Barracks near Watertown, New York, and another went to Fort Canby near Astoria, Oregon. Only one, Albert Todd, was directly involved in the Indian wars, but not until the Ghost Dance uprisings in 1890.

THE SALUTARY LESSONS

The salutary lessons to be learned from hard service in what most easterners considered the wilderness were largely reserved for the twenty-eight graduates commissioned in the infantry and the thirty-three who entered the cavalry. All but one of the sixty-one served on the frontier. The exception was Ariosto McCrimmon who was at Jackson Barracks in New Orleans. His experiences were atypical as he wrote of the frequent grand balls; the "sumptuous" fare provided inexpensively because of the proximity of the French market; the "kindest feeling toward the army" that prevailed "in the best circles"; the warbling of birds; the fruit-laden orange trees and the magnolias; and the "pretty girls (who) are more numerous...than the festive and musical mosquitoes in summer."[20] These were not the lessons that General Hancock had in mind.

Frontier life for the remaining young officers was essentially void of the comforts and luxuries that McCrimmon enjoyed, a factor that might have contributed to the decisions of ten of them to resign within a few years after graduation.[21] More commonly, though, they eagerly sought the most active service available. One such enthusiastic second lieutenant was Harry Hammond, the first member of his class to engage in an Indian campaign.

Hammond arrived at his home in California two weeks after graduation. Hearing of the problems with the Nez Percé he promptly volunteered his services. Foregoing graduation leave, he was assigned to a lst Cavalry detachment scouting trails in northern Idaho. Three months and several hundred miles later he returned to San Francisco without, insofar as is known, firing a shot, and that December he resigned to attend law school.[22]

The initial experiences of McCrimmon and Hammond were not representative, of course, of those of their classmates, most of whom were assigned to small, dreary posts throughout the West. Moreover, eighteen of the novice leaders (far more than ever before) were assigned to companies in which all the enlisted men were black and, until that year, all the officers were white.[23] The highest ranking of the eighteen was Calvin Esterly, twenty-seventh on the order of merit.[24] The others graduated from fortieth to seventieth, but only two were in the bottom quartile of the class, where choices were quite limited.

In addition to Esterly, six graduates (Robert Safford, John Bigelow, Jr., Henry Flipper, Robert Read, Millard Eggleston, and Matthias Day) went to the 10th Cavalry.[25] Another five (John Guilfoyle, Harry Hammond, Charles Bradley, Robert Emmet, and Ben Butler) joined the 9th Cavalry.[26] Four members of the class (Charles Crane, Ammon Augur, John Brereton, and Sam Wayman) were commissioned in the 24th Infantry and two (John McMartin and Edwin Glenn) in the 25th Infantry.[27] Before long all would find themselves at places where some of the hardest lessons were to be taught—and learned.

Chapter 3

Blacks in Blue

THE STRUGGLE ON CAPITOL HILL

In 1866 Henry Wilson of Massachusetts, chairman of the Senate Committee on Military Affairs, introduced a reorganization bill that, among other provisions, would fix the army's strength at about 75,000, add two regiments of artillery (one composed of "colored persons") to the five then in service, increase the number of cavalry regiments from six to ten (two to be "colored"), realign the nineteen infantry regiments and establish others so that sixty (including ten "colored") would exist, and create a new "Veterans' Reserve Corps."[1]

The ink on Senator Wilson's bill could hardly have been dry before editorial writers for the *New York Times* indignantly sniffed that the nation had "no use whatever" for a standing army of the size proposed. In the view of that venerable publication, no more was required than a "limited military organization" to rally around if "the aggressions of any foreign Power should compel us to go to war; and...to restrain the savages who exist upon our frontiers and the plains of the West." Moreover, the *Times* opined (presumably with some literary license), "our" experience proved that Indian troubles "will be less the fewer soldiers we have."[2]

Aside from such bleatings about numbers from the eastern press, more vociferous reactions were generated by the proposals to create a Veterans' Reserve Corps and permit blacks to serve in the army. Commenting on the latter, one troubled letter writer expressed the conventional lore that:

> ...[A]rtillery should be composed *entirely* of white persons, and the Cavalry and Infantry of a large proportion of colored persons [because]...men of greater intelligence are required for an effective artillery...and it is a generally admitted fact...that [in the present generation, at least] the intellect of gentlemen of color is less brilliant than that of their white brethren.[3]

Less dispassionate opponents in both houses of Congress wasted no time in denouncing the measure and offering amendments to preclude blacks from serving. Sen. Willard Saulsbury, for instance, argued that if colored soldiers were in Delaware, collisions between them and white men would be inevitable. And Sen. James McDougall of California moved to completely strike out any authorization for "soldiers of color." But others, including Sen. Benjamin Wade of Ohio, rose in support of the bill. Asserting that blacks had fought as well as whites in the recent war and were less liable to desert, he moved to double the proposed number of colored cavalry regiments, but his effort was unsuccessful. Sen. Henry Lane of Indiana, however, persuasively argued that serving in the army was either a burden or a privilege, and if the former it should be borne equally but if the latter the entitlement should be shared equally.[4]

In the midst of all the clamor, the *Army and Navy Journal* came forth with a reasoned analysis of the issue. After pointing out that Negroes were common in the navy in 1860, it first asked why black troops would be considered so revolutionary in the army. At the beginning of the Civil War, it noted, using blacks as soldiers would have been regarded as inhuman and a desecration of the Union cause, but with mounting losses national sentiment changed after a couple of years, so eventually a few Negro regiments were formed. Ultimately more than a hundred thousand African Americans were enlisted, and although the effect they produced "on the Rebellion [was] over-estimated in some quarters," they "were probably better than the fears of their malignant enemies or even the hopes of their sensible friends [had] anticipated." In this connection, the analysis went on, "the best colored regiments, those which were carefully selected, drilled and disciplined, were very good indeed," while those "huddled together by bounty-hired brokers at so much a head, carelessly officered, and left to drill and discipline themselves, were exceedingly bad." In any event, citing the trail-blazing 54th Massachusetts Volunteers for its "daring assault of Fort Wagner and its brilliant conduct at Olustee" and elsewhere, the *Journal* concluded that such "gallantry...settled the whole question."[5]

In February the controversy over the strength of the army was significantly affected when Napoleon III, after negotations with John Bigelow, Sr., announced that he would remove French troops from Mexico "because of the emotion [that their presence] produced in the United States."[6] And in May Congressman Robert C. Schenck's obsessive objective of creating a Veterans' Reserve Corps of ten regiments was defeated by a vote of 55 to 83.[7] Subsequently Senator Wilson introduced a new bill that, as a principal feature, would have fixed the size of the force at only five artillery, six cavalry, and thirty-seven infantry regiments.[8] Once more, as General Sherman later noted, the congressional fetish for emasculating the armed forces after every conflict, despite continuing threats, was rampant.[9]

The acrimonious debates continued during the typically long and sweltering Washington summer, and various permutations occurred. Finally, the act became law in early August. It provided that the strength of the army would be just short of 55,000 (a number never reached), which included five artillery, ten cavalry, and forty-five infantry regiments, as well as a Veterans' Reserve Corps of four regiments. Although there was no provision for any black artillery units, two of the new cavalry units and four of the infantry were to be composed of African Americans, authorizing them to be part of the non-war army for the first time in the nation's history.[10]

THE AFRICAN AMERICAN REGIMENTS

The four new infantry regiments were designated the 38th, 39th, 40th, and 41st. The 38th's first colonel was William B. Hazen, the 39th's J. A. Mower, the 40th's Nelson A. Miles, and the 41st's Ranald S. Mackenzie. Three years later the army's forty-five infantry regiments were consolidated into twenty-five, two of which were African American. The 38th and 41st then became the 24th with Mackenzie as commanding officer, and the 39th and 40th became the 25th under Mower.[11]

The two cavalry regiments, numbered the 9th and 10th, were activated under Colonels Edward Hatch[12] and Benjamin Grierson.[13] The new units were organized essentially the same as their eight white counterparts, with a staff of a colonel, six other officers, and five enlisted men in addition to a surgeon and two assistant surgeons. Each was to have twelve companies, lettered "A" through "M" (to avoid confusion with "I" in handwritten communications, "J" was never used to designate an army unit), and each company was authorized three officers (captain, first lieutenant, and second lieutenant), sixteen noncommissioned officers, and sixty-four privates.[14] One difference was that with the high illiteracy rate among former slaves, each black regiment had its own chaplain who was responsible not only for tending to the spiritual needs of the troops but also for providing enlisted men with instruction in basic school subjects, principally reading and writing.[15] In contrast the army's thirty other chaplains were normally assigned to posts rather than organizations.[16] Another difference was that each black cavalry regiment had two veterinary surgeons instead of the usual one.[17]

Congress required all initial vacancies for lieutenants and two-thirds of the higher positions to be filled by officers who had at least two years of volunteer service during the Civil War. Consequently, thirty-four of the first forty officers in the 9th and 10th Cavalry were non-Regulars, and only two of the six Regulars were graduates of the Military Academy.[18] Neither Hatch nor Grierson was an academy graduate, but each had been breveted as a major general of volunteers for his distinguished Civil War service.

Although a number of officers avoided or refused to serve with African Americans (sometimes referred to as "Brunettes," "Nubians," "Moacs," "Mokes" or other even more uncomplimentary terms) or in black regiments because of the "inferiority" of their officers, others were willing to do so.[19] In some cases officers accepting appointments might have perceived a greater opportunity for advancement at a time when highly capable officers often stagnated as lieutenants after "forty and fifty years of age."[20] Nevertheless, for many years only a small number of West Pointers, especially those of "field grade," were members of black segregated organizations.[21]

Shortly after its activation the 9th, headquartered at Greenville, Louisiana, commenced to enlist large numbers of blacks from around the New Orleans area, many of whom were physically wretched men whose past conditions of servitude poorly qualified them for military service. Describing the recently emancipated recruits in 1866, one officer wrote:

> Physically as well as intellectually the negroes...were far inferior to the white soldiers. All had been slaves...and showed signs of overwork and of malnutrition. Nearly every one had malformed hands and distorted feet. Their skins were almost always blotched or rough.... The men speedily learned the necessity of cleanliness of body, arms and equipment, in which they soon showed pride.
>
> They took readily to drill and cadence, and among them were many who readily acquired an erect and soldierly bearing. They were averse, however, to immediate and strict obedience to non-commissioned officers of their own color.
>
> They accepted punishments without complaint or signs of dissatisfaction.... Almost without exception the men were free from the use of intoxicating liquor, but their fondness for sweets was noticeable. There was practically no sense of chastity, and most of the infractions of regulations were due to intimacies with the women camp-followers.... The men said that their plantation life had been marked by such practices, and why, they asked, should they change.[22]

In the meantime the 10th was off to an agonizingly slow start, in part because Grierson insisted on uncommonly high standards.[23] In its first regimental report from headquarters at Fort Leavenworth in September 1866, he alone was present while the only other officer, Lt. Col. Charles C. Walcutt (who soon resigned) was in Kentucky trying to recruit soldiers.[24] The sole enlisted man, William N. Beauman, was hospitalized at Jefferson Barracks.[25] Grierson remained by himself for three more months, but by December he was able to report the presence of fifty-eight men, and in January four captains (including Louis H. Carpenter and Nicholas Nolan) joined him. After recruiting efforts were concentrated in Philadelphia and the Northeast, the situation improved sufficiently so that by March there were eight officers and 185 men, about half of whom were transferred to Fort Larned the following month. And in May the available men permitted a nearly full strength company to be stationed at each of three locations in Kansas.[26] Thereafter growth accelerated so that by June there were sixteen officers (including Lt. Richard Pratt and Capt. George A. Armes) and 555 men, most of whom were assigned to scattered posts that included Camp Grierson, Tar Creek, and the intriguingly named Camp Buggy. In August regimental headquarters moved to Fort Riley, and by late fall the 10th reached thirty-one officers and 1,175 enlisted men, the most it would have for years to come. These troops were deployed at two locations in Indian Territory and eight in Kansas, one of such a transitory nature that it was identified simply as the "west end" of the railroad.[27]

THE FIRST DECADE

By the time Bigelow and his classmates joined their organizations, the African American troops (about 10 percent of the enlisted strength) were among the most seasoned soldiers in the army, having ten years of hard frontier service behind them.[28] In 1867 and 1868 the primary duties of the 10th Cavalry were to guard construction of the Kansas Pacific and the Union Pacific railroads and to protect the widely dispersed settlers and travelers. The first of several encounters occurred about forty miles northeast of Fort Hays on August 2, 1867, when a band of some three hundred Cheyennes attacked the two officers and thirty-four men of Company F, killing Sgt. William Christy and wounding the commanding officer, Captain Armes.[29] Less than three weeks later the same company and ninety Kansas Volunteers were involved in an all-afternoon fight with an estimated five hundred Indians. From then on armed encounters were not uncommon.

Units from the 10th also participated in the 1867–1868 winter campaign against Black Kettle's Cheyennes, and two skirmishes took place in mid-September 1868, one near Fort Hays and the other on Big Sandy Creek. Then in October near Beaver Creek, Kansas, two companies routed an attacking force of about five hundred Indians. During the 10th's first decade on the Plains, seventeen engagements with Cheyennes, Comanches, Kiowas, or Apaches were recorded.[30] In addition, in the fall of 1868 Captain Carpenter's H Company was the first to relieve Maj. George A. Forsyth on Beecher Island.[31]

In the spring of 1868 the 10th's headquarters moved to Fort Gibson, Indian Territory, and a year later it relocated to Camp Wichita (soon to become Fort Sill), where the unskilled African Americans built one of the Army's finest frontier installations. When not engaging in manual labor or other mundane duties, troops from Sill scouted to control not only belligerent Kiowas and Comanches but also white whiskey peddlers and horse and cattle rustlers. They also were prominent in the incident involving General Sherman and Satank, Big Tree, Satanta, and other Indians on Colonel Grierson's porch, during which Grierson grappled with Lone Wolf when he aimed a carbine at Sherman, and Satanta, who had drawn a concealed pistol, hastily dropped it when the shutters behind Sherman were flung open to reveal a number of black soldiers aiming carbines at him. Detachments under Captain Carpenter and Lt. Louis Orleman also had important parts in that dramatic confrontation.[32]

Although there are various accounts of when, by whom, or why the 10th Cavalry troops became the first to earn the sobriquet of "Buffalo Soldiers," it probably was bestowed on them by Comanches or Kiowas during the Sill years or by Cheyennes in Kansas a few years earlier.[33] In either case the apparent reason related to the resemblance between the scalp of black soldiers and buffalo fur. Another version has the Sioux originating the name when they observed 9th Cavalry soldiers wearing buffalo skin coats.[34] The most entertaining (but least credible) explanation, however, is that an enterprising Ute found a way to transform pieces of buffalo hide into something that passed for Negro scalps, which were highly prized because of the likelihood that they were taken from soldiers. According to the legend, the entrepreneur lost his own scalp when disgruntled customers learned of his deception.[35]

TOLERATING HEAT

In 1873 five companies of the 10th were transferred to Texas, but the headquarters and other companies remained in Indian Territory until after the 1874–1875 campaign. The balance of the regiment then moved south of the Red River where headquarters and five companies were garrisoned at Fort Concho and the remaining seven companies at other posts.[36] The concentration of all four African American regiments in some of the most parched and hottest regions of Texas, New Mexico, and Arizona, where they remained for years, was at least partly because of the belief that they were "better suited to that climate" than whites.[37] Physiologically such conventional wisdom turned out to be generally correct.[38] Nevertheless, a greater resistance to high temperatures did not assure immunity to heat stress,[39] and how best to avoid it was not established for many years.[40] Consequently, white officers and black soldiers, together with the rugged early settlers and the native Americans, all shared to some degree the climatic suffering of summer in the semiarid regions of the Southwest.

Chapter 4

Bound for the Rio Grande

Before they could commence their careers, the members of the Class of 1877 were subjected to a much longer than usual interlude after graduation because of the crisis generated by the disputed 1876 presidential election between Rutherford B. Hayes and Samuel J. Tilden.

With each faction accusing the other of massive fraud, by late February the "Bargain of 1877," which assured the election of Hayes over Tilden by an electoral vote of 185 to 184, was arrived at secretly. Under it the Hayes Republicans (as contrasted to the "Radical Republicans") agreed to withdraw federal troops from South Carolina, Louisiana, and Florida, hence ending Reconstruction and permitting control of those states to revert from Carpetbaggers to Democrats. In exchange the Southern Democrats (known as "Redeemers") promised to block any filibuster by Northern Democrats that would have prevented completion of the electoral count before Inauguration Day. By placing "Rud" Hayes and his teetotalling wife, "Lemonade Lucy," in the White House, the anarchy or armed conflict that threatened the nation was avoided, but at a collateral price.[1]

Shortly before the "Bargain" was struck the Democratic-controlled House voted to add a provision to the pending army appropriations bill prohibiting the use of troops to support a state government without Congressional approval. When the Republican-controlled Senate rejected this move (which raised a basic constitutional issue of whether the president or Congress controlled where and for what purposes troops could be deployed), the House adjourned without appropriating any funds, prompting the *Army and Navy Journal* to editorialize:

> [As] the Class of '77 steps out...to begin the life of men and soldiers...they may perhaps think the prospect somewhat flat and discouraging.... After the fiercest and most critical political struggle...since the Secession Movement, they find that...the Army has taken all the blows.... It may puzzle these young men to know what [it] has done to deserve this, or how cutting off its pay for a season is going to benefit the country.... However, even West Point graduates are not supposed to be familiar with the intricacies of a Congressman's moral code.[2]

Because there were no funds with which to pay them, the new lieutenants simply were not ordered to report to their regiments. They and other officers had to survive as best they could, often by obtaining help from families or friends who had the means or by seeking low-interest loans from sympathetic bankers.[3] The enlisted men were also denied compensation, but in most cases the subsistence and housing provided them was not interrupted. In a special session which Hayes delayed calling until the year was drawing to a close, Congress finally made the necessary appropriation.

THE LONG WAY FROM JUNE TO DECEMBER

Until the funds became available, the new lieutenants enjoyed a respite between the rigors of cadet life and the hardships awaiting them on the frontier. For example, Bigelow spent the first few weeks at the family's summer house in Highland Falls, just south of West Point, and in New York City.[4] Then in late July he vacationed at Long Branch, New Jersey, and during much of August he stayed at the Grant House in the Catskills, relaxing at clambake parties, tub racing, ball games, and "tableaux and charades" after supper. He also attended a ball at West Point where he was impressed by the large size of the "german" that was danced.[5] On October 10 he attended the obsequies for Lt. Col. George Armstrong Custer, whose remains had been shipped from Montana for final interment at the Military Academy.[6] Although the services had been postponed to permit a larger military attendance, fewer officers than Bigelow expected were there because many had not yet returned from suppressing the 1877 railroad riots.[7] Nevertheless, the post was crowded with people who waited patiently most of the day to pay their respects to the flamboyant young hero.

During the following three months Bigelow was at Bar Harbor, Maine, for a couple of weeks, and made several train or steamer excursions to destinations such as Poughkeepsie, Providence, Albany, Philadelphia, Baltimore, and Washington to visit or call on classmates. On frequent trips to New York City he usually stayed at the Westminster Hotel for reasons he neglected to explain, even though the family home was nearby at 21 Gramercy Park. During this period he occasionally corresponded with his father ("Pa"), who was in England, and his mother ("Ma") visited him once in Highland Falls. Commencing in late November the widely scattered members of '77 began receiving orders to join their companies. In Bigelow's case that involved a tedious trip to Fort Duncan, Texas, on the Rio Grande.

THE JOURNEY WEST

After arranging for his baggage to be picked up, drawing his mileage allowance of $146.08, and buying a .38 caliber Smith and Wesson "pocket pistol," Bigelow boarded an express train for St. Louis at 9 a.m. on December 1, 1877.[8] That evening he wrote:

> Dined at Lancaster...and supped at Altoona.... Read a good deal in Le Mexique.... Learned that the Mexicans hate the Spaniards more than they do any other people, and that they hate the negroes next in degree.

During the night snow fell and it was quite cold. Breakfast was at Columbus, dinner at Indianapolis, and supper at Effingham. At nine that evening the train reached St. Louis. The easiest and fastest part of the trip was over. Bigelow walked from the station to the Planters House, where he obtained what he thought was a "very good room." After eating he went to the Lindell Hotel "hoping to find some clue to Safford's whereabouts."[9] His friend Safford was not to be found, however. The following day Bigelow had different thoughts about his room.

> Ordered my trunk to be brought up and a fire to be made before I dressed. The man who attempted to make the fire did not succeed...but filled the room with black smoke which made me open the window to let it out. I had to dress in the cold. The window having been open all night a good deal of soot had blown in and had fallen over my table and the articles on it.... The bituminous coal fills the air with smoke, smut and smell while the Mississippi water with which the city is supplied is so dirty that it is hard to make anything very clean with it. Hence the many dirty hands & faces in this place.

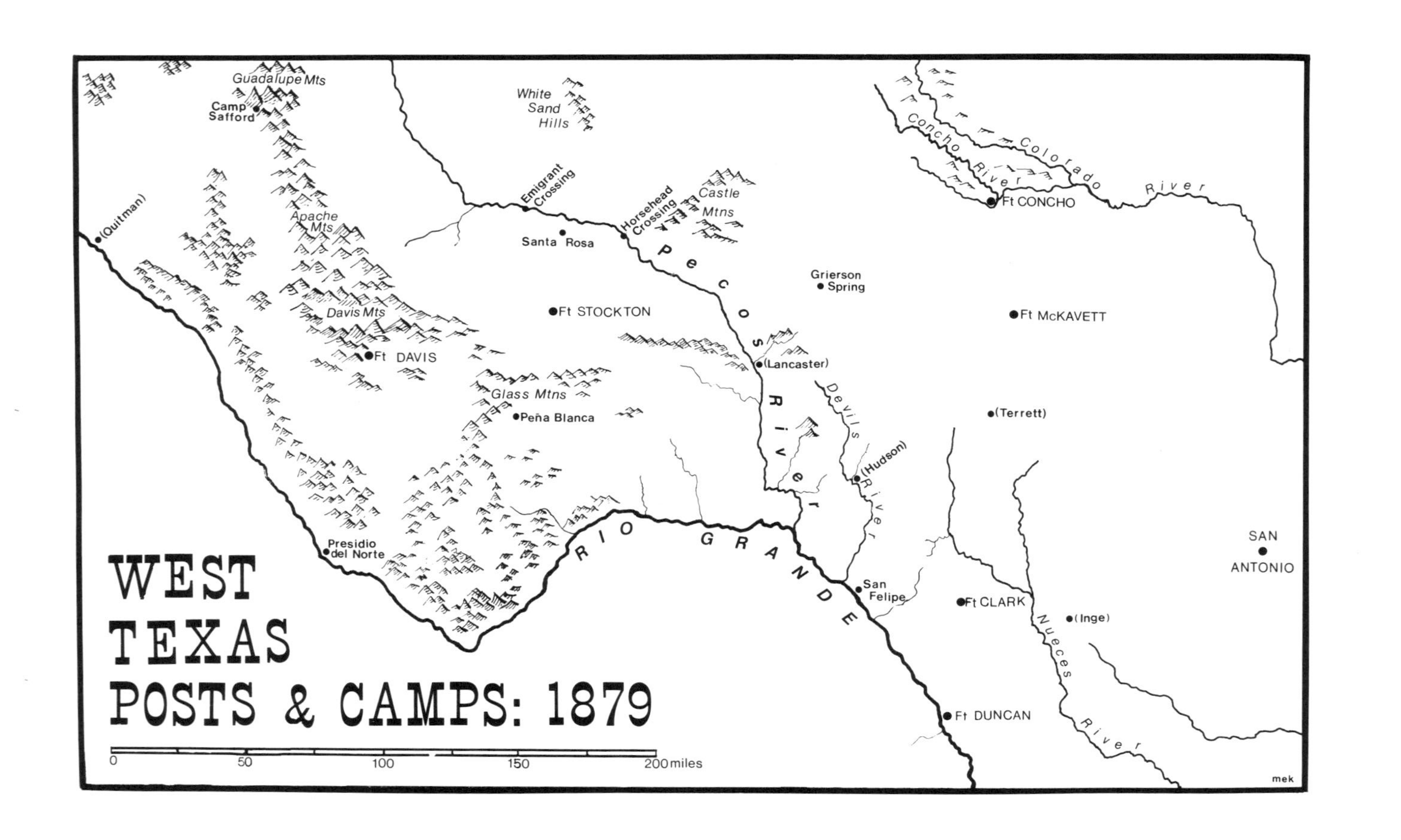
WEST TEXAS POSTS & CAMPS: 1879
Guadalupe Mts
Camp Safford
(Quitman)
Apache Mts
Davis Mts
Ft DAVIS
Presidio del Norte
White Sand Hills
Emigrant Crossing
Santa Rosa
Horsehead Crossing
Castle Mtns
Ft STOCKTON
Glass Mtns
Peña Blanca
Pecos River
Grierson Spring
(Lancaster)
Devils River
(Hudson)
RIO GRANDE
San Felipe
Concho River
Colorado River
Ft CONCHO
Ft McKAVETT
(Terrett)
Ft CLARK
(Inge)
Nueces River
Ft DUNCAN
SAN ANTONIO
0
50
100
150
200 miles
mek

The rest of the day was spent with another classmate, Ben Eggleston, who after noticing Bigelow's name in the newspaper as a recent arrival came over to see him.[10] As they were walking around they met 1st Lt. Steven Groesbeck of the 6th Infantry who was on leave to look after some coal-mining property he had acquired. Groesbeck believed that his coal would replace immense quantities being shipped from Pittsburgh, enabling him to resign and become wealthy.[11] Bigelow was skeptical, noting that Groesbeck was "so ignorant of mineralogy as to call FeSO-4 iron pyrites." The following day his rail journey to San Antonio resumed.

> We dined the first day at Hermann and...[took supper at] Sedalia. The next day we breakfasted at Muskogee, dined at Atoka, and took supper at Dallas. Breakfasted...at Hempstead & came into Houston at about 11 o'clock, too late to take the San Antonio train.[12]

> We went to the best hotel in Houston, the Hutchins House. After registering our names & preparing ourselves, we walked around the town. The climate was delightful to us, who only a short time before had been in St. Louis, where the smoke, smut, & smell are intolerable.... The Hutchins was a pretty poor house.

SAN ANTONIO: MORE CURIOUS THAN BEAUTIFUL

The next morning Bigelow and Eggleston departed for San Antonio where after arrival they obtained a room at the Menger Hotel, a hostelry superior to Houston's best. The Menger, located on Alamo Plaza, was separated from the historic mission San Antonio de Valero by an alternately muddy or dusty lane (or in the alliterative lyrics of a once-popular song, "across the alley from the Alamo.")[13] There were several stores scattered nearby, including a garish emporium known as Grenet's "Castle" north of the Alamo, a saloon on the south, and a stenchful meat market near the center of the Plaza.[14]

Earlier that year Harriett Spofford floridly described her arrival in the same town:

> Lights begin to twinkle below, and you descend into San Antonio. There is a crowd of dark faces at the station, a confusion of strange tongues. As the carriage goes along, soft wafts of balmiest fragrance salute you; you are conscious of being in a world of flowers. As you alight at the Menger, enter a narrow, unevenly-stoned passage, and come out upon a broad flagged court-yard, surrounded on three sides by open galleries, with the stars overhead, and the lamp-light flaring on a big mulberry tree growing in [the court-yard] below, you feel that you are in...Old Spain.[15]

MENGER HOTEL, SAN ANTONIO

For decades the Menger, opened in 1859, was San Antonio's finest hotel. In 1879 Bigelow stayed there for almost five months. (Courtesy Menger Hotel)

Bigelow later provided his impressions of the town that, while not as glowing as those of Miss Spofford, probably are more accurate.

> From what I have seen of San Antonio thus far, I am inclined to believe that...it is more curious than beautiful. There is a great variety in the type of people, in the style of architecture, and in the plants. Of the first there are Mexicans, Spaniards, Cubans, Germans, Americans and...Englishmen. Of architecture, there are specimens of the classic Doric, the modern renaissance, the Mexican wooden cottage and adobe huts; there is also Gothic and more or less of the log house style combined with the adobe, and, lastly, all kinds of tumbledown suburban hovels. In regard to vegetation we have the live-oak, china tree, mesquite, poplar, ebony, cactus and, in gardens, one or two plants that have probably been transplanted from a more southern country....
>
> There is a great deal in the streets that is new to a Northerner—the costumes of the Mexicans, their saddles, the mustang ponies mounted by men whose feet come pretty close to the ground, the mules, the teams of 8 or 10 oxen, in pairs, the Spanish sign boards...the numerous places or plazas.... There is nothing beautiful in all this, but it may be considered picturesque. That is not enough, however, to secure its admiration by every one for few...notice and appreciate picturesqueness.

Because all the new lieutenants assigned to posts in West Texas had to go through San Antonio, informal reunions were not uncommon. Three other classmates (Glenn, Kirby, and Brereton) arrived the next day.[16] They were later joined by another four (Crane, McMartin, Plummer, and Wayman).[17] Bigelow relates how they occupied themselves until transportation to take them farther west was available.

> We went out to walk after supper, intending to go to the Central Hotel...to see if any of our classmates were in town.... The next day Sat. Ben & I went with Major Wilson...to report to Col Taylor....[18] In the afternoon I...made arrangements to have my baggage sent out to my post.... Bob Safford arrived that evening. Lieut. Stretch & Major Wilson called on us.[19] Today, Sunday, Ben, Bob & I called on Stretch & Wilson at the soldiers barracks where we sat for awhile talking.... Upon our return we found an invitation from Lt Stretch to dine with him at 4 o'clock....
>
> *Menger Hotel, San Antonio, Dec. 10, 1877.* Bob Safford and I...took a Turco Russian bath. The latter we were very much in need of, not having had one since the completion of our journey. Safford had invited Lieut Bottsford to dine with us....[20] After dinner he took us out in an ambulance to the San Pedro Springs.[21] Upon our return, we called on Lieut Shaler of the Ordn Dept, who had called on us with Capt Comly; the latter has charge of the arsenal here....[22]
>
> [After] supper I went with Safford, Lt Bottsford, and another man, to take a glass of wine. According to Mexican custom, we threw dice to decide who should pay for the crowd. Lt Bottsford then proposed that we...should go...to play pool. I remained in the hotel.... The tourists...are now having a little "time" down stairs. Wine & music are the refreshments.

On his last day in San Antonio Bigelow thought he should make a courtesy call on Brig. Gen. Edward Otho Cresap Ord, commander of the Department of Texas, so he walked the short distance from the Menger to the Ords' house on Nacogdoches Street, directly behind the Alamo.[23]

> *Tuesday, Dec. 11, 1877, Menger Hotel, San Antonio.* Called this afternoon on Mrs Ord & family, the general being in Washington.... I saw Judge Ord, his brother, who had been at the legation when we were in Paris. Miss Ord showed us a...garment which she & the Judge together were constructing.[24] She had a wild cat skin which she proposed to hang over her back, tail downward, so as to bring...the forefeet around in front like a collar. This was to be sewed onto an undergarment...like a vest. The buttons, I suggested, should be covered with the fur.

BRIGADIER GENERAL E. O. C. ORD

Despite Ord's distinguished record, President Hayes retired him to promote Nelson Miles, who coveted Ord's rank. (Courtesy Fort Davis National Historic Site)

ORDEALS BY STAGECOACH

Having traveled as far west in Texas as the railroads operated, the new lieutenant took his next journeys by stagecoaches. Although stages were the primary means of travel until railroad branches were constructed, they were a singularly uncomfortable way to get from here to there.[25] For example, Calvin Esterly, who married soon after graduation, described their trip to Fort Concho:

> It took eight days to come by stage from Fort Worth, a distance of two hundred and twenty miles. The stage broke down in drenching rain, which mishap necessitated a ride of seventeen miles in an old lumber wagon. We waited four days at Bayou River for the water to fall so that we could cross. When the river went down there was no stage, and we crossed, Mrs. Esterly in a high-seated buggy and I on horseback without saddle or bridle.... I might as well have swum across with my clothes on.[26]

Similarly, Charles Gatewood, a tall, scrawny young man called "Beak" by his classmates and "Bay-chen-day-sen" by the Apaches because of his prominent nose, was equally disenchanted with the transportation. Within a few years Gatewood would become one of the best-known

CALVIN ESTERLY

As a boy in Ohio Calvin Esterly helped operate an "underground railroad" for escaping slaves. As a man he gave up a promising army career because of his wife's health. He then became El Paso's first superintendent of schools. (Courtesy USMA Library)

CHARLES GATEWOOD

His classmates called him "Beak" because of his hawklike nose. So did the Indian scouts he led. Although one of the most effective young officers in the Apache Wars, he was ignored at decoration and promotion times. (Courtesy USMA Library)

junior officers in the army, but first he had to join his 6th Cavalry company at Camp Apache.[27] In relating some of his experiences getting there he wrote:

> [Wilson] and I remained at Pueblo, Colo. a day, partly to admire Pike's Peak...but principally to await the next train...to El Moro.[28] At this latter place and at Trinidad the small-pox was "cleaning out" the Mexicans, who...have no especial liking for soap and water or disinfectant of any kind.
>
> From Trinidad to Santa Fe we had a nice little ride of two hundred and sixteen miles in a stage-coach. There were nine passengers in all, and the stage was about the size of a dry-goods box.[29] There was plenty of room inside for four men and for one man outside besides the driver. To seat nine men was a knotty problem only to be solved by paying the agent a dollar apiece for a larger coach. So we set out and made the trip in less than thirty-eight hours, only stopping for meals and a change of horses. Our progress was mainly due to the doses of "cheer" with which we continually plied the driver. Being "set up," he did not seem to care much if the coach did occasionally run on two wheels, much to the danger of our bones.[30]

Shortly before Gatewood rode the stage to Santa Fe, John Haden, 8th Infantry, made the same trip but suffered from an additional hazard.[31] As the coach was ascending a long, steep hill at night it was stopped and the passengers were told to step out. They complied since several shotguns were pointed at them. As they stood with their hands held up, one of the robbers searched all but Haden, saying disgustedly when he came to him, "Damn it, you Army officers never have any money." Haden concluded:

> My fellow passengers, a young man and a Roman Catholic priest, did not fare so well. The old padre had to come down with the *dinero*, and...[t]hey also relieved the young man of his little all. The robbers will not spend next summer at Saratoga on the proceeds of their enterprise, as they only got about five dollars all told. If they had searched me they would have obtained about twenty-five dollars.[32]

Henry Kirby also was waylaid during his 185-mile journey to Fort McKavett. He was somewhat better equipped for the encounter, however, having purchased a large revolver before departing because he heard of two recent murders on that line.

> Twelve miles out met a coach containing the corpse of a young man, who had been murdered the night before.... [The next morning] I again set out...in company with Mr. Blacker, a district judge in Western Texas. In Mason we were joined by a Jew from New Orleans.... [A]bout 11 P.M....I was awakened by a man yelling

HENRY KIRBY

One of his early army experiences was thwarting Texas "road agents" who held up a stage in which he was traveling to his first post. (Courtesy USMA Library)

at the driver to turn out from the road or he would blow his damned head off. The judge and I were on the back seat, and the Jew on the front.... I saw a man about ten yards off, pointing a gun directly at the door. I seized my pistols...and offered one to the judge, but he declined, saying "There is no use; there is a large gang of them and we will all be killed if we resist." I then offered it to the Jew, but he refused, being busy stowing away his money and...looking to see if he could jump out and run. I aimed at the only man I could see, but the judge caught my pistol and begged me not to fire. I told him that I did not propose to be robbed without fighting, but he insisted that...resistance would be rashness. As by this time the only man I could have shot had gotten out of view, I concluded that it would be better to surrender....

The stage was driven about two hundred yards from the road, and we were ordered to get out, one at a time, without arms.... I had time to take all my money except five dollars, and put it down my left boot-leg, putting my small pistol down my right boot and my watch in the case of a pillow.... They took me to the rear of the coach and demanded my money. I gave them my purse, and they, finding but five dollars in it, swore that I had more money, and that if I did not tell them where it was they would blow my brains out in case they found it. They then searched me, taking the studs from my shirt, and, not finding any money, repeated their threats. I...suggested they had better look in my boots but, as I expected, they declined with an oath.... [T]hey then proceeded to search the coach...[where] they found some money that the judge had hidden in the straw, and also my watch. They cut our valises all to pieces...then searched me a second time, tearing the lining from my hat, and were about to let me go, when one of them said, "Make the damned scoundrel pull off his boots any way."

Now if you have never looked down the barrel of a six-shooter within a few feet of your head, I can assure you that it is not pleasant.... I made a desperate resolve that, should they find the money, I would close in with the nearest robber and sell my life as dearly as possible. I pulled off my right boot first, telling them I had a pistol in it. While they were searching this and looking at the pistol, I pulled the other boot off cautiously, pressing my heel against the roll of money, and succeeding in throwing it out on the ground, and when they looked in the boot, it was empty.

Meanwhile, associates of the robbers farther down the road planned to hold up another stage traveling in the opposite direction. When the lights from the second stage came in view, Kirby, the judge, and the drummer were ordered to get back into their coach and not to make any noise or strike a light. During that time, Kirby "got out, crawled around on the ground, and found" his money.[33]

Other classmates also wrote of their adventures, but none was quite as harrowing as Kirby's. For example, Brereton, who accompanied Bigelow to Fort Duncan, merely noted that "We had a wretched stage journey from San Antonio, the roads being so bad that on one or two occasions we were obliged to walk several miles to relieve the horses. The stage was overcrowded...and we found it impossible to sleep inside, while to fall asleep outside was to incur the danger of falling off, not to speak of losing your hat, which I was unfortunate enough to do."[34] As for Bigelow, in a letter he mentioned only that "the most disagreeable part of my journey" was from San Antonio.[35] His journal provides somewhat more detail.

FROM SAN ANTONIO TO FORT DUNCAN

On the morning of December 12 Bigelow, Safford, and Brereton boarded a stage to Fort Duncan, some 183 miles and thirty-six hours away.[36] One of the other passengers was Mr. Schott, co-owner of the stage line, who "did not consider the Mexicans as treacherous as they were represented as being." Another was Joe Nye, a rancher who "made a sensation once by going into the front, and coming out of the rear door of the Menger Hotel on horseback." Nye rode with them from Castroville, where they had dinner, to D'Hanis, where they ate supper. Bigelow noted that he "was dubbed 'the parson' because" he refused to drink all the whiskey Nye wanted him to.

Nye told Bigelow about an incident suggesting that relations between the troops, who in effect were occupying former enemy territory, and the early settlers were not always harmonious.[37] Apparently when out on a scout Lt. Clayton S. Burbank, 10th Infantry,[38]

> ...had once come very near being attacked by a number of citizens of a small town through which he passed while scouting. One of his men shot a cow for fun and Berbank [*sic*] was demanded payment by the sheriff. Berbank told him...that he would not pay more than a certain amount, which amount did not satisfy the sheriff. The Lieut said that...he had a right to pass and that none but U.S. officers could arrest him...[and] expressed his intention of fighting his way through. The Sheriff told him to try it which he was not inclined to do, [as] there were three or four armed citizens to every one of his men. He paid the money to Joe Nye, who fixed the matter.... The sheriff was wrong in not allowing the Lieut to pass & then suing him. But Texans take the law into their own hands.

For part of the trip Bigelow rode beside the driver who "like others of the fraternity was very talkative." Much of his talk dealt with the railroads, which he opposed because teamsters would be thrown out of work and people would go farther west, lowering the value of land locally.

> *Thursday, Dec. 13, 1877, Stage Coach....* Slept very little during the night but was relieved of a headache by [a] short nap.... The roads are very bad, it having rained or drizzled almost continually since we left San Antonio. The light sprinkling does more harm to the roads here than a heavy shower, for the latter makes the mud of a fluid consistency so that it runs off the wheels whereas a small amount of water makes of this soil a very heavy mud...that sticks to the wheels in great clods that partially cover the spokes.
>
> We arrived at Fort Clark at about 7.30 tonight. Bob Safford took supper with us at the inn and then soon left us to go to the Fort.... I had to start off again very soon after supper...over a worse road than any that I had yet been on. We reached the Midway Station, where we took breakfast, at about two o'clock A.M. Meat & coffee were the principal nourishments, as they seem to me to be all through this

section of the country. In one of the houses that we stopped at we had brains and kidneys with pork meat and beef, also eggs & sauercrout [*sic*]. At another we had sausage & pigs feet. But no where did we have any variety at all of fresh vegetables.

Chapter 5

No "Hellisher" Land

Six months after graduation and two weeks after he left New York City, John Bigelow, Jr., arrived at Fort Duncan, which had an unenviable reputation as one of the most forlorn and least desirable posts in what many army members regarded as the most Godforsaken region on earth.

FORT DUNCAN: THE EARLIER YEARS

The first known United States military presence in the vicinity occurred during the Mexican War when a provisional camp was located next to an old Indian ford on the Rio Grande, some 650 miles from its mouth and near a principal road between Mexico and San Antonio.[1] When the war ended the troops were withdrawn, but in March 1849 two infantry companies returned to establish a fort, then the southernmost of a chain of Texas bases being built to protect the border and the advancing frontier.

The site selected was midway between the previous camp and a tent town about four miles upstream called "California Camp," where fortune seekers heading west rested and purchased supplies from enterprising merchants (the fortune finders) before venturing across the wilds of Mexico. As the gold rush declined the few semipermanent occupants of California Camp came to depend on sales to troops at Duncan, so they moved their flimsy shelters closer to the post. The next year a town called El Paso del Aguila (Eagle Pass) was laid out, and at about the same time the pueblo of Piedras Negras (Black Rocks) was taking shape across the river, about three-fourths of a mile from Duncan.[2]

FORT DUNCAN, TEXAS

Sketched from Piedras Negras on the Mexican side of the Rio Grande, probably in the late 1860s. (Courtesy USMA Library)

For the next twelve years troops from the post and its satellite camps protected trading caravans and settlers from roving bands of Indians, *bandidos*, and highwaymen. Among the officers performing such duties in 1854 were Philip H. Sheridan, a brevet second lieutenant recently out of West Point, and 1st Lt. Abner Doubleday.[3] Sheridan recalled that in the summer their time was "incessantly occupied in scouting" along the road to San Antonio. In some respects, however, the winters were even more trying; the accommodations were so austere (tents pitched under a shed) that Sheridan hauled poles thirty miles to build a crude shelter, windowless and with a roof of thatched prairie grass. Even though his only furnishings were a chair or two, camp stools, a cot, "a rickety old bureau," and a washstand made of a board resting on sticks driven into the ground, he regarded his shanty as relatively comfortable compared to the living conditions of other officers.[4]

That winter a young army wife, Lydia Lane, and her husband, William, passed through Duncan, which she described as "a wretched place to live in," on their way to Fort Inge.[5] Similarly Teresa Viele, the wife of a young officer stationed farther down the Rio Grande at Ringgold Barracks, wrote of conditions there in the early 1850s.

> There never was a country more unfitted...to be the home of civilized man.... It seems only to be intended as a home for desperate men, escaped refugees from the law; men who live in the saddle, and on the prairie seek their subsistence; such as give Texas any bad reputation its population might have.[6]

The lady's lack of enthusiasm for her surroundings can hardly be faulted considering that

> Under the most favorable of circumstances, the food was flavored with red ants, which were so thick that it was impossible to eat without devouring them by scores. They tasted something like caraway seed, and were not as disagreeable as a novice might suppose!... The vermin, the famine, hot winds, and dry soil, which caused clouds of dust to fill the sultry air of July and August and lodge on everything, made me begin to think...that it would have been better to remain in New Orleans and keep a thread and needle store than go to Texas.[7]

With the Civil War about to break out, federal forces were withdrawn from Texas in March 1861. By then the housing was less dismal than a few years earlier, but Duncan probably still deserved its reputation as "the most desolate and primitive post in all the army."[8] Confederate troops occupied the fort, and by the time the army returned in 1868 all windows, doors, and movable property had been damaged or destroyed. Extensive repairs were made, and negotiations to purchase the land commenced but failed because of the escalating price demanded by the owner, John Twohig, a San Antonio banker. In 1883 the army again abandoned the post, only to move back three years later.[9]

Privations were commonplace at the razed posts along the Rio Grande. After reading a complaint about conditions at an eastern station in 1867, an unsympathetic officer at an unnamed post below Fort Duncan responded that the adjacent border "city" was home to just three civilians (two men who were storekeepers and a woman who ran a boarding house), that rations arrived only monthly, and that he hadn't tasted a vegetable other than canned tomatoes since he arrived. He added:

> Our neighbors consist of a ranche of Greasers six miles above and another five miles below...[the post, and the troops are] morally certain any strange white man is an outlaw.... [Among the constant problems are keeping] cactus out of trowsers and rattlesnake fangs out of our flesh.... Boots cannot be put on safely without

> shaking them to dislodge any stray tarantulas, and mosquitoes are so big as to be frequently mistaken for curlew by newcomers.[10]

By the late 1870s living conditions at Duncan had improved, yet the wife of a lieutenant transferred there from Fort Clark, just forty-five miles north, found the post "inevitably dull."[11] She wrote from experience, having lived at some of the most depressing places in Nevada, Arizona, New Mexico, and Texas. The lady, who for more than a decade had uncomplainingly suffered through adversities that most eastern wives would have difficulty imagining, finally found her nadir on the Rio Grande:

> No station immediately on the river was ever considered desirable, on account of its unfailing sand and heat; and Fort Duncan...had no comfortable houses.... Our dwelling consisted of one room in a very dilapidated building...previously used as a store-room, and the barred windows made it seem prison-like.[12]

Militarily, Fort Duncan's most active days were from the early 1870s into the early 1880s, when several strikes into Mexico were launched against Kickapoos, Lipans, and Mescalero Apaches who had been raiding into Texas from their Mexican lairs.[13] The best-known incursion occurred in 1873 when Colonel Mackenzie led six 4th Cavalry companies and sixteen scouts on a highly successful foray against an Indian village near Remolino.[14] During the next few years a number of other raids were conducted by Lt. Col. William R. Shafter.[15] In addition, the Seminole Negro-Indian Scouts led by 1st Lt. John Bullis, known to the Indians as "Thunderbolt" or "Whirlwind," proved to be especially effective, whether used independently or with larger commands.[16]

FORT DUNCAN IN 1877

When Bigelow reported to Duncan, there were three companies of African Americans at the eighteen-square-mile post: B of the 10th Cavalry, E of the 25th Infantry, and F of the 24th Infantry. Some of the buildings were made of locally produced adobe, while others were sandstone hauled from about a mile away.[17] There were sufficient structures for the enlisted men, officers, and laundresses, but the accommodations were rather Spartan. John Brereton wrote a few weeks after arrival that he finally was assigned a room in which he "had to keep an umbrella over [his] head in rainy weather, and keep a sharp eye for chunks of adobe that occasionally fall from the wall."[18]

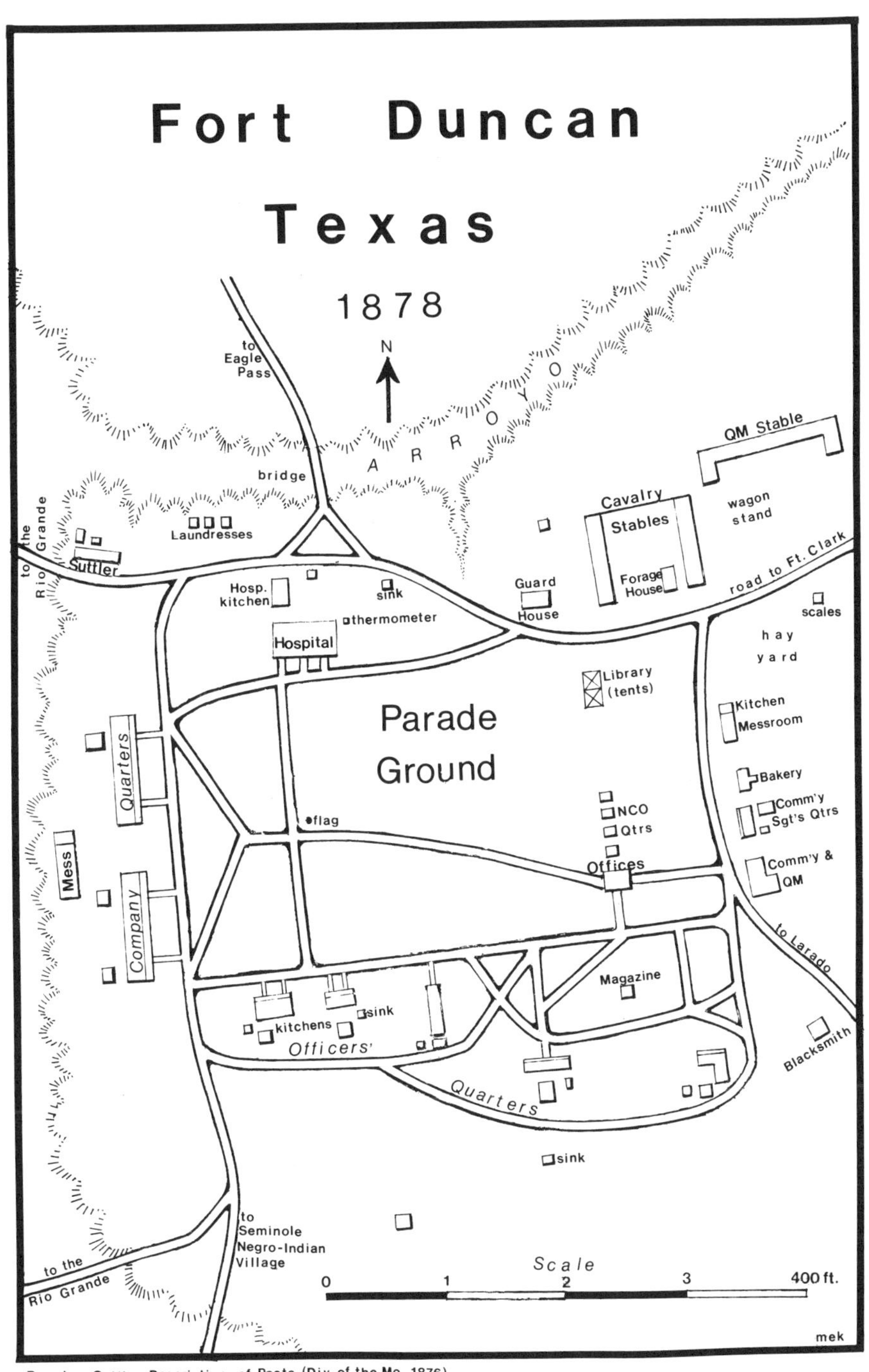

Based on Outline Description of Posts (Div. of the Mo., 1876) & Circular No. 8 (Surgeon General's Dept., 1875)

Inadequate and poorly constructed facilities were not unique to Fort Duncan, which at least was an established post instead of just another camp built, only to be abandoned as the need for troops shifted elsewhere. The usually sorry barracks and quarters resulted from the parsimonious refusal of Congress from 1865 to 1882 to permit anything other than "temporary huts and stables" at western posts—and even these were usually put up by soldiers with little or no skills as builders.[19] Most posts did not have adequate bathing facilities for the men, and at some locations nothing was provided but an outdoor basin of water or nearby river. Although small appropriations could have been used for temporary bath houses if the secretary of war approved, in that official's view troops should provide for their own needs without cost to the government.[20] In frustration, Sherman reported in 1882 that:

> ...troops have lived in holes in the ground; in houses made of green cottonwood logs, infested by vermin, [and] in temporary shanties, gently without murmur.... When this battle with poverty is over...[Congress should] appropriate funds for decent quarters.[21]

Despite the near-monastic conditions they had endured as cadets, several members of the 1877 Class found the frontier facilities even more austere. From the New Spotted Tail Agency in Dakota Territory George Baxter described the buildings as "simple, rough frame shells, made of unplaned lumber...[that] have shed roofs and are sunk about three feet into the ground."[22] And from Arizona Richard Wilson reported that "for pure monotony, dreariness, and general worthlessness [no place] could approach Fort Wingate."[23] Similar sentiments were widely echoed by observers elsewhere. For instance, a journalist described Fort Garland as "a rectangular group of brick-red adobe buildings, flat-roofed, squat...[and] in a state of increasing and unprepossessing dilapidation," which were "dispiriting in their unmitigated ugliness," conditions that moved him to commiserate for "all the unfortunate officers and men condemned to live in so desolate a place."[24]

Disparaging as most comments were, the consummate insult to all Texans was the barbed utterance of General Sheridan after a trip from San Antonio to Galveston in 1865. Fatigued and covered with mud, he entered the Washington Hotel where a gentleman whom he assumed was another guest asked him how he liked Texas. With characteristic candor he opined that "if I owned hell and Texas I would rent out Texas and live in hell."[25] The inquirer was neither a gentleman nor a guest at the hotel, but a newspaper reporter. Regardless, many of those garrisoned at Duncan probably shared Sheridan's assessment.

The officers and men might also have thought that the post was equally deserving of Sherman's description of Tombstone ("any common man would value the land...as dear at ten cents the hundred acres"),[26] and that West Texas was little better than that crusty officer's view of New Mexico (Sherman once told Gov. Lew Wallace that "the United States ought to declare war on Old Mexico and make it take back New Mexico").[27] Fort Duncan was not totally void of some redeeming assets, however. In 1875 a visiting assistant surgeon reported that the "general sanitary condition...so far as climate and locality are concerned, are [*sic*] very good."[28] But he did not have to remain there.

Eleven officers were at Duncan in late 1877; five were accompanied by their wives, two of whom had children.[29] In addition, Miss Stivers (sister of 1st Lt. Edwin Stivers) and Miss Winston (sister of Mrs. Gasman) were on extended visits, a common practice of young ladies related to officers or their wives stationed at frontier posts where the ratio of bachelors to single women was high.[30] Not uncommonly, romances (often abetted by matchmakers among the wives) were fostered by such associations.

By that time Eagle Pass had a population of about 1,500. Deer and antelope were nearby, and cougars, black bear, and ocelots could be found in the hills. Less welcome were the western diamondback rattlesnakes and copperheads, as well as the scorpions and tarantulas that thrived in the Southwest. And the vegetation was sparse, consisting principally of mesquite, mulberry, live oak, some cottonwood trees, and various cacti.

Views of those stationed elsewhere notwithstanding, for sheer physical discomfort, desolation, and barrenness, little could surpass the thin line of border posts that stretched more than a thousand miles between Forts Brown and Bliss.[31] And if not driven to drink (or perhaps because of it), some even resorted to verse to express their opinions. For example, in 1877 a disgruntled member of a garrison on the lower Rio Grande submitted to the *Army and Navy Journal* some doggerel describing the devil's delight with such a place, which commences:

The Devil was granted permission one day,
To select him a land for his own special sway;
He looked around for a month or more,
And ripped and snorted and terribly swore;
But at last was delighted a country to view,
Where the prickly pear, and the mesquite tree grew.
After a survey brief, he took up his stand,
On the eastern shore of the Rio Grande.

After detailing numerous satanic improvements to convert the region into something even less hospitable, including importing Comanches from hell, banishing all moisture, and fixing the minimum temperature at 107 degrees, it concludes:

He was satisfied now, He'd done all that he knew,
And vanished from earth in a blaze of blue,
And no doubt now, in some corner of H—l,
Gloats over the work he accomplished so well,
And vows that on earth is no "hellisher" land
Than the eastern bank of the Rio Grande,
For with his own realm, it compared so well,
That he felt assured it was "nearly H—l."[32]

Whether or not any place was "hellisher" then Fort Duncan, it must have provided a cultural shock to Bigelow, who had spent most of his young life in New York, New England, and western Europe. Nevertheless, he not only accepted his new surroundings without recording any dissatisfaction, but found much that interested him as he immersed himself in his duties and in learning all he could about the local community, customs, people, and language.

Chapter 6

Adapting to Army Life

For Bigelow and his classmates, reporting for duty at strange and far away places presented some situations for which their training had not fully prepared them. Finding their ways around was the initial requirement, after which arrangements had to be made for a variety of mundane essentials, such as a place to live, furniture, a bed and bedding, and meals. Fortunately the camaraderie and hospitality toward newly assigned officers made the transitions relatively effortless.

In Bigelow's case, however, his arrival at Fort Duncan was something less than auspicious. Reaching there about 11 a.m. on December 14, he walked to the commandant's quarters where he mistook the post commander, Major Schofield, for the officer of the day, and promptly proceeded to breach military protocol by reporting to him.[1] The minor gaffe apparently unnerved the young lieutenant, who tersely noted, "He told me to report to my Company Commander, which I immediately did."

Bigelow was not the only new lieutenant to bungle his introduction to the army. When the stagecoach carrying Charles Crane arrived at Duncan, he discovered that he should have alighted at Fort Clark where his company had been transferred. A couple of days later Crane caught a stage back to Clark; the reception provided him there by the post commander, Lieutenant Colonel Shafter, is not known.[2] Reporting to a post only to learn that a unit had moved elsewhere was not uncommon. Aside from the changing needs for troops at different locations, the policy was one of frequent moves if for no other reason than:

> Troops should never be permitted to remain long enough at any one post to acquire a home feeling, or for the development of the accumulative faculty. These are the most potent opponents to military efficiency, either of officers or enlisted men.[3]

After properly reporting, Bigelow was assigned a room, presumably in the "Long House," an 18-by-80-foot stone and adobe building with three rooms, a shared kitchen, and verandas along two sides.[4] The next necessity was where to eat. Unlike enlisted men who subsisted on government rations in company messes, officers were left to their own devices, and there were no restaurants or other dining facilities at frontier posts. Hence, as a matter of convenience and economy, an unaccompanied officer customarily joined a small number of others similarly situated (unless a married couple invited him to join their mess) and shared the expenses of the food and its preparation.

> I mess, for the present, with the Post trader, Dr. Byrne, and Lieut Wessals [Wessells],[5] the latter of the 25 Infty. The Dr. is an old friend of Mrs. Cornelius Lawrence who was very anxious to have me know him, as she does a great many other men.[6]

Bigelow's messing arrangements did not last long. Three weeks later he recorded:

> This morning...I had to wait longer than usual for my breakfast...and being pressed for time I...returned to my quarters in disgust.... I had my orderly Dilwood [Thomas Dillwood] go over to Eagle Pass and get a few eatables.... [When I met] Captain Schooley at the QM's office...he offered to take me in with Lieut Landon & himself [in] their mess.[7] I jumped at it. I intended after leaving the Sutler store this morning, to see Mrs Gasman and try to hasten her preparations for starting a mess.[8]

One perquisite of being an officer, even a lowly second lieutenant, was the availability of an enlisted man to serve as an orderly. Bigelow promptly acquired such assistance from Private Dillwood, but a few days later noted:

> Heard this m'g from officers who know, that soldiers are not required to act as servants. They do service in the officers' quarters only to accomodate [*sic*] them, though they accept pay for it. I had understood that they were required to wait upon the officers and I think they should be.

Despite a law prohibiting the use of "an enlisted man as a servant in any case whatsoever," soldiers who wanted to supplement their meager

Bigelow's brother, a Yale student, teased him with this cartoon.

incomes were customarily permitted to work for officers and their families.[9] Their employers usually paid them ten dollars or so a month from their own small salaries.[10]

The work performed ranged from cooking, cleaning quarters and miscellaneous housekeeping chores to grooming horses, watching over children, and otherwise relieving officers and their wives of many time-consuming and tedious tasks. Although some fellow soldiers derisively called them "strikers" or "dog robbers" (implying that they were fed scraps from an officer's table, hence depriving a family dog of food), they were often envied because of the added income and also because they frequently were excused from routine duties and might live and eat in the quarters of their employer.[11] Understandably, some strikers developed close and lasting affiliations with the officers and families they served.[12]

That evening Bigelow dined with his company commander, Capt. John Baptiste Van de Wiele, and his wife.[13]

> The Captain and Mrs. Van de Wiele did a great deal to make me feel at home and perfectly comfortable. The former, being post Qm. Mr. [Quartermaster], sent me what furniture I was in immediate need of...with the permission to retain them until I should buy what I wanted. After dinner, went to stable duty & walked around the post.[14]

Bigelow concluded the account of his first day by reflecting on the Mexican situation, the most pressing problem then confronting the troops in Texas.

TURMOIL ALONG THE RIVER

In late 1877 the long-brewing border controversies between the United States and Mexico were reaching a climax.[15] At the core of the disputes, which centered along the 400-plus miles from the mouth of the Rio Grande to Fort Duncan,[16] was the inability of either nation to effectively prevent Indians (and desperadoes of various ilks) from raiding into the other's territory to steal livestock, in the course of which incidental killings occurred.[17] As a result the number of American settlers decreased and cattle ranching retrenched because "stock cannot be raised there (between the Nueces and the Rio Grande) on account of its liability to being stolen."[18]

Resolution of the problems was made more difficult by such factors as political turmoil south of the border; the changing course of the river which often made the boundary location uncertain; the deep-seated animosities of many Mexicans toward Texans and other Americans, whom they contempuously called "gringos," and the reciprocal attitudes toward "greasers" held by the latter; and a fear that if United States forces pursued raiders into Mexico, the troops would stay there.[19]

Not all of the apprehensions were unfounded. At hearings in the fall of 1877 the House Military Affairs Committee was told that the legendary Col. John S. Ford, acting under the imprimatur of the governor of Texas to raise a regiment of volunteers, distributed handbills and held meetings in Corpus Christi and elsewhere urging people

> to defend their country and to repel invasion [because] a war was imminent, and that they would be called upon to uphold the honor of Texas.[20]

Maintaining Texas's honor might involve, of course, moving the boundary to the Sierra Madres, which would add territory surpassing that of several eastern states combined.[21]

Even though many Texans as well as some politicians and army officers thought that the nation was again on the threshold of war, Bigelow was less pessimistic.

> It appears that the Mexican question is passing through a crisis in Washington. I think that Congress is becoming conscious of the fact that bullying Mexico is as

unjust as fighting it would be. War and annexation, or civilization are the only two remedies to our frontier troubles. There will be squabbles wherever the line is drawn. Cooperation seems to be impossible.

After discussing the issues with some local residents a couple of days later, he added:

The [Mexican] troops...[are] doing the U.S. more good than harm in keeping down the insurrectionists as well as the raiders. The three generals in charge of the frontier...are supporters of Díaz.[22] More troops from the interior of Mexico...are coming to the frontier...for the same reason that additional American troops are now in the dep't: to protect the property of the people from thieves and robbers as well as to preserve peace between Mexico & the U.S.

The need for troops along the border echoed the opinion that General Sherman gave Congressman Bragg a few days earlier when the latter questioned where armed forces should be deployed:

...[Y]ou naturally place [troops] where chances of their being needed are greatest...[to protect Government property]...from thieves and other desperate and bad men. I do not refer to politicians now.[23]

TAKING CHARGE

The following morning Bigelow was given his first real responsibility with troops when he was unexpectedly placed in temporary command of the Company B and its sixty-six men—a formidable and heady duty for any second lieutenant on his first assignment.[24]

Saturday, Dec. 15, 1877. Fort Duncan.... I hope to get through my service as Company Commander without incurring any serious charge of incompetency. My lst Serg't is an intelligent darkey who has been in the Regiment ever since its organization. I have not found it necessary to do any writing as I was told the officers in colored regiments had to do on account of the ignorance of the men.

Apparently he performed his duties adequately, thanks in part to 1st Sgt. Jacob Young, the "intelligent darkey."

DIVERSIONS FROM DUTY

Not all of Bigelow's time was consumed by military responsibilities. For example, on Sunday, his second day at Duncan, Stivers called on him in the morning, after which he studied Spanish and wrote a letter. He then grumbled:

It is very annoying...to have to ask the commandant's permission to leave [the post] whenever one has occasion to do so. I asked him today if the permission which he granted was good for the whole day, to which he replied that it would be agreeable to him to know at about what time the permission would be taken advantage of.

Being miffed by Major Schofield's restrictions, however, did not deter Bigelow from going to Piedras Negras (which Brereton dismissed as a "picturesque mud-pile").[25]

A Mexican band passed through Eagle Pass...as is the custom when any merriment is to take place. Lieut. Landon said there would be a bull fight and that I should go over...as I might not soon have another opportunity. The Commandant gave me permission so I crossed the river for the first time....

Was astonished at seeing the Mexican quarter of a dollar cut in two for small change. The town is very dilapidated, there not being...a single fine house.... Most of the roofs appear to be flat,...the water running off through gutters of wood that project about three or four feet.... The appearance of Piedras Negras, or Black stones, is very much like what the name would suggest. The place stands on a bluff overlooking the river. The houses & bluff have the color of the mud along the banks.

...[After dinner] Dr Byrne and I...saw a bull fight.... I also saw...my ideal of Spanish beauty. I never had seen the large black eyes, long eyelashes and thick eyebrows represented in pictures of Spanish women. At the bull fight...was a young woman of an olive brown complexion, with a face between round and oval, whose eyes, mouth, hair, and expression, came nearer to what I had in my mind as the typical beauty of Seville, than anything that I have seen elsewhere.

Bigelow's greater interest in the señorita than in the bullfight is not surprising if Brereton's account is accurate: he wrote that the "bulls were mostly cows, all nearly paralyzed from fright, and without the slightest intention of injuring any of the men who danced around them and stuck barbs into their hides at every good opportunity."[26]

BORDER TOWN RIFFRAFF

Bigelow was also introduced to another aspect of life in the settlements that sprouted near military posts, especially along the lower Rio Grande: the toughs and derelicts who for whatever reasons—and whether in daylight or under cover of darkness—had left or escaped tamer regions of the country to live or drift in the West.

Monday, Dec. 17, 1877. Fort Duncan.... [Brereton and I] walked around town this morning. Met Lieut. Wessals [Wessells]...in the company of a rough looking crowd that was well armed; all were more or less under the influence of liquor.... I got

> him away from them to accompany [us] across the river...to inquire if there would be any bull fight in the afternoon. We found that none was to take place.

During much of the nineteenth century Texas had a reputation, not wholly undeserved, as a haven for killers, cattle and horse thieves, road agents, and other assorted pariahs who

> wear six-shooters, sombreros with snakes around them,...chew tobacco, drink whiskey, cuss the Yankees and vote for General Jackson, run off school teachers and hang Mexicans.[27]

The *St. Louis Globe-Democrat* even published a daily column headed "Texas Killings," which so enraged some Texas businessmen that they wrote the editor threatening to lynch any representative of the paper who showed up there.[28] And in a lighter vein there is the tale of a criminal caught red-handed while committing a crime; when his lawyer told him his only hope was to escape and run away, the confused client replied, "Where can I go to? Ain't I already in Texas?"[29]

Bigelow was not alone in commenting about some of the unsavory characters he encountered in town. Crane also noted:

> ...there were in the neighborhood of Eagle Pass some of the rough and ready desperadoes that have left such an impression of our border land. One of them, named King Fisher, had killed many men.[30]

LEARNING TO LEAD

Within a short while Bigelow's time and attention increasingly centered on his company duties, which included drilling troops, supervising target practice, correcting a lax soldier, helping another man rewrite an official letter, and serving as officer of the day.

> *December 18, 1877, Fort Duncan, Texas....* I drilled my company for the first time. The men...were rather slow...and did not seem altogether familiar with the drill. I kept them executing right by twos and eight by files till I thought none of the men could help knowing...how to do it. I then told them, that if any mistake were made I would presume that whoever made one...did not want to do it right, & that I would have him punished. My remarks had the desired effect....

> *Fort Duncan, Tex. Dec 19, 1877.* Spent most of the forenoon at home writing & studying. Went with the company to target practice at one o'clock. We shot...at 200 yards...while the Infantry...shot at 300 yards. The latter used the musket, while we used the carbine.... Walked to the village...for a little exercise and Spanish conversation this evening.

A few years earlier target practice was not part of the routine at many posts because of reduced appropriations, even though recruits often had never discharged a firearm.[31] Moreover, the nonmilitary labor required of them virtually precluded learning the basic skills of a soldier.[32] Following the defeat on the Little Big Horn, however, a concerted effort (including a general order that authorized using twenty ball cartridges monthly for each soldier) was made to improve marksmanship.[33]

That same day Bigelow again vented his annoyance with the limits imposed on how he used his off-duty time.

> When I asked...for permission to leave the Fort, [Major Schofield] said that I should not get too much in the habit of being away, that there was a great deal for me to learn and do etc. I told him that I asked to be absent for a number of hours in succession so as to be able to choose my time, but that I did not always want to be absent during the entire period.... I want to go to Eagle Pass or Piedras Negras...to learn Spanish by speaking it and also to make arrangements for eating at some place where I can hear Spanish spoken.
>
> The Commandant [also] told me...he had noticed [at drill]...a certain carelessness that he attributed to the scouting and like duty which allows the men to fall into loose ways. The same faults I noticed myself and have tried to have corrected. I spoke to Serg't Young about the guides and about a private, by the name of Dannels, [who]...instead of giving me a sergeant's salute, brought his left hand up to his cap while he held his carbine in his right.
>
> *Thursday, Dec. 20, 1877*.... I found a letter in my room, written for Pvt. Alfred Pride to Gen'l Ord:
>
>> Sir
>>
>> I wish to inform the Gen'l Comd'g of the unjust manner in which I was treated. My Company was paid...(on) Decb'r 13th 1877. Being absent on detached service I was not paid.... I presented myself to (the Paymaster) at 3 P.M. yesterday but he refused to pay me saying his safe was locked up. I have been nearly six months without pay and need the money, and request [it]...be sent to me in a check.
>
> ...[The letter] was not respectful enough to please me. The signature was not prefixed by any remarks as to the respect in which the writer held the person addressed.... Then the first sentence would give the impression that the writer had some personal ill feeling toward the paymaster instead of being simply desirous of obtaining his dues.

To remedy these shortcomings Bigelow composed a highly stylized revision replete with obsequious salutations and the customary close from "your obedient servant." He neglected to later mention, though, whether the impoverished Private Pride ever received his back pay.

Turning to a different subject, Bigelow wrote:

> My orderly Pvt Dillwood tells me that a Schofield Smith & Wesson is nothing but a pop gun, that no long range shots...can strike because the muzzle goes up every time it is emptied.[34] He told me that he was once chasing an Indian at close range, firing from his Schofield Smith & Wesson one shot after another until he had to give it up. He brought up his carbine and brought the Indian down.

Bigelow next relates an incident of the type that occasionally injected some comic relief into the largely humorless lives of the frontier troops. And the duller the conditions, the less humor was required.

> While passing from the sutler's toward my quarters, I heard a loud negro laugh. Looking towards the rear of our barracks I saw a soldier bending over the top of a barrel & laughing to split his sides while there resounded far and near the squealing of a pig whose feet were going through rapid movements very close to his face. The soldier had evidently stepped up while the pig had his head in the barrell *[sic]* and tipped it up so as to catch the pig. It had been eating swill out of the barrel.

On the last day of his first week Bigelow was appointed officer of the day, which placed him in charge of the guard for twenty-four hours and also required him to attend to numerous other matters prescribed in army regulations.[35] The next day he merely noted that he

> Did not feel so sleepy this morning...as I generally felt after such duty at West Point. I went to bed last night at about 9 o'clock, having instructed the Serg't of the Gd to wake me at 12.... Two parties are to leave the post tomorrow...to hunt game for the Christmas dinners.[36]

CHAPTER 7

LEARNING TO COMMAND

Despite his inexperience, Bigelow completed his first week as a company commander without causing his competency to be questioned. Before long different challenges would confront him, though, as disciplinary and personnel problems arose in B Company. Nevertheless his duties did not totally prevent him from pursuing his interests in the language and customs on the other side of the river, and with Christmas approaching the pace of social activities at Fort Duncan increased.

> *Fort Duncan, Texas, Dec. 21, 1877....* Private Harris...reported [to me] that Serg't [William] Givens had struck him.[1] The Serg't said that the man had been obstinate and insubordinate in continuing to talk instead of doing what he had been told to do. He said that, after he had allowed two men...on the feeding detail to go to the rear, Pvt Harris asked to do the same, which the Serg't would not allow, whereupon the private began to talk instead of obeying instructions. Serg't Givens told him to stop his talking, which he would not do, when the Sgt struck Private Harris on the arm with the back of a scoop shovel.
>
> I could not help smiling, but made Serg't Givens acknowledge that he had done...very wrong. He said that such men as Harris would defy his authority...and afterwards talk about it.... I said that...he would have to learn to...control his temper.... I think I will confine them both...to their qrs [quarters].

The next day Bigelow informed both men of his decision. When Sergeant Givens asked why he was being punished

> I told him that it was for [his] improper conduct.... He said that...what he had done was common in the Army. I said that it was well enough for an officer to

overlook such offences...when they were not brought officially to his notice but that he could not if they were so brought, without neglecting his duty....

I sent for [Pvt Harris who]...persisted in saying that Serg't Givens cursed him and that...a man had to seize Serg't Givens to keep him from beating him. I called this witness and peacemaker [from] whom...I learned more that was adverse than I did that was favorable to Pvt Harris.... Pvt Harris acknowledged the possibility of his having forgotten one or two things, which I told him...placed him in the position of one who had preferred false charges against a superior officer.... With due solemnity, I then pronounced his sentence—the same as that of Serg't Givens.

I found out later that I had not done enough [when] the Serg't came to me...with a private who, he said, had defied his authority...[by speaking] back to the Serg't instead of obeying him. I gave the private a talking to.... Serg't Givens told me that, being in confinement, he had lost a good deal of his influence over the men.... I immediately released him....

[He later] spoke to me about what I had said.... My remark was: "if this occurs again, the consequences will be different for both of you." He thought that the intimation...was unjust and he did not see why he should be punished.... I acknowledged that I had not understood the exact circumstances or I would not have made the remark. He was perfectly satisfied when I said that I had done wrong, that I felt very sorry and would try not to offend again in that way.

The several journal pages devoted to Sergeant Givens and his insubordinate subordinates indicate that Bigelow considered the matter somewhat as a conundrum without solution. Although he erred in chastising his able NCO in front of troops, the admission of fallibility suggests that he might have gained more from the incidents than any of the principals.

WHEN AN OFFICER'S WIFE IS NOT A LADY

Went across the river, this evening, with Dr Byrne,...Mrs Gasman, her sister, Mrs Stivers and her sister. Lieut Landon came over when he completed his duties.... Brereton was expected to go with us but was absent...so that, when we started, there was ill feeling towards him, on the part of the ladies, for having left four of their sex to only two escorts. Eddy Stivers said that Brereton was playing billiards in town.... That report did not smooth matters.

I thought that the ladies were going to the theatre, [but] we loafed around the Plaza de Torres [Toros], where the fair is held...looking in at the booths, where gambling was going on, and visiting shops. Mrs Gasman sat down at the Monte table with $6.50. She played for about a quarter of an hour, when she stopped without having lost or won. She was quite fascinated by the game.[2] It disgusted me to see her wedge in among a lot of ruffian gamblers...and then take a seat next to one. I believed her when she said that if she were a man, she would gamble and race horses; but, I did not believe what she had previously said—that as a woman, she would not gamble anywhere else. She said that all the ladies did it here.

We had a Mexican supper.... The nourishment was abundant, and very strongly favored. We had tortillas, tomales [*sic*], and one or two other dishes. I got a couple of cups of good frothy chocolate. It was a beautiful moonlight night, rather cool, especially...as I had not brought my cape with me.

OBSERVING THE SABBATH

Sundays at frontier posts usually involved an inspection and morning parade, with routine tasks such as stable calls interspersed between then and tattoo. Nevertheless some leisure opportunities might exist unless other duties were assigned.

Fort Duncan, Texas, Sunday, Dec. 23, 1877.... I ordered a horse "Pacer" from the stables and went out for a ride over the drill grounds and around Eagle Pass. The horse had been ridden by Lieut Orleman, first Lieut. of my company, a good deal.[3] It has a fine gait and is very easily managed.... A great many buffaloes must have been killed about here. Their bones lie bleaching on every side. Disgusting odors go up here & there from the offals around places where meat is cut. I do not know that this meat is buffalo, I suppose it is not....

Went across the river...to subscribe to the "Siglo diez y nueve," the Mexican paper; I was told...that it is the best in the country. I finally succeeded in finding a person...to order the paper for me. I then called on Captain Lopez, a Mexican officer. He cannot speak any English, so I try to see him whenever I can and get to talking Spanish with him....

The Commandant gave me orders to put Corporal [William E.] Carter in arrest and prefer charges against him under the 32d Art. of War [absence without leave]. It appeared...that he was over at the trader's establishment last night for about an hour and a half. His absence was detected by a check roll-call....

The Adjutant sent word to me while I was attending stables that there would be dress parade this evening. I sent the orderly to the Commandant to inquire if I should continue grooming or attend parade, and...that the Company could not do both. Major Schofield [said]...that he would like the whole Company to attend parade but that, in case it should not be possible, he would like the old soldiers to take part. The old men are the only ones who have a full dress uniform....

During the last few days my attention has been fixed at stable duty upon the tails...part of the grooming.... A great deal of carelessness had been allowed, and I decided to effect a reform.... Then, by going around examining tails, giving instruction,...and ordering some [men] punished for pulling out too much hair, I have effected a decided improvement in the appearance of the horses. My favorite punishment...is to unravel the tails of five horses.

Major Schofield has given over Pvt [George] Young...to the civil authorities. Major Van de Wiele told me that the Commandant is prejudiced against this private because he applied to be relieved...as servant to the Commandant. The latter told me that he had...stolen...whiskey while waiting on him.... The sheriff had a charge against him of having...ill-treated a woman in Eagle Pass. After he had received his sentence to be fined fourty [sic] dollars he asked Major Van de Wiele to lend him the money.... The Major is the cause of this familiarity. He is too unorganized and incautious in his intercourse with the men to maintain among them a proper respect.

To conclude the day Bigelow decided to attend a theater across the river at which a play in Spanish was performed.

Went over to Piedras Negras.... As no one would go with me, I took my revolver and went alone.... The [theater] door was guarded by dismounted Cavalrymen. My ticket cost one dollar which was [too much] considering that it did not secure a seat. The performance was in the open air, the audience being under a canvas awning. There were benches and chairs to accomodate [*sic*] a small number of people, the majority of the audience...having to provide their own seats.... There were a number of soldiers preserving order inside the theatre. [As] part of the "fiesta," it is under protection of the Military.... The play was not very exciting...[but] my strength in Spanish was somewhat increased by listening to the dialogues.

The following morning Lieutenant Landon mentioned that Major Schofield had once found fault with his (Landon's) punctuation. To avoid similar criticism, Bigelow thought "it would be well...to study the subject a little," so he copied numerous examples from his cadet textbook, Wilson's *Treatise on Punctuation*. Next he turned to his company duties, only to find that yet another soldier's unenthusiastic response to Sergeant Given's instructions demanded corrective action. This time he managed the situation differently.

After target practice today...Private [George A.] Sweat stood a few steps from the ranks cleaning his gun.... Sergeant Givens who was standing near me spoke to him; he continued cleaning his gun, moving slowly toward the Company.

> I...ordered him put in the Guard House. It was my intention...to prefer charges against him, but tomorrow being Christmas, I think I shall have him released to take dinner with the Company....
>
> Private Sweat...[later] told me that he was not thinking...and that if he were released this time he would not offend again. I told him that the example of his conduct was demoralizing and could not be allowed to go unpunished.... He was satisfied with my consent being granted to his going to the barracks in order to make such disposal of his effects as he should see fit.

Bigelow, who showed a glimmer of compassion, was not acting arbitrarily in having the private locked up, since soldiers charged with "crimes" were required to be confined prior to trial.[4] To prevent abuses, however, the officer of the day had to report the names of the prisoner and the officer to the post commander. Moreover, pretrial confinement could not lawfully continue for more than eight days or until a court-martial could be assembled—a requirement that went back at least as far as the 1686 Code of King James.[5]

A GUARDHOUSE IS NOT A HOME

The Fort Duncan guardhouse was a substantial building, forty-eight by twenty-seven feet, with a stone floor and a shingle roof. It was divided into three sections; the center one, which had a fireplace, was used by the guard and the other two were cells with grated windows for ventilation but no means of warming. The average daily prisoner population in 1875 was twelve men, or more than 6 percent of the garrison's strength.[6]

Confinement facilities had been a key issue a few years earlier when the *Army and Navy Journal* complained that "there is hardly a regular post at which soldiers are not undergoing sentences of courts-martial for periods varying from one week to several years. These prisoners are confined in the guardhouse with the ordinary minor garrison offenders."[7] Actually, authority existed to confine some longer-term prisoners in state penitentiaries, which often were designated as the place of confinement for soldiers who were discharged dishonorably. But there was a continuing need for a separate military facility for some prisoners, which Congress authorized the following year.[8]

MAKING DO

A remote frontier post such as Duncan provided few amenities and fewer means of observing holidays in a manner that was customary in eastern communities. Meal preparation with the limited foodstuffs available, possibly supplemented by wild game, challenged the culinary imaginations of the most talented hostesses.[9] A seasoned officer once commented that many a young bride finds that:

> Canned stuffs, such as peaches, tomatoes, and green corn, poorly recompense her for the eatables obtainable in New York, Philadelphia, Chicago, and St. Louis.... (M)ost old officers have seen a man put on a good many airs because he was the fortunate possessor of a cabbage or a mess of potatoes, while others had none of these toothsome comestibles. It does not take much to make an aristocrat.[10]

Despite the limited resources, though, the wives and officers at remote posts did their utmost with what they had to enliven their drab lives with some social cheer, especially at Christmas.

For entertainment in an officer's quarters, music (often supplied by a wife's guitar since pianos were seldom available), singing, charades, and card games such as euchre were popular.[11] And where facilities could accommodate them, dancing and amateur theatrics were in vogue.[12] Traditionally, bachelors were invited to share in all the festivities.

> *Dec. 24, 1877....* Was invited this evening to call on Lieut. Stivers, which I did. There was dancing in many styles. We began with a quadrille [and] I danced...the Cubana, which Mexicans dance in imitation of Cubans.

On-post recreational opportunities were even less for enlisted men. Except for laundresses, many of whom were the wives of noncommissioned officers, feminine companionship was virtually nonexistent, and apart from drinking at the post trader's or in barracks, there were few amusements other than playing cards or billiards, or occasionally hunting or participating in a sport such as baseball.[13]

> One of the greatest hardships of garrison life on the frontier is the privation...in regard to amusements, churches, and so forth. Private theatricals are not always successful...and the class of entertainments originated by the soldiers...are far from satisfying. Negro-minstrel shows are pretty slow affairs as rendered by the cavalrymen, there being a sort of woodenness about them.[14]

Off-post, of course, "hog ranches," saloons, and other unwholesome enterprises attracted those so inclined, assuming they could obtain passes to go into town.

Reading rooms that soldiers could use after retreat were popular but generally limited. Fort Duncan had a library with about 170 books and several newspapers located in two hospital tents, yet illiteracy was so widespread among African Americans that it was of little benefit to most soldiers. There were, though, two literary societies, and mail arrived twice a week from San Antonio.[15] And at Christmas sergeants' wives, like those of officers but with even less means, invited lonesome soldiers to join them for a home-cooked meal. But receiving permission to enjoy such hospitality could be a problem.

> Sadler [*sic*] [Sidney] Jones asked permission to be absent until twelve o'clock at an entertainment to be given by Mrs Stuart, the laundress.... I asked...Lieut. Stivers [who] told me that the Com'd't...would have to approve of such a permit.... Saddler Jones had therefore to be denied the privilege. I have no doubt, however, that he went without permission.... He was probably not the only 'B' Comp. man at that party.

CHRISTMAS 1877

At some posts, usually depending on what the commander and his wife encouraged, Christmas day was a festive time.[16] Elsewhere there was little to differentiate it from other days. Fort Duncan in 1877 tended more toward the latter.

> *Fort Duncan, Texas, December 25, 1877....* [Went] to Major Van de Wiele's house to dine.... We had quite a good dinner. The soup was followed by chicken salad and pickled tongue, then came chicken & venison with peas & potatoes. The desert [*sic*] consisted of pudding, jelly & mince pie followed by coffee. The Major had, also, some good Mexican wine. After dinner...he suggested that I go with him to see the Commandant.... I did not much like the idea of going without an invitation but Major Van de Wiele pressed me a little, saying that...the Com'd't being unable, on account of his wife's sickness, to exchange visits had invited the Major to call on him.
>
> ...I found that the Commandant was in an official rather than a sociable mood. He...talk[ed] about transportation [for] the American consular agent at Piedras Negras, who is summoned to Washington. I soon became convinced that I was hindering free discussion...and therefore took my leave. I hope Major Van de Wiele explained...how I happened to intrude.
>
> Lieut. Stivers called to tell me that a member of my company was very boisterous and unmanageable, evidently under the influence of liquor.... [W]e went together to the barracks where...I saw a man...who appeared to be a little unsteady but, not having conclusive evidence of his being drunk, I gave him the benefit of the doubt. I asked the non commissioned officer in charge if he had heard any loud and boisterous talking or shouting. He said he had and had just succeeded in

stopping it. I ordered him to put the next noisy man in the guard house. I am glad I did not have to lock anyone up, this being Christmas day.

Fort Duncan, Texas, December 26, 1877

to the Companey commander

Sir. I has the honor of Sending in my Resegnation to Resine my Rank as a Sergt. in Co B. 10th Cav. to be Redused to the Ranks as a Private Soldier in the Ranks.

Yours Very Respectfully

Sergt. Robert McDonald

I saw Serg't McDonald this morning.... He thought he could soldier better as a private, that the charge had been brought against him...that he was always concerned in any disputes between any private and a non commissioned officer,...and that some of the men were against him because he had belonged to the 9th Cavalry. I talked to him about the mistake he was making...and finally told him that the application was not authorized by usage or regulation and that if I were Captain of the Company I would have him in arrest.

Nothing momentous occurred the rest of the day, but when Captain Van de Wiele told him that Company B's property would be transferred to him, Bigelow noted with trepidation, "I hope to know more about it by that time than I do now." Turning to more mundane matters, he again groused about how Major Schofield was hindering his desire to learn Spanish.

The annoyance of having to get permission from the Commandant every time I wished to leave the post had got to be a serious obstacle in the way of my practising [*sic*} Spanish with people in town. He [plainly] did not like my going out every day and I therefore dislike...asking him permission to do so.... He said he would want to know how to find me [because] troops have had to start from here on short notice....

HOW WHITE OFFICERS AT DUNCAN REGARDED BLACK TROOPS

Bigelow also mentioned a talk he had with Lieutenant Stivers:

He said a great deal in favor of colored troops, especially their conduct under fire.... I have been told that they have outmarched white troops on foot.

Considering Stivers' fifteen years of experience with African American soldiers, his appraisal carried considerable weight. Not all views were as flattering, though. Captain Schooley, for instance, often talked "about the stupidity of colored troops," and Bigelow occasionally referred to the "ignorance" of blacks, most of whom, of course, were unschooled. His greatest exasperation, however, was what he considered their seemingly pointless frivolities. For example, after returning to his quarters one day to discover that someone had written on the pictures hung about the room, he vented his ire by writing:

> Childish thoughtlessness is the great weakness of these colored men. They will do things so foolish that it is impossible for a man of sense to anticipate their freaks & follies. Capt Schooley says that a colored soldier...would put the door of his barracks into the stove rather than go outside to get wood. He has seen such imbecility in his own company....
>
> A colored man cannot command the respect of another colored man. It is no wonder; they were all slaves together. Hence the colored soldiers are less apt than white soldiers to acknowledge any superiority...in their Non Com'd Officers, while the colored N. Com'd Officers themselves are less able than the white to make their subordinates feel and see what superiority they can justly assert.

Regardless, many knowledgeable officers attested to the battle prowess of blacks, who "make good troops" despite their lack of education or "habits of discipline."[17] And although Bigelow, the product of a strong abolitionist background, might express frustration when an African American trooper failed to meet the standards he expected, he also thought that

> Dignity, grace, and refinement go further I think with colored people towards inspiring respect than they do with coarse white men. In this characteristic, as in many others, they resemble children. A negro can be severe but he cannot be stern. A uniform air of serious earnestness would turn a negro white.

But despite the differing opinions that officers in Negro regiments might express among themselves, with outsiders most appear to have been staunch defenders of their troops. For example, when Joseph Bush transferred from a white to a black regiment and arrived at his new post, Bigelow pithily reported:[18]

> I have heard that Capt. French of the 25th when introduced to him made the remark: "Well, Major, what sort of soldiers do these white men make, anyhow?"[19]

MADDENING MINUTIAE

> *Fort Duncan, Texas, Dec. 28, 1877....* Upon marching on as Off. of Day, I found that [by using my name]...Sergt Young had confined Pvt [Arthur] Saunders [Sanders] on account of Sadler Jones having told Serg't Young that Private Sanders...said "damn Serg't Young." Serg't Young...saw Pvt Sanders [at the stables] walking with a strap in his hand and supposed that [he] was looking to the straps on the horses, which the Serg't knew was properly the duty of Sadler Jones. He made Pvt Sanders attend to his horse.
>
> ...I learned that the Corp'l of the stable detail had ordered Pvt Sanders...to perform some duty, [and] that...the strap was taken from the stall of his own horse. Also,...his profanity was directed toward Sadler Jones.[20] I had him released from confinement.

Coping with an occasional shirker was another problem that confronted Bigelow.

> Private Robinson was absent from reveille.... He had told the Sergt that he could not dress himself, in proof of which he [appeared] on the Company stoop without any pants on. I received a pass to sign for him, which I would not approve of, knowing that he affected to be, or was, sick.... [Captain Byrne] could detect nothing serious.... We concluded...that he had wanted very much to go to town tonight or get out of drill and that he knew there were two ways of doing [so].... One was to get on the sick report & the other to get a pass. He thought he would try both, thinking thereby to make certain of one, at least.

Chapter 8

Practicing Army Law

Having prepared courts-martial charges, ordered men confined, and taken other disciplinary actions, Bigelow was next appointed recorder on a garrison court-martial, which would immerse him more deeply in the Army's criminal law system, known as military justice. Once he became aware of all that was demanded of him, he might have regretted not devoting more time to the year-long cadet law course in which he finished seventy-third out of seventy-six.

LAWING IN THE ARMY

The court-martial system in the 1870s was essentially unchanged from that in 1806, with minor modifications made in 1874. The three peacetime tribunals were the general, regimental, and garrison courts-martial. Only a general commanding an army, a colonel commanding a separate department, or the president could appoint a general court-martial, which required from five to thirteen officers as members and a judge advocate. Its authority (jurisdiction) extended to trying officers or enlisted men for offenses that violated the Articles of War, and to imposing any prescribed or authorized sentence.[1]

The principal difference between garrison and regimental courts-martial was that a post commander convened the former to try enlisted men at his post, and a regimental commander convened the latter to try soldiers of his regiment.[2] Each was composed of three officers, and the sentences were limited to a fine of one month's pay and confinement at hard labor for one month. Until 1880 no judge advocate was appointed to these inferior courts, but the junior member, known as the recorder, performed similar functions and also voted on the findings and sentences.

To activate the lumbering military justice system, an officer would "prefer charges" against another officer or soldier, although customarily if a soldier was the accused (defendant) his company commander was the accuser. The charges (similar to an indictment or "information" filed in civilian tribunals) were forwarded to the "convening authority," usually the post commander.[3] If he determined that *prima facie* evidence existed and that trial by an inferior court was proper, he could refer the case to trial. However, if an officer was the accused or if the offense was serious, the charges were sent to the commander who was empowered to appoint a general court-martial.

As there was no judge as such, the highest ranking member of the court presided at the trial. Whatever legal advice might be desired was provided by the judge advocate of a general court-martial (seldom a lawyer except in major cases) or the recorder. After a witness was called, sworn, and examined by the side calling him, the other side could cross-examine, and then any court member could ask questions. Any evidentiary or other legal ruling was made by majority vote. After the evidence had been introduced and arguments made, the court closed for deliberation, then each member cast a secret, written ballot with a majority required to convict.[4] If the finding was guilty, the court closed again to arrive at the sentence. Unless Congress had specified a mandatory punishment, each member, commencing with the most junior, proposed what he believed to be the most appropriate punishment, and votes were taken until a majority (or two-thirds if the sentence was death) concurred.[5] Thereafter a report of the proceedings was prepared and submitted to the officer who convened the court who, if he concurred, could order the sentence executed unless it extended to dismissal of an officer or death, which required the president's approval.[6]

BIGELOW'S JURIDICAL BAPTISM

In addition to his prosecutorial and other responsibilities at trial, as recorder Bigelow also was responsible for notifying witnesses, administering oaths, and afterwards preparing a record of the proceedings.

> I found out a few points about my duty before the Court opened, but not much.... Had a hard time finding the oath to administer...and had not summoned

> any of the witnesses before opening of the Court so that we lost much time waiting for them.

The delay caused by Bigelow's dereliction prevented the trial from progressing beyond the preliminary stages that day since sessions were held between 10 a.m. and 3 p.m. only.[7] This practice once led Maj. Gen. Irvin McDowell to comment:

> ...how we cling to old notions prohibiting courts-martial from sitting after three o'clock p.m., because a hundred years ago in England officers were wont to dine and get drunk at that hour. Now...there is no reason why courts-martial should not sit all night if necessary to reach a verdict.[8]

Before the trial resumed Bigelow, who was still required to perform his officer of the day and other duties, "inspected the Guard at about half past one o'clock this morning [and] nearly froze during the night."

> *Fort Duncan, Texas, December 29, 1877.* The court met again at 10 A.M. and...adjourned at half past two P. M. Found the accused guilty of the first specification excepting the intent to deceive and guilty...of the second specification. We were not unanimous upon the sentence. I thought...that we should not have inflicted...the severest penalty that the law allowed [one month's imprisonment and forfeiture of pay] without having convicted him of the entire offence with which he was charged....

Bigelow then sought reassurance by consulting *Benet*, a law textbook used at West Point.[9] After devoting almost four pages of his journal to arguments for and against the issue, he concluded that:

> Upon second thought I do not think that we did commit any fault, for the punishment...was in our judgment sufficient for that part of the charge of which we had proven the party guilty; had we proven him guilty of more and awarded the punishment while we held it to be insufficient...we would have erred.... Military law is not so imperfect as I had thought.[10]

Other legal issues troubled Bigelow, who on occasion sought advice from officers more experienced than he.

> Talked with Capt Schooley...about the unfairness of a trial of a Private soldier [who] had not a counsel. He said that the Judge Advocate...is so far counsel for the defence as to see that he does not suffer from want of legal knowledge and that he can advise the prisoner even to impeach the veracity of a witness for the prosecution if he conscientiously believes that witness to have sworn falsely.... In other words the Judge Adv. should be an impartial seeker after truth.

Bigelow had a valid point. Although Captain Schooley correctly stated the existing law, at times a judge advocate's responsibility was bound to strain the limits of fairness. Within a few years this defect was partially remedied by requiring a separate defense counsel, if requested, for general courts-martial.[11] What Bigelow did not mention, however, was that the Sixth Amendment ("in all criminal prosecutions, the accused shall enjoy the right...to have the Assistance of Counsel") was then limited to federal courts so did not apply to either state courts or courts-martial, which were created under the power of Congress to "make rules for the government and regulation of the land and naval forces."[12]

Showing his customary inquisitiveness as well as a willingness to challenge practices with which he disagreed, Bigelow also questioned departmental orders that

> forbad the trying of two or more for the same offence except in cases of conspiracy or in which the offence could not have been committed by the individuals separately....[13]

And in a subsequent case he related:

> We had quite a scene in court...as to whether or not, when the prisoner pleads guilty and introduces no evidence, the recorder has the right to reply. I wanted to make a reply but it was objected to by a member.... I should like to know whether or not the Court in sustaining the objection was in the right.[14]

Then when a B Company trooper who had spent thirty days in the guardhouse awaiting trial for stealing asked for help in obtaining a copy of the charges, and another soldier who had been locked up for nine days for insulting an NCO made a similar request, Bigelow complained to the commandant. Not sharing his young lieutenant's concern, however, he curtly dismissed the matter by saying he could not furnish charges "as he had none" and that prisoners "had no right to any." Major Schofield erred, for the policy was to serve charges on an accused when he was arrested or as soon as practicable, with more than eight days considered arbitrary and oppressive under most circumstances.[15]

OFFICERS AND QUASI-LAWYERS

Bigelow's interest in the law was by no means unusual considering that almost all officers had to devote substantial time to disciplinary and criminal problems. During the pre–Civil War years military lawyers were virtually nonexistent, and they remained rarities even in the latter part of the century,[16] perhaps in part because of the conventional view that:

> [I]t will be a grave error if...we permit the *Military Law* to become emasculated by allowing lawyers to inject into it principles derived from their practice in the civil courts which belong to a totally different system of jurisdiction. The objects of the civil law are to secure to everyone all the liberty, security, and happiness consistent with the safety of all. The purpose of military law is to govern armies of strong men, so as to be capable of exercising the largest measure of force at the will of the nation....
>
> Civilian lawyers are too apt to charge that army discipline is tyranny. We know better.... To obtain...the largest measure of force and the best results, [a commander] must possess the absolute confidence of his command by his fairness, his impartiality, his sense of justice, and devotion to his country, not from fear.[17]

With the scarcity of lawyers, commanders and line officers were routinely required to perform legal and judicial functions for which most had little or no formal training.[18] Consequently, many officers marched off into the frontier figuratively clutching a firearm in one hand and a law book in the other. Such references often were the only guidance available when investigating suspected offenses, drafting court-martial charges, prosecuting or defending an accused, and sitting in judgment at trials.

Over time some officers became skilled advocates and a few even authored insightful legal articles (such as General Sherman, who had briefly been a lawyer of sorts and believed that military law was "the most interesting subject possible to all army officers").[19] At least an advantage held by academy graduates was a basic familiarity with the nature and purposes of law and the military justice system.[20] One even thought:

> There is no course of study at the Academy which subsequently enters more constantly and generally into the professional life of...officers than that of the law.... Not that it is expected or desired that they will become lawyers. Far from it. But...the great majority of officers frequently perform duties that call [for] legal knowledge.[21]

THE MORIBUND LEGAL SYSTEM

The principal problem, though, was not so much the absence of legally trained officers as it was archaic laws. The army's criminal law had its roots in ancient Roman law and the seventeenth-century Articles of

Gustavus Adolphus, and there had been scant change since the Mutiny Act of England was adopted almost verbatim at the time of the Revolution.[22] But what might have served the needs of the miniscule antebellum force had become grossly inadequate even before the Civil War. In 1868 General Sherman chaired a board to propose revisions, which were submitted with the remark that "the old Articles of War...had become in great part inapplicable to the present state of the military service."[23] Yet for years Congress did nothing and even then the changes were little more than cosmetic.

Among the greatest shortcomings was the fact that there simply was no way of dealing promptly, fairly, and effectively with minor derelictions. The infamous "disciplinary" or "company" nonjudicial punishments that had been commonly employed in earlier decades had never been authorized by law nor sanctioned by usage, and they were repeatedly prohibited in general orders and by the judge advocate general.[24] Although not wholly eradicated, such practices had decreased markedly since an *Army and Navy Journal* editorial in 1867 denounced the flogging of a Fort Sedgwick soldier who stole a gun, the bucking and gagging of another man, the spread-eagling of a third, and administering a hundred lashes to a civilian who gave a bottle of whiskey to two soldiers.[25]

The only lawful means of dispensing justice and maintaining discipline (other than administratively by such methods as withholding passes or assigning unpleasant duties) was by court-martial; consequently the number of cases, often for trivial offenses, was staggering. For example, by 1885, when the total enlisted force was less than 25,000, there were 14,179 trials, including 2,292 general courts-martial of soldiers (plus 28 of officers and 8 of cadets) and 11,851 garrison or regimental courts-martial, which cumulatively required enormous amounts of time.[26] No wonder one disgruntled medical officer who was a member of a court-martial complained:[27]

All day I sit and swelter
Upon this hard, hard chair,
My liver's out of kilter,
There's a pain beneath my hair.

The worst of our dreary routine
Upon the bleak frontier,
Is to meet in solemn conclave
And these stupid cases hear.

'Twill make damn little difference,
One hundred years from now,
Whether this fellow stole two dollars,
Then, wherefore all this row?[28]

MORE TRYING TIMES

Instead of abating, the time and effort Bigelow had to devote to disciplinary matters, stupid or otherwise, escalated. Early on Monday he commenced to transcribe the record of his first case, which concluded the previous Saturday. Before very long, however, he testily noted that

> the president of the recent Court Martial sent word to me to find out if I were through with writing up the record.... I sent him my compliments & informed him that I had not yet completed my labors. I did not feel it incumbent on me to write the record on Sunday. Beside it has been so cold...that I have often been unable to write well at my table it being so far from the fire.

Bigelow's less than lustrous initiation to the military justice system was further tarnished a few days later.

> My first Court Martial [did] not meet with the Com'd't's approval. He...object[ed] to some of the questions as assuming what was not proven and to others as tending to prove what was beyond the Court's legitimate range of inquiry. Said that cross questions should be by the prisoner to the prosecuting witness and that the re-examinations should be confined to the matter brought forth by the prisoner's questions.[29]

Not all trials were as vexatious. During the next month most of Bigelow's dozen or so cases involved little more than guilty pleas to minor offenses such as off-duty drunkenness or AWOL for a few hours. For example, a couple of days after transcribing his first trial Bigelow mentioned:

> Recorded for another court martial...this m'g. Pvt. Wiley Jones was tried for [absence without leave].... He had no witnesses so the case was disposed of in about a half an hour.... Yesterday tried...Dixon, Nunley & Robinson. Today continued the trial of Private [Phillip] Washington which was begun yesterday.

THE PERILS OF PAYDAY

Saturday evenings, especially after being paid, were a common time for lonesome soldiers to indulge (or at times wallow) in activites that weekday duties and the lack of money otherwise prevented. The most prevalent were gambling and excessive drinking in barracks, nearby settlements, or at the post trader's store, frequently leading to other transgressions. And although as a group black troops were less addicted than whites to these vices, Fort Duncan was not free of misbehavior.[30]

The propensity of some soldiers to gamble probably existed in most armies since time immemorial, but commanders still struggled to control it because of the deleterious affect it could have on some losers. Hence, to "discourage and prevent" soldiers from gambling, Major Schofield directed all officers to break up any "games of chance [they] noticed or heard of" and to arrest any NCO who engaged in a game with privates.[31] No arrests were recorded that January, but the problem is not likely to have been eliminated so simply. Drunkenness, however, was involved in an incident Bigelow relates:

> [A] man tried to run away this afternoon.... Brereton told me that he had jumped across the ravine making the biggest jump he had ever seen. He succeeded in gaining a few feet on the other side but there were sentinels on both sides who could reach him at a thousand yards. He...came back. This is the first cause of trouble due to this morning's payment. This man got drunk and beat a sergeant's wife over the head with a chair.

Another over-imbiber was Saddler Sidney Jones who ended payday in the guardhouse. Unfortunately for him, a sober prisoner, George Young, was already there.

> *Fort Duncan, Texas, Jan. 13, 1878*.... Jones was put in the Guard house...very much under the influence of liquor and while in that helpless condition was assaulted by [Private] Young who had a grudge against him for his having testified against Young before a Court Martial. The blow was given right over the eye with the flat of a spade. Sadler Jones was a sorry sight...this morning, with his right eye shut and water running freely out of both the right & left. I immediately determined to prefer charges against the cowardly brute who had struck him but, alas!—he is now over the hills and far away.
>
> ...The Commandant...had ordered him put in irons.... He was sent out with shackles on his ankles and his arms free, to work in a squad of four prisoners.... While chopping wood, he probably cut his chain through—at any rate, he made a leap over some wood, ran off, and although fired upon three times, made his escape. About a half a dozen mounted men...could not catch him. He had good cause to attempt running away as he had been retained by the civil authorities for assault[ing] a woman in Eagle Pass, had been in the guard house for a long time, was awaiting trial by a Gen'l Court Martial and awaiting my charges.... He is the

> happiest man now for miles around, may he turn out a decent character some day.

Whatever happiness Young might have experienced was short-lived. The following day Bigelow recorded:

> Pvt Young was apprehended last night. Jones...guided a patrol to a place in Eagle Pass where he knew Young would go, and there the Sheriff took charge of him. His feelings towards Jones must be anything but kindly.... He will be kept in irons and will probably not be allowed to run away again.

GUARDHOUSE LAWYERING

With other charges already pending at departmental headquarters, Major Schofield referred only one allegation against Young, that of aggravated assault, to the garrison court. And what should have been a simple case took five days to try and filled twenty-one, eight-and-one-half by twelve-and-one-half-inch pages of the book in which Bigelow recorded the proceedings, producing a classic example of the origin of the phrase "guardhouse lawyer."[32] The alleged victim testified that he was taken to the guardhouse where

> He [Young] struck me with a spade standing sort of to my right over my temple and saying to the sergeant take me out if he didn't he'd kill me.[33]

Private Fred Hayes then testified that he had "seen [Young] strike Pvt Jones...with a shovel," and another witness added that afterwards the accused said that unless "the son of a b——h was taken out he'd kill him." Two defense witnesses testified that they had been in the guardroom and did not see any blow struck, but when they entered the cell they observed Jones lying on the floor. Although Young declined to testify, he made an unsworn statement (thereby avoiding cross-examination) that "Saddler Jones...[bought] a bowie knife...and carried it purposely for me and from that I think they [Jones and the government witnesses] have prejudices against me."

After convicting the accused, the court sentenced him to "forfeit one month's pay and serve...a term of one month's confinement at hard labor. The labor during fifteen days to consist in carrying a log weighing twenty-five pounds from 7 a.m. until retreat, one hour being allowed for each meal."

THE COST OF MISTREATING A HORSE

As Young's case ended another was about to commence. Bigelow wrote that during stable call one day he

> saw a man jump back from his horse which had reared up a little, and standing about five or ten feet from him and facing him, throw his curry comb...right in the horse's face. It glanced off and flew over the top of the stables.... I could hardly believe my senses, but as soon as I realized the man's brutality and stupidity, I had him put in the guard house.

The inhumane soldier, Pvt. Cunen McReynolds, was soon arraigned on charges preferred by Bigelow, who noted that "I shall be prosecutor, sole witness for the prosecution and recorder or counsel for prosecution."[34] At trial the accused introduced mitigating evidence that his horse had a mean disposition and would paw and strike out with his front feet or bite him, which might account for the lenient sentence to forfeit only five dollars.

THE MORE SERIOUS OFFENSES

Despite Bigelow's complaint that "there is a great deal of writing for me to do as recorder of the Courts," he soon was appointed as a member of a general court-martial, which would preempt even more of his time. At least, though, the cases referred to it went beyond mundane transgressions. For instance, one trial involved Pvt. William Maulsby of F Company, 24th Infantry, a very tall, powerful, and finely formed person. After three days of taking evidence, deciding motions, and hearing arguments, Bigelow wrote:

> The prisoner appeared to feel very blue. He is accused of having beaten Mrs O'Connor the hospital matron with intent to murder her.[35]

Maulsby had little reason to feel "blue" since he received only eight months in confinement.[36] Three and a half years later at Fort Elliott the same soldier was again tried, this time for malingering. After his company marched from Dodge City to Elliott in extremely cold weather, he complained that a knee was stiff from rheumatism. His condition did not respond to treatment, and he continued to walk with a rigid leg. The surgeon finally admitted him to the hospital, where his symptoms failed to suggest any disability. Finally, as several men held him down, chloroform was administered and a determination made that "the big fellow" was malingering, apparently to obtain a disability discharge. Instead, all he received was a conviction and imprisonment. Feeling uneasy about the severity of the punishment, however, his company commander, Lt. Charles Dodge, later visited the prison where he saw his crippled giant walking about as well as anyone.[37] Passing nearby, Maulsby gave him a pronounced wink that might have assuaged the troubled lieutenant's conscience.[38]

RESOLVING PETTY SQUABBLES

Despite spending increasing amounts of his time on criminal cases, Bigelow also had to resolve other conflicts more akin to civil disputes, such as who owned an overcoat.

> Sadler Jones and a private...were at variance [this evening] as to the lawful owner of an overcoat.... Sadler Jones had bought the coat for about $2 from a man who had been discharged &...sold it to [another] man. The private with whom Sadler Jones was disputing came to the one who had bought it from the Sadler and claimed it as his own.... The man who last claimed it had bought it...from a man who was discharged. He...said that the initials of the seller were on the coat. I found them....
>
> The Sadler proposed to return to the man who had bought [the coat] from him what he had given for it. I told the latter that he ought...to be satisfied with...one half of his money. This he assented to.

RUDE AWAKENINGS

> *Fort Duncan, Texas, December 30, 1877....* At half past two o'clock this m'g...the Officer of the Day Lt Stivers turned me out to make a check roll-call. It was a cold morning and I had been sleeping very nicely. I crawled out and clothed myself as comfortably as possible, then...got the sentinel to wake up Corp'l [Steven] Ford [who]...went with me to Sergeant Young's quarters.... He lived in a framed canvas tent, in the form of a plain house with a door at the side. I went with the sergeant, who was followed by his dog, to the soldiers' barracks where there was a large wood fire in an open hearth which looked very cosy and comfortable. Sadler Jones had moved his mattress from the bunk to the floor immediately in front of the fire. He like most of the men, grunted & growled when the Serg't woke him up by pulling down his covering to recognize the person under it. He saw what was up & made the remark "Oh! I'm right here, Sergeant." The Sergeant's dog would follow him around, jump up on the men's bunks, sniff around their heads and occasionally crawl under the covering and startle the sleeper. We found every one present.

I have observed the custom among the soldiers, I do not know whether or not it is confined to the colored ones, of covering up the head with the blanket so completely that it is impossible to see who is under it without taking hold of it & pulling it down. Then some remarks are heard like "Quit dat! Wat yo doin dere? G'way, I tell yo—Oh, hello! Is dat you Sergeant Young, wat yo want, golly dis a check roll call an't it? Yo don't catch dis chicken out dis cold mornin."

Chapter 9

Life outside the Courtroom

Although Bigelow toiled for countless hours prosecuting and transcribing cases, trivial or otherwise, other matters also demanded his attention. Following Christmas celebrations, the next few weeks were filled with an assortment of activities. On the last day of the year, for instance, he was confronted by Sergeant Young:

> [he said] he would like to...tender his resignation as First Sergeant.... This afternoon the horses were not drawn up as I had ordered.... It irritated me & I showed it....
>
> To cap the climax...I happened to look toward the [stoop of] barracks where...I had asked [the saddles, bridles &c] to be placed for the Comd't to inspect. Serg't Young, who did not know what I had had them placed there for, ordered them taken in.... I ordered him to have the company marched to the barracks at double time and have my work done over again.

NEW YEAR'S EVE IN EAGLE PASS

After quelling Sergeant Young's feelings, Bigelow joined other officers and their wives at a celebration hosted by a prominent physician in town.

> Went to a party this evening at Dr Monte's.... The dancing was accompanied by a guitar & violin. The floor was very good and the company also but there was no good dancer present.... Miss Winston went through the dance as if she were going to a funeral, lapsed occasionally into a smile as she replied: "Yes, Sir" or "No, Sir" that would momentarily light up...the gloom of her countenance.... The Dr had

plenty of wine, cake & cigars but did not give any supper for which he should [be] ashamed of himself.

Although the few ladies at Duncan might have been less than proficient dancers, they tried to inject some levity into the otherwise somber lives of the officers, such as when

The ladies of the post dressed themselves in white and covered their faces under a white mask, in which disguise they called upon Lt Brereton.... This was a birthday call, he being 21 yrs old today.

THE PRICE OF INEXPERIENCE

Earlier that day Major Schofield told the young commander that he expected to attach a more senior officer to B Company. With a hint of disappointment, Bigelow commented:

He said that it was important that there would be an experienced person...in case the Cavalry should have to go on a scout.... [He] told me that it would make no change in the responsibility for the property, so that...the most difficult part...will therefore be left to me while the glory & honor will go to an older & more experienced officer.

On the following day an order appointed Lieutenant Stivers as Company B's temporary commander. Although the move might have deprived Bigelow of the "glory & honor" of command, he "could not have selected one who would suit [him] better." Also, the presence of a second officer had some advantages.

Fort Duncan, Texas, January 2, 1877 [1878]. Did not go to reveille this m'g, Lieut Stivers having taken that duty & m'g stable call. Wrote & studied tactics until 1.30 when I went to drill. Lt Stivers commanded the Co. He made a great many mistakes to some of which I called his attention.

With Bigelow's help Stivers's proficiency at drill soon increased, leading Bigelow to concede the following day that he "did a little better...but there is still room for improvement."

Fort Duncan, Texas, Jan. 3, 1878.... Looked over some property in charge of the QM Serg't to see if Major Van de Wiele really turned over to me as much as is shown in his invoices. Found quite a number of articles missing, some of which are in the possession of officers which I must see before I receipt for them.

THE NEW YEAR'S CUSTOMS

At Fort Duncan as elsewhere throughout the army, 1878 started with what was an obligatory tradition: calls on commanders, other military superiors, and friends.[1]

> *Fort Duncan, Texas, January 1, 1877* [1878].... Dr Byrne called on me. We went with Capt Schooley...to make our New Years calls. We took in the Comd't first, then Capt Hood, Mrs Stivers, Mrs Van de Wiele & Mrs Gasman.[2] Lieut Stivers & I then went to Eagle Pass where we called on some Mexican people by the name of Dresch, also on Mrs Monte. The Dr had been celebrating New Years so gloriously that he had had to retire.

The Dresches soon became the recipients of frequent visits from Bigelow. A couple of days later he mentioned that he again called on them and "talked some Spanish, but not much." Before long, though, speculation about his motives for seeing the señoritas chilled his interest.

> I am getting discouraged in my attempts to learn Spanish. My opportunities for speaking it are so rare that I might almost as well be in N.Y. as here. Miss Dresch...has the idea, I think, that my only object in making her acquaintance was to be instructed free of charge. Mrs Gasman...made a remark which has led me to suppose that *she* thinks it to be so and that is sufficient to keep me away from there.... But even if there were no thought...that kept me from these people, the mother would be an objection. She sits...with her visitors, listening and observing without speaking, in short, she acts the part of a suspicious parent.

A DESPOT IN COMMAND?

After finishing his calls, Bigelow returned to his room where he found a pass he had submitted for Major Schofield's approval to permit Private Dillwood to be absent in Eagle Pass from 9 p.m. until midnight. The adjutant had scrawled across its face, "This pass is not granted for the reason that it is believed that Pvt. Dilwood tried to shield Corp'l Carter from justice in testimony before a late Gar. C.M., By order of Maj. Schofield." Bigelow indignantly noted:

> The pass...was denied on grounds which I do not think are reasonable and just. The commandant is either punishing a man out of malice or on pure suspicion. I told Dilwood...that if he wanted to entitle himself...to his rights as a soldier...to apply for a court of inquiry to establish his character.[3] The Major thinks and believes that Dilwood committed perjury, yet does not charge him with it but treats him as if he had been convicted of it.... I think it is very unmilitary for him

> to acknowledge officially that he is so arbitrary, in fact despotic, as to punish a man who is charged with no offence.

Perhaps still smarting from being replaced as company commander, Bigelow showed thinly disguised contempt for what he regarded as Major Schofield's lack of professionalism, further heightened that evening.

> The commandant compared the muster rolls tonight.... Capt. Schooley was treated rather badly...by Major Schofield, who...[was] irritated at the mistakes [he] made.... He writes badly & does not see well. The slurs cast by the Commd't on the Capt's handwriting were, I thought, very unbecoming one in his station.

And a few days later when armed guards were ordered to surround the post at night to prevent soldiers from slipping into town without permission, Bigelow protested in his journal that

> sentinels have been posted outside the limits of the garrison to keep the men in. Such strict confinement...cannot be, and ought not to be, enforced.

THE IRREVERENT OBSERVER

Chaplains were allowed by law at only thirty posts, and Fort Duncan was not among them.[4] And while each black regiment was authorized a chaplain, they were part of regimental staffs at larger posts.[5] On Sunday, however, Bigelow (an Episcopalian) went to a Roman Catholic mass in town with Dr. Byrne and Misses Stivers and Winston, the post's two young, unmarried ladies.

> *Fort Duncan, Texas, January 6, 1878....* I never was in such a dilapidated church before. The belfry looked...as if it could hardly hold itself up. In ascending to the choir, we had to climb up a ladder in the tower, in doing which I got entangled among the many ropes hanging in it and came near ringing the bell. The ladies were very much amused. The ceiling had been once covered with canvas which is...hanging here & there in shreds and exposing to view the plaster & timber beneath.... In the church, supporting what is left of the ceiling are a few large heavy pieces of rough timber, propped and fastened without much regard to appearances. The style of architecture is Mexican, the roof being flat & the exterior perfectly bare. Here & there a crucifix hangs on the interior walls and a few tin candlesticks fastened to them in small groups relieve their barreness [*sic*] to some extent. The altar is ornamented with all kinds of church furniture, such as candlesticks, crucifixes, pictures, symbols, draperies, &c. These ornaments are all flimsy & cheap but I suppose they are attractive to the ignorant & superstitious worshippers. There were frames, four or five feet square, covered with boards, laid...on the floor as a protection to the kneeling & crouching devotees, from the cold hard

stone beneath. I saw but very few men. The priest was very fat, disgustingly ugly and sensual. He went through the service in a mechanical sing song way common to the ministers of established churches. I could not stand the odor of the incense & therefore excused myself.

FROM THE HORSE'S MOUTH

Fort Duncan, Texas, January 7th, 1878. Got the farrier of our Comp. to show me how to tell a horse's age. He looks only at two teeth of the lower jaw.... The black spot shows at [6 years of age] & leaves at [12].... The cavity over the eye is generally deep in old horses...[and] the angle between the upper & lower teeth [is] small.... A horse's tushes or eye teeth do not appear until...three years...[and their] absence in a mare is sure indication of barenness [*sic*].

I study the physiognomy of horses...to see if I can make much out of it in reading their character.... A horse that evinces curiosity & inquisitiveness toward a stranger is generally more tractable than one who is coldly indifferent. To examine a horse's mouth, approach him boldly and stand...close to him without appearing to take too much notice of him. If he turns his head towards the person and thrusts his nose towards his face or body, he should be allowed to continue the investigation, the person moving slowly & gradually...may begin to stroke him, bringing the hand close to the head by degrees. If he resents the latter liberty the stroking should be suspended occasionally & begin again in the body & carried toward the head as before. When the head is reached, it is easy...to open the mouth.... The thumb of the right hand should be forced between the jaws and the lower one strongly held & pulled down by...the other fingers. The left hand and arm should be used mainly in retaining the horse's head in the proper position.

OUTSHOOTING A VETERAN

The following morning provided an unexpected opportunity for Bigelow to demonstrate his superiority over Lieutenant Stivers, an experienced officer several years his senior, in a martial skill. He was too diplomatic to gloat openly, but crowed about his feat in his journal.

Fort Duncan, Texas, January 8, 1878. Remained in the target ground after the company had gone, and fired against Lieut Stivers whom I beat badly. My astonishment was not less than his, I never having fired a carbine before in my life.... The importance of preliminary training...has not been properly appreciated by him, nor by the men. Lieut Stivers has undoubtedly done a great deal of shooting...and is considered a good shot.... I attribute my success, simply, to my having learned, at West Point, the theory of correct aiming and shooting.

"SCHOOL" FOR OFFICERS

> Attended officers school this evening for the first time. The recitation was heard in my room. Lt Stivers and I are the two pupils of Major Van de Wiele. The Major did a great deal of reading from the tactics and I began to think that his instruction was going to be in the nature of a lecture.

In mentioning another "officers' school" session three days later, Bigelow noted:

> Recited in officers' school, tonight.... Learned [from Major Van de Wiele] that I have been right in thrusting my forefinger through the trigger guard as far as the joint next to the hand. Major Schofield told him [so].... The Major...who patented [a] feature of the Schofield Smith & Wesson pistol...is quite mechanical & works...in his workshop & private office which are in...the same room.

The informal meetings Bigelow attended could only be described as a "school" in the loosest sense. Although nothing in army regulations or orders directed that officers should convene to discuss or receive instruction on military issues, an occasional mention of such gatherings appears in journals or other writings. For example, at Fort Keogh, Montana, in 1889 a young lieutenant recorded that:

> In the evening at officers call the officers assembled in the Post Hall and decided that these meetings would be held at 6:30 p.m. on Mondays and Thursdays until March 31st and would be devoted to lectures by the officers on Military subjects. On Monday...I lecture on Military courtesy.[6]

Charles King, whose frontier army novels were based on his extensive personal experiences, also alluded to such instruction, which occurred at some garrisons because the officers (or the post commander) thought it would be beneficial.[7] They probably were right, as most other training devoted "too much time to theory and too little to practice."[8] At Duncan the sessions were held on Tuesday and Friday evenings, but apart from the above remarks Bigelow's only references to them are that on one occasion he "absented (himself) yesterday from officers school. Had forgotten all about it" and on another that "Major Van de Wiele postponed the officers' recitation [Tuesday] until next Friday." In any event, such casual gatherings appear to have been the precursors of the lyceums ordered by John Schofield, then commanding general, in 1891 to encourage professionalism.[9] Other techniques, such as playing kriegspiel, a popular game in the German army, were also used to help assure that unlike the Austrians in 1866 and the French in 1870, the United States Army could be improved other than by defeat.[10]

WORKING TWICE AS HARD

Fort Duncan, Texas, January 10, 1878. Yesterday afternoon I took the place of Landon as Post Adj't, he having obtained leave of absence to go to Ft Clark, where a ball is to come off....

This morning I was very busy & bewildered in the Office. The Com'd't did not allow me much time in which to learn, but gave me the same work he would have given to Landon. Had to correct some of the errors of the latter as well as my own. The Com'd't made me come in from drill...and started me on some dispatches he wanted sent. Then came a great deal of office work for this evenings mail.... I hope tomorrow's work will be easier.

Simultaneously being acting post adjutant, a company commander, and the recorder for courts-martial were arduous undertakings, yet assigning more duties than could be accomplished comfortably was all part of making a competent officer out of an inexperienced new lieutenant, which appears to have been Major Schofield's purpose.

Jan. 11, 1878, Fort Duncan, Texas. Have been so well employed during the last few days that I have kept no record of the time.... I would not like to be permanent adjutant under Major Schofield. There is too much work, especially for a man who has no privileges connected with the station to counteract the irksomeness of the duties. The Adjutant not only has to be prompt & punctual at all the roll calls & ceremonies, he has to go to target practice [the most tiresome & unprofitable of all drills to an officer], he has to be officer of the day when his turn comes and has an unlimited amount of detail work...[that] may require him at any time of the day or night to go to the Adjutant's Office.... I [do not] see why one officer on the post, the adj't, should be worked twice as hard as any other.

Fort Duncan, Texas, Jan. 12, 1878.... Reported to the Com'd't...the absence of Brereton from retreat last night & Lieut Wessels from reveille this morning. Hesitated before doing it...and finally concluded that I would ask the Com'd't first if it were my duty to make such reports. He replied "Yes, certainly." He required me to send a letter to the Com. Off. of the absentees calling for information as to the cause of the absences.... Wessels has no satisfactory explanation to offer [and] I have not yet heard from Brereton.

UNIFORM MEANS UNDIVERSIFIED

> Issued clothing to the men this morning. It is a shame that there cannot be clothing sent here of sizes needed by the men, instead of forcing them to take such as does not fit them and making them pay full price.[11]

Ill-fitting and poorly made uniforms were a chronic problem for years.[12] With huge surplus stocks from the Civil War and frugality the priority, procurement of clothing and other items was abruptly halted and depots were closed. By the 1870s depletion and deterioration of existing supplies required limited new production, but until available the troops had to make do with what they received, which included garments made in only four sizes. To accommodate the differing dimensions of soldiers, unfinished uniforms that required alteration and fitting (for which recruits received a five dollar allowance) often were provided, resulting in anything but a uniform appearance. By 1883 the number of standard sizes of trousers was increased to twelve and of blouses to six, which improved the misfit situation somewhat but did nothing to address the issue of regional and seasonal clothing.[13]

For years the army pleaded for different uniforms for different climates, but appropriations were routinely denied. Consequently, on the northern plains soldiers had to purchase privately whatever protective garments they could afford, although until they became too expensive buffalo overcoats might be issued. However, layering clothing, advocated as early as 1868, was ignored. Those in hotter climates fared no better. In the summer of 1878, Bigelow wrote:

> It is about time something were done toward providing rational clothing for our soldiers. We have...but one full dress for all latitudes and an undress cloth blouse almost as warm.... The same external clothing is issued to soldiers exposed to the heat of a Texas summer as to...those suffering the cold of a Canada winter on the Lakes.[14]

In 1879 a board of officers recommended lighter clothing in the South and arid desert regions, but the surgeon general believed that heavy woolen fabrics were more healthy. Gen. D. S. Stanley, however, thought that a primary cause of desertion in Texas was "the thick clothing worn...in the summer."[15] About the only concession was to permit straw hats "in extreme southern latitudes." Based on later experiments, though, in 1886 soldiers stationed in Texas were issued cotton duck clothing.[16]

WEARYING OF GARRISON ROUTINES

Fort Duncan, Texas, Jan. 14, 1878. I have been at this post a month today.... [My duties have] been full of instructive experience, [but] I hope to be a little more employed...in active field service.

Fort Duncan, Texas, Jan. 20, 1878. Corp'l [Alfred] Myers...and Pvt Arthur Saunders...were reported absent from [bed]check.... Confined the former to his quarters and the latter to the Guard House.[17] Spoke with Dilwood, my servant...about some crackers that I had missed. He confessed that he had eaten some of them and thrown the rest away. Of course I had to scold him again.... Captain Schooley called this morning. We talked about society...[and] former times when the officers at this post were not as moral in character and habits as they are now.

Fort Duncan, Texas, January 21, 1878. Dined with Lieut & Mrs Gasman, Miss Stivers and Brereton & Miss Winston. We had canvas back ducks, rabbits, quail, mashed potatoes, mushrooms, tomatoes, grape jelly and a salad in which rabbit was used as chicken. For desert we had custard pie, wine jelly and cake, followed by chocolate & coffee.

That day Bigelow finally decided that Pacer, the horse he had previously rejected, was the one he preferred. Consequently a board of officers was appointed to determine how much he would have to pay for it.[18] Bigelow later wrote:

Heard today that my horse will cost me eighty five dollars which I think it is worth. The price is in fact small.

STARTING THE TONGUES OF FEMALES

To reciprocate for the hospitality of the married officers and their wives, the bachelors planned a party. Bigelow describes their soiree:

Fort Duncan, Texas, Jan. 23, 1878.... [W]ent over to the room that was being decorated for this ev'g's ball.... I assisted in decorating the walls...[with] American flags & guidons. Over the two doors were cross sabres & cross muskets representing the Cavalry & Infantry. On the wall at one end of the room were the American & Mexican flags...illustrative of the bond of friendship uniting the two countries.... The entertainment was given in the Cavalry barracks. There was a tent on the porch into which ladies could enter from the dancing room, which served as a dressing room. Another tent served as a refreshment room.... In there, on a large table, were spread the numerous contributions made by the ladies of the post, forming altogether an elegant and abundant repast. Wine and beer were also provided. Quite a number of Mexican officers were present, among others Gen'l Falcón....[19]

Miss Stivers took offence because I said...no teetotaller need invite me to any party.... She said she had thought that I did not drink much. I said she was right. She made a remark...referring to a social gathering at her brother's quarters, on Christmas Eve.... She said it was a pity that, on account of there having been no wine, I should have failed to enjoy myself.... She said that ladies get along without wine. Without questioning the truth of that statement, I told her that they "take it out" in coffee & tea.

She has got something now by which to start the tongues of all the females on the post.... It is hard to keep one's name out of the mouths of these idle people who have very little occupation other than interesting themselves in one another....

I have found, since the party, that [someone] entered my room and carried off my nickel plated pistol, my regulation pistol and from ten to fifteen dollars of my money.... I shall not hereafter make much of a stand in support of...the honesty of negro soldiers. When I think of what the rascals might have taken I consider myself fortunate.... They might have taken my journal or record of court martial proceedings either of which I would have missed more than what they *actually* took. I had about eighty [dollars] in the pocket of my fatigue blouse which was hanging on a peg.

Fort Duncan, Texas, January 24, 1878.... Have been appointed adjutant today.... I am now Post Adj't, Recorder of a Garrison Court Mart., member of a Gen Court M., act'g 1st Lieut of the Company, beside which I am on the roster for duty as Officer of the Day and have the Company property & funds in my charge.

"CROSSING OVER"

....I talked for some time with my orderly: Dillwood.... Learned from him...that there have been cases of enlistment of the same man first in a colored, then in a white regiment & the reverse.... I had thought there were such cases and that the gradual discoloring of the race by intermarriage with whites would, of itself, in course of time lead to the abolition of the colored reg'ts as distinct organizations.... Said that officers often appointed men to offices of trust & honor in proportion to the extent to which their blood had been mixed with the white but he did not think it just & right.[20] He is black as ink himself.

For a light-skinned Negro to "pass" as a white had gone on for centuries. A variety of reasons have been advanced for doing so, but in the post–Civil War army the desire for better treatment and opportunity, or in some cases to hide one's past life, probably were the primary motives.[21] A couple of days later Dillwood provided Bigelow with additional information about the "passing" or "crossing over" of some soldiers.

> Goldsborough, George, 7th Cav. White to black 65–67—67–77 10th Cav. Sherfield, George, 6th Inf. Mother colored & father white. [A colored man] F Co, 8th Cav. Men who enlisted with him at Governor's Island say the latter is colored.... The first man, Goldsborough, served two years in the white Cavalry [the 7th] and then 10 yrs in the colored, the 10th.[22]

TIME TO MOVE ON

> *Fort Duncan, Texas, January 26, 1878.*
>
> Mrs Gasman & the Lieut are going to leave tomorrow. I called on them this evening.

In view of the amount of time Bigelow had spent with the Gasmans and Miss Winston, his seeming lack of concern about their imminent departure might suggest a degree of indifference. Perhaps, though, he realized that frequent transfers made personal relationships fragile and fleeting, but that the small size of the army made probable future encounters or assignments together. Or possibly he had been informed that on that day orders were issued transferring B Company to Fort Stockton, so his time at Duncan also would soon be over.[23]

> *Fort Duncan, Texas, Jan. 27, 1878.* Marched myself on this morning as Officer of the Day.... Attended dress parade for the first time as a Post Adjt. Made no great blunder so I am satisfied.... Sergeant [no name mentioned] came this evening to borrow five dollars from me. I am distrustful of enlisted men and therefore did not lend him anything.... I almost believe that he only wanted me to show him where I keep my money that he may conveniently rob me.
>
> Was at a private concert at Lieut Stivers' quarters yesterday evening.... Talked for a while with the Justice of the Peace.... He spoke of coming to an understanding with the military authorities by which citizens could obtain redress for wrongs done by soldiers without causing the latter to be tried twice, that is by the civil & military courts. Such an arrangement, I think, is possible.[24]
>
> *Jan. 29, 1878, Fort Duncan, Texas....* It has been blowing Norther almost all day. The air is laden with dust and everything...is covered with it. I have had to buy a couple of blankets from the Quarter Msts Dept., none of my things having arrived from home. Major Van de Wiele has promised me two blankets, which in addition

to my horse's blanket & my overcoat will be covering enough I expect for the coldest night.

Gave the Company books and funds to Major Van de Wiele.... It was a relief to get rid of them.

Fort Duncan, Texas, February 1, 1878.... My bedding arrived today.... The mice had gotten into the blankets and eaten a big hole into one or two. The camp table was broken in half and parts of the iron about the bedstead were bent....

February 2, 1878, Fort Duncan, Texas.... Received my books and large valise.... Had Dilwood grease & blacken my Freibey boots, which I shall probably wear on the road. Capt Van de Wiele...[and I] chatted awhile about our plan of travel. To help me get my...shotgun from Col. Shafter, he offered me...his buggy to ride in from San Felipe to Fort Clark....

Sunday, February 3, 1878, Fort Duncan, Texas.... After having finished my office work this m'g, I...rode around Eagle Pass. Looked with wonder upon the curious tombs in the churchyard. They were no doubt Mexican,...appearing to be but a solid mass of masonry resting...over the dead. Here and there was a plain mound of earth with a stake at one end, no doubt the covering of an American, if not of a Christian.

Perhaps appropriately, the local cemetery was among Bigelow's final glimpses of Eagle Pass before commencing the march to Stockton.

Chapter 10

The Long March to Fort Stockton

From late 1877 into 1879 some major relocations of troops took place in Texas in response to worsening conditions. After Mackenzie's 1873 attack on the Kickapoo village near Remolino and the strikes by Shafter and Bullis that followed, forays from Mexico had temporarily tailed off. By 1877, however, the activity had stepped up again, causing citizens and politicians to clamor for more protection, which led to General Ord's receipt of authorization from Washington to pursue the raiders across the Rio Grande when "necessary."[1] Later that year one of the army's most successful Indian-fighters, Col. Ranald Mackenzie, and six companies of the 4th Cavalry were transferred from Fort Sill to Fort Clark, and a new subcommand, the District of the Pecos, was created under Col. Benjamin Grierson, 10th Cavalry, and located at Fort Concho.

Grierson's mission was to protect the settlers, railroad workers, and mail contractors throughout the vast region bordered by Fort Concho on the east and Fort Bliss on the west, and New Mexico on the north to the Rio Grande on the south. His plans centered on using cavalry patrols to detect, intercept, and prevent incursions, while denying the Indians access to waterholes. To position the available forces to accomplish these goals, several units were reassigned.

A few months earlier the only cavalry company (M of the 10th) at Fort Stockton had been sent to Fort Clark because the area around the former post had not yet experienced the rash of depredations requiring the pursuit capabilities that only cavalry could provide.[2] The predictable result was to trigger Indian raids against which the three remaining infantry companies were virtually helpless.[3] In January 1878, Bigelow's company was selected to fill the void by moving from Duncan, and that summer the number of mounted troops was further increased with the arrival of Company L of the 10th Cavalry.[4]

Fifty-two days after he reported to Fort Duncan, John Bigelow matter-of-factly prepared to depart for his new post, expressing neither regret nor pleasure at leaving friends or familiar places. The traveling party included two officers (Captain Van de Wiele and Bigelow), three women (Mrs. Van de Wiele and two servants), and sixty-three enlisted men.

VENTURING FORTH

February 4, 1878, Fort Duncan, Texas.... The company has gone into camp between the garrison and target range. I did not have time to say good bye today as the Capt. ordered me to remain in camp.... The men are provided with tents as well as the officers so that we are all insured [against] great hardships. Our camp is layed [*sic*] out as follows.

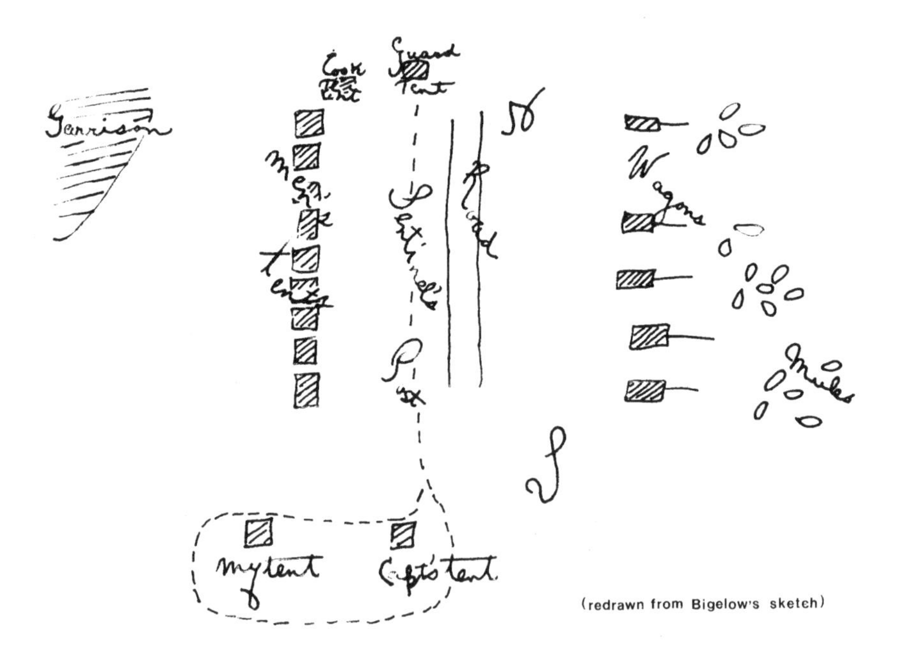

(redrawn from Bigelow's sketch)

TYPICAL PLAN OF CAMPS ON MARCHES

Had to put a man in charge of the Guard...for intoxication.... He had to be bound hand and foot and could not be kept in place even then. His name is Andrew Petry, who I believe is generally sober.... From his ravings I infer that his grief at having to part with some fair one in Eagle Pass has made him take to the flowing bowl....

On the road to Stockton, Canyon Grande, Feb. 5, 1878. Did not sleep at all well last night. I think the bracing and stimulating effect of the night air was the cause.... I put a flannel shirt over my head toward m'g and slept a little better afterwards.

At mid-morning the column finally took to the road with Captain Van de Wiele and his trumpeter at its head, followed by Mrs. Van de Wiele and her servant in an ambulance, a buggy with a male and a female servant, Bigelow and the company, and twelve pack mules.[5] The wagon train, which had left Duncan a half hour earlier, was soon overtaken and fell in at the rear where the dust stirred up by the horses and mules was heaviest.

We left at about half past nine.... At about 10.45 we reached...a water hole said to be seven miles from Duncan. At about 1 o'clock we reached the Canales ranch, 16 miles from Duncan, and at about half past three we went into camp...about 25 miles from Duncan.[6]

After having had the horses hobbled and put to grazing, the officers took a little lunch consisting of bread & butter, Schweitzerkaze and lager beer.... [I later]...took my carbine and started off from camp in search of game. I fired at a rabbit and several birds but did not hit anything. When I got back I found my tent put up. I immediately went in and refreshed myself by taking a good wash. I then walked out to overlook the feeding & grooming of the horses.

FOOD FOR THE STOMACHS ON WHICH TO MARCH

When the means and circumstances permitted, the meals for officers and their families on a march were far more palatable than a soldier's daily field ration of eighteen ounces of bread or flour, one and a quarter pounds of beef or three-fourths of a pound of pork, one and six-tenths of an ounce of coffee, two and four-tenths ounces of sugar, about one and a quarter ounces of vinegar, and a little salt.[7] Compounding the problem of less than appetizing foodstuffs, each company messed separately and on a ten-day rotating basis untrained privates were detailed as cooks.[8] Although an army board in 1878 asked Congress to permit commanders to appoint a permanent chief cook for each company and detail an assistant for up to thirty days, reforms were years in coming.[9] Consequently, those preparing meals often knew little about how to do so, resulting in "underdone pork, soggy beans—covered with greasy water for soup—and miserable coffee [that caused] discontent, a big sick-report, duty poorly done with much grumbling, and finally...men [who] are anxious to leave and...never return."[10]

> When I visited the kitchen they were frying bacon and making coffee in preparation for the double meal of dinner & supper [which] consists of a double allowance of hard tack or army biscuits,...a piece of bacon as big as a man's fist, and a pint of coffee. The bacon is fried dry or in its own grease which is sufficient to float it. Bacon was also being prepared to boil with beans in the m'g. All this meat had to be cleaned by being washed in soap and water before it was cooked. [At] the officers' dinner...we partook of beefsteak, mashed potatoes, stewed tomatoes and mince pie.

WITH NONE OF THE COMFORTS OF HOME

> The twelve pack mules were the charge of six men.... Each one carried two sacks of corn and two or three tents according to the animal's strength. The weight of the average load is about 250 lbs. The horses and mules stood the exertion very well. The latter made some trouble before starting by...attempt[ing] to lie down with their load.... As soon as they were freed from their harness [they all] laid down & rolled and kicked to their great satisfaction.
>
> *On the road to Stockton, Feb. 6, 1878.* Left camp this m'g at 7.30.... Learned that [Private Peter] Morris...has deserted.... The first Serg't...said he did not report him abst [yesterday] on account of his being on special duty as battalion clerk.... Capt Van de Wiele sent Sg't McDonald back to Duncan after him.... Morris carried off the clothing receipts, so that I have nothing to show in evidence of what I have issued to the men. The Capt says that I can make out an affidavit, which will answer the purpose.
>
> The wind blew pretty hard during a part of the night and kept on blowing all day.[11] It is still blowing from the North with considerable force.... Our tents are facing south and a wall of earth around the bottom of each tent keeps out the wind and dust.... Stopped shortly after leaving camp...to send a sg't ahead to look for the way.... Watered horses between 9 & 10...[and] at 10.45. Halted at 11.40. Watered horses at 1.25. Reached camp near Rio Grande at about 2.30. Got my eyes full of dust.
>
> Started out to hunt...but came back on account of the wind, which was strong and chilling. The sun was so hot that I was in a continual perspiration, yet when-

ever I would rise from a ravine or emerge from a sheltered spot the wind would chill me at once.... I wore my overcoat almost all day although...the sun burnt my face so that my nose is beginning to peel.

On the Road to Stockton, Feb. 7, 1878.... [Inspected the Guard] at 12.30 A.M. Started from camp at 7.15 [and] arrived at San Felipe Creek at 2.15. Encamped...at the post. The latter is new and commanded by Capt Kelly [Kelley], Co E of the 10th Cav.[12] He showed me his machine for making adobe. It was a kind of mill in which the mud & hay are thoroughly mixed.

On the Road to Stockton, Feb. 8, 1878.... Left camp at 7.20. Met Lieut. Hunt returning from a scout.[13] I gave him a letter to Flora [one of Bigelow's sisters]. Halted at Painted Cave at 1.15. Halted at 2.15 at the top of a hill. Halted at 3.25. M'ched on foot till 4 P.M.[14] Reached camp at 6.45. Dinner at about 9. The ground was so hard that it was almost impossible to drive tent pegs.... The men had to sleep without tents.

NEITHER COOL NOR CLEAR, BUT WATER

Wood was very scarce in consequence of which cooking was very difficult.... The Capt did not seem to know where he was going to find water. He had passed the water hole which the driver told him about.... Not finding any himself, however, he...very humbly asked the driver to show him the water hole. The water was so dirty that I would not even wash in it....

On the Road to Stockton, Feb. 9, 1878. Inspected the Guard at about half past three this m'g.... Started at 8.15.... Reveille was an hour later this m'g. This shows that it takes about three hours to get our party on the m'ch.... Halted at about ten [and] then...at 11.45 passing through Dead Man's Pass.... Lunched at 1.15. Stopped & encamped on the Devils River about 7 miles from the Rio Grande, near Fort Hudson.[15] The latter has not been occupied since '69.

THE HEAVENLY DEVILS

...This is a beautiful spot in a deep valley. The Devils River is of a pale light blue color and its banks are fringed with green grass, shrubs & trees. The capt is afraid of Indians stampeding his horses tonight. He has...placed a strong guard over them and posted a vedette on a high spot.... He is also afraid of its raining and of his camp being flooded....

Feb. 10, 1878, On the Road to Stockton.... Started at 8.15. Halted for rest at 10.15. Halted at about twelve thirty at Pecan Springs for lunch. Tried to find the boiling springs but could not. Encamped at 4.15.... It was so cold last night that the water froze in my bucket and in my canteen.

THE
LONG MARCH TO
FORT STOCKTON
February 5–18, 1878
Horsehead Crossing
PECOS RIVER
Adobe Walls
(3 springs)
1st Escondido
Leon Spg
El Paso
Fort Stockton
(Comanche Springs)
Riffles
Spg
Pecos Spg
Live Oak Ck
Old Fort Lancaster
Fort McKavett
Howard's Well
Johnson's Run
Beaver Lake
Bonita
Mtn
Comanche Trail
Painted Rock Ck
Spg
Rio San Francisco
RIO GRANDE
(Rio Bravo del Norte)
Pecan Spg
Old Fort Hudson
Dead Man's Pass
Painted Cave
Devils Riv.
W. Fork Nueces R.
Camp San Félipe
Fort Clark
San Antonio
Fort Duncan
Scale
10 20 30 40 50 miles
mek

THE SECOND HALF OF THE MARCH

> *On the road to Stockton, Feb. 11, 1878.* We are now probably half way to Stockton. I took my carbine...this m'g and went out with my present orderly [Robert] Reinhart to shoot turkeys.[16] We found them roosting. I shot an immense fat turkey gobbler.... Last night opened the package sent me from home through Col. Shafter. Was disappointed at not finding any ammunition with the gun.... The captain had one vedette out last night & two this m'g.
>
> As today's m'ch was to be a long one and as we were to make a dry camp without any wood, we carried both wood and water with us. We took five kegs containing ten gallons of water each; one keg for the officers, three for the men, and one for the teamsters. We struck a water hole about five miles this side of Johnson's house.... Cooks were not wakened this m'g until...6 A.M. Left camp at about 11.15. The late start was made in order to water the horses late when they would drink more.... Found good grass tonight but very dirty water. The horses will just drink enough of the latter to make them want more of a better kind but it will suffice to keep them quiet for tonight....
>
> *On the Road to Stockton, Feb. 12, 1878....* Had reveille at 5, Bfst at 6. Started at 7.30. Our first halt was at 9.20. Halted at 11.15. Halted & lunched at 12.15. Made a short halt at about three, came into camp at Howards Well about 4. The captain sent a man ahead...to see if there were water two miles from here.
>
> The man, Serg't McDonald, looked dubiously at the capt for a moment; the latter told him then that he could take one or two men with him. The Serg't had been here before. He was on this ground when a Mexican train was attacked by Indians and all the men were burnt, having been tied to the wheels of their wagons. He came in a company of the 9th Cav to rescue them but too late. Lieut Vincent who was with the Company and led his men three times to the charge was killed and is buried near the road. We will pass his grave tomorrow.[17]
>
> The water in Howards Well is very good. This road was formerly a California stage road.... Water had to be drawn in buckets for the horses....
>
> *On the Road to Stockton, Feb. 13, 1878....* [R]eveille sounded at 3.30. This attempt at an early start was made...on account of having a m'ch of 37 miles to look forward to. The train started out at 5.30.

Maintaining discipline on long marches under trying conditions was essential, yet the tools provided under the obsolete Articles of War fell far short of an effective means of doing so. Consequently, instead of postponing punishment until a court-martial could be convened, infractions often were handled by unjudicial but pragmatic measures.

One man, [Richard] Kimball, was required to walk on foot and lead his horse all day for having refused to go to the well and help fill the water kegs. He looked pretty tired after his 37 miles dusty tramp; he will probably fill the kegs next time he is ordered to.

...Halted...at 5.30 just twelve hours after the time of our departure from Howards Well.... We passed a herd of about 4000 or 5000 sheep this m'g, that had come all the way from Los Angeles, Cal. It was in charge of only six men. They had started about a year ago and were travell'g with their charge to Frio City.

...After lunch...the Capt came across a stray sheep that had probably been lost or abandoned by the herders whom we had passed. He had it put into a wagon.... It is rather a meager animal. We are now eating the big turkey which I shot the other day....

On the Road to Stockton, Feb. 14. Valentine's Day. Had Reveille...at about day light. There was no necessity for an early start as the captain had decided not to make a long march on account of the horses having had no grain last night, but as they had had good grazing he determined upon a march of from 10 to 15 miles. Left camp at 10 A.M. Halted, and forded the Pecos at 11.25. My horse got his belly wet but I kept my feet dry by crossing my stirrup over his withers and holding my legs over them in a horizontal position.... The wagons were pulled across without any trouble. The river, where we forded it, is about 50 feet broad.

We met our forage within half a mile of our destination. It was escorted by four Inftry privates & one serg't from Stockton.... We arrived at [Lancaster] about 1.30. My tent...is being very harshly treated by the wind. It is so well put up and banked, however, that I do not get much dust. There are excellent water cresses here and we will have some for supper with part of the mutton which we found yesterday.

The capt had 21 men, or 1/3 of the Command, guarding the horses last night for fear that the Indians would stampede them. He thinks it would only take 4 or 5 to do it. One of the men was bit [*sic*] today by a dog. The Capt first ordered it killed but I dissuaded him from having that done yet....

On the Road to Stockton, Feb. 15, 1878.... Left camp at 8.15. Halted at 10, at 12, at 2.30 and lastly at 4. We were joined in our camp last night by a party of 2 or 3 men who are travelling...to Arizona. They talked with the Major about the mineral wealth of that state.

I spent much of my time today...in representing to myself an imaginary foe coming out from some defile on the road, and making my plan of battle. I took the topography of the country as it is and supposed our two armies to be equal.

The lay of the land is very favorable to the maneuvering of an army on the defensive. As a protection against Mexican invasion the Rio Grande River is nothing, compared to the hills, ravines, gorges, wet & dry river beds &c which we have passed since our departure from Duncan. The barrenness of the soil would be an additional advantage to us. The numerous minor valleys and passes would enable us easily to assume the offensive with advantage.

The water froze in my bucket last night. When I inspected the Guard...I found the teamsters sleeping on the ground.... The water of the Pecos is alkaline here and I have been told that it is that way as far as Stockton. This place is called the Riffles, the name is applied to the rapids in the Pecos....[18]

On the Road to Stockton, Feb. 16, 1878.... Left camp at 10.5. Halted at 11.45 & 12.45 when we camped. We are at the "Adobe Walls."[19] There is a Mexican here who has a ranch. He keeps about 150 head of goats. The captain bought a goat and I bought a pie. The latter was not very savory. It was made with pumkins [*sic*].

This is the first place where I have seen a habitation since I left San Felipe. I talked with a Mexican, from whom I learned that the settlement around Stockton is growing very rapidly, that there were four stores there and several families....

On the Road to Stockton Sunday, February 17, 1878. The cooks were waked at 4. Reveille at 5. Started at 6.40. Halted at 7.50, 10.10, 12.30 & lastly at 1.55. There was considerable firing near our camp last night, from which the Capt. infered [*sic*] that there would be some cartridges missing.... He was right. A man...this m'g report[ed] that his cartridges had been stolen. He probably lost them all gambling, and the firing was done by ranch men who had bought ammunition. [The man] should have been charged with them and been made to walk on foot all day....

We passed a Mexican train today. The Capt. says that it rallied for a fight when we first made an appearance. It is no wonder that there [*sic*] trains are easily surprised & frightened. They travel without any advance guard.

Camp Stockton, Texas, Feb. 18, 1878. Reveille at 6. Left camp at 8 A.M. Halted at 9.15 and longer at about 12, when we lunched. The Captain then changed his coat and put on his sabre. I put on my sabre & belt...and so equipped we marched into Stockton.

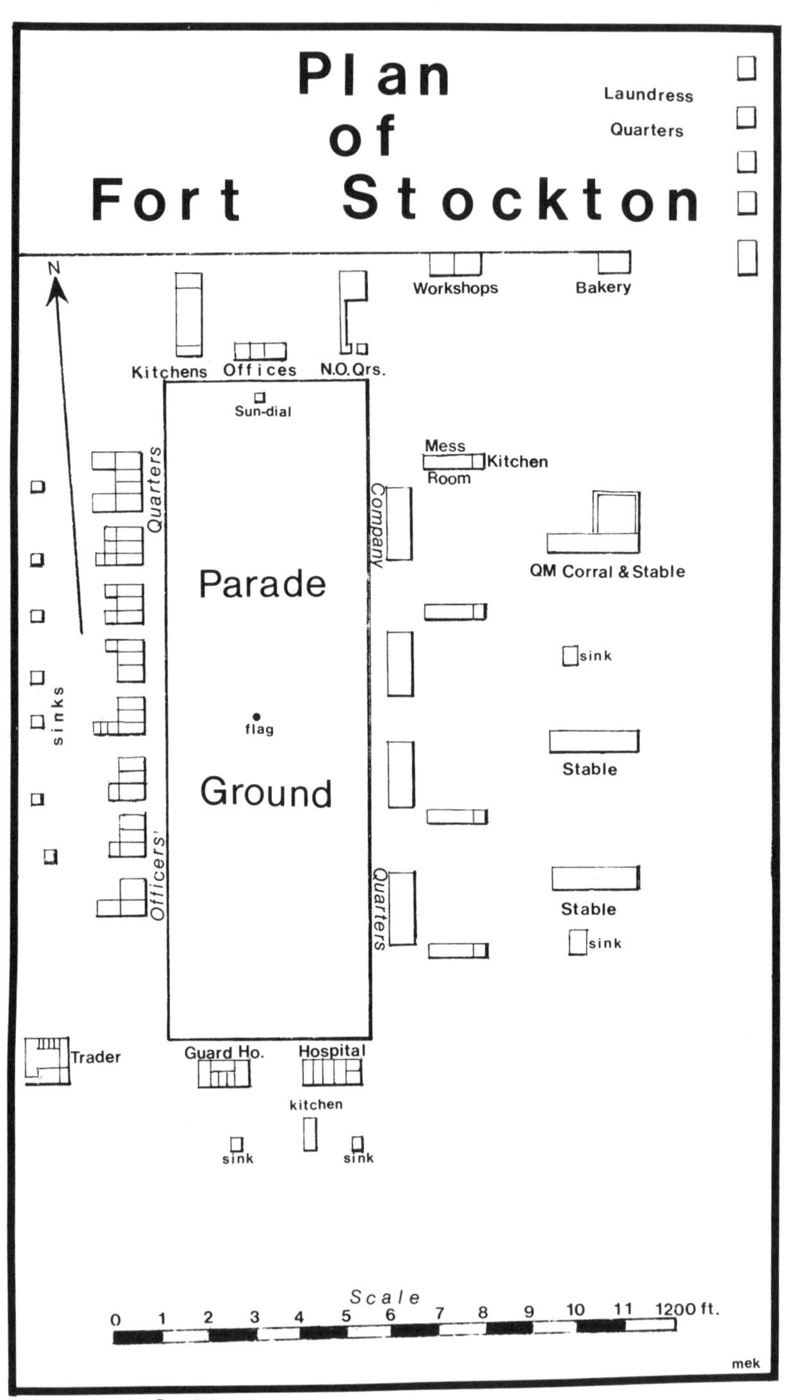

Based on *Outline Descriptions of Posts* (Div. of the Mo., 1876)

Chapter 11

Fort Stockton: Home of the Lonesome Tree

With B Company's arrival at Fort Stockton young Bigelow had successfully passed the first phase of his army initiation. Much more lay ahead.

Although established two decades before Bigelow reached there, Fort Stockton had predecessors in West Texas. The earlier forts (Clark and Inge) on the 674-mile stretch between San Antonio and El Paso were designed to guard the mail route between those towns and to protect emigrants and other travelers. In 1854 they were augmented by Fort Davis and the following year by Fort Lancaster, but increasing disruptions by unpacified Indians and other marauders required a still greater ability on the part of the army to respond to threats and attacks. Hence in 1858 an additional chain of bases was established. One of these, called Fort Stockton, was on the storied Comanche Trail near Comanche Springs (a major campground for various bands on their perennial raids into Mexico), near the crossroads of the principal stage routes.[1] The post was abandoned in May 1861, and toward the end of the Civil War Confederate forces burned most of the buildings. In July 1867, though, Colonel Hatch and troops of the 9th Cavalry arrived to erect new structures of thick adobe on rock foundations about half a mile from the original site.[2]

Fort Stockton's location was strategically well suited to its purpose, if not the comfort of those stationed there. In 1875 two visiting surgeons reported:

> It is on a line of travel across a vast and barren prairie, far removed from any city or town, and is thirty-five miles southwest from the nearest river, the Pecos, and fifty miles north of the nearest mountains. The nearest post is Fort Davis, seventy-four miles southwest.... The nearest town is Presidio del Norte, in Mexico, one hundred and forty-seven miles southwest. The nearest American town...is three hundred and seventy miles west. San Antonio is three hundred and ninety-two miles southeast....
>
> There are no indigenous trees at or in the vicinity of the post, except one cotton-tree in the post garden.[3] Mesquite bush covers the entire surface.... A school room has been erected for enlisted men and children...[but] there is no post library...[nor any] special arrangements for bathing, but the men, and all who desire, bathe in the creek.... The only means of communication...is by stage coach, which is...liable to interruption from Indians and floods.... The mail arrives and departs twice weekly.... The inhabitants of the vicinity are chiefly Mexicans, a cross between the Spaniard and Indian, which seems to have deteriorated both races....
>
> The general sanitary condition of the post is and has been excellent. In the winter and spring, in consequence of the "northers," catarrh is the prevalent affection; during the summer and autumn there are many cases of mild diarrhoea (apparently from vegetables, especially watermelons and cucumbers) and a few of intermittent fever. The atmosphere is warm, dry, and pure.[4]

LIFE ON THE NAKED PRAIRIE

In comparison with Fort Duncan, which at least had two towns nearby that offered a variety of diversions, Stockton was centered in what even its tough, hardscrabble pioneers must have initially thought was little more than a barren wasteland. But adequate water was nearby, enabling the early settlers to raise cattle and produce crops. No military reservation had been declared, but the government leased 960 acres in addition to 25 acres for the post garden.[5]

In late February 1878 the post housed four companies of African Americans (C, D, and F of the 25th Infantry and B of the 10th Cavalry), fifteen white officers (twelve of whom were then present), 163 enlisted men (all but 38 of whom were away on field service), and two civilian employees (a wheelright and a blacksmith).[6] Lt. Col. Matthew M. Blunt,

25th Infantry, was the commandant.[7] The other officers, in addition to Van de Wiele and Bigelow, were Captains David D. Van Valzah (D Company), Charles F. Robe (C Company), Daniel Hart (F Company), and Benjamin F. Pope (post surgeon); 1st Lieutenants Owen J. Sweet (post adjutant) and Henry P. Ritzius (F Company); and 2d Lt. Harry Reade (D Company) as well as two members of the Class of 1877, John McMartin (F Company) and Edwin Glenn (C Company), who helped facilitate Bigelow's transition, which went much more smoothly than it had at Duncan.[8] The other three officers were on detached service or sick leave.[9]

Three days after B Company arrived Bigelow made his initial journal entry, noting that he had taken care of essentials such as where to eat by joining a mess that included Mrs. Hart, her sister (Miss Hattie Lamond), Glenn, and McMartin. Bigelow had not yet met the lady's husband, Captain Hart of the 25th Infantry, who was confined to his room with malaria, but in at least one respect he found the arrangement more to his liking than the alternatives.

> *Fort Stockton, Thursday, Feb. 20th [21st] '78....* The style about the [Harts'] house, the furniture, ornaments &c show more taste and refinement, and bespeak more means than I have found in any other quarters on the frontier. There is an advantage...of my being in as good society as I can find here.... I would probably have joined Capt & Mrs Van de Wiele had they invited me, but...I accepted [Mrs. Hart's] invitation.... [At least] I am not subjected to the demoralizing example which [Captain Van de Wiele] sets by such expressions as "I don't want no this or that."

Bigelow and the other members of the Harts' mess soon decided to take turns reading aloud after supper. Glenn was the first to do so with the "Rime of the Ancient Mariner," which Bigelow thought he "read very poorly." The readings, which soon became an almost daily routine, embraced various works, often by Dickens, but on occasion they gave way to hymn singing. Frequently the performances were interrupted by visits from members of the community, which included the officers and their wives as well as the post trader, businessmen, and ranchers from the small town nearby. And at times the visitors participated in the convivialities.

> Lt. Read [Harry Reade]...gave us some singing & Mr Jacobs, in the store at the Post Office, played on the violin. His performance of the mocking-bird elicited great applause.... We read Dickens' Battle of Life.

EDWIN GLENN

As a cadet Glenn was noted for the number of demerits he accumulated. Later his casual approach to his duties irritated Bigelow. In the Philippines he did more than irritate people, but nevertheless went on to command a division in World War I. (Courtesy USMA Library)

JOHN McMARTIN

McMartin was with Bigelow on field service at Peña Blanca and at Santa Rosa. Neither seemed pleased with the arrangement. (Courtesy USMA Library)

The relaxed atmosphere during meals helped offset the loneliness and dreariness that otherwise might engulf those separated from families, friends, and familiar surroundings. In this vein, Bigelow related that at supper one evening:

> Glenn [received]...a telegram today from [Robert] Read, of our class, which winds up with "love to Hattie".... We had a great deal of fun at table talking about it.... [Miss Hattie] says she always thought he was conceited but thought also that he was a gentleman.... She said she wondered what the next communication would be. I ventured to say: "Please return my letters."

Bigelow had barely found his way around the post when he was disturbed one morning by a nonroutine but all-too-familiar incident at flimsily-built frontier posts.

> *Monday, Feb. 25th 1878, Fort Stockton.* The post traders' corral caught fire at about 7 o'clock.... I was waked by the sound of the long roll and numerous shots.... Being Officer of the Day I rushed to the Guard House [then] reported to the Commandant.... The Col. & I started out for the fire together but after having been forced violently against each other by the wind that was blowing almost a hurricane, and having repeatedly stepped on each others toes we took divergent lines of march and effected a junction again at the scene of action.... [By then] the men had thorough control of the fire and...every spark was extinguished.

The lot of an unmarried, lowly lieutenant in the assignment of quarters was no better than at Duncan. After enduring his dark, cramped room for several days, Bigelow wrote:

> I spoke to the Com'd't...about my quarters, telling him that I would like to change.... The porch [has] a very low roof and being surrounded by a thick trellis shuts off...light from my only window.... As Lieut. Orleman [who had been on sick leave since November] will turn me out when he comes, I should like to move now.[10] The colonel objected to me taking hired rooms in Mr. Corbett's store, near the stables, on the ground that they were too far from the...officers' quarters....[11] I expect to be put in one of Lieut. Sweet's back rooms where I shall be between two families with babies.

Entertainment or other diversions were quite limited at Bigelow's new post, but he soon managed to engage in some simple recreational activities. The first was to accompany Hattie Lamond on a horseback ride, after which he reported:

> She kept at a gallop & walk, alternately, all the time.... I do not propose to escort her...on my horse again. This was the first time that I have left the post since my arrival. We went to the Company gardens.[12] Saw the only tree that Fort Stockton

boasts of. Miss Hattie said that when she was on her way here, her sympathetic friends told her...there was but one tree & one gentleman [Lt. Read] here at the time. How much better off she must consider herself now, when there are two batchelor [*sic*] officers living in the same house and a third one favors her with his company three times a day.

Apparently Bigelow did not again go riding with the young lady, but he occasionally spent an evening with her reading such works as the poetry of Bryant or Tennyson. On an unrelated subject, he noted that "It is no wonder that Miss Hattie is so thin. All she ate for dinner...was a plate of soup, a pickle and cup of coffee. Sometimes she breakfasts on pickles and coffee."

He also went duck hunting occasionally, even though after his initial venture he reported:

Went out duck shooting, for the first time in my life, this m'g, with Glenn. I do not think I shall go again very soon.... I shot one duck but could not get it.... I came in with a headache and took a bath after which I felt a little better.

Still committed to learning Spanish, Bigelow arranged to resume his studies under the tutelage of Captain Van Valzah's wife. Before long, however, he discontinued lessons with her because she usually "excused herself from hearing me recite after I had taken the trouble to walk over to her house." He found a substitute teacher in Señor Lujan, a local Mexican tailor.

He talks good Mexican, not the best Spanish.... Dr. Pope says he is very "grandiose" and sensitive.... [H]e was once justice of the peace which so impressed him with his importance that he had to assert it by keeping drunk as long as he was in office. He called on Mrs Corbett one day and said to her: "My brother is dead, I must get drunk," whereupon he proceeded to show his brother the respect to which he considered him entitled. That evening he was picked out of the creek by a soldier who saw him fall off the bridge.

As at Duncan, Bigelow's principal escape from the monotony of post life was studying and analyzing subjects that appealed to him. For example, he commenced the sixteen-volume *Official Report of the Franco-Prussian War*, which he critiqued in many pages of his journal. He later noted that he was

getting on slowly with the French & Prussian War. Reading Jomini's Art of War and Paley's Philosophy at the same time. These books, together with my newspapers and the evening readings at the Major's keep my mind well enough employed.

CALLING FOR COMPANIONSHIP

Informal evening calls among officers, their wives, and the seemingly ubiquitous unmarried sisters were as frequent at Fort Stockton as at Duncan. If nothing else, the practice probably helped some participants mitigate tedium and promoted esprit de corps. As a well-bred and urbane young officer who was keenly aware of what was expected of him, Bigelow devoted part of most evenings to visiting or being visited, even though the usual banality often bored him.[13] On his fourth day on post, for example, he confessed, "Lieut Reade...called on me this evening for a few minutes. He is the first officer who has made me a formal call without staying so long as to weary me."

The next evening Bigelow was visited by Dr. Pope, Glenn, and Captain Robe. He reciprocated by calling on Dr. and Mrs. Pope, finding her to be "a very bright and cultured lady—the most perfect lady on the post, [and he] the most polished gentleman." Apart from the gossip and rumors that seemed to engross some officers and wives, calls often involved a discussion of current events and, unless the presence of ladies might make such topics boorish, an exchange of ideas on military matters. One concern in early 1878, for instance, was a proposed bill to forbid gambling among officers, as to which, according to Bigelow, some wag at Fort Stockton "suggested that a member of Congress be assigned to each military post as an example of a moral and well behaved gentleman for the officers to copy."

Another subject that generated concern among most officers was the on-again, off-again congressional plans to further "reorganize" the already debilitated army. Bigelow thought that doing so would be a mistake "if we are to expect anything of our army as a preparation for war," while conceding that "if it is to be a mere police force and protection against Indians it matters little in what form it is kept up."

In the Southwest, the key issues were still the perceived likelihood of another armed conflict with Mexico, and the even more imminent problems posed by those Indians who sporadically resisted with violence the uninvited and unwanted intrusions by travelers, freighters, stages and stage stations, ranchers, and other settlers. At the outset Bigelow was rather blasé about such threats, merely wondering:

> *Fort ~~Duncan~~ Stockton, Feb. 26, 78....* I do not know yet what the object was of moving the Cavalry company...to this place unless it was to put a stop to the Indian scares. No Indians have been heard of...since our arrival. Not long ago a Mexican was killed...between here and Fort Davis. Troops were sent out...after the Indians who were thought...to have murdered him.

POST ROUTINES

Most days at Fort Stockton, as at Fort Duncan, were devoted to familiar military activities such as the interminable drills, target practices, inspections, stable calls, officer of the day duties, and other routines. In addition, Bigelow was placed in charge of a School of Tactics for noncommissioned officers, which met for an hour every Tuesday and Friday evening. The experience led him to conclude that

> Some of my pupils are shockingly ignorant.... It is no wonder that the company is in bad condition when the instruction of recruits is left to such men. A great defect in them all is their weakness of character. They have no backbone or self-respect.... At drill [they] occupy themselves in looking wise & ornamental but never think of speaking to a man in ranks.

An occasional death, seldom a direct consequence of hostilities but instead a result of some illness then beyond the ken of medical men to cure, was an inevitable part of life at a frontier post. For example, before B Company arrived at Fort Stockton plans had been made for a party to celebrate Captain and Mrs. Hart's twenty-fifth wedding anniversary in early April. The festivities were postponed, however, because by then Captain Hart's deteriorating condition necessitated surgery. At Dr. Pope's invitation, Glenn and Bigelow observed the operation, after which the latter recalled:

> Glenn nearly fainted. Although not as old as I am, his nerves are so unstrung by smoking and drinking that the unsteadiness of his hand is perceptible whenever he raises a cup of coffee to his lips.[14]

Four days later Captain Hart died of pleuropneumonia and suppuration of the liver.[15] The next day he was buried in the post cemetery. Bigelow read the funeral service since no clergyman was available, and two days later Major Van de Wiele presided over a memorial service. Subsequently, a committee was appointed to prepare a statement to

FORT STOCKTON, TEXAS

From the southwest corner of the post in 1884. The building in the foreground is Joe Friedlander's store. (Courtesy Historic Fort Stockton)

OFFICERS' ROW

Looking southwest from the northeast at Fort Stockton. The flagpole was midway across the parade ground. (Courtesy Historic Fort Stockton)

eulogize the deceased.[16] In the meantime, the wives of other officers did what they could to console the widow as they helped her dispose of household furnishings and other possessions before commencing her lonely journey home and fading into their memories.

JUST BEING BLUNT

At Fort Stockton, as elsewhere, court-martial duties were interspersed with everything else. Soon after his arrival at the post Bigelow replaced the then-ailing Captain Hart on a general court-martial. Thereafter he served as a member or counsel on other general courts and recorded numerous garrison court cases that, except for names and places, closely resembled those that had occupied so much of his time at Fort Duncan.[17]

Not everything that might arise during a trial was related, of course, to the ultimate question of an accused's guilt or innocence. On March 14 a general court-martial convened with Colonel Blunt as president, Bigelow as a member, and McMartin as judge advocate.[18] During a recess McMartin began to transcribe the proceedings. When Bigelow casually observed what was being written, he received a mild upbraiding from Colonel Blunt. The young lieutenant's reaction illustrates the concern that officers of his time had for anything that might be construed as an affront to their integrity or gentlemanliness.

> [At the trial today] Col Blunt took it upon himself to teach me manners. He commenced by saying something about its being unpleasant to the Recorder to have some one looking over him while writing and then went on to say that it was bad manners to do so to which I replied "I do not know, Sir, whether you mean to rebuke me for my manners or my behavior as a member of the court." He said: "Yes, your manners, it is ungentlemanly," and something to the effect that he knew it to be so, to which I replied: "I don't." In making the latter reply, I had in my mind the distinction between looking over private papers and...a public writing in which I had a right to interest myself.
>
> Whether or not my looking over McMartin's record was objectionable to him & whether or not my doing so was ungentlemanly, Col Blunt made a mistake in speaking about it...in the presence of enlisted men. I am not certain that he was free from personal ill feeling toward me on the score of my having...declined to alter my record of...the Board of Survey of which I am a member. I have written an official letter to the Asst. Adj. Gen'l of the Dept requesting a court [of inquiry] to examine into and report upon my conduct as a gentleman...and have preferred...charges & specifications against the Col....[19]

An apology would be small redress for such an offense. If made to me alone or even to the Court alone it would not be commensurate with the insult for the latter was as public almost as if it had been made in the presence of the battalion in line.

For a junior second lieutenant to prefer court-martial charges against a senior officer for remarks such as those in question demonstrates an almost reckless disregard by the accuser for his future military career. This might have been of little moment to Bigelow, however, judging by his testiness a few days later when McMartin approached him with a soldier in tow. McMartin said that the company commander wanted Bigelow, who was officer of the day, to order the soldier to carry a log because of a minor infraction that the suspect denied. Bigelow flatly refused to do so.

McMartin had a long talk with me at dinner on the subject of log carrying & told me...that if I wanted to stay in the army & get along I would have to change my ways. I told him that I did not expect to remain in the service all my life and that the army of the U.S. would find it an easy matter at any time to relieve itself of me. He said it was a matter of courtesy for the Officer of the Day to punish a soldier as requested.... [I said] I would not out of courtesy to any man turn a deaf ear to a soldier's solemn protestation of innocence and earnest request for a fair trial.

Bigelow's apparent indifference to the consequences of his actions might be attributed in part to the low esteem in which he held several of the more experienced officers with whom he served. In addition, some animus already existed between him and Colonel Blunt, whom he and Dr. Pope both "look[ed] upon...as an unreliable treacherous man. His blandness does not conceal as much from us as he perhaps thinks it does." Also, Bigelow rationalized:

The 25th Art. of War...is intended as a protection to an officer's honor. [It] says that officers shall not insult each other, and the 26th Art. prohibits dueling.[20]

Having convinced himself of the righteousness of his indignation, and still smarting from the ignominy, real or imagined, of the censure, Bigelow gave the charges to Lt. Sweet, the post adjutant, to forward to departmental headquarters at San Antonio. A few days later he wrote:

Have heard nothing yet concerning my charges.... Am perfectly satisfied with the course I have taken although...[Dr. Pope] thought I should make an application to the department commander requesting, for myself, either a trial by court-martial or an apology. McMartin only advised me not to do anything rash, not to get the older officers "down" on me as I would, should I, a young graduate 2 months out of West Point, have the presumption to prefer charges against an officer of thirty years standing.

Bigelow went on to explain that he rejected Dr. Pope's recommendation because a request for a trial or an apology

would, I think, have been pigeon-holed or put in the waste paper basket.... There is no certainty about the redress...[which] is left entirely to the...judgment of the person applied to. The latter, too, is sure to be an old officer, more favorably inclined toward the party complained of than toward the complainer. Courts-martial and Courts of Inquiry, however, are governed by precedents and laws. They are also apt to consist of officers of low as well as high rank and therefore be impartial tribunals.

In early April Colonel Blunt and his wife departed for the East on a leave of absence, but not before Bigelow made a call to wish them a pleasant journey and to invite them to visit his parents in New York City.[21] He later speculated:

I presume [Col. Blunt] will go to West Point before he attends to me. I rather doubt that Mrs. Blunt will give the people at home as good an account of me as she promised.... She probably did not know all about the relations...between the Col. and me.

A few days after the Blunts departed, Bigelow received some information about the charges he had preferred.

Sunday, April 14, 1878.... Capt Van Valzah, who is temporarily in command of the post, told me that he had found out...that my application...had been returned...endorsed "Forwarded by mistake." [The Adjutant's] books...contain no notice either of the application or of the charges. The presumption is, therefore, that [Lt. Sweet] only forwarded the former.... I shall probably prefer charges against him for neglect of duty. The Captain informed me that the Col...had been ordered to return here and prefer charges against me.... The court is to be convened at once.... I think I shall ask...for a stay of proceedings [to determine why my papers were not forwarded].

Notwithstanding Van Valzah's information, Colonel Blunt did not return to Fort Stockton to prefer charges. In fact, because of successive extensions of his leave, which was initially for thirty days, followed by detached service in San Antonio, he was absent for more than nine months. Bigelow made no further mention of the charges in his journal, perhaps in part because the next day he was dispatched on the first of eight scouts that kept him in the field almost constantly until August.

The brouhaha generated by Blunt's brusque comment in the presence of enlisted men and Bigelow's hypersensitive reaction to it was not unique. With dueling outlawed, virtually no practical way existed for officers to resolve personal differences except by courts of inquiry or courts-martial, which disputants not infrequently turned to as a means of assuaging insults or other grievances.[22] Moreover, at times such squabbles involved even high-ranking officers who should have known better.

DE MINIMIS NON CURAT LEX

One of the more notorious disputes, which raged in the press and in courtrooms during much of 1879, pitted Gen. David S. Stanley against Gen. John Hazen.[23] At the outset Sherman tried to pacify the participants, but in unconcealed disgust he finally wrote Stanley that

> I feel inclined to give you both a good scolding. Two such men, with such war records, ought not to...push a personal quarrel to the extent of forcing a court-martial. But I have exhausted my personal influence and must leave you to chuck for yourself.[24]

The animosities between the adversaries had been festering since the Battle of Shiloh in 1862, but might have lain dormant but for Hazen's testimony against Stanley's friend, former Secretary of War William Belknap, in the Senate's Court of Impeachment for selling post trader concessions.[25] In 1877 Stanley preferred charges against Hazen alleging, essentially, cowardice during the Civil War and perjury before the Senate court. The case was never tried, but in late 1878, after Hazen returned from detached service in Austria, Stanley resumed his denunciations of him. Thereupon Hazen, professing that "what virtue is to a woman, courage is to a soldier," preferred charges against Stanley alleging eleven offenses of conduct unbecoming an officer and three of conduct prejudicial to good order and discipline.[26]

Although the statute of limitations would have barred the trial of Hazen, the president referred both sets of charges to the same court-martial. Stanley, whose case was heard first, was convicted of prejudicial conduct, but the sentence was merely an admonishment.[27] And even though Sherman urged that the court then try Hazen so that he could waive the statute of limitations and present matters in his defense (much of which the court refused to admit in Stanley's case), the military procedures ended. Displeased by what he described as a "shabby, indecisive verdict" in Stanley's case, Hazen filed a civil action for defamation but later dropped the suit, presumably because of Sherman's growing annoyance with the entire affair.[28]

Not long afterwards Sherman's irritation was exacerbated when Generals Pope and Gibbon preferred charges against each other. During their sparring Gibbon wrote Sherman accusing the latter of intervening to prevent investigation of the charges against Pope. Sherman trenchantly responded:

> [I]n my judgment you do not manifest the wisdom and delicacy which should characterize you.... [Pope] has never influenced me in [my] conclusion...and therefore your fling at [him] is absolutely and unqualifiedly worse than a mistake on your part.
>
> ...The charges and counter charges made by our officers of late, of which I have some half dozen before me now...have done more to damage us in public estimation than any other single cause.... The army today has plenty of honorable employment...without resolving itself into a General Court to investigate...gossip dating back ten and fifteen years.
>
> The *Stanley-Hazen* court demonstrates that *military courts* are not the tribunals to settle such controversies. I advise you and all to let the past dead bury its dead and employ yourself to do manfully the duties of the hour, leaving us to guard the honor of the profession.[29]

HAIL AND FAREWELL!

Even before Bigelow's extensive absences on scouts from Fort Stockton commenced, a shuffle of people, duties, and units was under way and would continue for the next few months. First, because of Blunt's leave Van Valzah became the post commander. Bigelow's reaction was:

> Capt Van Valzah...will soon be relieved, I hope, by some more able & more conscientious officer. On the first night of his term...he deliberately absented himself from tattoo roll call and allowed the officers who were with him...to follow his example.

This hope was realized before long when Maj. Napoleon Bonaparte McLaughlen, then commandant at Fort Concho, arrived at Fort Stockton to assume the command there.[30]

PREPARING TO LEAVE

In 1884 L Troop, 10th Cavalry, was transferred from Fort Stockton to Fort Davis. This is its wagon train waiting to depart. (Courtesy Historic Fort Stockton)

MOVING OUT

The troop, in a column of twos, heads south past Officers' Row. (Courtesy Historic Fort Stockton)

Also, in early April Dr. Pope, Bigelow's confidant, was transferred and his place taken by M. W. Price, a civilian physician employed as an "acting assistant surgeon."[31] Then in early May a man of the cloth, Capt. Benjamin Baldridge, reported from Fort Richardson to provide religious succor at the clergyless Fort Stockton.[32] And later that month Andrew Geddes, a recently promoted captain, replaced the late Captain Hart as commander of F Company.[33] On May 21 Major Van de Wiele, suffering from severe ear problems, departed on sick leave. Six weeks later he wrote from New York City to let Bigelow know that

> [My journey] was very severe on me. I was taken very bad at Centralia...[and] I think my only ear is worse now than ever it was. I have to leech and blister it every few days and the aurist says...[the outlook] is not good for saving my hearing. I occasionally have a partial paralysis of the brain but they are not so severe as at Stockton.

Failing to recover, Captain Van de Wiele met a retiring board and was separated from the army for disability.[34]

For a few weeks Bigelow was the only officer on duty with B Company, but then 1st Lt. William H. Beck was detached from C Company, 10th Cavalry, to become its temporary commanding officer.[35] And on June 23 the number of troops at the post increased by about one-fourth with the arrival of 1st Lt. "Oucks Bijoucks" Maxon and fifty-five men of Company L, 10th Cavalry, which previously had been assigned to Fort Concho.[36] With them was Alice Esterly, the wife of Bigelow's classmate Calvin Esterly who was then on field service at Camp Peña Blanca; in August he was able to join her. Also in August Company L's new commander, Capt. George Armes, arrived from Washington. He was not greeted with unanimous enthusiasm, having been dismissed eight years earlier after sixteen arrests and five courts-martial between 1861 and 1870. In addition, Colonel Grierson and several other officers objected to his restoration, which Congress nevertheless approved earlier in 1878.[37]

Over time, some of the newcomers were to have a profound affect on Bigelow's life. For the balance of the year, though, he and most of the junior officers at Fort Stockton were busily engaged in scouring the vast District of the Pecos for renegades and thieves, a type of soldiering that most of them preferred to the often stultifying conditions in garrison.

Chapter 12

Patrolling in Pecos Country

Under the best of conditions, scouting in West Texas was a severe test of stamina. Traveling day after day on horseback, often in blistering heat, was debilitating by itself. In addition, there were other physical discomforts such as wearing coarse and scratchy woolen clothes, sleeping on the ground, and surviving on little more than bacon, bread or hardtack, beans, and coffee. Generally the only opportunities to bathe, shave, change clothes or relax were when detachments (usually five to twenty-five men) returned to their posts for a day or so to obtain provisions and other supplies, repair equipment, and rest the men and horses. In short, a couple of weeks of intense scouting was likely to produce a scruffy looking and malodorous assortment of human beings who would repel even their mothers.

PREVARICATING FOR PROFIT

In Pecos country, most scouting parties were dispatched to protect citizens and their property from small and scattered groups of Apaches from Mexico, the Fort Stanton Reservation or elsewhere who reportedly had inflicted or threatened harm. Often, though, the troops who sought to intercept, capture, or kill alleged marauders and recover stolen livestock were unable to do so, simply because there were no Indians to find.

For example, in June 1879 Company F, 10th Cavalry, was bivouacked at what remained of Fort Lancaster when they were notified of the murder of a woman and two children by Indians near Cedar Fork, between Lancaster and Fort McKavett. A detachment hastily rode out in pursuit. After seventy fatiguing miles it reached Howards Well where immigrants with about two thousand horses were resting. Shortly afterwards Capt. Stevens T. Norvell came up with M Company, which had been scouting for the same Indians between Dove Creek and Beaver Lake.[1] After learning that neither detachment had found any sign of raiders or their victims, the travelers happily started west again with their herd. As they were leaving the head drover muttered, "That's what I thought, but it's best for a man to be certain about such things." When a soldier asked what he meant, he replied, "I have to do this to get my ponies through guarded by you fellows."[2] If the troops had known of this admission sooner, they might have been tempted to create some victims themselves.

Merchants, traders, and others seeking safe passage were not the only sources of false reports. That same year an entire battalion of the 5th Cavalry was dispatched to scout the Sand Hills for Indians who, according to settlers, had committed depredations nearby. No trace of them was found because the settlers themselves, who had beef and hay they wanted to sell to the army, were the source of the rumors.[3]

And although he was still a relative newcomer to the frontier, it did not take Bigelow long to complain about the "frequency of false reports concerning Indian depredations, & the occasional occurrence of the loss & damage of property, attributed to Indians, having been caused by white men."[4]

THE MAKING OF A FIELD SOLDIER

For all but a few days from mid-April until August, Bigelow led troops of Company B on eight fatiguing patrols through vast regions of West Texas.[5] First, in mid-April he was dispatched with twenty-five soldiers to pursue "hostile Indians" who had attacked a stage and killed a passenger near Escondido Station.[6] Over a ten-day period the detachment covered 350 miles and recovered the stolen mail, but their prey disappeared after crossing the Rio Grande into the near-sanctuary of Mexico.

After arriving back at Fort Stockton on April 25, Bigelow and fifteen men were sent out to search for suspected marauders between Escondido and the Pecos.[7] Again, none was found. When he returned to the post on May 3 for supplies, he took time to answer a letter from his father in

"MARCHING IN THE DESERT"

This Remington sketch (the artist is behind the commander) portrays scouting conditions similar to those in much of West Texas. (Courtesy Fort Davis National Historic Site)

which he related how scouting detachments were provisioned and equipped.

My dear Father

...When an officer goes on a scout he receives orders, written or verbal, to take a certain number of men with rations for a certain number of days and a certain amount of ammunition. One ration is one man's daily allowance...[which presently] consists of:

12 oz of bacon	2 oz of coffee	Vinegar
16 oz of (bread or hardtack) or	2 2/5 oz of sugar	Salt
		Pepper
18 oz of flour (with yeast) or	2 oz of rice or peas or	Candles
		Soap
18 oz of fresh bread	2 2/5 oz of beans	

In garrison the men get fresh bread from the post bakery. It is cooked by soldiers. They also get fresh meat furnished by contract. The allowance is a quarter of a lb more than of bacon. At this post all of the garrison have fresh vegetables & fruit (water melons & mushmelons) from the company gardens.

> Scouting parties carry no wall tents and take no wagons. Their transportation is all on horse or mule back. They take forage, if they can, but it is heavy and transportation for it is sometimes not to be had, in which case the animals have to subsist on grass. The men have what are called shelter tents...composed of two pieces. Each man carries one piece attached to his saddle. Two men join their pieces, and tent together.... It is just high and long enough to keep two men dry when they are lying down close to each other.

On May 7 Bigelow again led a scouting detachment for another ten days. When he had "a little leisure," he wrote:

> I was ordered out with a view to intercepting a party of Indians reported between the Pecos & Concho R. Having no guide I took the wrong road and camped at Escondido Station instead of at Horsehead Crossing.... No one at Escondido could tell me how to go, nor if the hills...were passable.... I left camp at 6 A.M. and in the course of an hour was across them.... I came upon [Horsehead Crossing] without coming in sight of either of the two roads that meet there.... [On my previous scout] I had neither map, guide nor compass and expected to follow Indians into the Fort Stanton [New Mexico] reservation. I thought I would be safe as long as the Pecos did not run dry.
>
> I did not know...how close I was to the river until the Serg't, about 30 yds ahead...was close to the bank. If we had been marching in the night he would have had his horse to thank had he not gone over the bluff into the water.... As if conscious of being at variance with...the Texas landscape and ashamed of being in such a dry, sterile, inhospitable country,...the Pecos seems purposely to conceal its gifts and charms. No babbling brooks, or quiet lakes, or trees in rich and heavy foliage attract the fainting traveller.... Accessible only at points, sometimes 10 to 15 miles apart, it takes its swift and winding way between vertical bluffs with nothing on either side to mark its course. A man fifty yards from it might die of thirst ignorant of there being water....
>
> I reached Horsehead Crossing at 1 P.M. and camped there.... I rode to a cowboys' ranch about a mile and a half from our camp.... Cowboys' herds are very large, numbering sometimes 20,000 cattle. They live in camps about 15 or 20 miles apart.... Every evening two ride out from each camp in opposite directions to a point half way to the next and if any one finds tracks leading away from the range he has to follow them and bring the cows back. Should he be gone over a certain length of time another man goes out...and follows his trail.
>
> The cowboys had neither seen nor heard of any Indians, but one of them said he had seen...a signal smoke: a tall column of smoke that lasted about twenty minutes...between Castle Gap and the Sand Hills. The Indians, if there were

> any...would be either at the Gap, Horsehead Cross'g or the Sand Hills, for they were the only places where they could get water. I therefore engaged one of the men to show us the way to...Castle Gap. We left camp at 6 o'clock the next m'g. We saw numerous Indian signs but none less than a month old. In several of the cañons caves...had been dug out of shale rock.

Returning to Fort Stockton on May 13 for two days, Bigelow resumed his journal entries by first inserting a departmental order that, while encouraging cooperation with Mexican authorities when possible, in effect authorized the pursuit of thieves and robbers across the border.[8]

> *Fort Stockton, Texas, May 13, 1878.* The above order looks very much like the instigation to provoke Mexico.... Guided by these documents [from] General Ord, no officer would hesitate to cross the border.[9]
>
> Things have been for several weeks looking more & more as though a grand campaign or scout were on foot...with the object of scouring the country thoroughly and cleaning it of Indians. I have no doubt that the general plan is to run them all into the Rio Grande or Mexico.... There will soon be the same war excitement that existed last summer.

Bigelow was correct about being on the threshold of a "grand campaign" in Texas. From May 15 until June 3 he and fifteen soldiers combed the region between Forts Stockton and Davis, about eighty miles to the southwest, but did not come across anything of significance. Four days later he was again dispatched to scout for Indians reportedly approaching from the direction of Fort Concho. During that expedition he and his troopers covered an incredible 620 miles in eight days.[10]

The short time he had in which to get ready for yet another patrol was less than tranquil. In addition to preparing his returns and completing a report of a board of survey, he had to inventory and transfer all of B Company's property to Lieutenant Beck, who had arrived from Fort McKavett while Bigelow was in the field. Bigelow's impression of his new commander was:

> ...Lt. Beck talks a good deal about what "they do at McKavett" and seems to think that anything that is in practise there should be put in practise here. He has found it necessary to have his Quarter Master Serg't at the stables every morning a half hour before reveille. I can see no sense whatever [in doing so] in garrison, when the days are about 16 hours long.... In less than a year [the company] has had five different commanders, [from which] it has suffered a good deal.

FIRST LIEUTENANT WILLIAM H. BECK

His overindulgence in alcohol almost cost him his career, but a lenient president saved him from dismissal. (Courtesy Fort Davis National Historic Site)

Bigelow joined the mess provided by the Becks, but about a week later decided that doing so had been a mistake.

> *Fort Stockton, Texas, June 13, 1878.* I left Lieut. Beck's mess this morning. I cannot stand the ways of the family. Mrs Beck's ugly temper is none the less unbearable on account of its being...due to ill health. The mess is the poorest and the most expensive that I have ever joined. The Lt. charges a dollar a day and cannot give me even a glass of good fresh milk in the morning.... I obtained admission to [Dr. Price's] mess, much to my relief & satisfaction.

On June 14 he and twelve men once more left the post in quest of Indians. They returned on June 26 for provisions, then went out again from June 28 to July 4. From July 12 to August 1 he and nineteen men covered 415 miles to, from, and through the Guadalupe Mountains north of Fort Davis. Stopping at that post on his way back to Stockton, on July 28 he wrote to his father:

> My dear Father
>
> I am again at Fort Davis having arrived yesterday at 10 P.M. after a 15 days scout.... It appears that I was sent out on a false report. I found no fresh trail. On the 26 we reached Victoria, having marched about 40 miles...to get water. Being unable to get provisions [there] I had to come into Davis for them last night.... The distance is 35 miles.

If Bigelow recorded anything else about his scouts that summer, it has been lost or destroyed, leaving only the entries in the monthly post returns and a rough map of some of the territory covered during his three and one-half months of continual patrolling.

He was not, of course, the only junior officer at Fort Stockton to perform such arduous duty. But as there was only one cavalry company, its officers and men bore a disproportionate burden until L Company arrived in June. Without rapid response capability, the infantry's role was largely limited to accompanying stages and wagon trains or protecting property. For example, John McMartin and ten foot soldiers spent from May 29 until September 1 guarding a "newly discovered" spring (soon named "Grierson Spring") in the Llano Escatado (Staked Plains), about eighty-five miles northeast of Stockton. And sometimes an infantry officer would lead a cavalry detachment, as Glenn did from May 8 through 22 when he and some L Company troopers patrolled the road and scouted for Indians near Escondido Springs. Then from May 28 until the end of August he was attached to L Company at Camp Peña Blanca, where he, Esterly, and

Maxon headed groups of horse soldiers in scouts between the Pecos and the Rio Grande.[11]

THE AUGUST INTERLUDE

From August 1 until September 4 Bigelow remained at the fort. After of couple of weeks there he wrote:

Fort Stockton, August 15, 1878.... I have finished reading The Life of Custer by Whittaker. The author tries to make his hero appear gentle and refined, but occasionally lets his true character appear, as when he tells of Custer rising from his table and giving an Indian Chief a black eye.[12]

My returns and Board of Survey proceedings are finished. I shall be able to go into camp [at Peña Blanca]...without feeling that a mountain of red tape is to keep me engaged when I return.

Fort Stockton, August 18, 1878.... The officers gave a ball to Capt. [Charles D.] Viele & the officers & ladies of his company on their way to Ft Davis from Ft McKavett.[13] Safford was with them. He is the same as ever. Capt Viele has a wife who is the most attractive &, I think, the most accomplished woman I have seen in the army. She, the Capt's sister & Safford read French together. Mrs Viele...can talk about something besides the relative merits of lineal & regimental promotion, the abuse of the army by Congress, the attractions of the other post, &c. As yet, I have seen but few good looking officers wives.... Perhaps I have already seen the worst. Capt Viele is no credit to the service. He got drunk on the day of his arrival here, bragged about his dogs and horses,...and having been invited to dine with Lieut. Beck kept the company waiting without having declined the invitation. He was probably too drunk to go, or to know the impropriety of not going. Mrs Viele is too good for the Capt. Her experience on the frontier has not imparted to her that masculine independence & roughness that the wives of officers generally acquire.... She made a better appearance than did any lady of the garrison. Mrs McLaughlin [and she]...do not...offend by rudeness nor overdo the matter when they are inclined to be polite....

Miss Candelaria Garza was considered the belle of the ball. Her mother is pure Spanish & her father a Mexican....

Lieut Sweet has been requesting me...to mount guard for him. He...thought he had affected his brain by overwork. Dr. Pope said that the trouble with him was that there was not enough of it....

At the end of the month Lt. Maxon is expected to be in from San Francisco Creek and we to be going out.

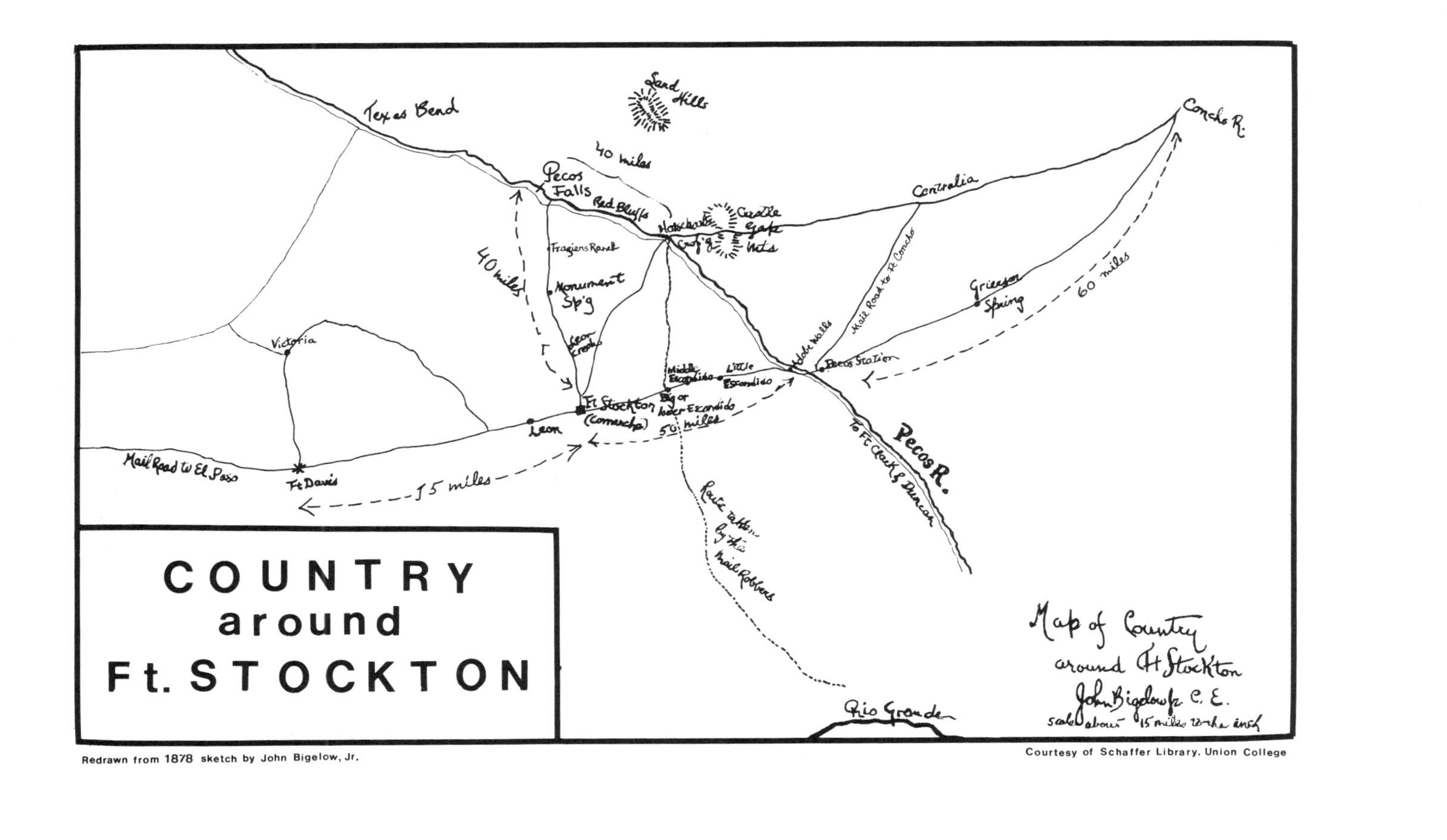

Redrawn from 1878 sketch by John Bigelow, Jr.

Courtesy of Schaffer Library, Union College

...The temperature has been 105° in the shade...[and] 140° in the sun. [The heat] that people here can stand is attributed to the dryness of the atmosphere, its purity and its almost constant motion.... Persons not in a town or near a military post eat plain, substantial food and drink nothing but water.... Those who live & travel over [the plains] know not at what time they may need all their wits....

Fort Stockton, August 19, 1878. I am now performing, in addition to my own duties, those of Lieut Beck who is sick. Mrs Beck told Dr. Price that the Lieut had a bad case of gout, causing the Dr to laugh...for he knows that Lieut Beck is only working off...a drunk. Judging the officers of the 10th Cav. by the specimens I have seen in command of Comp B, they are a poor lot....

Fort Stockton, Texas, August 20 1878.... Capt Armes...asked me to do some work for him while he was sick.... I excused myself.... If he had asked me to do something for him personally, as an invalid, I would have tried...although I believe his sickness is...a consequence of intemperance. I do not intend to run the affairs of every officer whose debauchery has unfitted him for duty.

Fort Stockton, August 25th 1878.... I went...this morning to see Capt [John W.] French off.... [He]...arrived here yesterday from Fort Davis to Fort Concho. Mrs. French, unlike a philosophical army woman, looks at the dark side of life. She says...[that] when she goes East she has barely time to get accustomed to...decent living before she has to...return again....

Major Geddes and Mr Corbett are at swords points. Mr Corbett incensed the major by allowing his clerk to write an article reflecting strongly upon him as an officer. Mr Corbett would not apologize...[and] has forbidden the major to enter his house...[because] of the badness of the major's private character.... I have heard it said that he was forced to marry his present wife by her father, who held a pistol to his head.... [Despite] the major's marriage, he has been very attentive to Miss Garza and has...present[ed] her with a ring.... She, as unsophisticated almost as any Indian maiden...continued to lend her ear to [his] seductive speeches. The Doctor and I...determined to protect female virtue against a man's infamous designs.... I broached the subject...by telling her...that I did not much like Major Geddes...[who] was already married. Instead of going into hysterics...she [said] she did not know much about him, with which disconnected remark our interview ended.

Having served with African American troops in both garrison and field for more than eight months, Bigelow was beginning to form some opinions of their soldierly qualities.

Fort Stockton, Aug. 29th 1878.... I find that colored troops, though not as observant of outward forms of respect as white soldiers, are more sincerely respectful.... They have, as a rule, the utmost confidence in their officers, which...though often misplaced, is very hard to shake. The excellence of an officer's private character will raise him more in the estimation of a colored soldier...than a white one, and the defects of character will lower him less.

Chapter 13

Scouting with Old Tanglefoot

After being delayed almost a week awaiting the arrival of provisions, B Company and a dozen infantrymen from D Company left Fort Stockton for Peña Blanca,[1] a subcamp about sixty-two miles southwest, where L Company had spent most of the summer.

In the field, Sept 4, 1878.... After breakfast I bade good bye to my friends.... An orderly [then] brought me the proceedings of a board of survey...[that] the Comm'd'g Officer wanted me to complete [so]...I delayed my departure about an hour.... While Dr. Price & I were on our way...McMartin came galloping up. He was ordered by Col Grierson to serve temporarily with the Company. McLaughlin [*sic*] protested but in vain.

At 6 P.M. we made camp after a march of 17 1/2 miles. We have two messes: Dr Price, Stilwell the guide, and I constituting one; Lieut Beck, McMartin & Willy Beck, the Lieut's son, the other. Willy is with us, I think, to keep him out of mischief during his father's absence from home.

In the field, Sept 5, 1878. Left camp at 7 A.M. Halted at 6.30 P.M. by a large water hole, having marched 21 miles. It rained hard....

Peña Blanca, Sept 6, 1878. Left camp at 7.15 A.M. and stopped here at 2.30 P.M., having marched 23 miles. We were...disgusted at the appearance of our camping ground.... The refuse and debris of Lieut Maxon's camp were strewn in every direction. Old empty cans, bottles, boxes, big heaps of manure, and rubbish of all kinds were conspicuously hideous in the midst of nature's works. Had it not been for [Col. Grierson's] express order we would not have camped here.

LEAVING THE FORT

A troop is about to leave Fort Stockton in 1885. (Courtesy Historic Fort Stockton)

For the next two days Bigelow was in charge of a detail of soldiers removing "all the filth" from camp and building the men's sinks, which was done in almost constant rain. Enigmatically, he concluded his September 8 entry with, "I heard one of the men say that he was more afraid of an Irishman than he was of an Indian."

> *Peña Blanca, Sept 11, 1878.* The camp is now pretty well established.... To the South about 7 miles is Sierra Caballo...from the top of it one commands a view in any direction of 100 miles.... A narrow sluggish stream runs...on the North side of camp.... At one time this country was the scene of extensive volcanic action.... The most common mineral is quartz. Fragments of jasper are numerous...[and] I have found specimens of common opal.... I am trying to add to my mineral collection and to start a natural history collection.... I have already a large tarantula...no where else, even in Texas, have I seen such spiders.

> *Peña Blanca, Sept 14th 1878....* One of our horses was bit on the nose...by a rattlesnake. The upper jaw...resembled that of a rhinoceros, [but it] is now looking almost natural....

> Dr. Price, Stilwell and McMartin are reading newspapers in my tent. Stilwell, like most guides, can spin yarns and is afraid of nothing. It was he who saved Forsyth's command when it was coralled [*sic*] by Indians on the Red Republican River. He and another guide got through the line of Indians during the night and carried the news to Fort Wallace on foot. He had to walk 125 miles and, until he got well out of range of the enemy, he...crept backwards so that his tracks should deceive the Indians had they been discovered.

B Company's guide, "Comanche Jack" Stilwell, was one of the most colorful characters on the frontier. When in September 1868 Forsyth and some fifty civilian scouts were besieged by a large band of Cheyennes and Sioux on what was later called Beecher's Island, the teen-aged Stilwell and another scout volunteered to seek help. After substituting rags and pieces of blankets for their boots so as to resemble Indian tracks, they escaped from the island under cover of darkness. As they hid in a buffalo wallow on the third day of their tortuous trip, a band of Indians stopped within a hundred feet of them, then shortly later a large rattlesnake slithered into their hiding place and approached them. Caught between the two potentially fatal forces, Stilwell reputedly spat tobacco juice in the snake's eyes, causing it to rapidly retreat.[2] Whether or not true, the story thrust Comanche Jack into a permanent place in frontier history, and also showed that the gauche habit of chewing tobacco might have some redeeming value after all.

> McMartin and Stilwell went out riding yesterday and came to a waterhole...[which] Mac's horse walked into and sunk. Mac was pulled out by Stilwell who threw him a lariat.... The water was so deep that he could not touch bottom.... He does not know how to swim; I should think that he would now want to learn.... He lost his carbine...but hopes to recover it when the command passes by on the way to Del Norte.

Two days later the company prepared to conduct a survey to determine the bearings and distances between Peña Blanca, Presidio del Norte (on the Rio Grande some ninety miles southwest), and San Carlos, a hotbed for Apache raiders fifty or so miles southeast of Del Norte and inland on the Mexican side of the river. There was no known road nor trail, no map, and Beck had not even asked Lt. Maxon for directions. Bigelow urged that they go to San Carlos first because an appearance at Del Norte

> will certainly be reported at San Carlos by Indian spies.... If we could go directly to San Carlos we would be more apt to overtake parties between the Indian Headquarters and our camp.

Lieutenant Beck rejected the recommendation, however, since he wanted to see Del Norte.

> *Sept 18, 78, in the field.* Left Peña Blanca at 8.30 A.M.... Halted...near where McMartin lost his gun. [It] was recovered by...men diving for it.

On the nineteenth the command covered twenty-four miles in about twelve hours before halting. The following day they continued on a southwesterly route until they reached some tablelands where they stopped for about half an hour while Beck and Stilwell searched for an ascent. Beck then led the command up what proved to be a box canyon. After a way up the steep slope was selected, a scramble in single file began. All but one horse reached the top after which

> The fun began when the mules were headed [up]. Some of them were pulled and pushed and beaten and shouted & sworn at which, notwithstanding all these incentives, persisted in returning to the bottom...after they had made half the ascent. The mule carrying the mess furniture & provisions for Dr Price, Stilwell and me rolled to the very foot.... It fell about 4 or 500 feet down a slope of about 45° strewn with...boulders higher than a man to small pebbles. The pack gave way and its parts scattered.... The mule got on its legs, whisked its tail, and began munching on grass...as if nothing had happened.... We went into camp at 6.20 P.M. where there was poor grass, no wood and no water.

> *Del Norte, Sept 21, 1878.* Left camp at 6.5 A.M., at 8.16 we came upon a path.... After following it about a mile we came upon a mounted Mexican who accompanied [us] part of the way to Del Norte.... I tried to get him to point out some prominent land marks in the distance...[so] that I might take bearings. But neither Stilwell nor I could get an intelligent answer from him. He would only point to the trail and say: "It don't go anywhere, here it is."

> *In the field, Sept 22, 1878.* Dr. Price & I rode to Del Norte after dark yesterday ev'g.... Presidio del Norte on the American side consists of about 4 or 5 houses. On the other side there are about three thousand inhabitants.... We left camp at 6.5 A.M. About 16 miles from Presidio we found Polvo, a Mexican settlement. I tried to procure a guide but the only [competent] person...was unwilling.... My belief is that he, like most Mexicans along the river, was afraid of incurring the vengence of neighboring Apaches for having assisted troops. He informed me that we could not follow the river down to San Carlos Crossing on account of the steep

cliffs...and that we would have to make a circuit to the north and come down again to reach it.

In the field, Sept 23, 78. Travelled about 20 miles. We had camped in a cañon which we could not find a way out of. We had to...retrace part of yesterday's march.... We stopped at a little hut [where]...the proprietor agreed to go with us.... He led us up two of the hardest hills I have ever travelled over....

Sept 24th 1878. In the field. Our guide led us today in the roughest country that a horse can travel over.... A little before dark we came in sight of the Rio Grande.... The first thing I did was to take a bath in the river and changed my underclothing. All the officers & the guide did the same. The water is muddy and shallow, the bottom rocky and the current swift.

ABUSE OF AUTHORITY

If scrambling up and down the rugged terrain northwest of San Carlos Crossing was arduous, it paled in comparison to the conditions to which the soldiers, voluntarily accompanied by Bigelow, were soon subjected.

Sept 25th 1878.... We had a great deal of hard climbing to do.... At about 11 o'clock Lt Beck ordered that the men should not mount again until ordered to do so. We halted at about noon...[for] about half an hour. The men walked about two hours and twenty-five minutes. Lt Beck, McMartin, Dr Price & the guide were all riding. I walked, with the exception of perhaps 15 minutes, all the time that the men were required to do so. As it grew very hot and the ground was rough and hilly...I expected that Lt Beck would have the men mount.... The Dr finally came riding by me and said that I should either halt or mount the men. I told him to see Lt Beck, that I had no authority to countermand the Lt's order. I told him however that he had the authority to order them mounted. He said, "Well, mount them then," which I did. He saw Lt Beck who said that the march was not a hard one, that the men were lazy loafers, that they had only marched about two hours, while he had, in his time, marched six, and cursed a great deal more than the Dr. liked.

Sept 26, 1878. In the field. Camped in a cañon about 2 P.M. [When the detachment halted only eight of fifty men remained.] The Dr ventured to speak to Lt. Beck again about marching the men too long without a rest. The Lieut's reply was, as usual, loud and coarse.... He [said] that...[they] were nothing but "damn paper men," that they would walk tomorrow "god damn 'em" and threatened to keep them going till 12 o'clock if necessary.... The Dr remonstrated that they were excessively fatigued.... The Lt replied "What the hell are they for but to work & get tired, that's what the government pays them for." The Lieut had the face to talk as he did, although he had ridden all day.

...The Dr said that he ought to care whether the men got fatigued...[and that] "I shall make my report to the Surgeon Gen'l." Lieut Beck answered: "I don't give a damn for you, Sir, nor for your report." The Dr repeated his threat to which the Lieut in a louder tone said: "If you repeat that again, Sir, I shall...march you under guard. You are insubordinate, Sir, and I shall not tolerate it." The Dr...said nothing and silence reigned supreme....

Sept 27, 1878. In the field. Left camp at 6.20 and camped at 3.40.... One of the men gave out.... The Dr and three men remained behind with him. I tried to make Lt Beck leave the Dr his bedding but he would not.... The men walked from 7 to 8 hours and I kept them company. My shoes are worn almost through.

Sept 28, 1878. In the field. The Lieut sent the Dr his blanket.... Another man got sick and had to be left on the road.... The men and I walked about 5 hrs. My shoes are worn through, but they will do me for two more marches which will take us to Peña Blanca. We had to walk about an hour after dark through brush and thorny bushes. We marched 25 miles.... We have lost two mules and two horses and...one or two other animals are permanently unserviceable.

There is no excuse for this damage. I have never seen the company...so run down.... Lt Beck got mad this noon because his lunch was not brought to him when he wanted it. He...abused everybody right and left. He called the men "damn worthless & scoundrels" & "sons of b——s," and swore that if he had charge of hell they should not come to it. One of the men [said] he would not want admission if the Lieut were there....

Sept 29th 1878. In the field. We remained in camp until 10.30 A.M. The men who were left behind arrived before we left.... The men rode most of the time. We travelled very slow. Lt Beck remarks that in three days everything will come out smooth.... I can show him a few horses that will not be smooth in three months.

Sept. 30, 1878
My dear Father:

I have returned...today having been to the Rio Grande in search of a favorable line for a road to San Carlos Crossing. We learned that San Carlos is about 22 miles from the Rio Grande.... [A road would] facilitate movement...in case of a war with Mexico.... The Indians are on good terms with the San Carlos people. Chief Asate has a band of about 50 Indians, mostly Lipans...at Las Palmas, about 50 miles from the settlement. He is a renegade Mescallero Apache.... Our troops want to get him.

As one goes south, [the country becomes] gently undulating, hilly, and then rocky & precipitous. [To] give you an idea of the roughness of my life during the past 12 days...I feel civilized and luxuriously provided for, now that I am again in a tent....

Lieut Beck says we start again to go East in about eight days. I am afraid our horses will not be ready for service in that time. At the end of next month I shall probably be back in Stockton.

I had very little time for reading or writing...[but] I read "Diderot in St Petersburg" while sitting in the shade...of a broad brimmed hat.... Allowing my mind to wander among Russian snows brought comfort to my heated body.

Peña Blanca, Oct. 3d 1878. Since our return I have been resting and reading. I have tried to learn something about the veterinary art by observing the treatment by the company farrier of the horses that were hurt while we were out. Dr Price has taught me a good deal about physiology.

I have been reading an article [about geology] from the Edinburgh Review.... The author thinks that...the general features of the crust of the earth have not changed since the Azoric time. He is, I think, greatly in error.

After a lengthy rebuttal of the author's premise, Bigelow turned to Lieutenant Beck, who he thought

is a pretty good company commander in the post. If [he] were as good in the field...he would make a fine officer.... He is now for the first time an independent commander...and shows it by the trouble and anxiety he allows the responsibility to give him.... The reason [for his actions] was that his mind was filled with forebodings.

Peña Blanca, October 4th 1878. Our wagon returned from Stockton [with] mail and provisions.... Lieut Beck has had me all ready today to take command of a detachment of 10 men...[to go] to the Rio Grande by way of Paint[ed] Rock Spring, about 60 miles East, and from there to find a line for...a road to the River. He has changed his mind and decided to make the trip with the entire company...the day after tomorrow.

It may be due to lack of appropriated money but it is probably due to the evils of our system of staff appointment that our commissary and quartermaster departments are in a deplorable condition.... Lieut Beck sent to the Q.M. at Stockton for 36 prs of boots [but] obtained 6 prs, all that were on hand.... I have worn out a pair of government boots, cowhides with half inch soles...[and] am reduced to wearing...low shoes on the coming scout. We are also greatly in need of carbolic acid for horse medicine but it is not to be had....

Peña Blanca, Oct 6, 1878 Sunday. We had Sunday Morning Inspection at 8 o'clock. The men are badly off for shoes. Our tent has become the loafing tent. Stilwell has an A tent, and he has no chairs so...his quarters are not a public resort. The Dr has fallen out with Beck and is therefore free from his intrusion. Beck is not sought for and has generally his tent to himself. He has consequently visited our tent almost every evening for company.... He & Stilwell remained until about midnight yesterday. They & McMartin were drinking whiskey which had been sent to them from Stockton. I undressed and went to bed but the hint was not taken.... [When] I told [Beck] I wanted to get to sleep, Stilwell...and he left.

Peña Blanca, Oct 7, 1878. Lieut Beck has changed his mind again and, instead of taking the entire company, took 20 men with McMartin, Stilwell & Willy...in search of a way to San Vincente. Dr Price & I are left in camp...[with] 37 men.... 25 are Cavalry and 12 Infantry.

Until the Dr joined us [last night] McMartin, Stilwell & I had been conversing upon the prospects of war with Mexico. We were all opposed to it out of sympathy with the Mexicans....

Peña Blanca, Oct 9th 1878. Sergeant Givens returned from Stockton yesterday with a dispatch for the com'd'g officer.... I opened it and learned that a party of Indians had killed three girls and a boy in Kerr Co. on Johnson's Fork of the Guadaloupe [Guadalupe] and that they are travelling toward the Rio Grande.... It [also] said that MacKenzie's movements might drive the Indians to Lancaster on the Pecos or into Grierson's District. Grierson directs that Beck keep a sharp lookout for the marauders and that they be captured or destroyed if possible.... [Beck] being away, I shall comply as well as I can. As Beck is on the way to San Vincente Crossing...[it] is guarded. There is no other one between it & Del Norte except...opposite San Carlos [which] I shall try to cover.... I picked out 15 horses which can be saddled and ridden. With that many men and two mules besides two spare horses...I shall start toward the River tomorrow.... I shall take 12 days rations.... The sketch on the next page shows, roughly, the line of our last march. It is not drawn to any scale but the distances are marked and the tents designate camping grounds.

...If I could spare a man and horse I would send Beck the dispatch...but he has so used up his stock, and the whole command is so much in want of equipment that I cannot spare a courier. The men have not even lariats for their horses. Yet if I should lose my stock by a stampede, I, and not the staff officer who failed to supply them, would hear the blame.

The horses have attracted a large number of blackbirds to Peña Blanca.... The Dr took my gun yesterday and shot a few with which our cook made us a blackbird

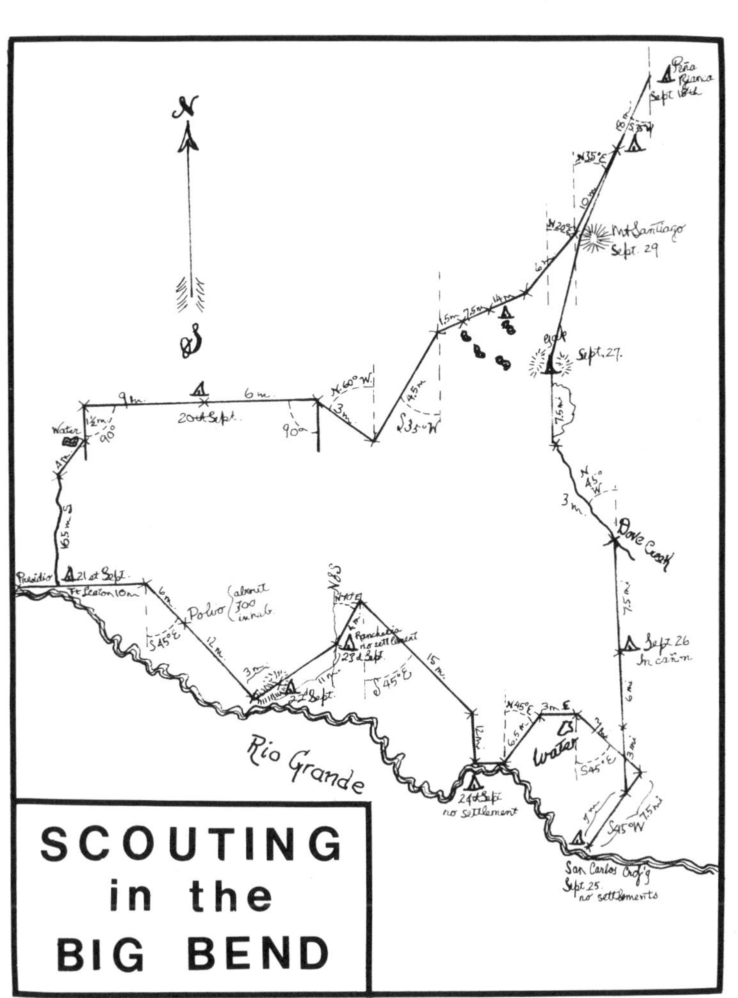

Redrawn from 1878 sketch by John Bigelow, Jr.

Courtesy of Schaffer Library, Union College

pie. There were not 24 birds in it nor did they begin to sing when it was opened, but it was, nevertheless, a "dainty dish."

Camp Peña Blanca, Oct 10, 1878.... I have changed my mind in regard to leaving Peña Blanca. My horse is very lame and I do not think it would do for me to take one of the company horses...[so] I have decided...to await Beck's return.

Camp Peña Blanca, Oct 12, 1878. According to...dispatches from Stockton the company is to remain here through November. Grierson says that he will order in all the troops in December and send them out in the field again in March.

The fall weather is setting in.... It will be quite cool before [we] return to Stockton. It would please me if I were never to see that post again....

Peña Blanca, Oct 14, 1878.... There are quite a number of Infantrymen in camp who are trying to learn to read. The Cavalrymen show fewer indications of a desire to improve their minds. This may be due to their being so much in the field and so hard worked in the post, that they have but little energy to devote to self culture, but it is due to a greater extent to their officers not having...taken any interest in their education.... At inspection of quarters I saw a couple of books in Corp'l Bowman's tent.... One was the New Testament and the other, Grecian Mythology. I do not know whether the two books represent a difference of faith between Bowman & his tentmate or whether they are the text books to the study of which they direct their unbiassed and unprejudiced minds in making a comparison of ancient with modern religion.

I have resumed the study of Spanish.... As there are six weeks between now and [our] probable return to Stockton, by studying and talking with Stilwell I may make considerable progress....

Most of the men do not drink coffee. Instead, they drink a kind of tea made with wild sage.... They are fond of grease in their food. Hence, their love of bacon, which they prefer to fresh meat. The fatter it is the more they like it.... They are economical of their grease, trying to get as much out of their bacon, and at the same [time] leave as much in as possible. They soak their bread, or drip their hard tack, in the melted grease or, as they call it, the gravy....

Camp Peña Blanca, Oct 17, 1878. A courier brought me...a dispatch from Lieut Beck directing me to send the wagon with a day's forage & rations to the water hole 12 miles from here. He expects to get there tonight.... I am glad we are going to have another month [here], but Beck, I expect, will be very mad when he is informed of it.

> *Camp Peña Blanca, Oct. 18, 1878.* Lt Beck returned today.... [He] has brought back a prisoner, whose offense consists in having told Lt. Beck he did not like to be called a ———, the most insulting name in the English language.

The incident Bigelow alludes to occurred on October 15 after Beck upbraided Pvt. Clayborn Mack by shouting, "You God damned black ignorant son of a bitch." Bothered by such unseemly conduct, the soldier was granted permission by the first sergeant to speak with the lieutenant. In a respectful and military manner he told Beck that his mother, "although a colored woman, was a lady." The devoted son's presumptuousness resulted in his being marched for three days, after which he had to perform hard labor from reveille until retreat for the next five days.

On October 22, while Private Mack still toiled away to atone for his indiscretion, Beck started back to Stockton, apparently to replenish his supply of what General Sherman called "Old Tanglefoot."[3] Bigelow, in temporary command, promptly released the prisoner.

> *Camp Peña Blanca, Texas, Oct. 28th 1878.* Lieut Beck and McMartin returned from Stockton this morning. Both were under the influence of liquor. They had been on a big spree in the post and were ordered off.... Beck has brought a supply of whiskey which he has drawn on this afternoon and on which Stilwell has got pretty drunk. He...told me that Beck [said] that I had no business releasing Private Mack, that my action was contrary to orders & regulations, and that I had better walk straight or would soon find myself in trouble.... Beck would have taken means to get satisfaction from me before this...and would have had Mack reconfined, if I were as plainly in the wrong as he says I am. He knows better than to put himself again in the situation from which I released him when I released Mack. He could not retire from his former position as gracefully as he can now.

Referring to Beck's comportment at Stockton as a "big spree" understates what happened. On the first day of his trip Beck frantically covered forty-five miles, killing one of four mules pulling his ambulance. Still resembling someone demonically possessed, he went the rest of the way at a torrid pace, causing another mule to collapse. After arriving he wasted no time in achieving a glorious state of intoxication, and then while in uniform rode a horse into Mr. Corbett's store, for which Major McLaughlen ordered him back to Peña Blanca.

The transgressions did not stop, however. Bigelow mentioned that Beck returned in an intoxicated condition, but he later failed to mention that the binge continued for at least three days. What is more, on his first night back Beck visited some government teamsters camped nearby, where he drank, caroused, sang, and shouted with them within the hearing of the soldiers and men at Peña Blanca. And on the next evening he invited a teamster to his tent where he again drank and sang. Then on the thirtieth he drunkenly staggered along the picket line during stable call.

When the company returned to Stockton on November 30, Beck's conduct was investigated, following which he was relieved of command and placed in arrest. Numerous court-martial charges were preferred, and on December 9 the accused, presumably sober, was escorted to Fort Davis by McMartin and a small detachment to await trial. A few weeks later Bigelow, McMartin, and several enlisted men from B Company would travel to San Antonio as material witnesses in the case. Before then, outpost life went on. On November 6 Bigelow answered a letter from his father:

> My dear Father
>
> The only taxidermists [another interest he was pursuing] instruments I need are a couple of scalpel knives. I have enough arsenic for [now].
>
> I am much obliged to Ma for her requests as to my wants for Christmas. I know of nothing that I need...except Scott's Military Law.... I cannot say whether I would appreciate Emory's report or not. It is highly probably though that $12 could not be better invested in other books.
>
> I expect to be back at Stockton by the 1st of next month. During...October I have been in camp reading from morning till night. I am therefore not continuing the existence of a savage.
>
> In a few days I shall probably start East toward the Pecos to look for...Painted Rock Spring.... We are now prepared for winter. I have a fire in my tent every night. A stone fireplace surmounted by a chimney...has been constructed in the rear of it...& by ripping open one of the seams...and drawing the canvas aside I admit the heat from the fire without much cold air.

> *Camp Peña Blanca, Nov. 17th 1878....* I started on the 8th to the Rio Grande with Gen'l Grierson, Lieut Beck, Stilwell and a detachment of men. We returned on the 14th. The trip was full of novelties to me. [For the 1st time] I served in the field under Grierson, marched until 3 o'clock in the m'g, saw Beck get a "cussing," saw several hot & cold water springs, swam the Rio Grande, and saw San Vincente. The place I saw was, according to Stilwell, not San Vincente but an old Aztec ruin. It was an adobe wall enclosure with a building in the wall on one side.... Grierson, in order to look for a crossing, had remained behind with me after the column under Beck had left the river. He had just found a place to cross with wagons. I swam over & forded back to satisfy him & myself of the practicability of the

> crossing. He nearly went wild over his crossing.... He is going to have a road built to...the ford which is almost directly south of Stockton in the most South point of the Great Bend. The road would be a very good thing if we should have a war with Mexico. Troops could be sent from Ft. Davis & Stockton to Del Norte, San Vincente & San Carlos in less than 8 days.

Grierson, similar to some other commanders, appears to have sought recognition by having his name associated with various landmarks.[4] And in West Texas, little was of more importance than water. Hence, a couple of days later he and Bigelow again ventured forth from camp.

> I returned today [November 17] from a trip to a water hole about 15 miles from here which I was ordered by Col Grierson to circumscribe by the sides of a square mile.... He thought the holes had never been visited by a white man until he discovered them. I found the remains of an old camp near the place where we camped and Sergt. McDonald told me that Comp. "I" of the 9th Cav. had camped there.... Lieut Beck will have to break the news to the General. It will be a great blow.

Whether or not Bigelow maintained his journal between late November and early January is unknown, but nothing during this period could be located. Military records permit reconstruction of some of his activities, however, and on January 3 he related some of his experiences and observations during December.

On November 26, four days before B Company arrived back at Fort Stockton, 1st Lt. Louis Orleman, a thirty-seven-year-old German immigrant who had been absent for more than a year because of his failing vision, joined the post.[5] He was accompanied by his eighteen-year-old daughter, Lillie, who cooked and kept house for him while his wife and the other children remained in Austin. Command of B Company was assumed by Orleman when Beck was relieved.

The next few weeks must have been unusually busy for Bigelow, who had to cope with the fallout from Beck's sudden deposal, a new commander to familiarize with changes in the company and current issues, the investigation of Beck's behavior, a plethora of reports to prepare, and the de facto responsibility for the company.

B Company was not the only organization to suffer a degree of turmoil. In the latter part of October the recently restored Captain Armes, commanding officer of L Company of the 10th Cavalry, experienced his twentieth arrest, and in early December he was in San Antonio to confront his sixth court-martial. This time he was accused of submitting a false guard report by listing a soldier who was not present. Armes claimed that the sergeant of the guard was at fault, and in any event the error resulted from no more than a misspelling. He later lambasted Grierson, McLaughlen, 1st Lt. Robert G. Smither (the regimental adjutant) "and company" as "conspirators trying to force [him] out of the regiment" on "false and malicious charges."[6] The court convened on December 3, but before arraignment the judge advocate announced that the charges had been withdrawn and the accused released from arrest.[7]

With Christmas approaching, various social affairs at the post kept pace. The most significant was a hop in early December at which Captain Geddes met Lillie Orleman. Their encounter marked the beginning of an entanglement that eventually would ruin careers, reputations, and lives.

As the month wore on, Bigelow decided to apply for a leave of seven days over the holidays to visit his close friend, Bob Safford, then garrisoned at Fort Davis. It was not as relaxing as he had hoped.

> *Fort Stockton, ~~Dec. 23~~ Jan. 3d, 1878 [1879].* I have my orders to appear before the court that is to try Beck at San Antonio. I shall probably get off Sunday or Tuesday, and hope to avoid Beck on the way....
>
> I was glad to get back here after my trip to Davis. It was a bore from the beginning almost to the end.... The people of the garrison were very kind and did the best they could to make us happy, but I was among strangers whom I was not anxious to know, and not comfortably lodged, and had duties unperformed that awaited me at Stockton weighing on my mind. My one little room with its comfortable bed, with my books and my clothes were often in my mind.... I made the acquaintance...of Capt. Carpenter of the 10th, who is now in command of the post. He is considered the best company commander in the regiment and one of the best in the service. He is a gentleman by birth and training. He is not a narrow minded "routinier" but a broad minded student of his profession. Many officers appear to advantage in the lower grades of the army who are incapable of rising and maintaining their reputation. Capt Lebo is a man of that sort.[8] But Capt Carpenter is not.
>
> There were not as many ladies at the hop...as we have at Stockton. The society was very much as Capt Viele represented it. He says that...he can dance with his shoemaker's wife or get drunk with the butcher, that he lets his 2d Lieut dance with the former while he does the drinking with the butcher.

I have made the acquaintance of a new contract surgeon [at Fort Stockton].... The Lieut & Miss Orleman liked him very well until he showed that he was only a "*spooney*" but not a polite man....

We had review on the last day of December. The performance of the command was enough to make an officer ashamed of his uniform. Drills are to commence again...but I shall start [soon] for San Antonio....

The Northers have set in. The ground is covered with ice. The wind is high and blowing rain, sleet and snow before it.

...Mrs Robe has consumption. She looks as if she has. Poor thing, her husband stints her and works her to death to pamper his appetite.... The hard work that army women are put to, and put themselves to, is one cause of their homeliness as a class. Many, I think, deny themselves the assistance of servants in order to save money for the purchase of dresses. I had rather my wife should dress like a servant and live like a lady than dress like a lady and work like a slave.

CHAPTER 14

SAN ANTONIO REVISITED

With the charges against Lieutenant Beck referred to trial by General Ord, Bigelow was once again immersed in military justice, but this time for an extended period and far removed from his company.[1] In mid-January he and the other prosecution witnesses departed for San Antonio.[2] Almost a month passed before he referred to why he was there.[3]

> *San Antonio, Feb. 21, 1879....* I was before the court this morning.... I had to state a remark made by Dr. Price about Lieut. Beck.... It was that the Dr. conceived a dislike to the Lieut. the first time he saw him. The Judge Advocate [Capt. John Clous, 24th Infantry] tried, indirectly, to make me express my opinion of Lieut. Beck, but did not succeed.[4] His object seemed to be to annoy me rather than to assist the prosecution. My opinion would have done his side of the case more harm than good....

> *San Antonio, Texas, Feb. 22d 1879.* Beck...called to borrow some money.... I told him frankly that I had the money and could spare it, but did not intend to lend it to him; that he would...only complicate his financial affairs by borrowing from one man to pay another, that no one could set him right but himself,...and that my lending him money might lessen his embarrassment...but had he reflected before he acted the embarrassment would have been foreseen and avoided.

The abrupt change from life in the field provided Bigelow with more than ample time for reading as well as calling on friends, attending dances, riding, picnicking, and strolling and talking with several young ladies. He often visited the Ords where he delicately balanced Mrs. Ord's attempts to get him to play croquet (which he despised) with his desire to walk and talk with Bertie, their twenty-two-year-old daughter, about abstruse matters such as the meaning of Longfellow's "The Bridge" (which they failed to discover).[5] Minnie Moore, the daughter of Major Moore, was another favorite companion.[6] He often rode with her and frequently was a guest in her home where they entertained themselves and others by singing German songs. He did not, however, reciprocate the interest shown in him by Florencita Garcia, the daughter of Hispanic friends, but he did acquiesce in her request to sign her autograph album, writing that "Memory is a crowded vestibule through which we pass in entering and on leaving the hearts of others," a suave bit of falderal that delighted the young lady. Describing some activities, he wrote:

> I have an invitation to drive out to the head of the River with the Ords tomorrow. Mrs Ord thinks she has provided a great pleasure...by having [me] meet six young ladies.
>
> *San Antonio, Tex. Feb. 23d 1879....* [The Ords and I] drove...to the head of the River. There we met a party of young ladies & gentlemen invited by Mrs. Brackenridge.[7] The afternoon was spent in talking, walking and singing.... At about half past six I rode with Howard to the Hord Hotel where I took supper.[8] He and I afterwards rode to Dr. Moore's [where] we were invited to spend the evening. The dancing ceased at 12 o'clock, today being Ash Wednesday. A number of the bachelors ...went to the Casino to take a look at the last ball of the season....[9] When a set was being formed for a quadrille...I placed myself with Miss [Harriett] MacKenzie [*sic*] opposite to Col & Mrs Andrews....[10] Mrs Andrews swelled up and pointed to the Col...then to herself and said: "*This* is the head couple." She should not have...presumed to take the lead on the ground of her husband's military rank....
>
> *San Antonio, Texas, March 1st 1879....* This afternoon Miss Moore and I rode on horseback.... [Later] Capt [Clifton] Comly called to get Miss Moore's guitar and asked us to...his quarters. We met...a number of young ladies & gentlemen [and] had the usual talking & singing.
>
> *San Antonio, Texas, March 2d 1879. Sunday.* Spent the forenoon...at the Mexican Catholic Church.... It struck me as democratic in comparison with the Episcopal church. I saw no reserved pews, the rich & poor appeared to worship together.... A large part of the lower class of worshippers, composed mostly of Mexicans, were standing in the rear...although there were many vacant seats...[they were] left by the common people for their social superiors out of courtesy or from a delicate sensitiveness....

San Antonio, Texas, March 3d 1879. Spent the forenoon at home reading. Rode in the afternoon with Miss Moore to the head of the River. Later...Miss Bowen and her brother made a call.... Miss B. has a very masculine face and wears a tremendous hat which she kept on during the whole evening. She afflicted us with a song, which...I thought was never going to end....

San Antonio, Texas, March 4th 1879.... Called this afternoon on the Garcias.... [Miss Garcia and] I talked about Spanish literature.... I called this evening at the Ords.... Miss Bertie and I sat outside and talked.... When I had lit a cigarette, with her permission, she wanted me to give her one which I would not. Mrs. Ord tried again, but failed, to get me...to play croquet.

As a reprieve from what was rapidly becoming a saturated social life, Bigelow was detailed to New Orleans to escort fifty-six recruits back to San Antonio.[11] After a ten-day absence he resumed the type of activities he resorted to during his enforced idleness.

San Antonio, Tex. March 15, 1879.... I escorted Miss McMillan to the Alamo Litterary [sic] Hall. There we heard several pieces read by...a professional reader.... Her best performances were the Charge of the Light Brigade and a Scene in a Private Mad House.

Because the bustling town of San Antonio was the core of the Army's far-flung presence in Texas, Bigelow also was able to renew acquaintances with officers stationed or passing through there. One was Lieutenant Stivers from Fort Duncan.

San Antonio, Tex. March 19, 1879.... After dinner I called on Lieut Stivers. The poor man is having all his teeth pulled out one after another, while being treated for a disease of the gums....

Called after supper at the Moores where I saw Gen'l Clitz....[12] I was surprised when informed by the General that the annexation of Mexico to the U.S. is favorably considered and often talked about by several leading men and a large number of intelligent people in that country....

I was called before the Court this morning and asked two or three questions; the Judge Advocate then directed me to report to the Adj't Gen'l that my presence was no longer required.

A few days later the court arrived at its findings and sentence. With minor modifications the bacchanalian lieutenant was convicted of all but one specification and mandatorily sentenced to dismissal. Pending action on the case by the reviewing authority and the president, Beck remained in arrest at Fort Davis. Two months later an order was issued from the Executive Mansion approving the proceedings, findings, and sentence, but commuting the sentence "to suspension from rank on half-pay for one year."[13]

The following day Bigelow dined with the Moores, then returned to his room at the Menger for his last night in town. Before retiring he wrote:

> *San Antonio, Texas, March 20, 1879.* I wish I was back at Stockton. The only objection I now have to that post is...Col. Blunt. MacMartin [McMartin] tells me that Beck is trying to borrow money from every one he meets, and that he spends a great part of the night in a gambling saloon.

THE RETURN TRIP TO STOCKTON

Five days later Bigelow arrived at Fort Concho, where he and McMartin interrupted their stagecoach trip. After noting that Lieutenant Smither "kindly took me into his quarters" where "[I slept] on a cot in his sitting room," he mentions a situation he found disturbing.

> *Fort Concho, Texas. March 25, 1879....* As I passed through this post [in January]...I heard something about Miss [Lillie] Orleman which greatly shocked and surprised me, but which was nothing to what I heard shortly after my arrival here this time. In the first case I heard that she drank her whiskey straight.... I had observed a taste of Miss Orleman's that placed the fact within the scope of possibility, if not probability. The second report is so disgusting as well as disgraceful that I cannot write it in my journal. Major Geddes I believe is the cause of the whole scandal.... It is high time that he were kicked out of the Army. Lieut. Orleman has been half paralyzed by the effect, I am told, of an [accusation] made against him by Major Geddes.

Although unaware of how extensive his involvement in the pending case would soon become, Bigelow quickly turned to another subject:

> I am to be placed in command of the Company upon my return to Stockton. Lieut. Orleman will probably go before the retiring board.... Smither tells me that I shall probably be in command during the summer. I hope...that I shall remain in command until shortly before I apply for a leave of absence next fall.

DIETARY DANGERS

Bigelow next relates a discussion he had with a doctor at Concho about a common frontier army concern: scurvy. Although not aware of its exact cause (inadequate vitamin C), physicians knew that the disease "could leave men with teeth dropping from their sockets, portions of their lips sloughing, multiple skin ulcerations, and bleeding."[14] They also realized that outbreaks were more likely in winter when diets consisted mostly of salt beef, bacon, and bread. Hence, when fresh or dried vegetables were unavailable, preventive substitutes were sought; these might include wild onions or artichokes, watercress, prickly pear, and even poke weed. In addition, army regulations directed that vinegar, "a most important part of the ration," should be used freely.[15] The preferable solution, though, was a post garden that could produce sufficient vegetables and fruits to prevent the disease, as well as provide some variety to the customarily drab and unpalatable meals.

> Called today on Dr Smith....[16] He showed me one of his scurvy patients, a number of which are in the hospital. They are all from the Cavalry companies. He ascribes this fact to the propensity on the part of Cavalry officers to pay undue attention to their horses and neglect their men.... The Cavalry officers pretend that they cannot get fresh vegetables; the pretension is evidently ungrounded, the Infantry officers being able to get them. Many company commanders stint their men of such necessities as antiscorbutics for the mere purpose of making large company savings [which] should be expended [for the men] as fast as made.

Chapter 15

Meanwhile, Back at the Fort

After completing the 170-mile trip from Concho to Fort Stockton, Bigelow found conditions much different than when he left ten weeks previously. Although he abhorred gossip, he was certain to have heard more about the Geddes affair, yet he refused to soil his journal with the details.[1] Instead, with Orleman awaiting a summons from a retiring board in San Antonio, he busied himself with his duties as a company commander.

> *Fort Stockton, Tex. April 2, 1879.* I have been very busy...assuming control of the property of the Company.... I am recorder of a Garrison Court Martial and of a Board of Survey. The men who were at San Antonio in Beck's trial have not yet returned.

GONE—BUT NOT FORGOTTEN

> Pursuant to Col Blunt's orders I detailed four privates and a [NCO]...to go in pursuit of a deserter from Fort Davis. He...is a desperate character and according to Lieut Orleman, he will not be caught alive. [The men] have forty rounds of ammunition, six days' rations and a hundred pds of forage.... Col. Blunt wanted me to ration them for four days and give them 10 pds of forage for that time and send them off without a packmule. He does not know much about Cavalry.

Desertion, the most common major offense on the frontier, plagued almost all units.[2] As repeatedly analyzed, the numerous causes included the harsh life, poor food, wretched quarters, arduous labor, tyrannical officers and NCOs, unnecessary restraints, inhumane treatment, insufficient pay, boredom, low social position of enlisted men, greater opportunities elsewhere, and even the discomfort of heavy woolen clothing in hot climates.[3]

Desertions of blacks, however, were dwarfed by those of whites.[4] Between 1876 and 1891 the eight white cavalry regiments lost 3,203 men (an average of 400 each), while only 238 men (an average of 119 each) deserted from the 9th and 10th Cavalry. Even more markedly, 5,585 men (234 each) departed from the twenty-three white infantry regiments, compared to a mere 14 from the 24th Infantry and 53 from the 25th.

Among the findings in studies of differences in rates was that "Those who do not lose in social position, i.e., the colored troops, do not desert to the extent" of whites.[5] In other words, poor as conditions were, they represented an improvement for most African American troops, many of whom were former slaves. Other studies concluded that high morale, discipline, and esprit de corps meant fewer desertions, and in these respects most blacks were proud men anxious to prove that they could soldier as well as whites, and who resented any derogatory comments or publicity.[6]

The 25th Infantry's chaplain at Fort Davis supported this view when he reported on the "Morals of Colored Troops." After praising their behavior and mentioning that even the small quantity of "ardent spirits consumed" would not be a serious evil were it not "frontier in Texas whiskey," he remarked that they "are possessed of the notion that the colored people of the whole country are...affected by their conduct" and that they were anxious "to be well thought of...throughout the states."[7]

HUNTING FOR BOUNTY

B Company's statistics also reflected a vast disparity in desertions between its black soldiers and the white soldiers of other companies, as shown in Bigelow's reply to a request from C. O. Smith, B Company's "late 1st Sgt," who wrote:

> Dear Sir. I am about to engage in the business of arresting deserters from the Army and I thought best...[to] ask you to furnish me with the names of such men as has [sic] deserted your company since May 1st 1867....[8] I have got my eye on some parties whom I am pretty sure deserted...while I was a member, but to prevent mistakes I write you before I proceed any further. Please keep this from the ears of the enlisted men.

Bigelow compiled a list of fifty-seven deserters during the preceding eleven years, then noted in his journal that

> I have politely informed him that...I shall not...grant his request until I have official sanction for so doing. I [shall] forward the list should he send me satisfactory evidence of...his intentions.[9]

Whether Bigelow ever sent the list isn't known. In any event, six years later Sergeant Smith's aspirations were thwarted by a Supreme Court decision that without a warrant or military order, neither a private citizen nor a police officer had authority to arrest and detain a deserter.[10]

MOLDING A MODEL COMPANY

During the next few days Bigelow neglected his journal, but on April 5 he resumed his narrative.

> I have just seen the Comp. blacksmith, farrier & saddler and ordered them to wear the insignia of their respective rank. Soldiers generally are the better for glitter & show of their apparel, and colored soldiers more than white....
>
> Lieut. Bullis called at the Orlemans yesterday evening while I was in their sitting room. He is short but not stout, and is high strung without being nervous.... He neither smokes nor drinks...and I am told...that he will sleep during a Norther using no other bedding than a saddle cloth.
>
> I wish the men would get back from San Antonio so that I could begin to drill the Company as a whole.... As soon as the Company sees that its Com'd'g officer will work as hard as any one to make it efficient...I shall commence...a complete & systematic course of instruction....
>
> *Fort Stockton, Tex. April 7, 1879....* I call[ed] on the Company saddler & blacksmith.... I found the former playing the guitar and the latter unoccupied for want of horseshoes. I gave them both plenty to do....
>
> *Fort Stockton, Texas, April 12, 1879....* I sent for Serg't McDonald yesterday and made him choose between resigning his rank...and being tried by a court martial. He chose the former.... He received money in trust from a sick soldier [but]...when it was called for had spent it all. He afterwards refunded part and gave a note promising to pay the rest.

In his written resignation, Sergeant McDonald grieved to Colonel Grierson:

> I heave the honor to tender my Resignation as a noncommission officer in company B 10th cav By Order of the company commander or else trial By Cort-

Marthiel. I am a Solder But yet this I think is all Predicas and my company commander said to me you Will Be Reduced to nothing But a Soldier. But [no] predice should exizst for I not think I is pest. I am in hopes this may meet you favorbel consideon and approval.

Pest or not, former Sergeant McDonald promptly became Private McDonald, which gave Bigelow "more satisfaction than anything that has ever come to me...in the shape of an order."

Still striving to turn B Company into a crack organization, a few days later the young commander was irritated with a classmate's more casual approach:

Issued clothing to the men today. Was short supplied by the QrMr as usual. I wanted to issue them yesterday but Glenn could not let me have them, giving as his reason that he was going to move.... A company should [not] be delayed in satisfying its wants by the QrMr's moving his private property during office hours.

...I gave Sergt Young...a plan of barracks, showing where each man's bunk belongs.... The next reform that I wish to institute is a separation of the N.C. Officers from the enlisted men. I do not at all like them living & sleeping together.

COPING WITH INEPTITUDE

Pvte [George] Mitchell of Comp L has been transferred to my Company. He is on daily duty in the Adjutant's office and Col. Blunt has not backbone enough to relieve him in opposition to the wish of his Adjutant. When I told him this morning that I wanted to get some work out of Mitchell as Comp. clerk he said I would have to consult with the Adjutant.... The Col's weakness made me inclined to take him by the nape of the neck & shake him.

Two weeks after this confrontation the young lieutenant was able to boast:

I received official information...this morning that Private Mitchell was relieved from daily duty as clerk in the adjutant's office, from which I infer that I beat Col. Blunt.... The man's services are of little value, but I am glad that Col. Blunt and Lieut. Sweet...recognize that I am company commander although a simple second Lieutenant. I am especially glad that Sweet is deprived of Mitchell's services, on account of the Lieut's meanness & deceitfulness toward me.

Aside from the dispute over Private Mitchell's services, a few days later Bigelow groused that

Col. Blunt informed me...that Dr Hall, thinking the presence of the saddles in the men's quarters unwholesome, I had better keep them...in the stables.... I told him that it was impossible to keep them in order in the stables on account of the dust.... [T]he Dr...knows nothing about Cavalry....[11]

I am now under the disadvantage...of being in a post commanded by an Infantry officer.... I called on Col. Blunt...to get him to have three water calls a day. He was very affable as usual...[and] said he thought it could be arranged. I wanted to tell him that I had not come to ask a favor of him but to do *him* one in teaching him something about Cavalry.

Bigelow was not the only officer to find fault with Matthew Blunt. In his rambling memoirs Captain Armes referred to him as "a boot-lick of Grierson" as well as a "cowardly sneak and an imbecile," but his objectivity might be questioned after all his arrests and courts-martial.[12]

THE POST GARDEN

Fort Stockton, Tex. April 11, 1879. I drove to the Company garden a few days ago with Miss Orleman.... The following vegetables are planted and will be ready for issue to the men at about the times set opposite them.

Radishes	End of April	Pepper	Jun
Beets Red	May or June	Onions	May
Carrots	Sept & Oct	Tomatoes	Aug
Parsley	1st May	Beets white	Jun
Peas	1st May	Squash	Jun
Cucumbers	Aug	Turnips	Jun
Bunchbeans	May & June	Lettuce	May
Sweet corn	July	Okra	Jun
Watermelons	Aug	Cauliflower	Jun
Cabbage	?		

Despite the semi-arid conditions, the garden flourished. Paralleling Comanche Creek, it had an "excellent system of irrigation," and produced vegetables that otherwise could not "be obtained...except in small quantity, small variety, and at enormous prices."[13] The site also was a favorite for picnics, although Bigelow once reported:

The Officers and ladies...went to the Garden today on a picnic. It was just about as tiresome as I thought it would be. My only object in going was not to make myself conspicuous by my absence.

BURYING ON THE LONE PRAIRIE

On April 12 Bigelow and Lillie again rode out to the garden in the post ambulance, and on their return joined a procession to inter a private in a lonesome plot of ground on the parched, wind-swept prairie, far from home and family.[14]

> This afternoon...there was a funeral of an enlisted man [Pvt. Milton Dannels]...who died at our hospital.[15] The hearse consisted of a government wagon drawn by two mules. The coffin was placed in it at the hospital where the companies, in full dress with side arms, were formed in line. A small escort of Inf & Cav was formed under arms. As the procession passed by the line of officers' quarters it was joined by a number of officers. Miss Lillie & I followed in rear.

Bigelow later received a letter from Mrs. S. E. Lathrop of Macon, Georgia, asking about Dannels.

> Sir,
>
> Will you please write me when Milton Dannels died and a few particulars of his death. His mother (a poor colored woman) is very anxious to hear.

After he furnished the details requested, Mrs. Lathrop wrote:[16]

> I have read [your letter] to Mrs Arnold, his mother...[who] was pleased to hear her son was kindly cared for...and she would gladly refund the money to Mr Russel if she were able to do so. She is very poor and works hard for the little she has.... If there was any back pay belonging to her son...[please] refund to Mr R the money he paid out...and if there was any left...she would be very grateful for it.... The poor woman...wished me to express her sincere thanks to you for your kindness.... My husband and self are working among the colored people here, and that is how I came to write for Mrs. Arnold.

SEVERING TIES

> *Fort Stockton, Texas, April 13, 1879.* Lieut. Orleman left...for San Antonio. Miss Lillie was in tears several times but managed occasionally to force a cheerful expression on her face.
>
> *Fort Stockton, Texas, April 14, 1879.* I did not realize until the Orlemans had left, how much I would miss them.... Monk, formerly his and now my dog, went off with him yesterday and followed the stage a distance of about 14 miles. It was then taken charge of by [Corporal Ford] who was in camp with Lieut. Wilson. The latter arrived this forenoon with 11 men of Comp B who were witnesses at San Antonio and with a number of recruits for Ft. Davis.

HAVING A BALL

The visit of an officer, whether a general or a lieutenant (especially if accompanied by his wife), was seized upon as reason enough to break the monotony with festivities of some sort. That evening:

> The officers of F Comp gave a hop for...Lieut. & Mrs Wilson and Miss Murphy, Mrs Van Valzah's sister. I was not feeling well nor in the mood to enjoy a hop [so]...I left at about 11 o'clock. There was the usual variety of dress and physiognomy. Mrs Sweet remarked, in regard to a couple of Mexican girls, that some of the ladies did not at all like to have these ranch girls brought to the hops. I replied that, if we know nothing against them and they are introduced by an officer, that ought to be sufficient. She said: "Yes, it *ought* to be" in a tone to imply that it was not.

Possibly because the Orlemans were no longer there and also because Stockton offered so few diversions, Bigelow began to reflect more petulance than usual. After attending church services on April 20th, for instance, he commented that he, three women (one the chaplain's wife), and one boy were the only worshipers from Officers Row, and that "the old chaplain [Baldridge] was as uninteresting as usual."

SHEPHERDS WITHOUT FLOCKS

Fort Stockton might have been fortunate to have a clergyman, uninteresting or not, to minister to the religious needs of the garrison and perform a variety of functions, such as officiating at marriages and funerals and providing instruction in elementary school subjects for the men.[17] With only thirty-four chaplains throughout the army, many of the smaller frontier posts went, for better or worse, without benefit of clergy.

The men of the cloth who served in this capacity occupied rather nebulous positions. They were ordained ministers (mostly Episcopalian, Methodist, or Baptist, together with some Roman Catholics) who were appointed to the rank of captains of infantry but had no command authority and no prospect of promotion; however, they had the same tenure and retirement benefits as other officers, but were assigned to posts instead of units (except for the Negro regiments), and in place of uniforms wore plain black frock coats with a standing collar and nine black buttons.[18] Their callings, however, generally precluded active participation in warfare or in another form of conflict as members of courts-martial.[19]

Disinterest in religion or religious services appears to have been widespread, with many officers and men substituting "worldliness" for denominational affiliations they might have previously held. For instance, in 1876 an agent of the Bureau of Indian Affairs reported:

> Fort Sill is a sort of young Sodom, and the garrison is mostly made up of men who neither fear God nor regard man.... Horse racing on [the Sabbath] is a favorite pastime. On their grounds they have built a neat stone chapel, and it has not been used for any other purpose than a theatre and a dance hall. Drunkenness is prevalent...[and] I can only speak of their conduct as reckless and depraved.[20]

An Indian agent in the mid-1870s was not necessarily an unbiased observer, of course, considering the efforts then under way to prevent some of that bureau's functions from being transferred to the army; regardless, many officers as well as soldiers regarded clergymen as more of a hindrance (or worse) than a help. For example, a 9th Cavalry lieutenant scornfully commented that the chaplain who wrote an article about intemperance among soldiers

> knows as much of the character of the enlisted man as he does of the personal appearance of Moses.... We know him to be profoundly ignorant of the subject [but]...the civilian reader does not know this.... [And] when he states that...the soldier should, by legislation, be classed with the Indian the civilian must believe the average enlisted man a drunkard.[21]

Another cause for many officers to resent clergymen was the practice of appointing elderly civilian ministers as chaplains and captains then retiring them after only a few years, while line officers might have to spend decades of hard service to reach the same rank. Basically, the "presence of ministers...was not because military circles wanted them, but rather because the religious sentiment of the country demanded that soldiers have spiritual guidance."[22] Sherman was typically blunt in explaining:

> [T]he whole system is a farce.... If Congress wanted the army to have the influence of religion, it would allow the Commanding officer of each [remote] post...to hire and pay for a minister while employed, like surgeons. Of such posts there are nearly a hundred, whereas Chaplains are limited to thirty, say half of whom are sick, or don't like the isolation of Texas, Arizona, etc.[23]

In the more sparsely settled frontier regions few civilian clergymen were to be found, even if funds had been available. Along the Rio Grande in pre–Civil War days, for instance, Teresa Vielé remembered that there were "but few religious observations kept," and "any Divine influence" that might prevail was "through the instrumentality of the Roman church."[24] At that time in Rio Grande City, a mile north of Ringgold Barracks, the only person owning a Bible was the postmaster (a Baptist), whose brother had "got religion and done well," so he thought of "getting it himself."

Although there were few Protestant missionaries, "the Methodists [were] more successful than any other sect," which might have been "accounted for by their being a less highly educated class of men than those of the Episcopal church, and assimilating better with the ordinary mind in consequence."[25] Regardless, almost any kind of religious rite would attract a large congregation. For example, when an Episcopal minister once preached at Ringgold he "had an overflow audience, who complained that he did not give them enough 'howling'—meaning a series of fearful denunciations that would serve to rouse the necessary degree of religious excitement."[26]

TAKING CARE OF STABLES AND OTHER MATTERS

> *Fort Stockton, Texas, April 21, 1879*.... I have not yet...[assigned] each man's horse to a particular stall [and arranged] the horses in a manner corresponding to [that of] the men in barracks. I think it of no use to mark the stalls with the names of the horses as the men do not trouble themselves to learn them.

Organizing the stables clearly had merit. And Bigelow's annoyance at soldiers who did not know their horses' names is understandable, as doing so might induce them to take better care of their mounts.

> *Fort Stockton, Texas, April 23, 1879*. [I feel] relieved now that I have got the store room in the stables cleaned out and the articles rearranged so that they can be easily found & counted. My QrMr Serg't, Givens, is an excellent man in many respects; he is clear headed, conscientious and energetic, but like most colored men, has no sense of order. He trusts entirely to his memory and rough notes...[hence] he is the only person who can render account of the property.

> *Fort Stockton, Texas. April 24th, 1879*.... [Sergeant Givens] felt hurt at my interference in his arrangement of things and...as the vulgar expression is, "got his back up." When I questioned him I found, much to my relief, that his only trouble was a dislike for the manner of the Commissary Serg't...[who] was overbearing and offensive, that he Sgt Givens was in danger of being so irritated by him as to...get into trouble. I told him...that I would see that he was properly treated and

that I would go with him to the store room when he should have occasion to draw anything....

Spent the evening with Glenn & McMartin in their quarters where Lt Quimby, Dr Hall, Mr Friedlander & Mr Edgar revelled over whiskey punch for a few hours.[27]

The next day, after first complaining about the "abominable German print" in his book on the Franco-German War which prevented him from reading it "in the glare of Fort Stockton," he turned to the subject of food for the troops.

I got two barrels of potatoes for the Company today. They will probably bring me in debt...but I do not mind that, as I shall be able to straighten out my accounts after the garden produces vegetables.... I have got to pay Capt Norvell for the bacon which I borrowed from him about a year ago and which neither Beck nor Orleman returned....[28]

Fort Stockton, Texas, April 26, 1879. I preferred charges this morning against Trumpeter [John] Baimer for beating his wife. I hope to have him reduced to ranks, as I do not think he will ever become a good trumpeter. His mouth is so formed that it is ordinarily open; I think he has a hair lip [*sic*].

The case of the harelipped trumpeter suggests that although few soldiers were married, wife abuse was not unknown, and on occasion even an officer might be tried for "conduct unbecoming" if he resorted to physical violence against his spouse. For example, a captain at Fort McKinney was convicted not only of beating his wife as charged, but also of disgracing the service by having married her, which had not been charged. The latter finding was reversed.

I heard a few days ago that Capt. Viele with his Company had stumbled on a couple of Indians and had got all their stock, but not an Indian; they got away among the rocks & escaped on foot. When Viele gets back to Davis he will talk louder than ever.

Little of importance occurred during the next several days, other than Bigelow's detail as a member of the Post Council of Administration to audit the accounts of Lieutenant Sweet, the post treasurer.[29]

On May 8 he received several birthday presents from home. These included an elegant tablecloth from the family, a picture of a little girl and a big dog from Flora (a sister), a photograph of Grace (another sister), a portfolio that rolled up from Jenny (also a sister), a picture frame, and a "looking glass." Most of these, he thought, would contribute "greatly to the adornment of [his] room." On his birthday (May 12) he celebrated with fellow officers by "purchasing 1/2 dz bottles of champagne, one of which Ford (Bigelow's orderly) dropped & broke between Mr Koehler's store & my quarters."[30]

After finishing his muster rolls one morning, which freed him "to breathe again for a short time," Bigelow led the company in mounted drills to "enliven the spirit and sharpen the wits" so that when the men went in the field they would not overly fatigue their horses. He also read extensively in Hamley's *Operations of War* and the two-volume *Life and Letters of Baroness Bunsen* (which he found "elevating in its effect on one's moral nature but neither strengthening nor nourishing to the mind"). That afternoon the boorish Sweet called on him.

> I thought he would never leave. He started and continued to talk upon his favorite subject: gossip, especially scandal. Upon his making a remark about Mr Friedlander & Mrs Beck, I...said: "Let's change the subject." The Lieut. is as bad a gossiper as Mrs Sweet. He likes to go among officers, I imagine, and draw them out on personal matters and then go home and have a good talk over them with Mrs Sweet.... The Orleman & Geddes affair...furnishes the kind of excitement that he & Mrs Sweet thrive on....
>
> *Fort Stockton, Texas, May 10, 1879.* Tried Pvte [Charles] Dixon this morning. His case was referred to a Garrison instead of a General C.M. merely because the money value of the package stolen was not stated in the specification.... If I had known that it was to be referred to a garrison Court and that the thief was to avoid imprisonment by a mere technical quibble I would not have preferred the charge.[31]

That evening Bigelow wrote about a homicide that provided some excitement at the post (and probably more grist for the Sweets' gossip mill).

RESOLVING FAMILY DISPUTES

> I have heard that Mr [John] Beckwith [a cattleman] was arrested here yesterday and that he is now released upon $1000 bail given by Mr Young [the post trader] & Mr [George M.] Frazier. Mr Beckwith had been having trouble with his son-in-law and shot him; Mrs Johnson, his son-in-law's wife, is now armed with a six shooter and determined, I am told, to take her father's life the first time he shows

himself to her. About two months ago she gave birth to a child of her dead husband.

Bigelow abruptly digresses to record his impression of a young lady who dazzled him. Although only tangentially related to the killing, perhaps his interest harked back to the señorita he had seen at the bullfight in Piedras Negras.

> Miss Helen Beckwith, Mrs Johnson's sister, is the most genteel looking girl I have seen on the frontier outside of a military post and not inferior to any that I have seen inside of one. Her father is American & her mother Spanish. Her face shows plainly that she has no Mexican blood, but that she has considerable of the pure Castilian. Her complexion is of that softness & fairness which is as characteristic of Spaniards as her large black eyes and heavy black hair. On account of her want of experience in society, her manners are the natural outgrowth of female gentleness & modesty; consequently when she is in the presence of strangers they are uneasy to an extent almost painful to observe.

THE SCANDAL AT STOCKTON

A few days before the homicide in the small town outside Fort Stockton, Bigelow related that:

> I heard...that I have become involved in the Orleman & Geddes trial.... It appears...that I shall be summoned to San Antonio.... I received this morning the annexed letter from Orleman. It contains the first mention he has made...of his trouble with Geddes.
>
> My dear Lieutenant,
>
> A court martial has been convened...for the trial of Capt. A. Geddes....[32] I am most of the time confined to my room, and poor Lillie cannot leave the house, as she has no one to take her anywhere....
>
> The Board recommended my retirement for disease contracted in the line of duty.... I have had so much trouble & sorrow...but thank God! since my arrival here, I...have been informed that I was completely vindicated, and the villain, who insulted my child and attempted to sully my honor and reputation will now be brought to trial, and I trust will receive full justice.

LILLIE AND THE LECHER

The sordid behavior that would influence Bigelow's life for the next few months resembled a melodrama, with an apparently licentious Captain Geddes as the villain and a naive Miss Lillie as the gullible victim of his loathsome designs. Unfortunately, though, with Bigelow in San Antonio at the time, no dashing hero was available to rescue her from a fate that if not worse than death was not much better.[33]

Geddes, a married officer separated from his wife, was about twice Lillie's age. When Orleman returned from sick leave the previous November, he and his daughter were assigned to a two-family building with quarters adjacent to Geddes, who became wildly infatuated with her. Before long he commenced visiting Lillie in her quarters when her father was away, and according to her proposed illicit intercourse, tried to kiss and fondle her, and begged for sexual favors. Disregarding his intense and ungentlemanly ardor, however, she did little to discourage him, and even maintained a cordial attitude despite several scurrilous advances. Her only explanation was that she thought he would divorce his wife and marry her.

In early March Geddes received a leave during which he, his friend Joe Friedlander, Orleman, and Lillie rode a stagecoach to Fort Davis, eighty miles west, to visit friends for a few days.[34] Allegedly, as Geddes and Lillie sat opposite each other in the cramped confines of the stage, he covertly squeezed her knees between his. He countered this assertion by claiming that her father had attempted to fondle her. After returning to Stockton Geddes asked Orleman to permit Lillie to accompany him to San Antonio. When he refused, Geddes accused him of incestuous acts with her which he threatened to disclose unless consent for the trip was given. It was not. He did. Because personal honor was the sine qua non of an officer, even the mention of such acts was sufficient, of course, to destroy her father's career as well as Miss Lillie's reputation.

Geddes then wrote to General Ord, claiming he had seen Orleman and Lillie in flagrante delicto one night when he peered through a bedroom window after hearing her beg to be left alone, and that he wanted to marry her out of pity to save her from further abuse. He also stated that he became aware of the situation from conversations he overheard through the fireplace in the wall separating their quarters.

Although Bigelow still did not record what he knew about the turmoil that raged around him, after he returned from Beck's trial he received a letter from Bob Safford concerning the early March Fort Davis visit by Geddes and the Orlemans.

> We had a very pleasant visit from some of your Stockton people. I don't think any one fell in love with Joe Friedlander. Geddes scarcely showed himself during the daytime while he was here: seemed to spend most of his time in bed. Orleman was previously known to most of the people here, & I found him very agreeable. Miss Lillie seemed to make a favorable impression upon every one.... [S]he is so entirely unsophisticated [though] that she ought not to hear a word spoken unless it's meant. I feel sorry, sometimes, for girls of her character, when I think of the awakening from their delusions, that must come sooner or later & is never a *pleasant* experience.

A charge of conduct unbecoming an officer was preferred against Geddes. The first of two specifications alleged that between mid-February and mid-March he attempted in various ways to corrupt Lillie for "his own illicit purpose," and the second was that on March 12 he attempted to abduct her. An additional unbecoming conduct charge was filed by Orleman shortly after his arrival in San Antonio. It also had two specifications: the first was that Geddes had falsely accused Orleman of having incestuous intercourse, and the other that he threatened to publicly expose Orleman for such conduct unless he allowed Lillie to go to San Antonio with him. Another additional charge averred conduct prejudicial to good order and discipline by false swearing.[35] When General Ord as convening authority determined that there was prima facie evidence of Geddes's guilt, a general court-martial was appointed and the charges were referred to trial.[36]

PREPARING TO DEPART—AGAIN

On May 14 Bigelow was notified that he was to go to San Antonio as a witness. He correctly inferred that his testimony would be used to rebut Geddes's claims about what he had seen and heard. Much of the next two days was spent packing and, at the judge advocate's request, measuring and conducting tests relating to the quarters occupied by the accused and the Orlemans.[37] He first determined the precise height of the walls and ceiling as well as the materials used in construction, then conducted tests which demonstrated that nothing could be heard through the fireplace or seen through the shutters on the windows. Another task was to acquaint McMartin, appointed to temporarily command Company B, with his policies and practices.

> *Fort Stockton, Texas, May 15, 1879*.... I took [McMartin] with me...when I inspected the barracks, kitchen, stables &c. I explained to him as much as I could about my

customs, rules, orders, &c.... I hope I shall not have to command [the company] long after my return...as I am afraid that it will have run down from the state of tolerable order & discipline to which I have managed to bring it.

Bigelow then relates the conversations he had with Chaplain Baldridge and Lieutenant Quimby.

The Chaplain informed me...that Miss Orleman had equivocated in pretending not to have had any correspondence with Maj. Geddes.... How, as a respectable young woman, she could have engaged in a clandestine correspondence with a man about whom she knew & surmised as much as she did about Maj. Geddes, I cannot understand....

Lieut. Quimby [said]...he had something...that might help Lt Orleman. I told him that I had no more interest in the Lieut. than he had, that I would like to see justice done, &c. He finally...said that...Mr Friedlander had hired a detective to take rooms opposite those of Lieut. Orleman...[and] watch the Lieut. & Miss Orleman. In case it is attempted to show that Maj. Geddes has systematically conspired with a number of villains to ruin the character of Lieut. & Miss Orleman, the clue...may be of use.

After less than seven weeks back at Fort Stockton following Beck's trial, on May 17 Bigelow once more boarded a stage that would return him to San Antonio.

WILLIAM HOWARD

The West Texas climate and the strain of his duties as acting judge advocate led to his early death from "softening of the brain." (Courtesy USMA Library)

Chapter 16

The Belles of San Antonio

In describing his journey from Stockton, Bigelow recalled that

> from Stockton to Concho I was accompanied by a consumptive invalid who had gone to Ft. Davis for his health. He coughed a great deal and complained of the dust.... We reached Concho at about reveille on the 19th...and left at 12 o'clock. We reached (San Antonio)...at about half past 12 on the 21st.... I took...a room at Hord [Hord's] Hotel.[1] I remained until this morning.... I am now living with Howard.[2]

The exhausting trip behind him, Bigelow was about to enter into one of the most vexatious periods of his career. The day he arrived Geddes's trial commenced before a general court-martial headed by Lt. Col. Nelson B. Sweitzer of the 8th Cavalry.[3] At the end of the first week Bigelow was told by the judge advocate that "the trial will be a long one, that it would probably last three weeks yet, and that [he] was to be retained until the close." The prosecutor's prediction notwithstanding, the case dragged on for almost three months.

With virtually no duties, Bigelow spent most of the time reading,[4] practicing at the firing range, attending various religious services and programs, pursuing social and other interests (usually involving young ladies he found intellectually attractive), and recording his activities and thoughts, hence preserving a unique glimpse of the people, events, customs, issues, and daily life in 1879 San Antonio.

San Antonio, Texas, May 27, 1879. Called on Gen'l Ord.... Miss Bertie & I sat in the shade in front of the house while she read Macbeth.... Mrs Ord...inform[ed] me that she had called at the Moores and had found the young lady very well.

The interest Bigelow had developed in Minnie Moore during his earlier stay in San Antonio had not gone unnoticed. In fact, Mrs. Ord's oblique reference suggests that it had been bandied about in the local gossip circles.

[W]hile on my way to the Headqr. Building I saw Lieut & Miss Orleman standing at Mrs Sappington's gate....[5] The Lieut. remarked that he had heard Mrs Sappington had a room to let, [so]...I introduced [them].[6] We looked at the rooms and Mrs Sappington offered to let the Lieut. have them.... After dinner as I was passing by the house, Mrs Sappington called me in, and said she had been told that there was quite a scandal in circulation in regard to Lieut. & Miss Orleman and that it would not be good...to have them, [so] she had written to the Lieut...that he could not have the rooms....

...I [later] learned that the Lieut. had gone to Hord's Hotel. I was in hope that I would be able to dissuade him.... Neither he nor Miss Lillie seemed to have the delicacy...to avoid publicity....

San Antonio, Texas, May 29, 1879. Went out to the range and fired...at 600 yards.... Called at the Ords. Miss Bertie read part of Longfellow's Golden Legend but was interrupted by [a visit from] Capt Kelly.

San Antonio, Tex. May 30, 1879.... [This forenoon] Miss Minnie and I played archery for a while. We soon found that game too heating and fatiguing; we then practised a few German songs....

San Antonio, Texas, June 1, 1879.... Went to the Episcopal church this morning with Howard and walked home with Miss [Georgia] Grimshaw.[7] Miss Grimshaw is one of the most attractive girls I have ever met.[8] She is not beautiful, but her face has a pleasing expression of frankness & intelligence. She is a hard student and has to wear glasses, but does not wear spectacles. She is clever & free from all mannerisms.... Most of the so called "smart girls" that I have seen keep up such a racket when they talk that it is impossible for me to get a word in "edgewise," and keep me in a state of mental and physical torture trying to become & to appear interested and amused. Her straightforward manner together with her intellectual countenance...make her...more admired by the other than by her own sex....

San Antonio, Tex. June 2, 1879.... Went this evening to the St. Mary's Catholic Church to hear the Rev. Father Garesche lecture on Parents' Love....[9] His discourse...appealed more to one's feelings & emotions than to one's reason....

San Antonio, Tex. June 3, 1879.... Went out...to the Depot where Capt Livermore instructed the competitors for Creedmoor [*sic*].[10] Went to St. Mary's Church this evening to hear Father Garesche lecture on Science & Religion.... His attempts at wittiness, made no doubt with the object of rousing the attentions of the less intelligent & therefore less appreciative part of his audience, were decided failures....

San Antonio, Tex. June 4, 1879.... Called at the Wilsons.... They insured themselves against a speedy repetition of my visit by professing that I should come to their house some afternoon to play croquet. While walking down Commerce St, I met Miss Hall, who...invited Howard & me to a horse-back party.... I did not like the idea....

I did not know what to do with myself this evening, so after reading until my eyes got sore I started out for a walk [and]...wandered into a Presbyterian Church.[11] There I heard a young clergyman deliver a fine eulogium on woman.... He appeared to think that the whole force of his eloquence backed by the power of his most impressive gestures were necessary to suppress doubt & controversy...whereas, not even on a Sunday m'g could he have found...a more acquiescent audience.... The greater part of it was composed of middle aged & elderly ladies who...were not disposed to take issue with the speaker, and...Sunday School children not over 10 yrs of age who would not have understood the discourse had they remained awake long enough to hear it....

San Antonio, Tex. June 5, 1879.... I am getting on slowly with Waverly.... It is like a Dime Novel, though not as interesting, nor as cheap.

San Antonio, Tex. June 6 1879. [Miss Ord and I] went riding yesterday ev'g.... This horseback party is a trick by which those young ladies whom the gentlemen do not voluntarily ask to go riding are to have an escort whether the gentlemen want them or not.

To further complicate his life, yet another young lady, Miss Baldridge (the daughter of Fort Stockton's chaplain), arrived in San Antonio for medical treatment. As a favor to her father, Bigelow had agreed to assist her.

San Antonio, Tex. May [June] 7, 1879. Went to Hord's hotel...to see if Miss Baldridge had arrived.... I sent up my card and called on her in the hotel parlor. She is a plain sensible looking country school girl, has apparently not been much in society but has nevertheless acquired an easy, if not graceful, manner.... I was very much surprised at her appearance, expecting to find her pale & emaciated from consumption, whereas she is as hale & hearty a young damsel as I've ever seen....

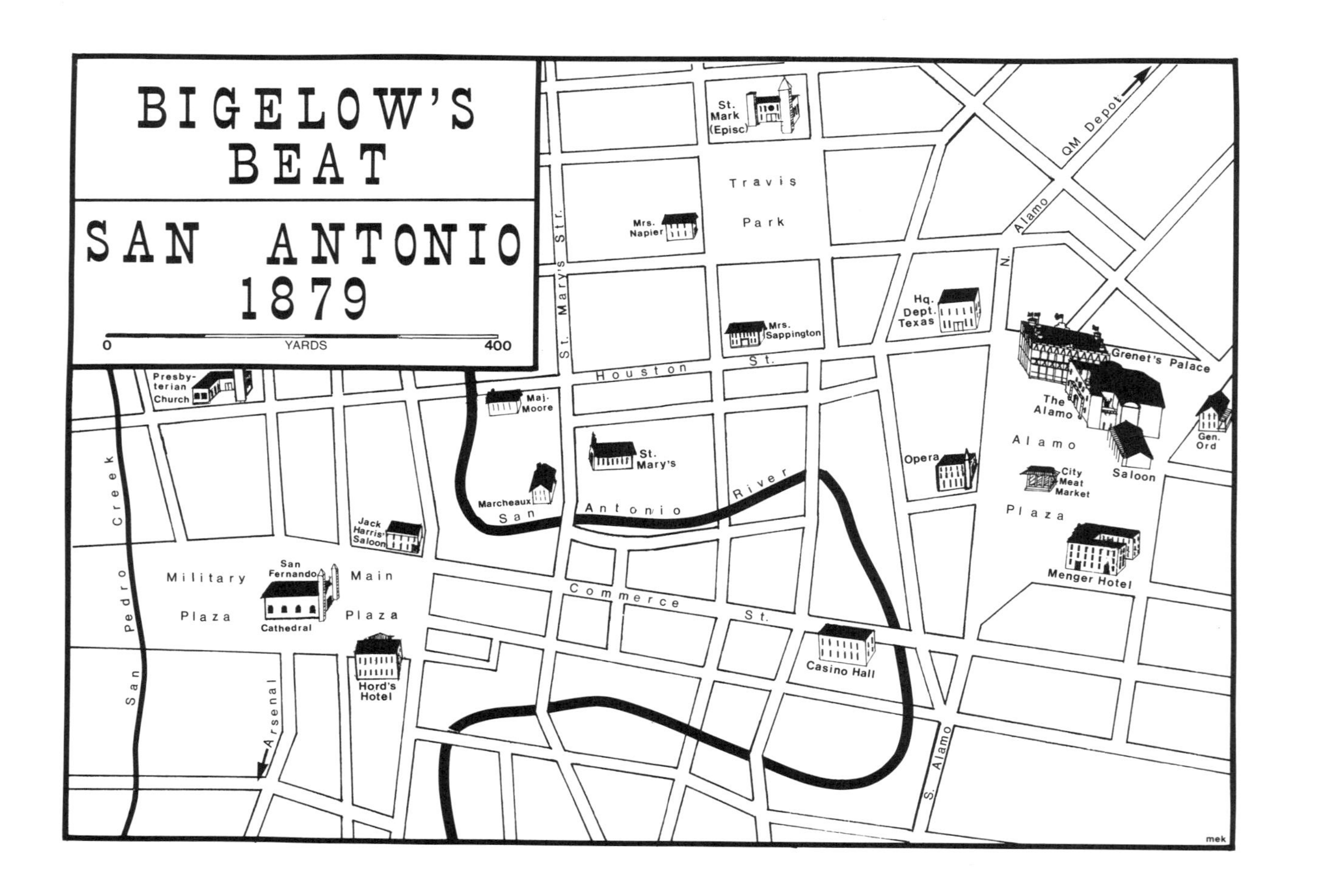
BIGELOW'S BEAT
SAN ANTONIO 1879
0
YARDS
400
St. Mark (Episc)
Travis
Park
Mrs. Napier
Mrs. Sappington
Hq. Dept. Texas
QM Depot
N. Alamo
Grenet's Palace
The Alamo
Gen. Ord
Alamo
Plaza
Saloon
City Meat Market
Menger Hotel
Opera
St. Mary's Str.
Houston St.
Maj. Moore
Presby-terian Church
St. Mary's
Marcheaux
San Antonio River
Jack Harris' Saloon
San Fernando Cathedral
Military Plaza
Main Plaza
Commerce St.
Casino Hall
Hord's Hotel
Arsenal
San Pedro Creek
S. Alamo
mek

Called this forenoon at the Moores.... Miss Minnie considers my situation as guardian & protector of Miss Baldridge a romantic one.

Possibly irritated by Minnie's characterization of his relationship with his tacit ward, Bigelow recalls an earlier situation involving the welfare of a young lady.

This is not the first time that I have been charged with the care of a strange young lady. When I left Fredericksburg...I found myself in the stage alone with a young lady whom an elderly gentleman had turned over to me having requested me as a gentleman to show her every courtesy. I at once did all I could to make myself agreeable; we carried on quite an animated conversation; the young lady appearing to be very intelligent & well informed. We left...at about 9 o'clock at night when it was so dark that I could not see her face.... I observed, as morning approached, that she became less talkative & appeared to be less cheerful. As the sun lit up the horizon...the young woman appeared to become uneasy and embarrassed. I noticed, while endeavoring to appear unconscious of it, that she avoided as much as possible presenting her face to my view...[and] spoke hardly a single word.

The fact was evident to me that the poor girl was conscious of her own ugliness. She did not know who I was nor whether I was enough of a gentleman not to express, by word or action, my disappointment at her appearance.... I did what I could to appear blind to everything but her internal worth and beauty, but all my efforts were in vain; she assumed and retained a mixed expression of sullenness & melancholy....

San Antonio, Tex. May [June] 8, 1879.... I went over...to say good bye to Mrs Ord who was going East for a change of air. I then called on the Col & Mrs Andrews. The Col has suggested to Gen'l Ord to get rid of the headquarters of the 4th or 10th Cav...[so that the] diminishing number of field officers in the Dep't...[could be given] commands suited to their rank and dignity. I do not suppose he considers the question of ability as of any importance, but the Gen'l does, which is a reason, I think, why the Col's desires will not soon be satisfied.

That evening Bigelow accompanied Miss Baldridge to the Moores' for tea. Two prospective rivals were also there.

We found Mr Bowen at the Moores.... [He] is a young man in business here, good at heart but exceedingly "sappy;" if I had formed any serious intentions to be carried out at the Moores, I would not consider him a formidable obstacle.... Lieut. James...came in full uniform except belt & sword, with white kid gloves and white & blue false necktie.[12] The evening was spent in looking over photographs and talking and singing....

San Antonio, Tex. May [June] 9, 1879. Remained at Headqrs during most of the forenoon prepared to appear before the Court but was not called up.... Called this afternoon...upon Miss Baldridge.... [She] invited me to join her and Miss Minnie Moore in a drive this afternoon...[but] she did not know when Miss Minnie was going to call.... [I told her] that I did not think it would pay for me to wait.... If I see Miss Minnie tomorrow...I shall probably be held to strict account for my apparent discourtesy....

San Antonio, Texas, June 11, 1879.... Met Rodgers of '75 at Headquarters this morning.[13] He says he will start for the Point, where he is to be Instructor of French, about the 1st of August. From what I know of him as a cadet & as an officer, I judge that he will not be much liked by his pupils....

San Antonio, Tex. June 12, 1879.... Wrote a letter to Safford this afternoon, and then called on Miss Grimshaw. I tried to get Miss G. to take a walk but she could not, having an engagement to go out with her "Auntie", Mrs Marucheaux....[14] The river is looking prettier than I have ever seen it. The tops of the trees...cast a deep shadow on its surface, and a luxuriant growth of vines, tall grass, and broad leafed tropical plants mirror themselves along its edges.... It appears for long distances to be inaccessible, except at regular crossings [where] a bridge or ford...invites the eye, wearied by the glare of ordinary sunlight, to rest itself in a sombre vista hung with every shade of vegetable green.

Bigelow's idyllic description of the San Antonio River neglects to mention such conditions as "a dead horse, one dead cow, five dogs, nine cats, and chickens and rats without number" reportedly found there that year.[15]

San Antonio, Tex. June 13, 1879.... Received a letter from Glenn this morning. It contained rather a gloomy picture of Fort Stockton, which reconciled me the more to San Antonio....

San Antonio, Tex. June 14, 1879.... Called on the Halls. They startled me with the information that they were preparing for another horseback party. I do not think they will get me in it. Called in the evening at the Moores. Miss Minnie was out riding with Lt James. When I learned who her escort was I thought of the remark made to the Lieut. by Curtis:[16] "Good heavens, man, I wouldn't be as spoony as you are, and as fat, during this hot weather, for all you could give me."[17]

After failing to make any entry in his journal for the next five days, Bigelow commented that he had moved from Lieutenant Howard's quarters to the Menger and had been busy reading and calling. He then opined:

San Antonio, Tex. May [June] 20, 1879.... The present custom of the service that leaves officers on duty as witnesses, unemployed in any other way, is rather an extravagant one. Since I have been away from my company...I have not done two good days work for the government. I have never seen as many loafers at a military post as there are here. Many of the officers, it is true, are here on leave but I should think they would nevertheless engage in some rational employment, instead of loitering around....

...[After supper] Howard and I [called on the Moores]. Miss Minnie...persisted in playing what all of us could sing or attempt to sing; [consequently] a great deal of good music was spoiled. Howard's voice is not more musical than that of an ass....

San Antonio, Tex. June 21, 1879.... Called this afternoon on Mrs Col Schweitzer [Sweitzer]....She told me that Mrs Stevenson had said that Lt Howard & I being interested in the same young lady [Miss Moore] when one of us wants to call there he locks the other one in his room. She also said that Lieut. James was trying to cut us out.

Although not mentioning how he responded to the story, wagging tongues soon brought another damaging assertion to Minnie's attention, assuming he did have an interest in her.

Miss Moore told me that...Miss Adele Grenet while walking with another lady some distance behind me was asked...who I was. She answered..."Why, he's Georgie Grimshaw's beau." I do not...object to being known as Miss Grimshaw's beau; but, as the young lady may, it is rather annoying that I should have received the appellation; it deters me from visiting her as frequently as I would were I free from it.

Bigelow's reluctance to visit Miss Grimshaw too often was short-lived, for on Sunday he provided those so inclined with even more to blab about by accompanying her to church for both morning and evening services, then spending an hour talking with her at her home.

On Monday Bigelow walked with Minnie to the falls, where she played her guitar and they sang German songs. That evening he called on the Ords, hoping to see General Mackenzie who was visiting them. Mackenzie, however, was with his mother who was "staying with the Cards and is not very well."[18]

San Antonio, Tex. June 24, 1879.... I spent the...evening in singing & playing duets [with Miss Moore].... I got a couple of silk handkerchiefs from Mrs Moore, for which I am to pay her $2.00 a piece. The money goes to the support of a

Catholic...charity. The price may be charitable to the poor little Catholics for whose benefit it is paid, but it is most uncharitable to the poor Protestant Lieut. who paid it.

San Antonio, Tex. June 25, 1879.... Mrs Moore asked...if I was going to see them off on the train.... I engaged not only to go to the station, but to accompany her as far as New Philadelphia.

Although Dr. Moore's pending transfer to New York had been known for at least a month, Bigelow had not mentioned it previously.[19] His stoic acceptance of the parting might suggest that if he were considering matrimony, either Minnie's Catholicism or his growing interest in Miss Grimshaw interfered.

I learned from Miss Minnie this evening why she suddenly and mysteriously gave up dancing. She had been prevailed upon by a Catholic sister of Charity...[and] thought she owed to her church the mark of respect of abstaining from a social custom of which it disapproved.... I told her that...she should not let the church tyrannize over her, that as she...did not think it wrong to dance, there was no good reason for denying that pleasure since the members of a sect, and not the ecclesiastical officers alone should make its rules and customs....

San Antonio, Tex. June 27, 1879.... At about half past eleven my eyes commenc[ed] to pain me, [so] I laid down my book and went out for a walk. I strolled into the Mexican Cathedral and wandered about looking at the pictures, statues, and other curiosities. After coming out, an orderly informed me that I was wanted by Gen'l Ord & Gen'l McKenzie [Mackenzie].... I immediately reported to the Gen'l...and found that he wanted to learn...about the country along the Rio Grande south of the Upper Escondido.... The Gen'l proposes to build a road...from the Pecos...to Davis, by which the trip from San Antonio...will be very much shortened. I told him I thought it quite impracticable.... He told me to be at his office at 10 o'clock tomorrow morning when Gen'l McKenzie would be there to interview me further.

Called this afternoon on Miss Grimshaw.... She showed me [General Lee's] house, not far from hers, in which the Gen'l lived.... She likes Capt. Kelly because he went to the war as a boy 16 years old.[20] He is the first man she has met who joined the federal army at that age [but] a large number of friends and relatives went into the Confederate army at 15 & 16....

San Antonio, Tex. June 28, 1879.... While at Headqrs this afternoon...Gen'l Ord...told me that General McKenzie had been unable to get to headqrs at 10 o'clock this m'g but that he was there at about half past ten. I did not make any apologies but expressed my regrets at not having met him....

On the way home I passed Dr & Mrs Moore...[who] asked me if I was going to call this evening, to which I replied, of course, in the negative.... I am more afraid of being too attentive to my acquaintances than not attentive enough. I would rather...have it asked a hundred times when I am going to call, rather than have it once asked when I am going to leave.

San Antonio, Tex. June 29, 1879, Sunday.... Dr Brown the Post Surgeon spoke to me...about Geo Young of my Comp. who is here in the post hospital.[21] He had a fight with another soldier, a white man who bit his finger causing it to mortify and requiring it finally to be amputated.... The Dr is going to discharge him on a Surgeon's certificate of disability.

When the day of the Moores' departure arrived, Bigelow joined other well-wishers, including the giddy Mr. Bowen, at the railroad station.

San Antonio, Tex. June 30, 1879.... Promised to write to Miss Minnie who promised to send me her photograph from New York.... If she keeps her promise, Miss Minnie will be my first young lady correspondent. I never could understand the great satisfaction that young men derive from correspondence with young ladies. I hope it will soon be explained to me.

Whether Bigelow ever received an explanation isn't known, and insofar as could be determined he and Minnie never wrote each other. Several days later he mentioned that

Howard informed me...that Lt James...confided to him that he, Lt James, was "gone" on Miss Moore and that the only person he feared as a rival was myself.

In light of the attention Bigelow increasingly showered on Georgia Grimshaw, the gauche Lieutenant James apparently need not have feared competition from him for Minnie Moore's affections. Anyway, she failed to reciprocate James's interest. Turning his attention to Fort Stockton's foremost gossipmonger, Bigelow scornfully remarked:

San Antonio, Tex. July 1, 1879.... Below is a letter received from Lt Sweet.... I have not yet thought it advisable to minister to his love of gossip.

Dear Bigelow,

...I am anxious to know the status of the G case...as it appears to you from public opinion in San A, as well as how Lt O. and Miss L are rec'd in society etc.... I will respect in confidence all you may choose to confide to me.... Geddes has written...that he would come out all right.... [H]is line of defense is to disaffirm abduction in that her father was willing she should go. Armes, Price, Esterly & the Co are having a disagreeable antagonism going on at Santa Rosa.[22]

Edwin Glenn, Bigelow's swarthy looking classmate, and Lieutenant Landon, who were witnesses in the Geddes case, arrived in San Antonio on July 1st. Both had lost their luggage along the way. Bigelow also learned that six hundred dollars would purchase three acres near the railroad station, but he passed up the opportunity. And on a stroll down Main Street he saw a friend, Mr. Oathout, and a British army captain mounted and equipped for a hunting expedition, which prompted him to observe:

> In San Antonio one may come across a man with a sunburnt & weather beaten face wearing a slouch hat, canvass or leather breeches, tremendous Mexican spurs, a knife & a six shooter, and might be quite at a loss to conjecture whether he is a Texas cowboy or a New York aristocrat.

IGNORING WITH APLOMB

> *San Antonio, Tex. July 2, 1879....* I have not spoken to Maj. Geddes since my arrival.... Most of the officers here appear to have nothing to do with him. While I was walking with Landon this afternoon we saw Glenn & Geddes coming toward us on the opposite side of the street; Landon proposed we should go over to see Geddes. I said I did not care to and kept on, leaving him to go alone....
>
> *San Antonio, Tex. July 3, 1879....* Saw Lt Wood of the 4th Cav. today for the first time since I left West Point.[23] He was sitting with Maj Geddes when I came down...to breakfast. As I passed them by, Wood called to me; I walked over to him and shook hands but said nothing to Geddes. Wood looked at me & at the Major & said "you know Major Geddes;" I replied "Yes, I know Maj. Geddes" and made a formal bow.
>
> Landon, Glenn & Friedlander were at a public ball at the Alamo yesterday evening. Being seen...with the friend, if not the accomplice, of Geddes does not look very well [for Landon & Glenn].... I made a call on Capt. Robe.... He asked me if I gave Maj Geddes more than a passing acknowledgment.... I told him I did not give even that....

CELEBRATING INDEPENDENCE DAY

> *San Antonio, Tex. July 4, 1879....* Saw the national salute fired at 1 o'clock today on the Alamo Plaza...from guns of the 2d Artillery.... After the firing had ceased...a couple of Army four-mule wagons wheeled around in rear of the pieces. The poles of the limbers were fastened by ropes to the wagons, which moved off...carrying in them part of the firing detachment.... There were no caissons...which necessitated the transportation by wagon of those men who could not be seated on the

limbers. As this mockery of the pomp & circumstance of war filed past the crowd...I congratulated myself that I was not in the Artillery.

...I rode out to the [San Pedro] Springs in a street car.[24] I heard the Declaration of Independence read in English to a crowd composed largely of Germans & Mexicans; the reader did very well but received very little attention. A beer garden is not, in my opinion, a proper place for a reading of the Declaration of Independence, a subject too sacred to be repeated [at]...an outdoor concert for the amusement of a crowd of idlers and pleasure seekers.

The Fourth of July was a major occasion for celebrations in the nineteenth century, and the reverence Bigelow expressed for the Declaration reflects the deep-seated patriotism that motivated him and most officers. In this light his reaction to the indifference of the beer garden's patrons is understandable, but even if they spoke English they might not have heard of that document or appreciated its significance.

THERE ARE MANY WEALTHY YOUNG LADIES

Went with Howard to a hop at the Casino Hall...[where] a small party of dancers was going through a square dance. Neither Howard nor I recognized a single lady in the room. We took our seats as wall flowers and contented ourselves with commenting upon what we saw.... I made the acquaintance of several ladies & gentlemen of the "bourgeoisie," among others: Miss Lacoste & Miss Gross. I took a few turns on the floor with the former; with the latter I danced from the beginning of a waltz to the end. When I got through I was dripping wet. Miss Gross & I talked German; I should liked to have taken her to supper...but she was already engaged.... A gentleman said to me...,"Do you know that you have just had $40,000 in your arms;" I said "Yes, and now my $40,000 are gone." I comforted myself with the thought that there were many $40,000 girls in N.Y.

THE EVILS OF SMOKING

San Antonio, Tex., July 5, 1879.... Rode out to Camp...to call on Dr Brown and consult him about my ears. My right ear has been troubling me of late.... I saw Geo. Young...and had a talk with him about his prospects. He thinks of going to his home in Georgia and being a waiter. I called on Lieut. Curtis. We talked about smoking.... I think the desire to smoke if gratified is always followed by a desire to rid one's self of the effect of smoking, which one is tempted to do by drinking. Smoking & drinking are..."counter irritants." My main objection to smoking is aesthetic rather than sanitary. I object to having my breath & my clothes smell of tobacco, to having my fingers tipped yellow from rolling cigarettes, to having my teeth blackened with nicotine, and to having my nose, lungs & tongue lined with foreign matter by which the usefulness of each of those organs is impaired.[25]

DERELICTION OF DUTY

George Andrews, of the 25th Inf. arrived here in the stage today.[26] He was in charge of prisoners from Ft. Stockton. He lost one at Leon...[and] has offered $30 reward for his recapture.... While we were walking down Main St after dinner a man said that...Gen'l Ord [ascribed] the prisoner's escape to pure carelessness.

We walked over to the Headquarters Building to see Howard.... He asked Andrews how often he inspected [the prisoner's] irons.... Andrews said he was not going to finger around the heels of any d__d nigger, that if the Sergt was not capable of doing that & the U.S. government chose to employ niggers as soldiers it would have to take the consequences.[27] He said that he really did not care what was done or said about it, that he was generally disgusted with the "Mokes." He remarked...that it was a long time since he had taken a real good "talking to" and that he believed he could button up his coat and stand up to it again with his palms to the front as...in the days gone by.

GEORGIA ON HIS MIND

San Antonio, Tex. July 6, 1879. Called this afternoon on Miss Grimshaw.... We visited the Mexican Cathedral [and] afterwards wandered into a [Presbyterian] church.... Finding [it] a pleasant place to sit in we remained there about a half an hour, Miss Grimshaw entertaining me with accounts of her past experiences in San Antonio.... She said of Lt Howard that in talking with young ladies...his conversation consisted of nothing but the most profuse & unmerited flatteries....

San Antonio, Tex. July 7, 1879.... As I walked toward [the Marucheaux's house] I...saw a female form which I recognized as that of Miss James glide from the porch into an adjoining bedroom.... Miss Grimshaw appeared...discomposed by my sudden appearance [and] moved about...with an ill dissembled expression of annoyance [so] I...went on my way.

Miss Laura James is a great friend of Miss Grimshaw's.[28] These two, together with Miss Stribling, constitute a gossip clique...which keeps itself & Miss Brackinridge [Brackenridge]...informed of all the society news in town. They form a trio calculated to develop masculine qualities such as strength & independence of mind & character. It were well for all three of them as aspirants to matrimony to cut loose from each other and seek [different] influences.

San Antonio, Tex. July 9, 1879.... After supper I...called on the Borups [where I met] Miss Bradley...a wonderfully precocious child.[29] She is 13 years old. The artlessness

& vivacity of a child are strangely united in her character with the decorum & understanding of a young lady. Howard once offended her very much by addressing her as if she were, as she actually is, a mere child. She told Howard that she always *did* despise little men.

Bigelow then inserted in his journal, without comment, a menu from the Menger that provides some idea of the cuisine then available at one of the more fashionable establishments on the frontier.

GENTLEMEN WITHOUT MANNERS

San Antonio, Tex. July 11, 1879.... Spent the evening at the Clouses.... Notwithstanding the many ladies present, I was the only gentleman in the room with them, during the greater part of the evening. The other gentlemen, with freedom of manners peculiar to army officers...spent most of the evening outside on the porch. The ladies...talked and ate their refreshments and listened to a little music from Miss Garrard & Mrs Clous, while the gentlemen had their cigars with their conversation & refreshments, the latter including perhaps a little more in the way of stimulant than the sherry wine that was handed around in the sitting room.... I had heard and seen a good deal of the informality of army society but had never before seen anything like this.

It opened my eyes to a cause...of the general disinclination on the part of army officers to establish social relations with civilians; they know that the latter would not allow them the same liberties that they enjoy in their own circle.

ENGAGED? MOI?

San Antonio, Tex. Sunday, July 13, 1879. Miss Grimshaw yesterday evening repeated her invitation to me to sit in her pew.... Accordingly I did not hesitate to take a seat. It will not be long before I shall be talked about in connection with Miss Grimshaw. While I may thereby be placed in false relation to the latter I will no doubt be placed in more correct relation to another young lady, Miss Moore. I have already been congratulated upon my engagement & infer that it is to her that I am supposed to be engaged. My present attentions to Miss Grimshaw will, I hope, have the effect of expelling that delusion;...whether or not my attentions to the latter are of more force than words might be in the refutation of gossip they are certainly better suited to my taste & disposition....

Learned...that Loder, of my class, had committed suicide.[30] According to the newspaper...he had been drinking hard, and I presume [was] heavily in debt.

San Antonio, Tex., July 15, 1879. Called...on Dr & Mrs Taylor. Heard...that Miss Orleman is very sick. Her temperature is at 104.

FRIDAY JULY 11, 1879.

SOUP.

Split Peas.

FISH.

Salmon, Parsley Sauce.

BOILED.

Leg of Mutton, Caper Sauce, Beef, Chow Chow Sauce.

ENTREES.

Calf Liver a la Creole,
Ox Tongue, Rarigotte Sauce,
Noodles, German Style,
Stewed French Prunes.

ROAST.

Loin of Beef, Ribs of Beef,
Lamb, Mint Sauce, Veal Brown Gravy.

VEGETABLES.

Mashed Potatoes, Cabbage, New Carrots.
Stewed Tomatoes, Onions Stewed,

RELISHES.

Worcestershire Sauce, Pepper Sauce, French Mustard,
Chow-Chow, Tomato Catsup, Pickles, Horse Radish.

DESSERT.

Cherry Pie, Bread Pudding, Sherry Wine Sauce,
Sponge Cake, Sugar Cake.

COFFEE.

BILL OF FARE, MENGER HOTEL

After calling on Lt. Orleman, Bigelow added:

...Miss Lillie was probably worse than she had ever been. Her temperature is now 105. She takes morphine & camphor to calm her nerves and is from time to time put in a cold bath to reduce her temperature. I am very much afraid that she is not going to live.

Chapter 17

Pour Prendre Congé

MISS LILLIE'S STRUGGLE WITH THE DEVIL

Lillie's illness led Bigelow to turn his attention to his friends, the Orlemans, and for the first time record his version of the situation confronting them.

> *San Antonio, Tex. July 16, 1879....* The history of that poor girl's experiences...has a sad and melancholy interest. First her father's trouble with his eyes...compelled him to go on a year's sick leave; during that time Miss Lillie...shared her mother's responsibility in caring for the Lieut and the children, and her mother's anxious fears that he might go perfectly blind. Then as her father's eyes improved, she advised and pressed him against his own judgment...to go back to the Company rather than to retire.... From this time on until Maj. Geddes conceived [his] villainous scheme their life was as bright & happy as it has subsequently been gloomy & miserable.
>
> ...[I once] heard Miss Lillie make a remark from which I inferred that she knew the character & reputation of Maj. Geddes.... He [must have]...used his devilish arts with such success as to have blinded her to the danger of his company.... Shortly after [the trip to Fort Davis] Miss Orleman's eyes were opened; then came the short & decisive struggle between herself & the devil, during which she would sit for hour after hour looking abstractedly at the fire, replying to her father's question by a nod or shake of the head but having no heart for work or recreation. The struggle over, she confided all that she had gone through, to her Father....
>
> When permission [to take Lillie to San Antonio] was asked & declined and the Maj. took the wicked & dastardly satisfaction of charging the Lt with a monstrous

crime [incest], Miss Lillie again had the care of her sick father, this time at the point of death and brought there...by circumstances for which she [felt] more or less responsible....

...[After] the Lieut. had brought the Charges against Maj. Geddes...she was then subjected to a judicial and medical examination most trying to her maidenly instincts, which double ordeal she endured...to the complete vindication of her own & her father's honor.[1]

...Mr Friedlander the friend, if not the accomplice, of Maj Geddes has done everything he could to damage her good name.... It is not improbable that the villain who destroyed the happiness of this guileless girl will ere long have accomplished the fiendish revenge upon her father of sending her with a crushed spirit to the grave.

Having unburdened himself of the indignation he felt, Bigelow ventured forth from the Menger to walk to the Marucheaux home from which he escorted Georgie to

the Alamo Building...[to discuss] erecting a monument in commemoration of the Defense of the Alamo.... On account of the small attendance we did not attempt to do any business....

San Antonio, Tex. July 16 [17], 1879.... Went...to a party at Mrs Moore's boarding house.... Mrs Moore was not present to receive me nor to introduce me, and...none of her boarders or other acquaintances...had the tact or politeness to present me to either the ladies or gentlemen.... Having danced one waltz and got well heated...I took leave of Mrs Moore & went home, disgusted with her & her entertainment.

San Antonio, Texas, July 19, 1879.... Called this evening at the Clouses. Learnt that the Capt. had been at school at Paris.... Mrs Clous...favored me with several Scotch songs which I enjoyed.... She says the Mexican military bands render the finest music she has ever heard, but that when she heard it her enthusiastic raptures were not a little dampened by the appearance of the musicians and the knowledge of the harsh treatment & severe discipline to which they were subjected. On one occasion, she told me, when a Mexican band was ordered over to an American post to honor & entertain the garrison...the Mexican commander not only had a guard of his own troops over the band, but so strong was the disposition of his soldiers to desert, he requested the American Commander to place a guard over the whole Mexican detachment.

San Antonio, Texas, July 20, 1879.... Spent most of the day reading.... Went to Church this evening with Miss Grimshaw; after walking home with her we sat in front of the house with Mrs Marucheaux and talked.

THE LOWLY STATUS OF A SECOND LIEUTENANT

Called this evening on Capt & Mrs Comly. The conversation turning upon the Menger Hotel, I gave them an account of my experiences & impressions as a boarder. I have been struck by the cool cheek with which certain ladies...who, considering themselves too good to eat at the same table with their servants, will send them off to another table at which they will sit with persons who, like myself, have no reason to consider themselves socially inferior to their mistresses. The servants should, of course, not be allowed to eat in the same room with the boarders and at the same time, yet it would be inconsistent to deny that privilege to them while it is left to hack drivers, stage drivers and other persons of that class. As for me, I would rather have a neat & comely nurse or governess at my table than an unshaven, unkempt, collarless & horny handed stage driver.

I observe a disposition on the part of Mr Menger to show preference to superior rank in his attention to his military guests. While I appreciate the respect & deference due to my superiors & elders generally and to those wearing the Army uniform especially I do not like to have a sense of my inferiority of rank forced upon me three times a day by a hotel keeper & his waiters, for whose attendance I pay as much as any Capt, Major or Colonel in the house.

DEPRESSING NEWS FROM THE GUADALUPES

San Antonio, Texas, July 24, 1879. Received by telegm. this m'g the sad news of Safford's death. He died of dysentery on the 19th of this month, in camp in the Guadalupe Mts. I have lost in him the best friend I had in the regiment, if not in the Army.

A few days afterwards Bigelow received a letter from Nannie Viele, the wife of Captain Viele, in which she wrote:

About the 27th of June Capt Viele started out on a scout...but as Mr. Safford was not feeling well, he remained in camp. Upon the Captain's return...he found that Mr. Safford had been very ill, but was then improving. He sent couriers to Davis at once for medical stores...and also for an ambulance to bring Mr. Safford in...but on the 13th inst. the disease assumed a most alarming form, and Mr. Safford...sank rapidly, and on the 19th...he sweetly, and almost painlessly, died, and was buried the same afternoon under a beautiful cedar at the base of one the the grand peaks of the Guadalupes.

ROBERT SAFFORD

Bigelow's close friend died of dysentery in 1879 while scouting in the Guadalupe Mountains. He is buried under a tree somewhere near Mansonita Springs. (Courtesy USMA Library)

> Capt Viele sent in a twig from the tree under which he rests, his class ring, and a lock of hair, which I shall send to his poor mother. The physician at the camp devoted himself entirely to the case, and Capt. Viele...was with Mr. Safford night & day. Everything possible was done to save him, but in vain...and we mourn him today, most deeply.[2]

When Safford's father telegraphed the commanding officer at Fort Davis asking that the body be sent home to Ohio, Captain Carpenter wrote to explain the obstacles of such an undertaking:

> Fort Davis...is 500 miles from the nearest railroad terminus...at San Antonio. The camp near the Guadaloupe [Guadalupe] mountains...is 130 miles from [Fort Davis].... [Because of] the extreme heat it was necessary to bury Lieut. Safford on the day of death. There was no material...to embalm the body.... There is no metal casket at Fort Davis. It will take at least a month before one can be delivered...and two weeks more before the body could be brought from the camp. In that time the decomposition will be such that...it would not be wise to think of moving [it].[3]

After Bigelow wrote to Safford's father, he received the following reply from his friend's sister, Edith:

> [S]ince he is dead and gone from us forever, we cling to everything with which we can associate him. Especially sacred, there are the friends who...knew him...as you did.... You cannot well know the terrible void which his untimely death has caused in our hearts and home, and we will always hold in sacred remembrance the friends of his young life.... Bobbie wrote us of your pleasant visit to him at Christmas. How thankful we are for any enjoyment he had, so far away from us and so many lonely hours as he must have passed. Is it not a hard, wearisome life you lead?

AN EMPTIER LIFE

That evening Bigelow escorted Georgie Grimshaw to the Alamo Literary Society meeting which was brief because so few people attended. On the following day he wrote:

> *San Antonio, Texas, July 25, 1879.* I have not since I left West Point felt the want of occupation as much as I have during the past two or three weeks. I cannot read as much as I should like to on account of a weakness in my eyes.... To reserve my reading strength for the hot & wearisome hours of midday, I rise at about 8 o'clock and immediately after dressing go down stairs to breakfast. After breakfast I walk over to the Headqr. Building to get my mail and see Dr Taylor. I then return to my room, having first attended to any shopping or other business...[and] take up whatever book I have and read until 1 or 2 o'clock, [then] go to dinner.

Immediately after dinner I walk over to Headqrs again, to see if any mail has come for me by stage from Stockton. That done, I return to the hotel having, as in the morning, first attended to my business in town. The remainder of the afternoon I spend in reading. At about 6 o'clock I...wander aimlessly forth from the hotel, alternately thinking of deciding upon some one to call on, and hoping to meet with something or somebody of interest.... I usually stay out until 8 o'clock & then go to supper. Supper over, I am again at a loss what to do with myself. Generally I have no engagement. I make one or two calls during the evening.

As Bigelow strolled about town that day with two companions, Lieutenant Howard and Terrell, a gratuitous comment triggered an uncharacteristic reaction in the usually congenial young lieutenant.

[W]e passed Miss Grimshaw who was walking on the other side of the street with two little children.... Mr Terrell said that the first time he met [her] she was very much disposed to flirt [and] made him promise to call on her the following evening.... Mr Terrell had formed an erroneous opinion of Miss Grimshaw, who I have no doubt formed a correct opinion of him [as]...a shallow pated youngster who could not talk with understanding upon any serious subject and thought that she would suit her conversation to his mental capacity & requirements. He probably went home thinking that she believed all he said, so Howard probably thought she believed all he said.... He should have heard her speak...of *"Poor little Howard."*

San Antonio, Tex. Sunday, July 27, 1879. Went to church this morning.... Got an oil color painting from Miss Grimshaw, representing a sunflower I gave her.... Went out to the Springs with [two friends].... We drank two or three glasses of beer, saw the German beauty & fashion of S. Ant. & heard some tolerably good music. On our way back I...called at the Halls.... I told Miss Lilly that, being engaged, I would not go out next winter. She congratulated me a week or two ago upon my engagement, but has not yet told me whom she takes to be the star of my hope....

San Antonio, Tex. July 30, 1879.... It rained a little this afternoon.... While in the North rainy weather gives me the blues, in Texas it cheers me more than the clearest skie that ever smiled upon the earth. In fact the clearer the skie, the hotter the air and...the greater my discomfort.... In winter when [a clear sky] is desirable it is not to be counted upon, but in summer when most undesirable, it is.

Occasionally Bigelow made a simple sketch of something in his journal. At this point he filled four pages with drawings, but other than a figure labelled "Talleyrand" (apparently the French statesman) none is identified.

SKETCH FROM BIGELOW'S JOURNAL

San Antonio, Tex. July 31, 1879. Got photographed in full uniform this morning [see frontispiece], pursuant to a request in Jenny's last letter. My photographer was Mr Bingham.... He charges $10.00 a dozen for Imperials, a high price....

...Miss Grimshaw showed me a daguerreotype of herself when she was 8 yrs old.... She said her heart would break should I not think it pretty.... I told her...that I thought it very pretty, but soon afterward remarked with unconscious naivety that I did not think it even looked like her.

San Antonio, Texas, Aug. 1, 1879. Mr Cross having suggested to me to join a party...in "our set" to attend a public ball this evening, I invited Miss Bertie Ord to go with me.... To our disgust & amazement we found a party of colored ladies & gentlemen all gaily arrayed in their ball costumes. We walked home discussing the probability of our having been sold by Mr Cross. I thought the joke, if one had been played on us, was too rough a one to play on a lady.

CULTURE ON THE FRONTIER

San Antonio, Tex. Aug. 2, 1879. Called this afternoon at the Garcias.... Miss Garcia [asked] me to escort her & her mother to the Hilgers.... The room [there]...was well filled with members of the Opera Club, most of whom were ladies.

At first blush an opera club in the midst of the ruffians, drifters, cattlemen, and soldiers on the still-raw frontier of West Texas might seem incongruous. Nevertheless it thrived because of the substantial German population, including refugee intellectuals, that had migrated to small towns such as New Braunfels and Fredericksburg in the mid-1840s, after which many gravitated to San Antonio where a more genteel life was possible. At the time German speech and guttural accents were common south of the Commerce Street bridge and between Alamo Street and the river (an area called "the Little Rhein").[4] Moreover, even the once-raucous saloons along Alamo Street became more sedate.[5]

By 1876 San Antonio's population, estimated at only 800 in 1846 and about 8,000 in 1860, had grown to more than 17,000, with the Germans and Alsatians the largest ethnic group, having edged out the Americans, English, and Irish by an estimated 5,630 to 5,475, and the 3,750 Mexicans a distant third. By then some of the Germans who had become wealthy merchants, businessmen, or bankers headed efforts to preserve their Old World culture by establishing such facilities as an athletic club (the Turner-Halle),[6] a German-English school, and the "Casino Hall."

I made the acquaintance of most of [the ladies at the Opera Club].... The Misses Wolf are Germans; the elder is the better looking. She talks English, German & Spanish. I wonder whether it is due to her good sense or good looks that she does not powder as her sister does. Miss Cotton is, I presume, a pure American.... She is more interesting in conversations than Miss Wolf [but] the Germans are becoming socially Americanized faster than any other foreigners. Neither the Spaniards, French nor English have gone as far toward the emancipation of women.... Hence...as regards refinement of mind & manners the German young ladies ranked next to the American....

ADIEU, BONS-AMIS!

San Antonio, Tex. Sunday, Aug. 3, 1879.... Went walking with Miss Bertie Ord this afternoon. The Misses Hall asked me if I could...take supper at their house next Tuesday.... I excused myself [because]...I might have to leave on short notice and would need my time for making P.P.C. calls.

A "P.P.C." (*pour prendre congé* or "to take leave") call was an almost-obligatory visit paid to friends and acquaintances when an officer was about to transfer to another post.[7] Army protocol prescribed that such calls, usually of short duration, should be made, and whether or not the callee was home the caller was expected to leave his card with the letters "p.p.c." written in the lower left corner.

San Antonio, Texas, Aug. 4, 1879. Notwithstanding my interview yesterday morning with Miss Hall a propos of her proposed tea party, she sent me an invitation which...I have answered by accepting, with pleasure.... Captain Patterson informed me...that I am detailed as a member of a board of Survey.[8] The government is going to get some work out of me, perhaps, before I leave.... I have not done a good day's work for Uncle Sam yet while I have been here.

San Antonio, Tex. Aug. 5, 1879.... Spent the evening at the Halls...playing cards, dancing & singing. I danced a waltz with Miss Lilly Hall [who was]...determined to hold out until the music should stop, while Miss Garrard who was playing appeared to have decided to hold out until the dancing should stop.... I had about as leave be invited out to chop wood as to dance in such weather as we are having now.

The following evening Bigelow wandered over to the Alamo to hear a lecture on petroleum, not then a burning concern. He "got very tired before it was over." Perhaps he should have paid closer attention.

San Antonio, Tex. Aug. 9, 79. Remained at the Headqrs this forenoon having been told to hold myself in readiness to appear before the Court.... Called at the

Marucheaux this afternoon.... Miss Grimshaw...had gone out.... Called after supper at the Grenets.

Rain nearly all day Sunday converted the streets into mud, which discouraged Bigelow from attending church and seeing Miss Grimshaw. It also provided some relief from the sweltering heat, enabling him to finish work on his board of survey report.

San Antonio, Tex. Aug. 11, 1879.... Finished my return of Garr. Eq. [garrison equipment] today, but cannot forward it to Washington on account of a couple of signatures...which McMartin...failed to witness.

Called this evening on Col. Withers, a West Point graduate and late Confederate officer.[9] He was Adjt Gen'l...under Lee before the War. He said that if...the Confederates had attempted to take Ft McKavett which post Gen'l Lee was commanding, there would have been trouble, the Gen'l having pressed his determination to protect the Gov't property under his charge until his resignation should have been accepted. The Col. said that Gen'l Twiggs was not treated right by the authorities at Washington who declined his several applications for leave to resign.[10]

San Antonio, Texas, Aug. 12, 1879.... Rode to the Government Depot this morning...and got blanks for Quartermaster's Returns.... After dinner I went to the Arsenal and got blanks for my Ordnance returns, which I have made out as far as I can at present.

Bigelow spent the next morning at the Headquarters Building expecting to testify in the Geddes case. His wait was again in vain. Later he made calls on the Halls and on Georgie, who reproached him for a comment he had made to Lilly Hall.

San Antonio, Tex. Aug. 13, 1879.... Miss Grimshaw informed me that Miss Lilly Hall charges me with having made the remark: "It is not my fault if all the young ladies fall in love with me." I...told Miss Grimshaw there were certain young ladies with whom one could not talk in jest.... I shall be glad when I get away from these gossipers; I find myself getting into their ways—the natural consequence of my being forced into ladies' society by want of profitable employment.

San Antonio, Tex. Aug. 14, 1879.... Went to the Alamo Litterary meeting this evening.... Miss Bertie read a piece entitled a Smack in School, a silly rhyme about a school boy kissing a school girl. I walked home with the Ords. While Miss Bertie, Miss H. [Adele Hall] & I were sitting out in the garden I remarked upon the scarcity of original work done by members of the Litterary Society.... Miss Bertie or Miss Adele then suggested that we constitute ourselves into a litterary society

.... We decided to meet next Saturday...and read something of our own composition....

San Antonio, Texas, Aug. 15, 1879. Held myself in readiness to appear before the C.M. but was not called up. Met Lt. Thompson of the 4th Cavalry at the Menger....[11] He told me that several officers of the 4th would like to have me join their reg't, that they had heard of my scouting propensities and wanted all the officers like me they could get. He told me to apply for a transfer, but I did not say I would.

Bigelow undoubtedly was flattered by the suggestion that he would be welcome in Mackenzie's elite regiment. If he wanted to get away this was his opportunity, but his noncommittal response implies that he preferred the 10th Cavalry.

Went out [to] the Government Depot on horseback this afternoon with Mr Cross. We called on Capt [George] Bradley, the Depot Qrmr, to get his consent...for an officers' hop.[12] He...said we would have to get Gen'l Ord's consent and that we were not to introduce any kerosene oil in the building.... [After supper] we started out to call on Mr Twohig, the banker.[13] The night was dark and being unable to open the gate...we climbed the wall.... I confided my apprehension of a meeting with a big watch dog, whereupon we were both so strongly impressed with the uselessness and impropriety of remaining...that we immediately scaled the wall & regained the street....

San Antonio, Tex. Aug. 16, 1879.... The Litterary Society held its first meeting at the Ords this evening. Each of the young ladies read a poem. Miss Bertie's was on the Riddle of Life and Miss Adele's on a young Cavalry officer from Fort Stockton, whose something or other *"outshone the sun."*

THE INDIAN AGENCY PROBLEM

San Antonio, Tex. Sunday, Aug. 17, 1879. Have just read a sensible article...on the Indian question. The [author] is in favor of a transfer of the Indian bureau to the War Dep't. He says the dishonesty among Indian agents and the inefficiency of their management are due to the short & uncertain duration of their terms of service, the smallness of their pay, their freedom from supervision, and their ignorance of the wants & customs of the Indians, none of which causes of dishonesty or inefficiency would exist or have effect in the case of Army officers having the control of the Bureau.

While the transfer would better the condition of the Indians, I doubt if it would not injure the Army. We have already too few active officers with their commands.... It is a question too, with me, whether the temptations that have ruined

> many a civilian of previous good character...would not be too strong for the honor & integrity even of army officers.

Control of the Bureau of Indian Affairs, which had been transferred from the War Department to the Interior Department when the latter was established in 1849, was a bitterly contested issue after the Civil War. Proponents of returning the bureau's functions to the army cited, among other things, the lack of qualifications, inexperience, and corruption of some agents that resulted in costly inefficiencies or worse. The opponents countered with assertions that officers lacked the ability, concern, and compassion to effect the "civilization" of Indians, and that vesting so much authority in the army would endanger the nation's democratic institutions. In 1867 and 1868 bills to effect the transfer were passed by the House but not the Senate. In 1869, however, as part of President Grant's "Peace Policy" some agents had to be nominated by Quaker church officials. More importantly, in a compromise that fell far short of a satisfactory solution, the bureau was given control and jurisdiction of Indians while on their reservations, but the army was in charge of them elsewhere. And despite further efforts in 1876 and again in 1878 when the House Military Affairs Committee voted in favor of transfer, neither bill passed.[14]

RETURNING TO A SOLDIER'S CALLING

> Went to church [with] Miss Grimshaw.... [We then] took our favorite walk to the bridge. After our return I talked with the family.... When I told Mrs Marucheaux that my mother was a Baltimorean and that I had relatives who were Confederates she said "Now that I know that, I think a great deal more of you."

> *San Antonio, Tex. Aug. 19, 1879....* Spoke to Gen'l Vincent about the hop.... It appears that Col [Charles] Terrell...objected to it on the ground of distance from town to the depot & other difficulties.[15] All the officers...ask: "What the Devil has he got to say about it." Gen'l Vincent...decided to let the matter drop.

Termination of plans for a hop did not seem to bother Bigelow, who later that day learned that he was excused from his duties as a witness. Almost gleefully, he noted in his journal:

> I got my orders today to return to Stockton.[16] Called at the Garcias.... Miss Garcia asked me to drop her a few lines now and then.... I [said] I would do so when I should feel sufficiently inspired. If I do not mistake myself the inspiration is not liable to come.

After supper Bigelow made P.P.C. calls on the Ords and the Stevensons.[17] His final farewell visit was with Georgie Grimshaw, but he did not disclose what they discussed.

Three months to the day after arriving in San Antonio, Bigelow headed back to Stockton. Although his testimony in Geddes's trial had been limited, it undoubtedly contributed to the findings and sentence of the court, which were not made known until the president took final action in December.[18] The court had convicted Geddes of three of the four unbecoming conduct specifications and of false swearing, but had acquitted him of attempting to abduct Lillie. He was sentenced:

> To be cashiered and dismissed from the service of the United States, and to be confined in such penitentiary as the proper authority may direct for the period of three (3) years.[19]

Subsequently, however, after reviewing the 750-page transcript, President Hayes concluded that the court erred in not allowing the challenge of a member, unduly restricting defense cross-examination, and not permitting various questions to test the veracity of witnesses. Because of the "undue restraint upon a free and full defense," he disapproved the findings and sentence, and ordered Geddes released and returned to duty.

Chapter 18

Commanding a Camp—of Sorts

Bigelow failed to mention whether anyone saw him off on his return to Fort Stockton, but he did describe his journey.

> Left San Antonio at about one o'clock this afternoon. The passengers beside myself were Mr Corbett, Mr Goldschmitt a "drummer," Dr Henderson, a boy...& another gentleman. The latter...carried a cage containing two canaries.... The other passengers [called] him the "bird man." Mr Goldschmitt was a roundfaced Jewish looking German [who] almost continually smok[ed] a cigar or cigarette or chew[ed] liquorice or tobacco, [so] he was always smelling of something.... We left our bird man at Mason.
>
> *San Ant. Tex. Aug. 23, 1879, Fort Concho.* Arrived here at about 11 o'clock this morning. Lieut. Smither being out with Gen'l Grierson, I went to Eggleston's quarters. Rode over to San Angelo...this ev'g with Lt Pratt, Eggleston, Mr Corbett & Capt Grey [Gray].[1] After our return...we sat on Capt Grey's porch and listened to the band playing on the parade ground.
>
> *Fort Concho, Tex. Aug. 24, 79. Sunday.* Went with Maj [Anson] Mills on his tour of inspection....[2] What I saw of the company quarters did not strike me as very creditable to Gen'l Grierson as Post Commander.[3]
>
> Capt. Norvell told me this morning that his company marched 100 miles without striking water.... When the company went into camp several of the men were out of their senses.... Hardly a man wanted to drink. As soon however as one had got a taste of water he had an almost insatiable thirst, and it was not many minutes before...[they] had given themselves the colic.... The march was from the head of Spring Creek to Beaver Lake and was made in about 30 hours.

Notwithstanding the exhausted condition of his men & stock, the Capt. marched his company to Howards Well, a distance of 45 miles, & on the following day to Camp Lancaster, 35 miles. Eggleston...says that he did not suffer from thirst and that he had water.... His statement goes to show that the men were careless and improvident, as they are apt to be.

I have heard that Gen'l Grierson is displeased with Maxon's inactivity while in the field. The Gen'l counted on his exploring the country [between] the Rio Grande...& the Pecos, but Maxon was so much concerned about his horses that he would not venture more than about a day's march from water.... I have in prospect pretty good opportunities for active service on the Staked Plains. Capt. [Alexander] Keyes is going to Moss Spring. He & I may operate together....[4]

Fort Concho, Tex. Aug. 25, 79. The following shows the disposition of certain comp's...for the next month.

Capt Lebo	K, 10th Cav	Guadalupe Mts
Capt Keyes	D, "	Head of N. Concho
Capt Kelly	E, "	Grierson Spring
Lt Tear[5]	G, 25th Inf	Rainbow Cliff Spg
Capt French	A, "	Camp Charlotte

I may find it convenient & advisable to call on a few of the com'd'g officers during my coming campaign.

CAMP SANTA ROSA

On the next day Bigelow resumed his journey to Stockton. After arriving he hastily prepared to rejoin his company, which had been under McMartin's command at Camp Santa Rosa, a small outpost about thirty miles north of the fort, since July 29.[6] Before he got there a detachment already had a brush with some Indians that was reported in the *San Antonio Express*:

Fort Stockton, Tex. August 27, 1879

Sergeant [Edward] Briscoe and nine men of company B, 10th Cavalry, from Santa Rosa, Texas, struck a trail of Indians on the 19th, who had stolen eight horses on the Pecos. They pushed it eight miles, capturing six of the horses, besides blankets, lariats, etc., near Castle Mountain, on the 20th 25 miles north of Centralia. They also caused the Indians to kill a horse for its blood, after which the trail scattered and was lost in the direction of Peck Spring. The horses being exhausted further pursuit was abandoned.

CAMP SANTA ROSA, TEXAS

For a few months Bigelow commanded this bleak outpost from which scouting detachments scoured the region for water and Indians. (From the William C. Wedemeyer Collection, Courtesy of Fort Concho National Historic Landmark, San Angelo, Texas)

> *Aug 29, 79, Camp Santa Rosa.* Arrived here about sundown yesterday, having left Stockton at about two o'clock.... The Camp is very unfavorably situated in a hollow...being insecure against both surprise and disease.... I have already broken ground with a view to moving the camp to the crest of a gentle rise....
>
> The members of the Company appear to be glad to see me back. When I arrived...Sergt Young swaggered up to me in a broad grin and said *"I am glad to see you back Lieut., I hope you are well Sir."* He held out his hand for me to shake; it went against my military instinct to take it but my natural instinct forced me to do so. What would a German martinet think of the Commanding officer of a Camp who would shake hands with an enlisted man, and a colored man at that.

Vast barriers separated officers from enlisted men, although reciprocal dependency and respect was essential to effectiveness. "Familiarity breeds contempt" was an unquestioned principle, however, that extended even to such seemingly innocuous acts as shaking hands. Nevertheless, Bigelow sensibly subordinated military propriety to his gentlemanly spontaneity.

The wretched subposts that companies on field service occupied, often for months, were far removed from any semblance of civilization and often void of any amenities, as Bigelow had discovered at Peña Blanca. The principal requirements for a site were the proximity of adequate water and if possible forage and firewood. Cooks prepared rations which the men generally ate sitting on the ground or standing. With utility instead of comfort the idea, the only protection from the elements for most soldiers was inside a cramped "A" tent, while officers usually had larger tents and the camp commander might even have two tents placed together with a cot, a chair or two, and a portable desk.

Diversions at Santa Rosa were extremely limited, and the scarcity of game made hunting unproductive where little moved besides the wind and nothing much grew but mesquite. Reading furnished an escape for Bigelow as well as many other officers and some enlisted men, but for Company B's troops (almost all of whom were illiterate) playing cards, singing, and swapping stories were among the few ways of fending off boredom, and going out on scouts became a welcome respite. Even Bigelow found the situation barely tolerable.

> It is fortunate for me that I have plenty to do. I do not know how I could otherwise live here. The glare is more than it was at Peña Blanca. I shall therefore have to do less reading than I did there.

Field service did not necessarily involve uninterrupted isolation, of course, since mail, dispatches, and orders were occasionally received and from time to time detachments had to go back to their posts for resupplies or other purposes.

> *Camp Santa Rosa, Tex. Sept. 3, 1879.* Returned yesterday afternoon from Stockton having marched to that post...to allow the men to get their cartridge pouches.... McMartin brought the Comp. out...with prairie belts [which]...have stretched so much that they are now unserviceable.[7] I left camp...at 7 A.M. and reached Stockton at 3.30 P.M. The weather was very hot & the road very dusty....
>
> Almost as soon as I arrived in the Post I asked Glenn the Post Qrmstr to furnish forage for my horses.... I wanted...to be able to leave early in the morning, but Glenn could not be induced to attend to my wants. If the Post had been under the command of a man like McLaughlen I might have [made]...an official complaint...but Col Blunt lacking energy & backbone even to a greater extent than Glenn, it would have done me no good.... Instead of leaving the Post at 7 o'clock...I did not start until 1/4 of 9....

> I have been working hard on my muster rolls, monthly status & official correspondence. I have to do all that writing myself. My Comp. Saddler has been...in the hospital at Fort Stockton...[and] I lost Private [James] Riley, who...got taken up and put in the County Jail for firing off his pistol in the settlement...& on my way back to Camp Private Mitchell, the only man who can do any clerical work, was kicked by a horse & disabled....
>
> *Camp Santa Rosa, Tex. Sept. 5, 1879.* Began yesterday and ended today the moving of the Camp. McMartin might have spared me all the trouble...by selecting the present camping ground [which]...would naturally suggest itself to any officer of slight experience...while the camping ground which he selected would strike any observer as the most unsuitable....
>
> Owing to the general flatness of the country, the slight elevation [of the camp]...affords me a very wide prospect. My eye ranges...in a NEasterly direction over five or six miles of mesquite bushes, and passes across...the Pecos basin, to a long line of purple, dotted & streaked with white: the distant and enchanting view of the bluffs of the Pecos and the sandy tracts & gentle undulations of the Staked Plains.

Either the unexpected leisure or too much time in the sun might have contributed to Bigelow's portrayal of the countryside. But in even loftier terms he describes the plight of a private undergoing punishment. Perhaps it was the sun.

ATONEMENT FOR A MISCREANT

> Returning from its wanderings, my wearied optic, looking for a place to rest, lights upon a human form wearily walking back & forth directly in front of my tent. The form is the earthly habitation of Isaac Wescott's immortal soul. Mr Wescott is a colored recruit who with a sledge hammer on his shoulder is doing penance for unsoldierly deportment toward his Com'd'g Officer. I had ordered Serg't Givens to have him carry a log, but as there is not a piece of timber within sight of Camp large enough to furnish such a thing, I changed his punishment, making his burden a sledge hammer. It must be getting pretty heavy and be making its bearer uncomfortable. The sun shines forth in all its glory while one side of Pvte Wescott's head has no protection but a soldier's cap, about a size too small, and the other side none but a scanty crop of black wool. I disliked to punish him, quite as much I think as he disliked to be punished, but of course he would not believe that, no matter what might be said or done to prove it.

THRIFTY TROOPS

To pay the troops (whether or not they had any place to spend the money) the department paymaster, making his circuit around the posts, camps, and outposts in Texas, arrived at Santa Rosa that evening. The next day Bigelow related that

> Maj. Wilson paid the Company this morning. A large proportion...made deposits which pleased me very much, but...amazed the Paymaster.[8] He did not like the trouble & detention caused by it....

RESULTS, NOT APPEARANCES, COUNT

> *Camp Santa Rosa, Texas, Sept. 7, 1879.* McMartin got back today.... His detachment approaching camp made a rather unique appearance. The apparent sameness of color of the dark uniform & dark skins of the wearers, brought into further harmony by a heavy coating of dust, gave the whole column a peculiarly sombre aspect. The unstudied neglect in the attire of the men was striking and picturesque. Most of them wore nothing over their shirts and had their coats hung to their saddles. Ford wore an Indian head dress. I took him for an Indian Guide when I first saw him. They brought in quite a number of relics consisting of a bow and arrows, lariats, &c.... Considering the work done by McMartin & his command I think his stock returned to camp in very good condition.

Although Bigelow does not elaborate, "the work done by McMartin" was a major achievement. For some time marauders from the Mescalero Reservation in New Mexico (about a hundred miles northwest of El Paso) had been striking isolated ranches and herds in West Texas. On this occasion McMartin's detachment covered an extraordinary distance of 963 miles, 742 of which involved the pursuit of raiders back to their reservation sanctuary. Denying that anyone from there could be guilty of stealing horses, the agent, S. A. Russell, refused to surrender the thieves.[9] Consequently none was apprehended, but ten of the horses were repurchased for two dollars each and a dozen or so more that had been abandoned on the trail were recovered.[10]

GRATIFYING DIFFERENT APPETITES

> *Camp Santa Rosa, Tex. Sept. 9, 1879.* The train came out from the Post today and brought me 18,000 pounds of forage.... Sergeant Briscoe...asked me to allow a mule to be taken in to the Post tomorrow...to bring out a few commissary stores for a mess which the Non-Com'd Officers have proposed to start among themselves.... It is the first evidence I have seen of any desire among the Non-Com'd

Officers to separate themselves.... I think I can turn it to advantage in my endeavors to awaken among the privates a livelier sense of respect for their Non-Com'd Officers.

The object of this...shows plainly what I have often inferred: the susceptibility of colored soldiers to any ministrations to their natural appetites.... Of course, [their] desire for nice food is not the craving of a diseased and pampered appetite, it is due more to the former stinting of the stomach than to its indulgence.... An ignorant man who for years has had to toil for other men while subsisting on the crumbs that fall from their tables will whenever he can do so, enjoy the newly attained privilege of eating the same fare as his former masters.

Since the Privates would like to do just as the Non-Com'd Officers are doing I anticipate no...dissatisfaction. The Non-Com'd Officers have no cause to make any and the Privates have no right to.

THE CONSOLATION OF FRIENDS' DEATHS

Camp Santa Rosa, Tex. Sept. 10, 1879.... I learned that Lieut Gasman died a short time ago.... It appears that he drank himself to death.... His death and Safford's, together, have raised me two files on the list of 2d Lieutenants.[11] What an inglorious way of advancing, that of merely replacing those who topple over, and what an unfortunate line of aspiration that which leads to self congratulation at the death of a friend. I think I have as little desire for rank...as any officer, yet I cannot think of the death of a superior without soon associating it...with my greater closeness to the last of the 1st Lieutenants.

GETTING OUT OF THIS PLACE

For those who found field service unbearable, one method of avoiding it might lie in a leave of absence. The amicable Sergeant Young could have been resorting to such a ploy when he was granted a furlough of sixty days.

I am glad the Serg't is off. Dr Price thinks it not improbable that he is a malingerer but, whether he is or not, as long as I can get no work out of him, I do not want him in camp.

EQUINE DISTRESS

Camp Santa Rosa, Tex. Sept. 13, 1879.... One of my horses died today of a complicated distemper that included apparently the bowels, bladder and kidneys. I had never before seen a dumb animal suffer as this horse did.... [H]e was lying on his side, his fore legs perfectly rigid, his eyes covered with a light film and partially closed, his lips drawn back so as to uncover his upper front teeth; now he would lie still, giving an occasional twitch and groan, now carry his head to the rear and well up off the ground and bring it down again with a heavy thud in the dust; he would now & then rapidly repeat this movement as if madly threshing the ground with his neck and head. His belly was covered with perspiration, brought out by excessive agony. The men...had to give him an occasional pitying glance as a groan, a heavy thud or a cloud of dust would draw their attention to his suffering. If he had been my horse I would have shot him, but he being government property I had not the authority to do so. If I had known that his disorder was incurable I would have shot him notwithstanding.

AMATEURS PLAYING SOLDIER

Camp Santa Rosa, Tex. Sept. 14, 1879.... Read Capt Wherry's pamphlet and I agree....[12] The Secretary of War is not a military officer nor is the President. In our republic, as well as in all monarchies, the executive commands the Army; the difference between our president and a monarch is essentially that the former is a civilian clothed with military power and the latter a soldier clothed with civil power.... The preponderance of the civilian over the military...is greater...in our republic than in a monarchial government. Our President [an ex-volunteer officer] is therefore more in need of military advice than the average monarch.... [Yet he] commands [the Army] as best he can with the assistance of his Secretary of War [George McCrary], a civilian who is more familiar with political than with military tactics.[13]

Bigelow's concern that a president and his secretary of war receive competent military advice in order to command the army effectively was well founded, but only part of the larger issue of how the army should be commanded. At the core of the problem was the failure of the Constitution to provide for "civilian control" in an institutional manner or to differentiate between political and military functions.[14] Consequently, the transitory solution came to depend on the interrelated and changing roles of the president, the secretary of war, the commanding general, and the heads of the army's staff departments.

Under the structure that developed in the nation's formative decades, the army had two principal components: the "line" (infantry, cavalry, and artillery) and the "staff" (such as the adjutant general, quartermaster, and engineers) that provided logistic and other support and services to the line.[15] As commander in chief, the president usually exercised his authority in military matters through the commanding general, and in fiscal, logistical, and other primarily nonmilitary activities, through the secretary.[16] Among the drawbacks of such divided responsibility, the staff departments, being independent of control by the commanding general, tended to become quasi-autonomous, creating a risk of not being as responsive to the needs of the line as military situations might require. Moreover, an aggressive secretary (such as Jefferson Davis in the mid-1850s), acting directly or through staff officers assigned to territorial commands, might be able to preempt the commanding general (then Winfield Scott) in purely military decisions.

Except when war or serious civil disruption threatened or occurred, military affairs were not a pressing concern to Congress or most of the nation. Consequently, none of the few attempts to legislate a solution was successful. A legally questionable Command of the Army Act, designed primarily to disrupt President Andrew Johnson's Reconstruction plans, passed as part of the 1867 Appropriations Act, but events overtook its implementation.[17] Then in 1879 Sen. Ambrose Burnside's ambitious reorganization bill was thwarted by the efforts of entrenched staff officers and their congressional allies.[18] So for the balance of the century the army remained subject to a system that under the best of circumstances was awkward, and under the worst seriously hobbled military effectiveness.

For example, when Sherman became commanding general in 1869, President Grant assured him that in the chain of command he would be between the secretary and the staff departments as well as the field forces. Shortly thereafter, though, direct control of the staff reverted to a new secretary, who nevertheless continued to send his directives through Sherman. A few months later, however, William W. Belknap became secretary, after which the commanding general's position became little more than titular as Belknap and the staff heads usurped more and more control.[19] By 1874 Sherman had become so frustrated that he decamped to St. Louis where he remained until Belknap resigned in 1876 to avoid impeachment for selling post sutlerships.

From then until his retirement in 1883, Sherman and successive secretaries avoided serious disputes, but it was not until 1903 that a framework for reform was created by the General Staff Act.[20] Among other changes, it eliminated the commanding general, created a small "general staff" headed by a chief of staff, and provided that assignments to the staff departments would be temporary instead of permanent. Both the line and staff were theoretically subordinated to the chief of staff, who was to assist the secretary, who in turn acted at the direction of the president. But because the old staff hierarchies remained little changed for several years, the act fell short of accomplishing all that was needed. Nevertheless, in time it helped eliminate the divisive arrangements that had intermittently lessened the army's effectiveness. Still unresolved, though, is how to assure that a commander in chief at least receives experienced military advice before making major military decisions.

RICE ISN'T WORTH BEANS

> *Camp Santa Rosa, Tex. Sept. 17, 1879....* I have had some trouble...about my rations. I wanted nothing but beans and Glenn sent me a lot of rice.[21] I did not care to lose any time by arguing with Glenn. I addressed myself directly to Col Blunt.[22] Although I did not get all I asked for...I accomplished a good deal in getting beans substituted for rice.... I expect to start for the Staked Plains this afternoon with...21 enlisted men.

THE SAND HILLS SCOUT

Later that day Bigelow and his small detachment set forth for the White Sand Hills, which stretch north by northwest from the present town of Monahans almost to the southeast corner of New Mexico, an area about twenty-eight miles in length and an average of some three miles in width. Earlier army expeditions and immigrants had crossed through or near these wind-swept hills, which also were a favored route of Indians because cool, clear water could be obtained by scooping shallow trenches in the sand between the dunes—if you knew which dunes.[23] Bigelow's mission was to explore the Sahara-like region, identify and record where water could be found, determine the best routes, and intercept any raiding parties they might encounter. Substituting a three-by-six-inch notebook for his bulky journal, he recorded how such an expedition was conducted. Unfortunately, the detachment did not get off to a very propitious start.

> *In the field. Sept. 18, 79.* Marched yesterday from Camp Santa Rosa to Pecos Falls [about five miles north]. Left the Falls at 5.30 this morning and camped here, on the outskirts of the Sand Hills [approximately twenty-two miles north of the Falls] at 12.15.... My camp is close to a hole...[that had] some water in it when I reached it. I had it dug deeper but without first having the water removed that was already in it. The latter being a little stagnant the horses will drink but very little...as the new water is all contaminated by the old.

I was very much annoyed...to learn from the packers that they had no spade.... With my experience in commanding colored soldiers I should have known better than to have left such an important matter...to the thoughtfulness of the packers and Non Com'd Officers.... Here I am...without a spade and dependent entirely upon digging for water....

Sept. 19, 79. Left camp at 5 A.M. having had reveille at 3. Walked the command for an hour & 1/4, then found myself at a place where Indians evidently camped.... There was about a quart or two of water in each of two holes.... Halted and set the men to work digging. The horses have not had hardly anything to eat since they left the Falls.

TOLERATING HEAT

I have heard it said that colored men could not stand the heat as well as white men. I do not believe the saying.[24] How can I, when I see Ford lying down on the sand with no protection for his head but his hat, exposed to the full glare of the sun when he might...have had the shelter of a willow tree, as I have. White men, on account of their greater intelligence and in general more sanguine temperaments, can *when they want to* endure greater unaccustomed physical trials than colored men can. They can bring more moral and nervous force to their support. Hence a Northern white man, much more a Southern bred white man, can stand perhaps a more intense heat than a Northern bred colored man. But generally speaking, white men will only show their greater endurance in such exceptional cases as will excite in them their moral & nervous stimulus.

TRAVELING IN CIRCLES

Having left the water at about 8:45, travelled about N50°E a distance of five miles then...due W. 1/2 mile and came upon a...trail which I took to be that of Lieut. Bullis & the Indians which he pursued...last March. We followed [it], which brought us...back to the water from which we had last started. We went into camp [there] at 1.30 P.M., having marched 13 miles. There is hardly any grass.... The water is good; the wood is barely sufficient for camping purposes.

The Sand Hills extend about NW & SE.... The country to the NE...is sandy; a belt about 2 1/2 miles broad...is almost level & made conspicuous by numerous mesquite bushes. Beyond this belt the country becomes more markedly rolling. The belt is a kind of valley between the Sand Hills and the rolling country beyond them. About 5 miles from the Hills we saw an abundance of grama grass. It was so dry however that the horses would not eat it.

RESPECTING OLD SOLDIERS

Sept. 20, 79. In the Field. I heard Pvte Willis McReynolds...lecture a Recruit who had charged him with pilfering his haversack. McReynolds spoke somewhat as follows: "What you gibin me fellah? What you a gibin me. Does you know who yoo's a talkin to? Does you know that I's an old sojer? You wait till yoo's an old sojer for yoo try to dominize over me. You ain't nothin but a recruit, that's all you is. Instead of dominizin ober old soldiers you ought to salute em bery time you sees em, dat's wot you ought to do. You try to *dominize* ober me, I knock you head off."

MANEUVERING THROUGH HELL

Having decided to give the horses a day's rest and such grazing as they could find.... I broke camp at 7 A.M. and marched out of the Sand Hills. Halted at 7.15.... Set my men to work digging. The earth is very dry and the work has not thus far promised to be very successful. I am reclining on my saddle blanket in the shade of another blanket spread over a mesquite bush. Behind me are the Sand Hills, their depressions as close and hot as so many furnaces.

In front of me lies a vast sandy tract sparsely covered with grass & mesquite.... Immediately in front of me is the hole...where my men have been digging today. After two hour's work, it was about 7 feet deep and showed no sign of water. About 3 or 4 feet beneath the surface was found a couple of pieces of iron off the hub of a wheel.... Bob Speakes, my guide, has walked a few miles from camp and found a trail leading just in the direction in which I want to go tomorrow along the E. side of the Sand Hills.[25] I hope to make a good day's march & then go into the Hills for water.

One of my horses while grazing this m'g was bit in the nose by a rattlesnake. Its head is swelling very fast. As bad luck would have it, the snake happened to strike one of the best horses in the Command.... [The men] are pretty tired of digging with buckets & camp kettles. I am getting tired of reading Les Deux Filles de Madame Plichon. I wish I had something else....

21 Sept. Left camp at 4.50. Walked the detachment out of the Sand Hills then mounted it & marched...3 1/2 miles from our last camp when we came upon an old trail running into the Sand Hills from the NE.... The guide...found signs of water.... I have had a hole dug & am waiting for it to fill. Opposite me is a large Sand Hill about 50 feet high, its top as bald and almost as white as the driven snow.... Went into camp at 11 A.M. in the Sand Hills. About 5 miles from our last camp...we found another trail.... We followed it about 5 miles and found that it led into the Hills.... [A]fter a march of a half a mile...[we] found signs of water...and have now a waterhole about 6 feet across and five feet deep....

In the Field. Sept. 22, 79. 6.35 A.M. Left camp at 1/4 of 5. Marched the men SE a third of a mile & came upon my own trail leading to our first camp.... Marched the detachment to it and from there travelled S 1 1/2 miles.... I am in a mesquite bottom covered with the best grama grass that I have seen on this trip. My stock is in good condition notwithstanding its having had little to eat; this is due to my having made the men dismount in the heavy sand and lead their horses over it. I have been able, thus far, to give my men & stock all the water they have needed.

On long, dreary marches in stifling heat the thoughts of most men were likely to stray from the tedium of leading their horses or riding them at a walk. Bigelow was no exception. But while most others might daydream about physical comforts, he chose to ponder another subject.

Painting as compared to music is of the earth.... A painter seeks his models and inspirations in a real world; the musician seeks his in an ideal world.... The artist wants to show us what we have seen and make us feel what we have felt; the musician wants to make us feel what he feels.... As soon as the artist goes into himself...he is in the world of musicians.... He is less sociable than formerly; he lets his hair grow longer and is seen at his work looking upward like the musician through the ceiling. The amateur critic in front of his picture instead of exclaiming *"How natural"* opens his eyes and either passes it as uncomprehended, or makes the remark: *"What a daub."*

12.10. I am now...a mile & 1/2 from last night's camp.... There is no grass here to speak of. After leaving our last resting place I marched the detachment about 4 miles rounding the S.W. point of the Sand Hills and returning to our last camp'g ground for water. Near the S.W. extremity of the hills I came upon a trail leading into them.... [The guide and I] are both now inclined to think it is the old Emigrant Wagon trail leading across the Staked Plains from the Pecos Falls. After watering the horses I marched to our present temporary camp. The horses can find nothing to eat in the Sand Hills. The weather being very hot and the travelling in the sand very fatiguing, I have to make short marches and halt frequently to let my horses rest and graze. Camped at 2 P.M.

Sept. 23. Left camp at 4.15 and the bald Sand Hills at 4.50. Marched 18 miles N80°W then 22 miles due 1 1/2°N of West. Made a dry camp at sundown.... The country was very gently undulating, presenting numerous large flats. The soil is in many places sandy and hard to travel over. Distance marched: 40 miles....

Sept. 24. Left camp at 4 A.M. and marched 1 1/2 N of West until 5.5 A.M. when I came upon the road. Followed it...about 20° N of West. After travelling 8 miles...arrived at Marboe's Crossing. Halted there 3 hours and marched 10 miles up the river to Sand Bend where the detachment went into camp at 7 P.M. Found good grass & water but little wood....

In the Field. Sand Bend, Sept. 25, 79. Am resting here today and grazing my stock.... I have never found grass as scarce in this country as it is now; it gives me as much concern as water does. When I left the Sand Hills, I thought from what the guide had told me that I was at least 75 miles from the River. Having the prospect of a march over that many miles without water I was made rather uneasy by the sandy character of the soil for the first 20 miles.... It was a great relief to me to learn from Speakes that he did not think the distance to the river greater than 45 miles.

He had never made the trip himself and did not know the topography of the country. During the first 5 or 6 hrs I let him guide us, after indicating to him the direction, taken from my compass. I found however that he...could not keep steadily in the same direction. I therefore had to be my own guide. I shall never again depend on a person without a compass to steer me across the plains.... Speakes is as useless as most of the guides that I have had, amount'g to nothing more than a trailer. He does not know as much about the country away from the river as I do, and had never been to the Sand Hills until I had taken him there. As a companion he is of some use to me.

He amuses me at times by the quaintness & originality of his language. Speaking of the course best calculated to quiet the Fort Stanton [Mescalero] Indians he said: "We ought to go in there some time, and make a killin' among 'em, and let 'em rest on *that* awhile. If that don't do 'em we can go back and give 'em another twist." On the biting power of a certain insect: "If you think one o' them won't make a man stop eatin', you got it put up wrong for sure." Referring to Comanches, "If a man goes after them and thinks they won't fight, he's goin' to get left, that's all."

Sept. 27, 79. Left camp at 4.15 A.M. I camped at 10.15 having marched 17 miles along the Pecos.

Sept. 28. Returned to Camp Santa Rosa. Arrived there at 7.15 P.M. having followed the Pecos to...about 5 miles above Emigrants' Crossing and then made a partial circuit around Camp Santa Rosa....[26] Struck the road to Stockton at dusk about a mile above Monument Spring.... Day's march 45 miles. Found no water.

Chapter 19

Au Revoir to the Wilderness

THE UPRISINGS OF '79

Soon after returning to Santa Rosa Bigelow planned another exploration, but his arrangements went awry.

> *Camp Santa Rosa, Tex. Oct. 4, 79.* I sent fourteen days' rations...to Bob Speakes' ranch...for McMartin's detachment, which is going out this afternoon. I want Mac to camp at the ranch...tonight, [then] at Horsehead Crossing, [then] at Castle Gap.... From [there] he is to travel to the Sand Hills then as far North as possible.
>
> ...While at dinner...I received the following communication...which decided me to change my instructions. I sent [McMartin] a letter, by courier...to scout the line between Hackberry Crossing & Castle Gap & to look for trails to the North....
>
> Fort Concho, Texas October 3d 1879
>
> To: Commanding Officer, Fort Stockton, Texas
>
> The following just received (from Colonel Hatch, 9th Cavalry):
>
> Large band of well armed Apaches are reported going south from Mescalero Agency.... Serious trouble in Ute country. Major Thornberg [Thornburgh] killed, and three officers wounded. *I have my hands full.* Merritt with nine hundred men moving on the Utes, most of my Cavalry in pursuit of Victorio.
>
> [Furnish] this information to all the officers commanding troops in the field...and [hold] the troops now at the Post in readiness....
>
> Smither, A.A.A.G.

Headquarters Fort Stockton, Texas, Oct. 4th 1879

Official copy respectfully furnished Commanding Officer Camp Santa Rosa, Texas....[N]otify the ranchmen in your vicinity to be on their guard, and...promptly report...any important reliable information...in regard to the movements of these Indians, also if any emergency should arise necessitating reinforcements or troops....

By Order of Lieut Colonel Blunt

Owen J. Sweet, 1st Lieut, Post Adjutant

Colonel Hatch's concern is understandable. In early September Victorio and his Warm Springs Apaches cut and ran from the Mescalero Reservation, then commenced a series of lightning-like strikes in southwest New Mexico. And that same month in northwest Colorado the White River Utes were doing their best to annihilate a large number of troops. More than three-fourths of the Class of '77 was then on the frontier. In the Southwest Matthias Day, Robert Emmet, and three others were with the 9th Cavalry.[1] Besides Bigelow, Eggleston, Esterly, Read, and Flipper were assigned to the 10th Cavalry.[2] Also, Gatewood and Augustus Blocksom, both of the 6th Cavalry, and James Maney of the 15th Infantry each led a company of Indian Scouts.[3] Most would soon be deeply engulfed in the spreading clashes.

WAR TO THE DEATH

Violent conflicts between the Apaches and those who disrupted their lives were not of recent origin.[4] In the sixteenth century these ferociously independent warriors had defied both the cross-toting Spanish friars bent on converting them to Catholicism and the saber-wielding *soldados* with their lances and fire-belching muskets. And for decades before the Americans became adversaries, the Apaches were the scourge of the Mexicans, whom they despised. In the early 1840s Mangas Coloradas, a physically powerful and highly intelligent Mimbreno, forged alliances with the Chiricahuas and other bands to drive the intruders from Apachería, and for years thereafter some of his ablest disciples, including Cochise, Victorio, and Geronimo, disrupted and delayed encroachments into their territories.

By the late 1870s most of the Apaches had been forced to submit to the growing United States strength that drove them from their homelands onto unhealthy and unproductive confines such as the infamous

San Carlos Reservation in Arizona. But a few, such as Victorio, refused to capitulate, choosing instead to wage a "war to the death."[5] The situation that culminated in the 1879 uprising was brought about largely by the ineptitude of Eastern bureaucrats coupled with the questionable competency of some Indian agents. Additionally, a contributing factor was the covetousness of some of the miners, merchants, settlers, squatters, and other whites who wanted the Indians' lands.[6] In this regard a few years later George Crook aptly observed:

> Greed and avarice on the part of the whites—in other words, the almighty dollar—is at the bottom of nine-tenths of all our Indian trouble.[7]

Despite inadequate manning and meager resources the army was called on to subjugate the natives who forceably resisted the Indian Bureau's policies and the avaricious wealth-seekers. Crook subsequently described such an undertaking:

> The mode of warfare of the Indians occupying the western slope of the Rocky Mountains is in many respects as dissimilar from that of their brothers living on the Plains...as the physical character of the country in which they live....The Apaches are representative of the Indians of America so far as ferocity, courage, cunning, and skill in savage warfare are concerned...[but] they live in the roughest part of the continent [with] rugged mountains and arid plains...[and] can endure fatigue and fasting and can live without water for periods that would kill the hardiest mountain men.[8]

Believing that they were to be forced back to the despised San Carlos, in early September Victorio and an estimated 42 warriors (a number thought to reach 125 to 150 as others joined him) left Ojo Caliente.[9] A few days later Colonel Hatch asked that the Mimbreños be permitted to remain in the mountains they cherished, noting that "These Indians have been often deceived."[10] The die, however, had been cast. After killing two herders and several sheep, the Apaches headed west. Then on September 4 they came across a grazing herd of horses from E Company, 9th Cavalry. They attacked, killing all eight guards and getting away with at least thirty horses and some mules.[11]

Two weeks later the first major engagement between troops and the runaway Apaches occurred high in the Black Range of the Mimbres Mountains. The battle commenced when Matthias Day and forty-six men under Capt. Byron Dawson were ambushed in a deep canyon near the headwaters of Las Animas Creek. Another detachment, commanded by

Capt. Charles D. Beyer and including 2d Lt. William D. Hugo and Bigelow's friend, Robert Emmet, was about three miles down canyon. Learning of the situation, they galloped to the scene and made a frontal assault to estabish contact with Dawson. When that effort failed, troops led by Hugo and Emmet made a flank attack on the Apaches' camp high above them to draw the Indians away. The maneuver distracted the ambushers long enough for Beyer to join forces with Dawson. Beyer directed a retreat but Day, refusing to abandon his wounded, dashed forward about two hundred yards under heavy fire to carry off a disabled black soldier.

As Beyer and most of the troops cowered under outcroppings of rocks on the canyon floor, Hugo and Emmet were making their attack on the Apache camp. A large number of Indians counterattacked, soon routing Hugo and most of their detachment, but Emmet, who with five men had been farthest in advance, was left behind. As the Indians headed for a position from which they could fire directly on the withdrawing soldiers, he kept shooting at them until the troops reached shelter. Then noticing that Hugo and several men had abandoned their horses, which were tied to bushes in the nearby camp, he held off the Apaches until his men, one of whom was killed, led the horses away. Emmet's gallantry was recognized with a Medal of Honor. After darkness Beyer withdrew the entire command to Fort Bayard where he preferred court-martial charges against Day for disobedience. Instead of being tried, however, "Daisy" also received the Medal of Honor. In all, five soldiers, two Navajo scouts, and one civilian were killed, one soldier wounded, and thirty-two horses killed and six wounded.

When word of the near-disaster reached Fort Bayard, Gatewood and Blocksom were promptly sent to the scene with their Indian scouts.[12] By then, of course, Victorio had moved his camp, but after a grueling pursuit for three nights in the rain, his new location was discovered and another fight occurred. This was followed by a month of frantic but generally unproductive chases and a few skirmishes; in late October "Old Vic" sought sanctuary in the northern Chihuahua mountains where he was pursued and engaged in an indecisive battle. From then until early 1880 the renegades remained south of the border.[13]

In the meantime, the imperiled settlers, miners, and ranchers, realizing that far more of them would have perished but for the sacrifices of

MATTHIAS DAY

Seemingly born to fight, he had numerous encounters with Apaches and was awarded the Medal of Honor, after which he fought the Sioux, then Spaniards in Cuba and Moros in the Philippines before going to sea to chase pirates. If he harbored a death wish he lost, living to age seventy-four. (Courtesy USMA Library)

ROBERT TEMPLE EMMET

His courage matched that of his Irish great-uncle, resulting in a Medal of Honor for the lives he saved in Las Animas Canyon. (Courtesy USMA Library)

the troops, replaced the disdain many had previously shown with tributes such as:

> The "Buffalo Soldiers," as the Indians call the colored troops, returning with interest...the intense hatred the savages have for them, have won the respect and regard of all our people, and the prejudice existing against them at one time has entirely disappeared.[14]

BLOOD IN THE MILK

Eleven days after the Las Animas fight and several hundred miles north, another conflict was taking shape near a stream called Milk Creek.[15] Triggered by an alarm from the Indian agent, Nathan Meeker, at the White River Reservation, 150 troops under Maj. Thomas Thornburgh, accompanied by a twenty-five-wagon supply train, were sent from Fort Steele, Wyoming.[16] The detachment included James Paddock and Sam Cherry, both of the 5th Cavalry.[17] Some miles north of the agency Cherry met about ten Utes who asked, "What troops come for? What matter?" He persuaded them to accompany him back to camp, where Thornburgh assured them of his peaceful intentions and that he was going down to see what the problem was with the agent, Nathan Meeker.[18] On September 29 the command arrived at Milk Creek, the northern boundary of the reserve. Leaving the wagons and infantry there, Thornburgh crossed with the cavalry to find a suitable campsite closer to the agency. Sam Cherry relates what happened next:[19]

> I had been ordered...to take ten or twelve men ...in advance of the command.... About half or three-quarters of a mile beyond Milk River [Creek] I saw three Indians disappear from [a] ridge, about 500 yards in advance....I crossed a little stream and got up on the ridge....By a mere fortunate circumstance, Major Thornburgh happened to take that trail instead of the road....I was within a hundred yards of the Indians, and I could see [300 or 400 of them] lying down on top of the second ridge,...packed as close as they could be, their line extending at least 400 yards....
>
> I motioned to Major Thornburgh to move back ...[then] I rode down the slope...and told him what I had seen....[He] told me to...communicate with the Indians if possible....About fifteen or twenty Indians came in sight from behind the ridge...and I took off my hat and waved it in a friendly way. I was replied to by a shot...that wounded a man right behind me....I sent word to Major Thornburgh that...I would hold that point until further orders...[and] that the Indians were riding round upon the flanks, trying to cut us off from the wagons. [He ordered

SAMUEL CHERRY

Cherry survived Milk Creek, but a few months later a soldier shot him through the heart for no apparent reason, then rode off into the sunset. (Courtesy USMA Library)

> me] to hold the point...until the other companies had fallen back, and then I was to fall back slowly....
>
> The Indians set fire to the grass and sagebrush above our positions soon after we reached the wagons....We at once set about getting the bundles and grain sacks out...to make defenses; we also covered ourselves behind our horses, and half of them were shot that afternoon....That night the Indians made a charge...but we repulsed them by a heavy fire that killed a number of them....We had to drag out the dead horses and bury our dead, and care for the wounded, and dig trenches, so that we did not sleep at all.

For the next six days a type of warfare rarely waged on the frontier took place. Inside the circled wagons the only available water was what little could be brought at night from the creek, about two hundred yards away, and the only food was corn from the wagons. The situation was further aggravated by the stench from more than three hundred dead animals. On October 2 Capt. Francis Dodge arrived with forty members of Company D, 9th Cavalry.[20] One grateful soldier later wrote:

> Why, we took those darkies in right along with us in the pits. We let 'em sleep with us, and they took their knives and cut off slips of bacon from the same sides as we did.[21]

And with a touch of unconcealed pride, another cavalryman declared:

> You ought to have seen them niggers and watched how they behaved. You know it wasn't any fun going for water even in the night time, let alone the daylight. But one afternoon one moke got terribly thirsty; the firing had stopped for quite a spell, and says he, "Well, boss, Ise powerfully dry, and somebody's got to get water fo' me, or Ise got to get water for somebody," so what does that moke do but take two pails in broad daylight and go down and bring 'em back full of water, and the Injuns never lifted a hair on him.[22]

The thirsty "moke" was Sergeant Henry Johnson of Boynton, Virginia, who had enlisted at Baltimore. The citation accompanying his Medal of Honor further relates that he

> Voluntarily left fortified shelter and under heavy fire at close range made the rounds of the pits to instruct the guard [and] fought his way to the creek and back to bring water to the wounded.[23]

Notwithstanding the racial terminology of the times, the black soldiers earned new-found admiration and respect from the white troopers with whom they shared the dangers at Milk Creek.[24]

Disengagement occurred on October 5 when a rescue party under Col. Wesley Merritt arrived and the Utes withdrew. Apart from Sergeant Johnson, Capt. J. Scott Payne, Sam Cherry, and young Jim Paddock were among the many who distinguished themselves.[25] The casualties included Major Thornburgh who was killed before he made it back to the wagons and Paddock who was shot five times. In addition to them and the other dead or wounded, the bodies of eleven adult civilians (including Meeker) and one boy were found at or near the agency.[26] Also Meeker's sixty-four-year-old wife, twenty-two-year-old daughter, and the sixteen-year-old wife of an employee and their two children had been carried off. The Utes lost thirty-seven warriors.[27]

IMPOVERISHMENT ON THE PLAINS

Back in the Southwest, Victorio remained relatively secure in his Mexican mountain refuge during November and December 1879, so the frequent and intense encounters of early autumn abated until his incursion into the United States in January. Nevertheless, the risk he posed continued, and within a few months 10th Cavalry troops would augment those of the 9th as operations spread into West Texas. In the meantime, as B Company remained on the *qui vive* to intercept any Indians who might try to penetrate its territory, camp routines continued.

> *Camp Santa Rosa, Tex. Oct. 6, 1879....* A few days ago a number of Mexicans settled down in a delapidated [*sic*] old ranch about a mile from camp.... I called on the new tenant. He had been bringing me milk for a shilling a quart...and suddenly went back on me.... I asked him why he did not bring me any more *"leche."* His answer was "Manana traere, senor," so I said "Bueno" and went on. This man has rented the ranch and a few acres of ground from Mr Frazier. The men with him are terribly poor. I saw one of them picking up rags and other rubbish on the former camping ground of Comp. L. All the Mexicans around here are in a deplorable condition.... I have seen them...go over....and pick up the corn that remained where the forage pile had stood. There were many cases of smallpox among the Mexican children when the Company first came out here....

DRIVEN TO POETRY

> I ordered a number of men punished...for not having their side lines on their horses while they were out grazing.... The neglect exhibited by the Non Com'd Officers in not reporting the delinquents annoys me a great deal more than does the neglect on the part of the men. While in the mood in which I wrote the foregoing remarks on colored soldiers I wrote:
>
> *A soldiers's likes and dislikes*
> To sit with his grub in a shady nook
> And curse the captain and curse the cook
> And damn the Army till every thing's blue,
> That's what a soldier *likes* to do.
>
> With empty canteen, with no grub in his sack,
> To dismount from a horse with a sore on its back
> And walk without rest for an hour or two,
> That's what a soldier *hates* to do.
>
> With his pay in his pocket and pistol in hand,
> To shoot and shout till he makes your hair stand,
> Or with his "dulcina" to dance the night through,
> That's what a soldier *likes* to do.

To wake in the morning with head very sore
On the cold hard stone of the guard house floor
And find he can't think where he was at tattoo,
That's what a soldier *hates* to do.
And, generally speaking, to draw their pay
And sleep all night and rest all day,
I don't know yours, but I tell you,
That's what *my* soldiers *like* to do.

WINDING DOWN

On October 7 Bigelow's only journal entry was inspired by rereading Hamley's *Operations of War*, from which he concluded that a study of the lives of successful leaders was of increasing importance in military training. Next, an October 10 entry examined Moreau's mistakes in his 1800 Danube Campaign. Then after a three-week hiatus he wrote that he had been drilling the men in firing so they would be proficient if the company should go after Indians. On November 12 he simply noted that "as soon as my horses shall be shod I shall be ready for another scout."

Before he could depart on the scout, however, he was abruptly ordered to West Point to replace Ranald Mackenzie's cousin, Lieutenant Rodgers, who Bigelow had predicted would not be "much liked" by his students. Consequently, as soon as a new commander arrived, Bigelow left.[28]

The next few weeks undoubtedly were hectic. After returning to Fort Stockton on November 25, he had to pack and ship his goods, inventory and transfer the company equipment and accounts, and perform his P.P.C. calls.[29] Thereafter he faced the four-hundred-mile stage trip to San Antonio, followed by whatever time he had to visit friends before commencing the week-long train ride back to New York. On January 1, 1880, the still young but now successfully tested lieutenant reported at West Point as an acting assistant professor of French, ending his initiation on the frontier.[30]

Epilogue

'77 Fades Away

The departure from Fort Stockton of Bigelow's eastbound stage signaled the end of his first phase as an officer in the Indian-fighting army. Among the memories to take with him were the deaths of his closest friend, Bob Safford, as well as three other classmates who also had exchanged the comforts of homes and families for lonely posts in the desolate West. Many other contemporaries went on to earn fame (if not fortune), while a few ended up less than gloriously.

THE FORT DUNCAN COTERIE

Among Bigelow's associates at Duncan, Maj. George Schofield was court-martialed later in 1878 for seeking a medical excuse to avoid sitting on a court-martial. He was acquitted, but in December 1882 killed himself with his Schofield Smith and Wesson.[1] A year after arriving at Stockton Captain Van de Wiele was retired for disability, and ten years later he died. Henry Landon resigned in 1880 to become a New York banker, and then-toothless Eddy Stivers retired in 1891. John Brereton married twice but both wives died, leaving a daughter in his care. In 1898 he was wounded on San Juan Hill, and the following year took his own life.[2] "Pecos Bill" Shafter, then a major general, headed the Cuban Expeditionary Force during the Spanish-American War, by which time he had ballooned up from 230 to around 300 pounds on his five-foot, eleven inch frame, which provided editorial cartoonists with a sizable target to caricature.

FORT STOCKTON'S FRIENDS AND FOES

Perhaps Edwin Glenn, somewhat listless as a post quartermaster, had just been conserving energy for later. In 1888 he became PMS&T at Minnesota where he also studied law and subsequently wrote leading legal textbooks.[3] In the Philippine Insurrection he gained notoriety in some circles and admiration elsewhere for his aggressiveness, which culminated in two courts-martial: one for ordering "water cures" for natives on Samar Island and the other for causing the execution of misleading guides.[4] Afterwards he served in a variety of legal assignments, led expeditions to Alaska, headed a regiment on the Mexican border, commanded the 83d Division in France as a major general, and received five honorary degrees.[5]

In 1894 John McMartin was convicted of being drunk on duty and dismissed, with President Cleveland noting that it was not a single lapse "but a tendency...very discouraging to any hope of reform."[6] Despite William Beck's egregious alcohol-related offenses, his dismissal was commuted to suspension. Apparently he took (and kept) "The Pledge," as he became a colonel during the war with Spain, later served in the Philippines, and was promoted to brigadier general a year before retiring in 1906. He died five years afterwards.[7] Robert Read also survived a bout with the bottle that led to his conviction for being drunk on duty. He, too, reformed, then remained on frontier duty until 1898 when he was sent to fight in Cuba and later in the Philippines, after which he was retired as a colonel for disability. Five years later he died.[8] Other than marrying Colonel Grierson's niece, "Oucks Bijoucks" Maxon did not have much more success in the army than he had as a French student. He was promoted to captain in 1889, but advanced no further after being retired for disabilty in 1891. From 1902 to 1911 he returned to active duty with ROTC detachments at the Universities of South Dakota and Arizona and was on recruiting duty in Cincinnati.[9] Matthew Blunt was promoted to colonel and served as commanding officer at other frontier forts before retiring in 1894.[10]

In 1879 and 1880, George Armes, one of the most vexatious officers to plague the frontier (or any other) army, survived two more courts-martial. Hayes reduced the dismissals adjudged in both to suspensions and forfeitures.[11] Finally, after twenty-three arrests, eight trials, and a sanity board, he was (in his opinion) "forcibly and arbitrarily" retired in 1883.[12]

Although Andrew Geddes' convictions involving the Orlemans were reversed, his army days were numbered. In 1880 he was tried at Fort Randall on eight allegations of drunkenness. Although convicted of only one, he finally (as Bigelow had hoped) was kicked out of the army.[13] There was more behind the case, however, than appears in the record of trial. In July 1880 Sherman sent General Terry a report that Geddes had fathered the child of a 10th Cavalry major's wife. Despite Sherman's reluctance "to touch" such a "dirty subject," he asked Terry to show the report to Geddes.[14] Perhaps preferring to be branded a drunkard instead of a lecher, he slithered away. In 1879 a retiring board found Louis Orleman incapable of further service, but he lived another fifty-six years before dying at age ninety-four.[15] What happened to Miss Lillie is unknown.

John Clous, the "Dutchman" who prosecuted Geddes, Beck, and (on more than one occasion) Armes, completed formal law studies. During the Spanish-American War he was a brigadier general and then served briefly as judge advocate general before retiring in 1901.

WARRIORS IN BLUE

Because of his transfer to West Point, Bigelow found his role in the Victorio Campaign was limited, but numerous classmates and other friends continued to clash intermittently with that fierce libertarian. From September 1879 to October 1880 thirty-five battles occurred. Ninth Cavalry troops were involved in sixteen, the 10th in twelve, and the Indian scouts in almost all.

After Las Animas Canyon, a five-week pursuit of Victorio culminated in the Guzman Mountains of Mexico where Charles Gatewood distinguished himself in close combat.[16] Eleven weeks afterwards Victorio returned to New Mexico. Seven fights took place between January and early April when in Hembrillo Canyon of the San Andres Victorio's small but tenacious band was pitted against five 9th Cavalry companies and Indian Scouts led by Gatewood, James Maney, Stephan Mills (all of '77), Timothy Touey ('76), and Thomas Cruse ('79). But for a fluke that enabled Victorio to escape, the uprising might have ended then and there.

As the Apaches dispersed, Colonel Grierson and five 10th Cavalry companies were on their way to help disarm the Mescaleros, who were providing reinforcements as well as succor to Victorio. While en route K Company, with Robert Reed, found some Indians at Shakehand Spring.

They killed one warrior and captured eight women and some twenty horses.[17] After attempting to disarm the Mescaleros, the 10th returned to Texas to patrol between the Rio Grande and New Mexico and guard the water holes. That May Calvin Esterly led a detachment on a chase of horse thieves from Stockton toward the Mescalero Reservation. After three days and 220 miles (90 without water) he caught up with his quarry, killed one raider, and recovered eight horses.[18]

In the meantime, Victorio returned to Mexico, but in July he again crossed into Texas in an effort to reach New Mexico. On July 30 Grierson, Beck, and about twenty men waited behind rocks on a ridge near a minor water hole in Quitman Canyon as a large force of Apaches approached. After an almost two-hour firefight, Viele's company arrived, then an hour later the Indians withdrew as Nicholas Nolan and Henry Flipper approached with Company A.[19]

During the first week of August there were five other engagements in Texas, including a skirmish in the Guadalupes near Camp Safford, named after Bigelow's friend. And on August 6 at Rattlesnake Springs, after a gruelling sixty-five-mile march from 3 a.m. until midnight, Grierson and Companies B, C, G, and H ambushed and inflicted a severe blow on Victorio's waning forces.

In October 1880 Victorio was killed by Mexican troops, but the Apache problem lasted another half dozen years. Among the recurring confrontations was one at Horseshoe Canyon, New Mexico, in 1882, when David McDonald, six scouts, and two soldiers held off an estimated 150 Apaches until 4th Cavalry troops arrived.[20] During that battle Wilber Wilder was awarded the Medal of Honor for rescuing a wounded comrade.[21]

Of all the members of '77 in the Apache campaigns none was as involved or performed more valiantly than Gatewood, not only in the Victorio Campaign but later against Geronimo. In the latter he risked his life by entering Geronimo's camp where after two days he persuaded him to surrender. Regardless, he never received much recognition, despite (or because of) his assignment from 1886 until 1890 as aide to Nelson Miles, a competent but vain and ambitious officer disposed to self-aggrandizement.[22] In 1892 Gatewood was seriously injured at Fort McKinney while trying to blow up a burning barracks. He died four years later, still only a first lieutenant.[23] Like Gatewood, Augustus Blocksom was in the Victorio fracases from the outset, and also took part in the 1890-1891 Sioux Campaign. He was wounded at San Juan Hill in 1898, and in 1900 was involved in the Boxer Rebellion, receiving Silver Stars in both conflicts. He then participated in the Philippine Insurrection, and as a major general in World War I commanded the 34th Division.[24]

Matthias Day, seemingly born to fight, took part in ten battles and countless scouts. After Las Animas Canyon he headed an assault in the Guzmáns, then organized stragglers and the sick to capture a hill. The next January he led two successful charges near Percha Creek, and in 1885 he and his scouts attacked Geronimo's stronghold in the Sierra Madres. In Cuba he headed a volunteer cavalry regiment, later fought the Moros in the Philippines, and then went to sea with the "Bamboo Fleet" chasing Fikara pirates. In 1912 he retired as a colonel.[25] The unpretentious Robert Emmet resigned after twelve years on the frontier to manage a large estate in New York, but returned to duty during the Spanish-American War.[26]

Capt. Charles Beyer and Lt. William Hugo had checkered military careers, raising a question of whether their future conduct might have been predicted by their unseemly haste in withdrawing from action at Las Animas. In 1881 Hugo was dismissed for drunkenness and dereliction of duty, and in 1884 Beyer was dismissed for misappropriating troop funds.[27]

In 1893 James Maney killed his company commander, Capt. Alfred Hedberg.[28] A federal district court acquitted him of manslaughter, but the following year he was court-martialed for having kicked and shot Hedberg, using insulting language toward him, and sending him a disrespectful letter.[29] Failing to obtain a writ of prohibition, the defense unsuccessfully moved to dismiss, arguing that the court-martial lacked jurisdiction and that former jeopardy barred trial.[30] Maney was convicted of disrespect but acquitted of the other charges on grounds of self-defense. The sentence, however, was merely a reprimand.[31] Thereafter he campaigned for seven years in Cuba, China, and the Philippines before retiring as a colonel in 1911.

Henry Ossian Flipper might have attained greatness if he had not lied to conceal a shortage of commissary funds at Fort Davis. In 1881 (with Clous prosecuting and Capt. Merritt Barber defending) he faced trial for allegedly embezzling $3,791.99 and making five false official statements.[32]

As "commissary of subsistence" Flipper was required to exhibit weekly whatever government funds he had (in cash and checks from sales) and submit a written report, then send the funds and report to department headquarters. Among the funds he showed Shafter on July 2 was a $1,440.43 check he had drawn on a bank in which he did not have an account. Then on July 8 Shafter, informed that nothing had been received at San Antonio, told Flipper to send the amounts due. He prepared a report, which he gave to Shafter, stating that $3,791.99 was in transit. It was not. Similar false reports were made on July 16 and 23 but never mailed. Learning that nothing had arrived, on August 10 Shafter asked Flipper about it and was told, "I did mail those checks just as I have told you."[33] He had not.

The defense vigorously and successfully contested the embezzlement, but the false official statements were another matter. Although Flipper elected not to testify (thereby avoiding cross-examination), he read an unsworn statement in which he implicitly admitted lying.[34] With respect to the $1,440 check he even told Shafter that "I had to deceive you in some way...and I took that way to do it." Essentially, his defense amounted to thinking he would receive money to cover the shortage, fearing Shafter too much to admit carelessness, and having no one in whom to confide.[35] Notwithstanding, Flipper was convicted of all five misrepresentations and, as required by law, sentenced to dismissal.[36] His career ended on June 30, 1882.

Commencing in the late 1890s numerous petitions and bills urging reinstatement were submitted to Congress, but the evidence of guilt was overwhelming.[37] Flipper's inexperience, apprehension of Shafter, and naive trust in others might have been factors in his efforts to conceal the shortages, but he alone compromised his honor.[38] He later had an illustrious civilian career before his death in 1940. In 1966 the Army Board for the Correction of Military Records changed his discharge from dismissal (dishonorable) to honorable. However, while this removed the effects of the conviction, it could not alter the fact.[39] Nevertheless, Flipper's otherwise exemplary achievements clearly marked a path for other African Americans to follow.[40]

After surviving Milk Creek, Sam Cherry soon had his life snuffed out. In 1881 four soldiers deserted from Fort Niobrara and assaulted some citizens in a dance hall about ten miles away, killing one man and wounding another.[41] Cherry, heading a small detachment, was sent in pursuit. As he and a sergeant rode side-by-side followed by two privates, a shot rang out. Wheeling around, they saw a soldier named Thomas Locke holding a pistol. He promptly sent a bullet through Cherry's heart, then shot the other private. The sergeant fled in one direction and Locke, who was never located nor his reasons determined, went elsewhere.[42]

Another survivor of Milk Creek, the intrepid Sgt. Henry Johnson, who risked his life to obtain water for the parched defenders, remained with the 9th Cavalry until he retired in 1898. Seemingly his thirst was never fully quenched, for in 1889 at Fort Robinson he was reduced from sergeant to private for using abusive language toward a bartender who told him that he could not have any more beer. He retired from the army in 1898, died in 1904, and now rests in Arlington National Cemetery.[43]

THE SAN ANTONIO "SET"

In 1880 Ord's eldest daughter Roberta ("Bertie"), then twenty-three, married Gerónimo Treviño, a 41-year-old Mexican general. Treviño, commander of the forces south of the border, apparently was equally successful on the croquet courts—or unlike Bigelow at least was willing to play the game.[44]

Edward O. C. Ord was involuntarily retired in late 1880 to make way for the promotion of Nelson Miles, which was possible only if one of the six active brigadiers was eliminated.[45] Hayes' desire to placate Miles' political allies at the expense of the army's effectiveness enraged Sherman, demoralized other officers, and disappointed most Texans, none of which seemed to bother the insouciant president, who soon left office.[46] While traveling to Mexico by steamer in 1883 Ord contracted yellow fever, disembarked in Cuba, and died.

In December 1883 Ranald Mackenzie became commander of the Department of Texas. He also planned to marry within a few days, but before then his suddenly bizarre behavior, which involved drinking and public brawling, caused him to be taken to the Bloomingdale Asylum in New York for evaluation.[47] The following March a Retiring Board heard testimony that he suffered from "general paralysis of the insane" and was unlikely to recover. Despite his haunting plea that "I would rather die than go on the retired list—the Army is all I have got to care for," the board found him incapacitated for further service.[48] That June he was released to his sister on Staten Island. In 1889 his tormented existence ended.[49]

After General Ord retired, William Howard became aide for Brig. Gen. Christopher C. Augur and acting judge advocate for the Department of Texas. In 1881 the "severe mental strain" of his legal duties and the climate of San Antonio caused him to be placed on sick leave. He returned to South Carolina where he remained until his death in 1888 from "softening of the brain."[50] The maladroit Lt. William James, who was "gone on" Minnie Moore, remained a forlorn bachelor after she went the other way. He served in Cuba and the Philippines, then retired in 1903.

In 1886 Minnie's father, Dr. John Moore, became the army's surgeon general. Minnie married Capt. William A. Thompson of the 4th Cavalry. Thompson, an older man, had not been among the entourage of Minnie's aspiring suitors, but he might have won her affections when he was sent to the New York Cavalry Rendezvous in the fall in 1879.[51] He was aide-de-camp to Nelson Miles during the final phase of the Geronimo Campaign, in which Minnie played a small but significant role. As the end of Chiricahua resistance neared, President Cleveland planned to turn the Apaches over to Arizona authorities for trial, but Miles, claiming he was not fully informed of what terms he might accept, told Gatewood to assure the renegades that they would be held in Florida with their families. After Geronimo and his band were brought to Fort Bowie, where Minnie was living, Miles and Thompson departed with the prisoners for Bowie Station, thirteen miles away. Shortly after they left, a telegram arrived from Washington directing that the prisoners not be removed. Minnie could have had the message transmitted to the railroad station by telegraph, assuring that it would arrive in time to prevent the movement east. But knowing that Miles did not want to hold the Apaches at Bowie, she instead sent the telegram by courier, enabling Geronimo to be shipped out before it arrived. Her accolade from Miles was, "Minnie, you are a smart woman."[52]

A furious President Cleveland had the train stopped in San Antonio, demanded an explanation from Miles, and threatened to have the Indians returned to Arizona. He relented, but two years later when a vacancy for major general occurred, the promotion went to George Crook, who died in 1890. Minnie's husband never advanced beyond the rank of major before retiring in 1897. In the meantime Miles became commanding general of the army in 1895; he fell short, though, of realizing his presidential ambitions. After heading the Puerto Rico Expedition in 1898, he retired in 1903 but thereafter lived another twenty-two years.

Bigelow's journal entries with respect to his "engagement" are so enigmatic that any conclusion as to whether he ever was engaged to marry—and if so whom—would be conjectural. There is little doubt that he had been interested in both Bertie Ord and Minnie Moore until Georgie Grimshaw entered his life. What happened to their relationship remains a mystery. After his abrupt departure for West Point, Bigelow apparently did not resume his journal until September 1881. What is more, despite efforts to learn what became of Miss Grimshaw, she seems to have vanished without a trace.

"JUST KEEP UP THE CHARGE"

After reporting to West Point, Bigelow taught French and Tactics. In 1883 the following item appeared in the *Army and Navy Journal*:

> The marriage of Lieut. John Bigelow, Jr., 10th U.S. Cavalry, to Miss Mary Dallam took place at the residence of the bride's father at Baltimore on Saturday, April 28. Miss Dallam is a daughter of Judge H. C. Dallam, and the groom is the son of the Honorable John Bigelow. Lieutenant Bigelow has taken his bride to West Point, his present post of duty, the requirements of the Military Academy at this season not permitting a lengthened absence. His brother, Mr. Poultney Bigelow, was best man.[53]

Bigelow returned to the West with Mary in 1884. He was assigned to K Troop, 10th Cavalry, at Fort Davis until the following April, then at Fort Grant, where he conducted extensive scouts during the Geronimo Campaign. His journal of these experiences was published serially in Poultney Bigelow's Outing magazine between March 1886 and April 1887 under the title, "After Geronimo," with sketches by Frederic Remington, Poultney's then-obscure artist friend and Yale classmate.[54]

In 1887 Bigelow was assigned to Washington, then in 1890 he returned to Fort Grant, serving there and at Fort Assiniboine until 1894 when he became PMS&T at the Massachusetts Institute of Technology. In 1898 he was able to rejoin his regiment just before it departed for Cuba. Most of the officers he knew at Forts Duncan and Stockton had transferred, resigned, retired or died, but a few remained. Thomas Baldwin, then a lieutenant colonel, was the regimental commander. Major Norvell

MARY BIGELOW

Leaving several attractive and interesting young ladies behind him in San Antonio, Bigelow married Mary Dallam, the daughter of a Baltimore judge. (Courtesy Fort Davis National Historic Site)

JOHN BIGELOW, JR.

A photograph taken when he was about thirty years old. (Courtesy Fort Davis National Historic Site)

headed the 1st Squadron, and Captains William Beck, Charles Ayers, Thad Jones, Levi Hunt, and Robert Reed were all troop (formerly known as company) commanders, as was Bigelow.

Less than a month elapsed from the time the United States forces (which included all four African American regiments) landed in Cuba in late June 1898 until the enemy surrendered on July 14. The 10th Cavalry, along with the 1st U.S. Cavalry and Lt. Col. Theodore Roosevelt's 1st Volunteer Cavalry (the "Rough Riders," some of whom had been recruited in the Menger Hotel bar), constituted the Cavalry Division's Second Brigade, which was in the thick of the fighting.[55] The principal battles occurred at three locations within a few miles of Santiago de Cuba: Las Guasimas (where 10th Cavalry troops helped save the inexperienced and militarily inept Rough Riders from annihilation), El Caney, and the infamous San Juan Hill.[56]

On July 1, in conjunction with the First Cavalry Brigade and six infantry regiments, the Second Brigade launched a dismounted attack on the enemy's blockhouses atop San Juan Heights. As commander of D Troop, Bigelow, together with General Ord's son, 1st Lt. Jules Ord, led their soldiers on an almost fanatical charge up the steep slope into the enemy's blistering fire.[57] Bigelow was soon shot, but being unaware of it he continued forward until about midway up the hill when he fell, pierced almost simultaneously by three more Spanish bullets. A participant remembers him imploring, "Men, don't stop to bother with me, just keep up the charge until you get to the top of the hill."[58] They did, led by their NCOs and the only remaining officer, Jules Ord, who was shot in the throat as they routed the Spaniards. Ord's dying utterance was, "If we had the rest of the Tenth Cavalry here, we could capture this whole command."[59]

On that one day and at that one place, one-half of 10th's officers and one-fifth of its soldiers became casualties.[60] Bigelow, who was awarded the Silver Star for gallantry, was hospitalized and on sick leave until October. First Lt. John J. Pershing, the 10th Cavalry's quartermaster, became temporary commander of D Troop.[61] Pershing, a taciturn person, subsequently said, "We officers of the Tenth Cavalry could have taken our black heroes in our arms. They had again fought their way into our affections, as they here had fought their way into the hearts of the American people."[62] Bigelow echoed this appraisal when he wrote:

> The officers of the colored regiments are not surprised at the way their men behaved in battle. They knew that the colored troops would do their duty. Had they not seen them, in Indian campaigns, march and fight, go hungry and thirsty, and as scouts and guides carry their lives in their hands across weird, silent wastes of curling grass and chaparral, through gloomy, resounding canyons, and over wild crags and mountain-tops, as if they did not know what fear was.[63]

Other lavish praise was heaped on the African American soldiers and numerous poetic tributes were written, including an anonymous one titled simply, "The Fighting Tenth."

> There wasn't any color line
> At San Juan that day;
> They didn't look so very fine,
> It was their dogged way
> Of going straight where duty led
> That made their record bright;
> A nation cheered them when they said:
> "We're simply here to fight."
>
> And many a happy man has grasped
> Again the sable hand
> Whose rifle, resolutely clasped,
> Answered to each command.
> And many a heart bereft would pine
> Were it not just to say
> "There wasn't any color line
> At San Juan that day."[64]

Moreover, thirty African Americans received commissions in volunteer regiments for their performances.[65] Six were from the 10th Cavalry, including William Givens, who years before had struck the obstinate Private Harris on the arm with a scoop shovel. Over many years of hard service together on the frontier, the mutual respect, trust, and friendship between the white officer and the black NCO were demonstrated on San Juan Hill. After Bigelow fell, Givens, then first sergeant, courageously led D Troop the rest of the way up that hazardous slope. Bigelow wrote that in doing so he "conducted himself like the thorough soldier which I have long known him to be." That he did.[66]

When Bigelow resumed active duty he was in Alabama and then back in Cuba before going to Fort Clark in 1899. That August he declined a lieutenant colonelcy in a volunteer regiment to remain with the 10th. For the next three years he investigated Spanish war claims in Cuba, after which he went to Fort Robinson, followed by Ord Barracks and the Presidio of San Francisco. In 1904 he became superintendent of Yosemite National Park, and that September he retired.

From 1905 until 1910 Bigelow was professor of French and head of the Department of Modern Languages at MIT. Afterwards he devoted himself to studying strategy, tactics, and international relations, and to writing several books.[67] During World War I he volunteered for active duty and until 1919 served as a lieutenant colonel in Washington, at Rutgers as PMS&T, and in the War Department's Historical Branch.

He and Mary suffered a devastating loss in 1917 when their only son, Braxton, a captain of the British Royal Engineers, was killed in action near Loos. John died in Washington, D.C., in 1936 at age eighty-one. Mary as well as a daughter, Jane, and one granddaughter, Joan Benjamin, survived him.[68]

'77 FADES AWAY

Despite the often harsh conditions and intermittent jeopardy under which most members of the Class of 1877 spent much of their lives, fifteen of the seventy-six graduates outlived Bigelow. Between 1877 and 1891 four-fifths of the class had participated in the Frontier Indian Wars, and many served in one or more of the nation's subsequent conflicts, including the Spanish-American War, the Boxer Rebellion, the Philippine Insurrection, the Mexican Punitive Expedition, and World War I. Thirteen died on active duty, and thirteen were retired for disability because of severe wounds or service-incurred illnesses. Hence, few experienced for long the "seductive influence of peace" that Professor Thompson predicted would be their burden when as eager young men they exchanged cadet grey for army blue.

Seven who graduated in 1877 became generals, and twenty-three attained the rank of colonel. Eight served as faculty members at the Military Academy, four as tactical officers, and one as superintendent. Thirteen others were PMS&Ts of ROTC units at various civilian colleges and universities. Among those who pursued civilian careers, four became lawyers, one a university president, one a governor, one a school superintendent, and others were journalists, civil engineers, educators, stockmen, legislators, or businessmen.

DID THEY MATTER?

The members of the Class of 1877 and, with rare exception, most officers were true patriots who sacrificed their youth, their opportunities to live in comfort, and in some cases their lives on the altar of uncomprising integrity, loyalty, discipline, courage, and perseverance. They placed country before self, and when their course was run could leave knowing that they had done their duty.

Regardless of how "manifest destiny" and the nation's westward expansion might be viewed by some today, the services rendered by Bigelow and his friends helped tame the frontier, thereby facilitating the migration of pioneers seeking better lives and leading the United States farther down the road to international preeminence.[69] Also, the thin blue line contributed to American society in many other ways. For example, the eventual integration of black with white troops, which Bigelow anticipated, might have been delayed even longer than 1948 but for the respect and acceptance that the once-downtrodden ex-slaves earned as soldiers on the Plains and in Cuba.[70]

Within the army, deficiencies magnified by situations encountered in the wilderness spawned numerous changes. Commencing in 1881 with Sherman's founding of a School of Application for Infantry and Cavalry at Fort Leavenworth, military training took on entirely new meaning as basic branch schools became prerequisites for initial assignments of second lieutenants, and post-graduate command and staff schools, war colleges for each of the armed forces, and the National Defense University were created to enhance professionalism and the effectiveness of commanders and staff officers.[71] Additionally, enlisted service grew far more attractive as significant improvements were made in living conditions (including the introduction of centralized messes and trained cooks), treatment, and educational opportunities.

The reform in military justice also traces its origin to the experiences from that era. General Sherman's tenacity in urging modernization of the outmoded system was partially rewarded shortly before he died by creation of summary courts-martial, the first major innovation in military jurisprudence since the nation won its independence.[72] Other significant advances followed in the 1890s, the 1920s, the 1950 enactment of the Uniform Code of Military Justice and the promulgation of a new Manual for Courts-Martial, and since then through various amendments, executive orders, and decisions of military appellate courts.[73] As a result the criminal law system in the United States Army, Navy, and Air Force progressed far ahead of that in the civilian sector, which one of the nation's foremost defense counsels, F. Lee Bailey, recognized when he wrote:

> [I]f I were innocent, I would far prefer to stand trial before a military tribunal...than by any court, state or federal. I suppose that if I were guilty and hoping [for] an acquittal or to create a reasonable doubt in the face of muddled evidence, I would be fearful of a military court because their accuracy in coming to the "correct" result...[is] far better...than any civilian court has even approached.[74]

EPITAPH

When John Bigelow wrote Robert Read's obituary, he unwittingly provided a fitting epitaph for all of those who devoted so much to their country on the now-vanished frontier:

> [L]ong and faithful performance of duty, sometimes arduous and dangerous, generally monotonous, and rarely, if ever, glorious or thrilling, has become a common thing in the traditions of the Army.[75]

Appendices

Appendix A

Abbrevations

AAAG:	Acting Assistant Adjutant General
AAG:	Assistant Adjutant General
Adj't:	Adjutant
AGO:	Adjutant General's Office
ANJ:	Army and Navy Journal
AOG:	Association of Graduates, USMA
Art'y:	Artillery
AW:	Article(s) of War
AWOL:	Absent without leave
BCMR:	Board for the Correction of Military Records
Cav:	Cavalry
CG:	Commanding General
CE:	Corps of Engineers
CM:	Court-martial
Co:	Company
Comp:	"
Comd't:	Commandant
Com'd't:	"
Corp'l:	Corporal
Cpl:	"
Ev'g:	Evening
GarCM:	Garrison court-martial
GCMO:	General Court-Martial Orders
G'd:	Guard
GO:	General Order
GPO:	Government Printing Office
Inf:	Infantry
JSMI:	Journal of the Military Service Institution

LC:	Library of Congress
MCM:	Manual for Courts-Martial
M'ch:	March
M'g:	Morning
Mt'g:	Mounting
NARA:	National Archives and Records Administration
NC:	Noncommissioned
Off:	Officer
OpJAGAF:	Opinion of The Judge Advocate General, USAF
PMS&T:	Professor of Military Science and Tactics
P.P.C.:	Pour prendre congé (to take leave)
QM:	Quartermaster
QtrMstr:	"
Qrs:	Quarters
RG:	Record Group (at NARA)
ROTC:	Reserve Officers' Training Corps
SecWar:	Secretary of War
Sgt:	Sergeant
SO:	Special Order
UCMJ:	Uniform Code of Military Justice
USMA:	United States Military Academy
WD:	War Department

Appendix B

USMA Class of 1877

		Appointed From	Assigned To
1.	Black, William Murray	PA	CE
2.	Fisk, Walter Leslie	IA	CE
3.	Roessler, Solomon William	IL	CE
4.	Patterson, Thomas Calvin	PA	1st Art'y
5.	Todd, Albert	KS	1st Art'y
6.	Gordon, William Brandon	PA	4th Art'y
7.	Springett, Howard Abraham	OH	4th Art'y
8.	Galbraith, William Watts	PA	5th Art'y
9.	Massey, Solon Frederick	NY	5th Art'y
10.	Haden, John January	MO	8th Inf
11.	Woodward, Charles Gwinn	MD	3d Art'y
12.	Slaker, Adam	IL	1st Art'y
13.	White, John Vasser	MS	1st Art'y
14.	Marsh, Frederick	MO	2d Art'y
15.	Price, David Jr.	IA	1st Art'y
16.	Blair, Francis Preston Jr.	MO	3d Art'y
17.	Shofner, James Clayton	TN	21st Inf
18.	Foster, Fred Waldron	NY	5th Cav
19.	Parker, Theophilus	NC	8th Inf
20.	Plummer, Edward Hinkley	MD	10th Inf
21.	Martin, Medac Chapman	VT	22d Inf
22.	Blocksom, Augustus Perry	OH	6th Cav
23.	Gatewood, Charles Bare	VA	6th Cav
24.	Galbraith, Jacob Garretson	PA	1st Cav
25.	Murray, Cunliffe Hall	NY	4th Cav
26.	Wilson, Richard Hulbert	MI	8th Inf
27.	Esterly, Calvin	OH	10th Cav
28.	Chynoweth, Edward	WI	17th Inf
29.	Patten, Francis Jarvis	ME	21st Inf
30.	Philbrick, John Herbert	ME	11th Inf
31.	Goldman, Henry Joseph	NY	5th Cav
32.	Wilder, Wilber Elliott	MI	4th Cav
33.	Thorington, Monroe Parker	IA	5th Inf
34.	Paddock, James V. Seaman	IL	5th Cav
35.	Hoppin, Curtis Bushrod	NY	2d Cav
36.	Mann, James Defrees	IN	7th Cav
37.	Stevens, Robert Ratcliff	TX	6th Inf
38.	Kirby, Henry	NC	10th Inf
39.	Barry, Thomas Henry	NY	7th Cav
40.	Guilfoyle, John Francis	MD	9th Cav

41.	Brown, William Carey	MN	1st Cav
42.	Wood, William Thomas	IL	18th Inf
43.	Safford, Robert Eliel	OH	10th Cav
44.	Crane, Charles Judson	TX	24th Inf
45.	Hammond, Harry Truett	CA	9th Cav
46.	Bigelow, John Jr.	NY	10th Cav
47.	Augur, Ammon Arthur	MI	24th Inf
48.	Baxter, George White	TN	5th Cav
49.	Bradley, Charles Allen	IL	9th Cav
50.	Flipper, Henry Ossian	GA	10th Cav
51.	Brereton, John James	NJ	24th Inf
52.	Brown, Oscar James	GA	1st Cav
53.	Emmet, Robert Temple	NY	9th Cav
54.	Butler, Benjamin Israel	MA	9th Cav
55.	McMartin, John	NY	25th Inf
56.	Read, Robert Doddridge, Jr.	TN	10th Cav
57.	Wayman, Samuel Pierce	KY	24th Inf
58.	Glenn, Edwin Forbes	NC	25th Inf
59.	Mills, Stephen Crosby	IL	12th Inf
60.	Chase, George Nathan	WI	4th Inf
61.	Eggleston, Millard Fillmore	IN	10th Cav
62.	Baldwin, William Herbert	PA	7th Cav
63.	Baxter, John Elston	NJ	9th Inf
64.	Creel, Heber Mansfield	MO	7th Cav
65.	Jackson, James Berryman	KY	7th Inf
66.	Patch, Alexander McCarrell	PA	4th Cav
67.	Hunter, George King	OH	4th Cav
68.	Frederick, Daniel Alfred	GA	7th Inf
69.	Clark, Wallis Olwin	MA	6th Cav
70.	Day, Matthis Walter	OH	10th Cav
71.	Loder, Samuel Howard	NJ	7th Inf
72.	McDonald, David Newton	TN	4th Cav
73.	Maney, James Alison	TN	15th Inf
74.	Hegewald, John F. C.	IN	15th Inf
75.	McCrimmon, Ariosto	GA	13th Inf
76.	French, Frederick Halverson	VA	3d Cav

APPENDIX C

Organization of Cavalry and Infantry Regiments and Companies, 1880

Cavalry			Infantry	
10 Regt's (each)	12 Co's (each)		25 Regt's (each)	10 Co's (each)
1	0	Colonel	1	0
1	0	Lt Col	1	0
3	0	Major	1	0
1	0	Adjutant*	1	0
1	0	QtrMstr*	1	0
12	1	Captain	10	1
12	1	1st Lt	10	1
12	1	2d Lt	10	1
1	0	Chaplain**	1	0
1	0	Sgt Maj	1	0
1	0	QM Sgt	1	0
1	0	Chief Musician	1	0
1	0	Saddler Sgt	0	0
1	0	Chief Trumpeter	0	0
12	1	1st Sgt	10	1
60	5	Sergeant	40	4
48	4	Corporal	40	4
24	2	Trumpeter	0	0
0	0	Musician	20	2
24	2	Farrier	0	0
12	1	Saddler	0	0
12	1	Wagoneer	10	1
600	50	Private	360	36
44	3	Total Off'rs	36	3
797	66	Total Enl'd	483	48
841	69	Aggregate	519	51

* Extra lieutenants.

**Each African American regiment had a chaplain; the other 30 were assigned to posts instead of regiments.

Appendix D

Monthly Pay of Officers in Late 1870s

Rank (No.)	<5 years	>5 yrs	>10 yrs	>15 yrs	>20 yrs
General(1)	1,125.00	+10%	+20%	+30%	+40%
Lt Gen(1)	916.67	"	"	"	"
Maj Gen(3)	625.00	"	"	"	"
Brig Gen(6)	458.33	"	"	"	"
Colonel(49)	291.67	320.83	350.00	375.00	375.00
Lt Col(57)	250.00	275.00	300.00	325.00	333.33
Major(104)	208.33	229.17	250.00	270.83	291.67
Capt*(480)	166.67	183.33	200.00	216.67	233.33
Capt**	150.00	165.00	180.00	195.00	210.00
1st Lt*(532)	133.33	146.67	160.00	173.33	186.67
1st Lt**	125.00	137.50	150.00	162.50	175.00
2nd Lt*(449)	125.00	137.50	150.00	162.50	175.00
2nd Lt**	116.67	128.33	140.00	151.67	162.33
Chaplain(34)	125.00	137.50	150.00	162.50	175.00

*Mounted
**Not mounted (numbers of officers are for both categories)
Compensation consisted of two components: "pay" and "allowances." Pay might be increased if an officer was assigned certain duties; for example, an aide-de-camp to a major general received an additional $200 a year, and a "commissary of subsistence" was allowed $100 (*Act of July 15, 1870*, sec. 24; Rev. Stat., sec. 1261). The 1870 Appropriations Act increased the basic pay of all officers in order to eliminate some of the maze of allowances, but entitlements to fuel, quarters (housing), and forage were retained. The 1879 Appropriations Act rescinded the fuel allowance but permitted firewood to be purchased from the quartermaster, and if quarters were not provided approved commutation of up to $10 per room for the number of rooms authorized an officer (which depended on rank, with four rooms for a colonel and one for a lieutenant). Also, the number of horses for which forage could be provided was reduced to two for mounted lieutenants through colonels and three for general officers (Sec. 8 and 9, *Act of June 18, 1878*, 20 Stats. 145). See Adjutant General's Office, *Legislative History of the General Staff* (Washington: GPO, 1901), pp. 11–48.

Monthly Pay of Enlisted Men in Late 1870s: Cavalry and Infantry

			1st enlistment***			1st	2d & later
Rank	Yr 1	2	3	4	5	Re-enlsmt	Re-enlsmts
Private	$13	$13	$14	$15	$16	$2/mo. more	$1/mo. more
Corporal	15	15	16	17	18	during next	during each
Sergeant	17	17	18	19	20	5 years	subsequent
1st Sgt	22	22	23	24	25		enlistment

***From years three through five $1, $2, and $3 a month, respectively, was retained, and thereafter $1 a month, to be paid on discharge. Hence, the sums actually received in first enlistments were those indicated for the first year. Wagoneers and artificers (who received $15 and $17 monthly for their first five years) were exempt. Musicians & trumpeters were paid as privates, and farriers, blacksmiths, and saddlers as corporals.

As with officers, the pay of enlisted men performing certain duties was increased. For example, a post ordnance sergeant received $34 a month, or twice the sum paid other sergeants during their initial two years of service. For a comprehensive view of enlisted pay and problems, see Coffman, *The Old Army*, pp. 346–50.

Appendix E

HEADQUARTERS DEPARTMENT OF TEXAS
San Antonio, Texas, May 4, 1878
General Orders)
No. 9)

The following extracts from orders and instructions, relative to the crossing of United States troops into Mexico, in pursuit of marauders, have been compiled from the original official communications, and are promulgated for the information and guidance of all concerned:

[The secretary of war's letter of June 1, 1877, to the General of the Army, is first set forth. It commences with "The President desires that the utmost vigilance on the part of the military forces in Texas be exercised for the suppression of...raids...[and] he is...convinced that the invasion of our territory by armed and organized bodies of thieves and robbers, to prey upon our citizens, should not be longer endured."

The secretary's directive is followed by General Ord's letter of June 9, 1877, to the commanding officer of the District of the Rio Grande, which states]:

The Brigadier General Commanding...directs that you confer with the Mexican authorities and invite co-operation. Local Mexican authorities will be notified in every instance, when practicable, of our troops crossing into Mexico...; and such authorities will be furnished with particulars of the raid...to enable them, when practicable, to co-operate in the capture of the robbers, and return of stolen property.

Military commanders, while on Mexican soil, will maintain discipline and prevent injury to persons or property of peaceable citizens, by prompt execution of sentences of military commissions, when such may become necessary, or by such other summary action as may be called for. Supplies will, in all cases, be paid for in cash, and every means taken to cultivate the most friendly relations with the local authorities or with commanders of any troops, which may be sent to co-operate with those of the United States.

As the parties, who have been committing the raids, are either bandits and enemies of civilization in both countries, wild Indians, who live in the mountains, remote from settlements—at times in Mexico and at other times in the United States—and who commit raids on either side, as opportunity offers, the same courtesy* and co-operation will be extended to Mexican troops, who may, when in pursuit of such raiders, cross into the United States...when operating on their side of the river.

United States troops will not remain beyond the border any longer than absolutely necessary to carry out the orders of the Secretary of War....

*This courtesy and co-operation...(is not) applicable to revolutionists....

BY COMMAND OF BRIGADIER GENERAL ORD:
Thomas M. Vincent
Assistant Adjutant General

Endnotes

PROLOGUE

1. Bigelow's journals from mid-October 1877 until mid-February 1878, and from early February 1879 until mid-November 1879, are in the Manuscript Collections of the U. S. Military Academy; those from February 20, 1878, through January 3, 1879, are among the holdings of the Schaffer Library of Union College, Schenectady, New York.

2. After graduating from Union College in 1835 and practicing law, the senior Bigelow, an outspoken abolitionist, became editor and co-owner of the *New York Evening Post.* In 1862 Lincoln named him ambassador to France, where he is credited with preventing the French from assisting the Confederacy. He later persuaded Napoleon III to abandon imperialism in Mexico, and in 1867 he negotiated the French army's withdrawal from there. After a term as New York's secretary of state he retired to pursue literary interests, but with close friends such as Andrew Carnegie he remained influential throughout his life. *New York Times,* December 20, 1911, p. 9, and March 1, 1936, p. 10; Dumas Malone, ed., *Dictionary of American Biography,* vol. 1 (New York: Scribner's Sons, 1936), pp. 258, 259; see John Bigelow, Sr., *Retrospections of an Active Life,* 3 vols. (New York: Baker and Taylor Co., 1909).

3. Edward M. Coffman, *The Old Army: A Portrait of the Army in Peacetime, 1784–1898* (New York: Oxford Univ. Press, 1986), p. 250; Russell Weigley, *History of the United States Army* (New York: MacMillan Co., 1967), p. 271.

4. Francis B. Heitman, *Historical Register and Dictionary of the United States Army,* vol. 2 (Washington: GPO, 1903) (hereafter Heitman); *1936 Annual Report, Association of Graduates of the U.S. Military Academy* (Newburgh, NY: Moore, 1930), pp. 103, 104 (hereafter *AOG Report* for a particular year, by various publishers); William H. Powell, *List of Officers of the Army of the United States from 1779 to 1900* (New York: Hamersly, 1900).

5. Bigelow's order of merit declined from eighteen out of one hundred (including first in French and fifteenth in mathematics) his first year to the bottom quarter his final year. *Official Registers of the Officers and Cadets of the U.S. Military Academy for 1874–1877.*

CHAPTER 1

1. Morris Janowitz, *The Professional Soldier* (New York: Free Press, 1960), p. 127 (hereafter Janowitz).

2. See P. S. Michie, "Education in Its Relation to the Military Profession," *Journal of the Military Service Institution* (hereafter *JMSI*) 1, pp. 154–84 at 155, 156. At the beginning of 1879 there were 2,126 officers; 829 were West Point graduates, 1,123 from civilian life, and 174 former enlisted men.

3. Jeffrey Simpson, *Officers and Gentlemen: Historic West Point in Photographs* (Tarrytown, N.Y.: Sleepy Hollow Press, 1982), p. 182.

4. See Janowitz, pp. 215–32.

5. Thayer, a graduate of Dartmouth in 1807 and West Point in 1808, was in the War of 1812 and later conducted a two-year study of the education and training at l'Ecole Polytechnique. Many of his initiatives were based on what he observed there. See George S. Pappas, *To the Point: The United States Military Academy, 1802–1902* (Westport, Conn.: Praeger Press, 1993), passim; Stephen E. Ambrose, *Duty, Honor, Country: A History of West Point* (Baltimore: Johns Hopkins Press, 1966), pp. 62–105 (hereafter Ambrose); George Fielding Eliot, *Sylvanus Thayer of West Point* (New York: Julian Messner, 1959), passim; Sidney Forman, *West Point: A History of the United States Military Academy* (New York: Columbia Univ. Press, 1950), pp. 36–60; R. Ernest Dupuy, *Where They Have Trod: The West Point Tradition in American Life* (New York: Stokes, 1940), pp. 137ff (hereafter Dupuy); and Ed Cass, "Sylvanus Thayer 1817-1833: A Personal Glimpse," *Assembly* 40, no. 4 (March 1982), pp. 8ff.

6. The accomplishments of Thayer, who has been described as the father of science and engineering education in America, hastened changes at civilian colleges, where utilitarian courses soon made inroads into classical studies. James L. Morrison, Jr., *"The Best School in the World": West Point, the Pre-Civil War Years, 1833–1860* (Kent, Ohio: Kent Univ. Press, 1986), pp. 111–13 (hereafter Morrison); William B. Streett, "West Point and the Rise of American Science in the 19th Century," *Assembly* 55, no. 2 (November/December 1996), pp. 20–22, 49, 50.

7. See Janowitz, pp. 128ff. The strict disciplinary system was also designed to assure that each cadet suffered equally and was rewarded equally. Dupuy, pp. 137ff.

8. For example, cadets could not bring money from home nor receive any outside financial assistance, so those from poor families were on the same footing as the wealthy. Dupuy, p. 141.

9. Most cadets were unenthusiastic about the Sunday pulpital exhortations. One reluctant worshiper even hyperbolized that "there is not one here who professes Christianity. The two who did have left." Such indifference helped avoid the revivalism that swept through many colleges in the early to mid-1800s. Ambrose, pp. 151, 152; Morrison, pp. 56–58, 85, 86.

10. The methods were adopted to (1) assure that assignments had been studied, (2) train the student to present clear, concise, and methodological statements, and (3) replace erroneous impressions with correct principles. Michie, "Education in Its Relation to the Military Profession," pp. 154–84.

11. See Thomas E. Griess and Jay Luvaas, *The Centennial of the United States Military Academy at West Point, New York, 1802–1902,* vol. 1, pp. 374–438; also see Peter Karsten, ed., *The Military in America from Colonial Times to the Present* (New York: Free Press, 1980), pp. 160–63.

12. Ambrose, pp. 85, 86; Morrison, pp. 19ff. The experiments with new weapons and tactics related primarily to improving conventional warfare.

13. The origin of the Honor Code ("a cadet will not lie, cheat, or steal, nor tolerate those who do") is ascribed to Thayer's principle that the word of a cadet was always accepted. It became a formal part of academy doctrine after an 1871 incident in which three cadets lied to conceal a minor violation of a directive. Some seniors confronted them, gave them civilian clothing and money, and told them to leave. They did, but a congressional investigation followed. Subsequently, cadets organized a "Vigilance Committee" of elected representatives to deal with offenders. In Dwight D. Eisenhower's widely-shared opinion, "West Point gives its graduates something that far transcends the techniques and knowledge involved in developing, training, and leading an army. It helps them build character, integrity." Ambrose, p. viii; U.S. Corps of Cadets, *The Cadet Honor Code and System* (West Point: USMA, 1967), p. 2.

14. In 1866 control of the academy was transferred from the Corps of Engineers to the secretary of war who was authorized to appoint the superintendent, instructors, and staff from any branch. Act of July 13, 1866; Rev. Stat. of 1878, sec. 1314; *Army and Navy Journal* (hereafter *ANJ*), March 17, 1866, p. 470.

15. A new curriculum was adopted in 1867 but few substantive changes were made. The primacy of mathematics, science, and engineering continued, while English, geography, and history were ignored. Morrison, p. 147.

16. Ambrose, pp. 222–31; Simpson, *Officers and Gentlemen,* pp. 99–101. Although upperclassmen in the 1850s played humorous tricks (called "running the plebes") on fourthclassmen, hazing was not tolerated. S. W. Ferguson, "West Point before the War," *Assembly* 43, no. 3 (December 1954), pp. 18ff.

17. T. Harry Williams, *The History of American Wars from 1745 to 1918* (New York: Alfred A. Knopf, 1985), pp. 189, 190. Randolph B. Marcy, Class of 1832, who was no stranger to hostilities involving defiant Indians as well as rebellious Mormons, wrote that "The education of our officers at the Military Academy is doubtless well adapted to the art of civilized warfare, but can not familiarize them with the diversified details of border service; and they often, at the outset of their military career, find themselves compelled to improvise new expedients to meet novel emergencies." Randolph B. Marcy, *The Prairie Traveler* (New York: Harper & Brothers, 1859), pp. xi, xii. See Robert M. Utley, *Frontier Regulars: The United States Army and the Indian, 1866–1891* (Bloomington: Univ. of Indiana Press, 1972), pp. 44–58.

18. Rpt. of the General of the Army in H. Exec. Doc. 1, 48th Cong., 1st sess., vol. 1 (1883), *Report of the SecWar* (Serial 2182); *ANJ,* November 10, 1883, p. 292.

19. Three classes (1859, 1860, and May 1861) were in the five-year program. The thirty-four-member Class of June 1861 (in which George Custer was thirty-fourth) reverted to four years. In 1860 a commission headed by Sen. Jefferson Davis examined the five-year program, which Robert E. Lee had recommended when he was superintendent. Lee testified that without schools of application the course at West Point should be five or six years; and Capt. E. O. C. Ord proposed five years, adding that it should include one year of practice followed by two to three years with troops before joining a corps. See Edward S. Holden, "Training of Cadets for the U.S. Army," *JMSI* 34 (1904); 1990 Register of Graduates, pp. 282–84.

20. Schools for artillery and engineers were created in the 1820s and endured, while one for infantry was short-lived. In 1881 an infantry and cavalry school was

established at Fort Leavenworth, but the curriculum was designed for experienced officers. See James S. Pettit, "The Proper Military Instruction for Our Officers," *JMSI* 20 (1897), pp. 1–54, and Coffman, *The Old Army*, pp. 269ff.

21. Recognizing the shortcomings in military training, Bigelow ordered two books from New York "to study the 'principles' of tactics...(which) are not taught at West Point." Bigelow Journal, February 16, 1879.

22. By June 1865 all but one of the eighteen major generals commanding departments of the Union Army were academy graduates, and the records of senior commanders such as Grant, Sherman, Sheridan, and Thomas were highly lauded throughout the North. Similarly, most of the principal commanders in the Confederate Army also were products of West Point. See "Military Education," *ANJ*, March 3, 1866, p. 437.

23. In the early years no conditions were specified for becoming a cadet nor any times prescribed for entering, remaining, or graduating. Consequently, young boys as well as commissioned officers and reportedly even a middle-aged married man with children were accepted. Appointments were made throughout the year, and cadets were graduated whenever they demonstrated sufficient understanding of the courses offered (the first two graduates finished in seven months). In 1816, though, a four-year program was adopted, and in 1843 statutory requirements for appointments were enacted. By the 1870s each congressional district, territory, and the District of Columbia was permitted to have one cadet at West Point, and the president was authorized ten appointments at large, resulting in a corps of slightly more than 300. *Acts of March 1, 1843* and *June 11, 1878*, Rev. Stat. of 1878, sec. 1315; *Regulations of the Army of the United States and General Orders in Force on the 17th of February 1881* (Washington: GPO, 1881) (hereafter *1881 Regulations*), p. 325; *Official Register of the USMA for 1877*, p. 37; Morrison, pp. 1–22; Dupuy, p. 138; Ambrose, pp. 1–61.

24. Albert Todd, *The Class of '77 at the United States Military Academy* (Cambridge, Mass.: Riverside, 1878), p. 2 [hereafter Todd].

25. Through the late 1870s an average of about one-third of the nominees failed to pass the qualifying examination, and of those who did only about 60 percent graduated; hence, only two of five nominees were ultimately commissioned. Michie, "Education in Its Relation to the Military Profession," p. 158.

26. *1881 Regulations*, pp. 325, 326; *Official Register of the USMA for 1877*, p. 37.

27. "Turnbacks" were former members of the previous class who, having been disenrolled because of an academic failure or a temporarily disabling injury or illness, nevertheless were believed to possess sufficient ability and potential to be readmitted as members of the next lower class.

28. Through most of the pre–Civil War era the percentages of cadets who were sons of lawyers (12.2 percent), editors (1.7 percent), and army officers (5.4 percent) were larger than the small percentages of the population represented by their fathers; conversely the sons of farmers (the largest category at 24.8 percent), merchants (12.4 percent), and clergymen (1.9 percent) were underrepresented. The financial status of 4.2 percent of parents was regarded as "affluent" and 83.2 percent as "moderate," while 12.6 percent showed either "reduced" or "indigent." Morrison, pp. 155–59. During the 1842–1899 period 20.0 percent were sons of farmers, 13.2 percent merchants, 11.8 percent lawyers, 6.6 percent army officers, 2.3 percent clergymen, and 1.1 percent editors. Griess and Luvaas, *The Centennial*, vol. 1, pp. 482, 483.

29. In remarks after graduation Flipper reportedly said, "(Cadets) always treated me fairly, would speak to me, and some came to my room and talked with me, but the only thing they did that was wrong, perhaps, was that they would not associate with me openly." He added, "As to Mr. Bigelow's son...I know him well, and his whole family—his father, the distinguished ex-Secretary of State, his mother and his two sisters, and met them at their home. Mrs. Bigelow, recognizing my position, and thinking to assure my feelings, sent me a nice box of fruit with her compliments." *ANJ,* July 21, 1877, p. 796; also see Henry Ossian Flipper, *The Colored Cadet at West Point* (1878; reprint, New York: Johnson Reprint, 1968), pp. 264–66, and George L. Andrews, "West Point and the Colored Cadets," *The International Review* 9 (November 1880), pp. 477–98.

30. Charles Judson Crane, *The Experiences of a Colonel of Infantry* (New York: Knickerbocker, 1923), passim; *AOG Report for 1928,* pp. 159–61.

31. Wilhelmi recovered sufficiently to obtain a commission in 1875, two years before his classmates.

32. Ferguson, "West Point before the War," p. 20. By the 1870s cadets were organized into a battalion of four companies with seventy to eighty cadets each. Segregation by height was practiced until the second half of the twentieth century.

33. Their ages ranged from a low of just over seventeen to almost twenty-two, with the mean a few days short of nineteen. *Official Register of the USMA for 1874,* pp. 15–17; Todd, p. 4.

34. Studies the first year included algebra, trigonometry, descriptive geometry, and French. *Official Register of the USMA for 1877,* p. 35.

35. Second-year courses included surveying, analytical geometry, calculus, and topography, with military training in artillery, infantry, and cavalry tactics. Ibid., p. 35; Todd, p. 11.

36. The missing cadet, James Shofner, inadvertently stepped off a train between Washington and Baltimore; a few days later he was found, semiconscious, in a swamp, little injured except for a slight case of malaria. Todd, pp. 13, 14. The courses that year were natural and experimental philosophy (mechanics, astronomy, acoustics, and optics), chemistry, and landscape drawing. Military instruction was in artillery, cavalry, and infantry tactics and in signaling and telegraphy. *Official Register of the USMA for 1877,* p. 36.

37. Cadet officers usually were from the senior (first) class, sergeants from the first and second class, and corporals from the third class. *Official Register of the USMA for 1877,* p. 34.

38. "Confinement" of a cadet did not involve incarceration in a cell, but instead restriction to his room except for attendance at classes, military training, chapel, and meals.

39. The senior courses were civil and military engineering, mineralogy and geology, ethics and law, and practical military engineering (e.g., pontoon bridges, reconnaissances, field fortifications, batteries, and siege works). In military training, ordnance, gunnery, and pyrotechny were added to instruction in artillery, infantry, and cavalry. Ibid., p. 36.

40. Todd, p. 22.

CHAPTER 2

1. *New York Times,* June 15, 1877, pp. 4, 5; *ANJ,* June 23, 1877, p. 736.

2. Charles O. Thompson, a professor of the Free Institute of Worcester, Massachusetts, was in his mid-twenties when the Civil War erupted but spent most of those years as a principal in New England schools. There is no indication he had ever been west of the Mississippi. Malone, *Dictionary of American Biography,* vol. 18, pp. 453, 454; Griess and Luvaas, *The Centennial,* vol. 2, p. 370; *Annual Report of the Board of Visitors for 1877* (Washington: GPO, 1877).

3. The tensions resulting from Maximilian's policies had been resolved, partly through the efforts of John Bigelow, Sr., in negotiating the French withdrawal, but the Benito Juárez government was largely impotent in controlling border problems. See H. Misc. Doc. 64, 45th Cong., 2d sess., vol. 6 (1878), *The Texas Border Troubles* (Serial 1820) (hereafter H. Misc. Doc. 64 for 1878).

4. In his 1877 report, Sheridan wrote that "The troubles on the Rio Grande border, the Indian outbreak [in]...New Mexico, and the Indian war in the Departments of the Platte and Dakota, have kept the small and inadequate force in this division in a constant state of activity, and almost without rest, night and day." H. Exec. Doc. 1, 45th Cong., 2d sess., vol. 2 (1877), *Report of the SecWar,* p. 58 (Serial 1774).

5. H. Exec. Doc. 1 for 1877, p. 58; *ANJ,* November 24, 1877, p. 250; see Russell F. Weigley, *History of the United States Army* (New York: Macmillan, 1967), pp. 265–94.

6. James W. Dixon, "Across the Plains with General Hancock," *JMSI* 7 (1886), pp. 196–98; Lonnie J. White, "The Hancock and Custer Expeditions of 1867," *Journal of the West* (July 1966), pp. 355–78; *United States v. Custer,* GCMO 93, AGO, November 20, 1867; *ANJ,* August 3, 1867, p. 481; see U. S. Grant, *Personal Memoirs,* vol. 2 (New York: Webster, 1886), pp. 539, 540.

7. *New York Times,* supra note 1; *ANJ,* June 23, 1877, p. 738.

8. In late 1877 the average enlisted strength was 701 in a cavalry regiment and 65 in a company. An infantry regiment had 355 men and a company 35, while the numbers for artillery were 462 and 36. Congress authorized enlisting up to one thousand Indians as scouts with the pay of cavalry soldiers, but funds were never sufficient for more than a few hundred, so on occasion others were hired as civilians. H. Misc. Doc. 64 for 1878, p. 5; *Act of July 28, 1866,* as amended by *Act of March 3, 1869;* Rev. Stat. of 1878, sec. 1112; Robert N. Scott, *An Analytical Digest of the Military Laws of the United States* (Philadelphia: Lippincott, 1873), pp. 219–26 (hereafter Scott). By 1883, when the strength of the army was 2,143 officers and 23,335 enlisted men, only 210 of the latter were Indian scouts. H. Exec. Doc. 1, 48th Cong., 1st sess., vol. 1, p. 44 (1883), *Report of the SecWar* (Serial 2182). See Thomas W. Dunlay, *Wolves for Blue Soldiers* (Lincoln: Univ. of Nebraska Press, 1982), pp. 50–57.

9. By 1875 the authorized strength, which totaled 54,641 in 1866, was 25,000 enlisted men and 2,151 officers in addition to 9 professors and 312 cadets. *Acts of July 28, 1866; March 3, 1869; July 15, 1870; June 16 and 23, 1874;* and *June 26, 1876;* Heitman, pp. 606–13; see Utley, *Frontier Regulars,* pp. 15–18. When a former senator begged Sherman to rescue another ex-senator's son, supposedly captured by Apaches, he replied, "You ask of me impossibilities. The Apaches never take prisoners alive. With full knowledge of all the facts Congress reduced the Army to an impotent state when you yourself were a Senator. The men we have, have done all that was possible...."

Telegram to Stanley Matthews, *Sherman Papers,* LC, Container 95, p. 52, July 8, 1881.

10. In 1878 there were 23,701 enlisted men and 2,153 officers. Heitman, p. 626; Theodore F. Rodenbough and William L. Haskin, eds., *The Army of the United States: Historical Sketches of Staff and Line* (New York: Maynard, Merrill, 1896).

11. H. Exec. Doc. 1, 45th Cong., 2d sess., vol. 1 (1877), *Report of the SecWar* (Serial 1774); *ANJ,* November 24, 1877, p. 250.

12. Of 2,395 officers in the mid-1870s, 96 had been born in Ireland, 48 in Germany, 34 in England, 19 in Canada, 14 in Scotland, 9 in France, and 24 elsewhere. *ANJ,* December 4, 1875, p. 271. Similarly, of 183,659 soldiers who enlisted between 1865 and 1874, 21 percent were from Ireland, 13 percent from Germany, 5 percent from England, and 3 percent from Canada. *ANJ,* March 25, 1876, p. 529.

13. Martha Summerhayes, *Vanished Arizona: Recollections of the Army Life of a New England Woman* (Glorieta, N. Mex.: Rio Grande Press, 1970), p. 157.

14. July 18, 1882, Endorsement, *Sherman Papers,* LC, Container 99, p. 580. Also see May 31, 1876, Letter, Container 90, p. 403; Jack D. Foner, "The Socializing Role of the Military" in James P. Tate, ed., *The American Military on the Frontier,* Proceedings of the 7th Military History Symposium, U.S. Air Force Academy, 1976 (Washington, D.C.: Office of Air Force History, 1978), pp. 85–99; and Oliver Knight, *Life and Manners in the Frontier Army* (Norman: Univ. of Oklahoma Press, 1978), pp. 94–96.

15. Robert Temple Emmet was raised on a Pelham, New York, estate, attended exclusive schools, and developed skills as a marksman, horseman, and yachtsman. At West Point he excelled only in drawing, perhaps influenced by his artist sister, Rosina, the first woman member of the American Watercolor Society. Heitman; *1990 Register of Graduates; AOG Report for 1938,* pp. 106–12; Summerhayes, *Vanished Arizona,* pp. 247, 248.

16. Sherman concluded by advising Mrs. Emmet that "your son is a fine manly fellow. Let him alone.... We cannot fight Victorio, Sitting Bull, and the devils who rise up in every quarter with men at home...." *AOG Report for 1938,* pp. 108, 109.

17. After each cadet listed his preferences, assignments were made commencing with the first graduate on the Order of Merit, so once a particular vacancy was filled it was eliminated for those lower on the list. Thomas Cruse, *Apache Days and After,* ed. Eugene Cunningham (1941; reprint, Univ. of Nebraska Press, 1987), pp. 19, 20.

18. Sherman, who also detested politicians and despised Washington, regarded officers who wanted to be there as "barnacles" who eventually "degenerate into toadys." *Sherman Papers,* LC, Container 96, pp. 241, 242, and Container 90, No. 302.

19. See Appendix A. *Official Army Register for 1878* (Washington, D.C.: 1878) (hereafter *1878 Army Register*). In 1875, only about one-third of all officers were Military Academy graduates. *ANJ,* December 4, 1875, p. 271. Nevertheless in 1877 all 107 officers in the engineers were from West Point, as were 51 of the 54 ordnance officers and more than half of all field grade (major and above) officers in cavalry, infantry, and artillery, while the Adjutant General's and Inspector General's Departments each had only one non–West Point graduate. *ANJ,* July 21, 1877, p. 801; *1876 Army Register.*

20. Todd, pp. 78–80. McCrimmon resigned in 1879, after which he practiced law, taught, and edited and published the *San Diegan* newspaper. Heitman, vol. 1 (unless

otherwise indicated all Heitman references are to vol. 1); *Official Registers of the USMA for 1874–1877*; *AOG Report for 1918,* pp. 91, 92.

21. Four of the ten became lawyers, two stockmen, one a university president, another a high school principal, one a businessman, and the other a railroad executive whose military career had been shortened by the loss of a leg in an 1879 skirmish with Indians. *1990 Register of Graduates.*

22. Hammond's father was an 1841 West Point graduate. After attending Columbia Law School Harry joined a Bay Area law firm and became a lieutenant colonel in the California militia. He died in 1883. Todd, pp. 61–63; *1990 Register of Graduates.*

23. In 1876 seven of the thirty-three graduates (21 percent) were assigned to African American regiments, but all but two (6 percent) soon transferred to white units, in part because of vacancies in the 7th Cavalry after the Little Big Horn. Heitman; *1878 Army Register*; *1990 Register of Graduates.* Although blacks were ineligible to enlist in white regiments, a Negro officer could legally be appointed in any regiment. In fact, "one of the first colonels appointed by the Continental Congress in 1775 was Louis, a half breed (Negro and Indian, and therefore most richly colored) chief of the Cayugas." There was no known African American officer after the Civil War, however, until Henry Flipper graduated from West Point in 1877. *ANJ,* June 23, 1877, pp. 736, 737.

24. Esterly, the underground railroad helper as a boy, declined Harvard to accept a West Point appointment. Following a promising early career, he reluctantly resigned in July 1883 because of his wife's failing health (see Epilogue). Heitman; *1990 Register of Graduates*; *AOG Report for 1921,* pp. 158, 159.

25. The 10th had headquarters at Fort Concho with one company at each of Forts Duncan, McKavett, Griffin, Davis, Richardson, Clark, and Stockton, and Camp San Felipe. Of the thirty-nine officers assigned when the new appointees reported, only seven were from West Point. See *1878 Army Register*; John Bigelow, "The Tenth Regiment of Cavalry," *JMSI* 32 (1902) pp. 205–14, reprinted in Rodenbough and Haskin, *The Army of the United States,* pp. 288–97; Herschel V. Cashin, *Under Fire with the Tenth U.S. Cavalry* (New York: Arno, 1969 reprint of an 1899 publication); Maj. E. L. N. Glass, *The History of the Tenth Cavalry, 1866–1921* (Tucson: Acme, 1921), micropublished in *Western Americana: Frontier History of the Trans-Mississippi West, 1550–1900* (New Haven: Research Publications, 1975); John M. Carroll, compiler, *Buffalo Soldiers West* (Fort Collins, Colo.: Old Army Press, 1971); and William H. Leckie, *The Buffalo Soldiers: A Narrative of the Negro Cavalry in the West* (Norman: Univ. of Oklahoma Press, 1967).

26. The 9th was headquartered at Santa Fe with companies at Forts Union, Wingate, Stanton, and Bayard in New Mexico, and Lyon in Colorado. Before the new graduates arrived just five of the thirty-nine officers were from the Academy. See *1878 Army Register*; Grote Hutchinson, "The 9th Regiment of Cavalry," *JMSI* 16 (1895), pp. 666–73; and Leckie, *The Buffalo Soldiers.*

27. The 24th's headquarters and three companies were at Fort Clark, two at Fort Brown, one at Fort Concho, and four at Ringgold. Three of its thirty-two officers were Military Academy graduates. See *1878 Army Register;* H. W. Hovey, "The 24th Regiment of Infantry," *JMSI* 15 (1894), pp. 1341, 1342; William G. Muller, *The Twenty-Fourth Infantry, Past and Present* (Fort Collins, Colo.: Old Army Press, 1972); and Arlen L. Fowler, *The Black Infantry in the West, 1869–1891* (Westport, Conn.: Greenwood, 1971).

Headquarters and five companies of the 25th were at Fort Davis, three companies at Fort Stockton, and one each at Forts Clark and Concho. Exclusive of McMartin and Glenn, only three of thirty-four officers were West Pointers. See *1878 Army Register*; George Andrews, "The 25th Regiment of Infantry," *JMSI* 13 (1892), pp. 224–26; John H. Nankivell, *The History of the Twenty-Fifth United States Infantry, 1869–1926* (Fort Collins, Colo.: Old Army Press, 1972); and Fowler, *The Black Infantry in the West, 1869–1891*, passim.

CHAPTER 3

1. *Congressional Globe,* 39th Cong., 1st sess., p. 265 (January 17, 1866); *ANJ,* January 13, 1866, p. 331.
2. *New York Times,* January 12. 1866, p. 4; and February 8, 1866, p. 4.
3. *ANJ,* January 27, 1866, p. 362. The writer's views were similar to those of most whites at the outset of the Civil War. See Joseph T. Glatthaar, *Forged in Battle: The Civil War Alliance of Black Soldiers and White Officers* (New York: Free Press, 1990), pp. 81–98 and passim.
4. *Congressional Globe,* 39th Cong., 1st sess., p. 3667 (July 9, 1866).
5. Almost two-thirds of the 54th's 22 officers, including its commander, Col. Robert Shaw, and 225 of its 650 enlisted men, were killed or wounded storming the Charleston Harbor fort on July 18, 1863. Reportedly, Shaw's body was stripped, mutilated, and thrown into a common grave with his black soldiers. Charles Eliot, president of Harvard, wrote that on that day black and white together "gave to the nation...undying proof that Americans of African descent possess the pride, courage and devotion of the patriot soldier." Joseph T. Glatthaar, *Forged in Battle,* pp. 121–68; Page Smith, *Trial by Fire,* vol. 5 (New York: McGraw-Hill, 1982), pp. 318–20; Bruce Catton, *Never Call Retreat* (Garden City, N.Y.: Doubleday, 1965), pp. 220, 221; Hondon B. Hargrove, *Black Union Soldiers in the Civil War* (Jefferson, N.C.: McFarland, 1988), pp. 150–62, 216; Dudley Taylor Cornish, *The Sable Arm* (New York: Longmans, Green, 1956), pp. 152–56, passim. On February 20, 1864, the 54th, one of three black and six white regiments attempting to conquer Florida, was repulsed by an overwhelming Confederate force after a bitter battle at Olustee. The Union commander reported that "The colored troops behaved creditably.... It was not their conduct that [was]...the cause of failure, but the...yielding of a white regiment [the 7th New Hampshire]...when everything depended on its firmness." *ANJ,* March 31, 1866, p. 501, and April 7, 1866, p. 525.
6. *New York Times,* February 8, 1866, p. 4.
7. *ANJ,* May 5, 1866, p. 588.
8. *ANJ,* May 19, 1866, p. 621.
9. "They are resolved to cut down the Army,...[with] more than 1/4...posted on the Texas frontier, thereby...utterly ignoring the [Northwest's] claims...for protection against the savage and brave Sioux." Moreover, "after every war...the Army underwent the same process of 'Reduction.' Instead of cutting off the leg, once for good, Congress cut off the foot, then the knee, and finally at the hip joint." M. A. DeWolfe Howe, ed., *Home Letters of General Sherman* (New York: Charles Scribner's Sons, 1909), pp. 386–89.
10. *ANJ,* August 4, 1866, pp. 791, 797.

11. Mackenzie, who transferred to the 4th Cavalry in 1870, was succeeded by Abner Doubleday for one year, then by Joseph H. Potter who was the 24th's commander until 1886. Heitman, pp. 123, 124. After ten months Joseph J. Reynolds assumed command of the 25th, but he was soon followed by J. D. Stevenson who two weeks later was succeeded by George L. Andrews, the regiment's commander for the next twenty-one years.

12. Hatch entered military service in August 1861 as an Iowa Cavalry captain. He became a colonel the following January, a brigadier general in 1864, and a brevet major general in 1866. He died in 1889. Heitman.

13. Grierson, a musician and storekeeper before the Civil War, became aide-de-camp to an Illinois volunteer general in May 1861. That October he was appointed a major in the 6th Illinois Cavalry, six months later was the regiment's colonel, and in 1865 became a brevet major general. During the Siege of Vicksburg he led a daring, 800-mile cavalry sweep from LaGrange, Tennessee, to Baton Rouge, destroying huge quantities of property and ruining two railroads. His compassion, distaste for consistent discipline, penchant for showing favoritism toward some subordinates, and Sheridan's animosity limited his potential. Heitman; Ezra J. Warner, *Generals in Blue* (Baton Rouge: Louisiana State Univ. Press, 1964), pp. 189, 190; see William H. and Shirley A. Leckie, *Unlikely Warriors: General Benjamin H. Grierson and His Family* (Norman: Univ. of Oklahoma Press, 1984); Leckie, *The Buffalo Soldiers,* passim; Utley, *Frontier Regulars,* passim; and Frank M. Temple, "Discipline and Turmoil in the Tenth U.S. Cavalry," *West Texas Historical Association Yearbook* 43 (1982), pp. 103–18.

14. During the Civil War, a few cavalry companies used the term "troop," which first appeared in legislation in 1862. However, "company" remained the prescribed name until 1883. Mary Lee Stubbs and Stanley R. Connor, *Armor-Cavalry, Part I: Regular Army and Army Reserve* (Washington, D.C.: GPO, 1969), p. 18.

15. Sec. 30, *Act of July 28, 1866*; General Orders (hereafter GO) 56, AGO, August 1, 1866; Rev. Stat. of 1878, sec. 1124.

16. By law chaplains had the rank of infantry captains, without command. *Act of July 15, 1870*; Rev. Stat. of 1878, sec. 1122.

17. Stubbs and Connor, *Armor-Cavalry,* pp. 18–23.

18. Bruce J. Dinges, "Scandal in the Tenth Cavalry," *Arizona and the West* 28, no. 2 (Summer 1986), pp. 125, 126.

19. Custer reputedly refused the 9th Cavalry lieutenant colonelcy before securing similar rank in the 7th. Leckie, *The Buffalo Soldiers,* p. 8. Conversely, Mackenzie (first in the Class of 1862), who like Custer (last in the Class of 1861) had been a brevet major general during the Civil War, accepted the colonelcy of the 41st Infantry in 1867. Joseph H. Dorst, "Ranald Slidell Mackenzie," *Journal of the United States Cavalry Association* 10, no. 39 (December 1897), pp. 367–82. *ANJ,* June 23, 1877, p. 736. Leckie, *The Buffalo Soldiers,* pp. 25, 26. Both legislation and army orders used the term "colored," which included "blacks" as well as "mulattoes." Lowell D. and Sara H. Black, *An Officer and a Gentleman: The Military Career of Lieutenant Henry O. Flipper* (Dayton, Ohio: Lora, 1985), pp. 13–29. In addition to "the inferiority" of the officers "stocking" the 10th Cavalry and other black regiments, Bigelow ascribed the regiment's "lowness of...tone" to "the easy, *laisser aller,* character" of Colonel Grierson. Douglas C. McChristian, ed., *Garrison Tangles in the Friendless Tenth* (Bryan, Tex.: Carroll, 1985), p. 26 and passim. Also see Shirley A. Leckie, ed., *The Colonel's Lady on the Western Frontier:*

The Correspondence of Alice Kirk Grierson (Lincoln: Univ. of Nebraska Press, 1989), pp. 1–4; Temple, "Discipline and Turmoil in the Tenth U.S. Cavalry."

20. *JMSI* 3 (1882), p. 87.

21. In 1877 there were fifty officers above the rank of captain in the ten cavalry regiments. All five in the 4th and 7th were academy graduates, as were all but one in the 5th and 6th, but the 9th had none and the 10th only two. *ANJ*, June 23, 1877, p. 732; *1878 Army Register*; also see Erwin N. Thompson, "The Negro Soldiers on the Frontier: A Fort Davis Case Study," *Journal of the West* (April 1968), pp. 217–35; Robert Wooster, *Soldiers, Sutlers, and Settlers: Garrison Life on the Texas Frontier* (College Station: Texas A&M Press, 1987); and Leckie and Leckie, *Unlikely Warriors*.

22. Adolphus W. Greely, *Reminiscences of Adventure and Service* (New York: Charles Scribner's Sons, 1927), pp. 98, 99.

23. Leckie, *The Buffalo Soldiers*, pp. 3–18; GO 6, Hq. Div. of the Missouri, Aug. 9, 1866; Bigelow, "The Tenth Regiment of Cavalry," pp. 205–7.

24. Charles Walcutt commenced his military service in 1861 as a major in a volunteer regiment, and later became a brevet major general. He was commissioned in the 10th Cavalry in July 1866 but resigned that December. Heitman.

25. 10th Cavalry Organizational Return for September 1866, NARA, RG 391, M744 (*Returns from Regular Army Cavalry Regiments, 1833–1916*), roll 95, *10th Cavalry, 1866–1872*.

26. Company A was at Larned, while Company B (commanded by Capt. J. B. Van de Wiele) was at Buffalo Creek and Company C at Mud Creek. Ibid., 10th Cavalry Return for May 1867.

27. Ibid., 10th Cavalry Returns for 1867, passim.

28. In 1875 there were 25,989 white soldiers and 2,530 Negroes. Surgeon General's Office, *Circular 8: A Report on the Hygiene of the United States Army with Descriptions of Military Posts* (Washington: GPO, 1975) (hereafter *Circular No. 8*). See Leckie, *The Buffalo Soldiers*; Glass, *A History of the Tenth Cavalry*, pp. 96–103; and Fairfax Downey, *The Buffalo Soldiers in the Indian Wars* (New York: McGraw-Hill, 1969).

29. George Augustus Armes enlisted in 1862, and by the end of the war he was a brevet major. He was commissioned in the 2d Cavalry in 1866 but transferred to the 10th Cavalry that July. See Epilogue. Heitman; George A. Armes, *Ups and Downs of an Army Officer* (Washington, D.C.: n.p., 1900), passim.

30. For a chronological account of the 10th's engagements see Glass, *A History of the Tenth Cavalry, 1866–1921*, pp. 96–103.

31. The Beecher Island battle is frequently chronicled in accounts of the Indian wars. See George Bird Grinnell, *The Fighting Cheyennes* (1915; reprint, Norman: Univ. of Oklahoma Press, 1956), pp. 277–97, and John H. Monnett, *The Battle of Beecher Island and the Indian War of 1867–1869* (Niwot, Colo.: Univ. Press of Colorado, 1992), passim. Carpenter, a Civil War colonel, became a 10th Cavalry captain shortly after mustering out. He was awarded the Medal of Honor for his 1868 rescue of Forsyth and his detachment of frontiersmen, and a brevet promotion to colonel for his service on Beaver Creek. Forsyth enlisted in the Chicago Dragoons in 1861, and by the end of the war he was a brevet brigadier general. In 1866 he was appointed a major in the 9th Cavalry. He served as Sheridan's military secretary from 1869 to 1873, and his aide from 1878 until 1881 when he joined the 4th Cavalry. Heitman; *1879 Army Register*.

32. During the Civil War Louis H. Orleman, a German immigrant, enlisted in a New York regiment and eventually became a captain. In 1867 he was appointed in the 10th Cavalry. He received a brevet promotion for his services at Beaver Creek and at Wichita Agency in 1874. Heitman; *1879 Army Register*; Clayton W. Williams, *Texas' Last Frontier: Fort Stockton and the Trans-Pecos, 1861–1895*, ed. Ernest Wallace (College Station: Texas A&M Press, 1982), pp. 199–200. See Col. W. S. Nye, *Carbine and Lance: The Story of Old Fort Sill* (Norman: Univ. of Oklahoma Press, 3d ed., 1969), pp. 134–43.

33. Glass, *The History of the Tenth Cavalry*, p. 19; Leckie, *The Buffalo Soldiers*, pp. 25, 26.

34. Richard Wormser, *The Yellowlegs: The Story of the United States Cavalry* (Garden City, N.Y.: Doubleday, 1966), p. 430. The difficulty with this version is that the 9th Cavalry was stationed in the Southwest for more than two decades before serving in Sioux country.

35. Ibid.

36. Grierson wrote his wife that "if I knew that I should be compelled to stay a very long time at Fort Concho or in the Dept. of Texas, I think that either *drunk or sober*, my decision would be to resign and get out." Leckie, *The Colonel's Lady on the Western Frontier*, p. 73. His opinion apparently changed, since he invested in ranch land near Fort Davis and lived there intermittently after retiring. Leckie and Leckie, *Unlikely Warriors*, pp. 281, 282.

37. H. Misc. Doc. 64 for 1878, p. 20. General Sherman explained that black troops were stationed in Texas because they were "better adapted to that latitude"; "the death-rate in that climate [was] greater among white troops than among the black"; they were "less liable to typhoid fevers"; and "there was an implied understanding when we employed the black troops that they were better qualified for Southern stations than troops of our own Anglo-Saxon race."

38. The physical characteristics of soldiers with the greatest tolerance to heat stress is important because of the impact it has on combat effectiveness and logistical support. Various studies have since confirmed that persons "with brunette skin and low body fat" are best suited to hot climates, and that a "very significant fraction of the phenotypic appearance of these attributes is determined by genetic structure." Extensive measurements showed that African American soldiers in the U.S. Army had a mean of only 8.2mm of skinfold on their arms and 13.6mm on their backs, compared to 11.4mm on the arms and 13.6mm on the backs of white soldiers of identical ages. In contrast, American businessmen measured 14.4mm and 19.9mm, respectively, while Chinese soldiers were only 4.2mm and 7.9mm. Paul T. Baker, "Theoretical Model for Desert Heat Tolerance" (Tech. Rpt. EP-98) and "American Negro-White Differences in Heat Tolerance" (Tech. Rpt. 75), Environmental Protection Research Division, Quartermaster Research and Engineering Center (Natick, Mass.: 1958).

39. For instance, during a march in West Texas in 1880 Charles Crane came across "several colored soldiers apparently insensible from heat and fatigue," one of whom fell, "his head landing among the thorns of a...cactus bush without awakening him." Crane, *Experiences*, p. 104.

40. A comprehensive study determined that (1) fully clothed men lose less sweat and gain less heat than scantily clothed men; (2) the kind of clothing or material does not influence sweat loss if it adequately covers the body and does not prevent evapora-

tion; (3) white outer clothing is advantageous; (4) if the sun does not shine directly on an individual, less clothing produces greater comfort despite increasing heat exchange; (5) lying on the ground produces more heat and loses more sweat than sitting or standing; (6) shade is a most important factor; and (7) eating less does not modify the need for water. E. F. Adolph and Associates, *Physiology of Man in the Desert* (New York: Interscience Publishers, 1947), pp. 345–51.

CHAPTER 4

1. See C. Vann Woodward, *Reunion and Reaction: The Compromise of 1877 and the End of Reconstruction* (Boston: Little, Brown, 1951), pp. 3–9; H. J. Eckenrode, *Rutherford B. Hayes: Statesman of Reunion* (Port Washington, N.Y.: Kennikat, 1930), passim; Harry Barnard, *Rutherford B. Hayes and His America* (New York: Bobbs-Merrill, 1954), passim; and Crane, *Experiences,* p. 53, 54.

2. *ANJ,* June 23, 1877, p. 736; also see *ANJ,* October 13, 1877, p. 152. Sherman wrote, "The debates of 1860 were not as mean and vindictive as those of 1877." Letter to Mrs. W. T. Sherman, November 12, 1877, Howe, ed., *Home Letters of General Sherman,* p. 387.

3. Drexel, Morgan, and Company and other New York banks advanced money against assignments of pay accounts, discounted at a nominal interest, and one New Orleans bank did the same without remuneration. Frederick Bernays Weiner, "Service without Pay," *The Infantry Journal* 58, no. 2 (February 1946), pp. 38ff.

4. See Poultney Bigelow, *Seventy Summers* (New York: Longsman, Green, 1925), pp. 43, 44.

5. "Germans" were cotillions to waltz melodies that were popular throughout the army. Knight, *Life and Manners,* pp. 132, 133.

6. After arriving by boat from Poughkeepsie, the coffin was escorted to the chapel by post detachments and the pallbearers (Generals Marcy, Devin, Fry, and Forsyth, and Colonels Lyford, Ludlow, and Mitchell). As superintendent, Maj. Gen. John M. Schofield accompanied Custer's widow, Libby, and his father, Emmanuel. *ANJ,* October 18, 1877, p. 153.

7. *ANJ,* September 29, 1877, p. 118. A Baltimore and Ohio walkout soon spread to other lines, and riots resulted in about three dozen deaths and heavy property losses. Because some 30,000 militiamen were incapable of controlling the strikers, about 3,000 army troops were used to do so. See Elwell S. Otis, "The Army in Connection with the Labor Riots of 1877," *JMSI* 5 (1885), pp. 292–323; also see Allan Pinkerton, *Mass Violence in America: Strikers, Communists, Tramps and Detectives* (1878; reprint, New York: Arno, 1969); Paul Andrew Hutton, *Phil Sheridan and His Army* (Lincoln: Univ. of Nebraska Press, 1985), pp. 175ff; *ANJ,* August 4, 1877, p. 835.

8. When transportation was not provided by the government, the rate paid an officer was then eight cents a mile, so the distance between New York City and Fort Duncan was 1,826 miles. *Act of June 23, 1876,* 19 Stat. 97.

9. Robert Eliel Safford of Ohio and Bigelow were close friends. Both became members of the 10th Cavalry. Heitman; *1878 Army Register; AOG Report for 1880,* pp. 38–40.

10. Millard Fillmore ("Ben") Eggleston, 10th Cavalry, resigned in 1890 and became a journalist. Heitman; George W. Cullum, *Biographical Register of Officers and Graduates* (New York: Van Norstrand, 2d ed., 1891).

11. Steven W. Groesbeck, a volunteer lieutenant in the Civil War, afterwards received a Regular Army commission. In 1903 he retired as a brigadier general, apparently never having become wealthy. Heitman; *1878 Army Register.*

12. The Southern Pacific had been extended to San Antonio only ten months earlier. WPA Writers' Program (hereafter WPA), *San Antonio: A History and Guide* (San Antonio: Clegg, 1941).

13. The Alamo, which dates from 1718, was abandoned as a religious compound in 1793 and then used by Spanish and later Mexican troops. On March 6, 1836, after a thirteen-day siege, Santa Anna's forces overwhelmed and killed all 187 defenders. Most of the buildings and walls had been torn down to accommodate business expansion. In 1883 the state purchased the chapel, and in 1905 the "long barracks" was acquired. Ray Miller, *Texas Forts* (Austin: Capital Printing, 1986), p. 181; Mary Ann Noonan Guerra, *The Alamo* (San Antonio: Alamo Press, 1983).

14. The Menger, constructed of stone in 1859, had ornate, wrought-iron balustrades across the balconies on the front of the building, as well as a rotunda with a marble floor and columns supporting the interior balconies. Because of its luxurious appointments it was an anomaly in the rough-hewn San Antonio of that time, and the choice of most visiting luminaries, including Grant, Lee, and Sam Houston. See Charles Ramsdell, *San Antonio: A Historical and Pictorial Guide* (Austin: Univ. of Texas Press, 1968), pp. 52–54, 151, 152; Menger Hotel brochure, "The Grand Lady of the Plaza" (n.p., n.d.); WPA, *San Antonio,* p. 51; Frank H. Bushick, *Glamorous Days* (San Antonio: Naylor, 1934), pp. 32, 33.

15. Harriet Spofford, "San Antonio de Bexar," *Harper's New Monthly Magazine* 55 (June-November 1877), p. 834.

16. Edwin Glenn's cadet performance was relatively low; "his swarthy complexion won him the title of 'Mohawk,' and his intense enjoyment of life, many demerits." Later events brought him widespread publicity, not all of which was favorable (see Epilogue). *AOG Report of 1928,* pp. 67–70. Henry ("Buncombe") Kirby was on his way to join the 10th Infantry. John J. Brereton studied law in Paterson, New Jersey, before being appointed as a cadet. He was on frontier duty from 1877 to 1890. *AOG Report for 1900,* pp. 88–91; Heitman; *1878 Army Register; 1990 Register of Graduates.*

17. Although Charles J. Crane, a Texan called "Longhorn," had preferred an appointment in a white regiment after graduation, he "never regretted" his assignment to the 24th Infantry. After retiring in 1916 he returned to duty in World War I as PMS&T at Rice Institute. Crane, *Experiences,* p. 59. A fellow New Yorker about two years younger than Bigelow, John McMartin had an unremarkable career as a cadet as well as an officer. He graduated 55th in the class, was commissioned in the 25th Infantry, and served on the frontier until 1894 (see Epilogue). Edward Plummer, 10th Infantry, was on the frontier for twenty-one years, then from 1898 until 1901 was aide-de-camp to Maj. Gen. William R. Shafter. He retired in 1918 as a major general. Heitman; *1990 Register of Graduates.* Samuel Pierce Wayman served in the 24th Infantry for just a year and a half before being granted sick leave. He died seven months later. Heitman; *1878 Army Register; 1990 Register of Graduates.*

18. Robert P. Wilson, a 10th Infantry captain, was the post commander at San Antonio. He was killed by the accidental explosion of a gun about three months after befriending Bigelow and Eggleston. Joseph Hancock Taylor, an 1856 West Point graduate, was a major and AAG for the Department of Texas. He had been a brevet colonel in the Civil War, so was addressed by that rank. Heitman; *1878 Army Register*; *1990 Register of Graduates.*

19. John F. Stretch, a tactical officer at West Point when Bigelow was a cadet, was assigned to the 10th Infantry. Heitman; *1878 Army Register*; *1990 Register of Graduates*; Todd, p. 7.

20. Charles E. Bottsford, an enlisted man in the Civil War, was commissioned in the Regular Army in 1867. Heitman; *1878 Army Register*; Powell, *List of Officers.*

21. An 1878 photograph of San Pedro Springs, which gushed out of limestone a few miles north of town, depicts a meandering stream in a shady setting. A nearby pavilion, bathhouse, museum, zoo, and tropical garden made it a favorite place for picnics and political rallies. Ramsdell, *San Antonio,* passim.

22. Charles Shaler, Class of 1867, had been one of Bigelow's instructors at West Point. An 1862 graduate, Capt. Clifton Comly had been in the cavalry but later transferred to the Ordnance Department. Heitman; *1878 Army Register*; *1990 Register of Graduates.* The arsenal was built in 1860 to support the forts in West Texas. The original buildings are still in use.

23. Ord was rumored to be the grandson of the Prince of Wales and his morganatic wife, Lady Fitzherbert. After graduating from West Point in 1839, he served in the Second Seminole War and the Mexican War, then in several Indian expeditions on the West Coast. While there he supplemented his pay by mapping Los Angeles; returning a few years later, he commented that the town had "improved in appearance tho not in morals." As a major general he was in numerous Civil War battles and was severely wounded. Heitman; *1990 Register of Graduates*; *Dictionary of American Biography,* vol. 7, pp. 258, 259; Dan L. Thrapp, *Encyclopedia of Frontier Biography,* vol. 2 (Glendale, Calif.: Clark, 1988), pp. 1086, 1087; Bernarr Cresap, *Appomattox Commander: The Story of General E. O. C. Ord* (London: Tantivy, 1981); Edward O. C. Ord, *The City of Angels and the City of Saints,* ed. Neal Harlow (San Marino, Calif.: Huntington Library, 1978).

24. Mrs. Ord (Mary Mercer Thompson before marriage) was called "Molly." They had thirteen children; seven lived to maturity. Placidus Ord had been a U.S. attorney and a member of the 1849 California Constitutional Convention. The daughter was Roberta Ord, then twenty-one. Cresap, *Appomattox Commander,* p. 399.

25. See Oscar Osburn Winther, *The Transportation Frontier: Trans-Mississippi West, 1865–1890* (1964; reprint, Albuquerque: Univ. of New Mexico Press, 1974). For entertaining accounts of stagecoach travel see Carrie Adell Strahorn, *Fifteen Thousand Miles by Stage, vol. 1, 1877–1880* (1911; reprint, Lincoln: Univ. of Nebraska Press, 1988).

26. Todd, pp. 41, 42.

27. Ibid., p. 123; see Britton Davis, *The Truth about Geronimo* (1929; reprint, Lincoln: Univ. of Nebraska Press, 1976); Odie B. Faulk, *The Geronimo Campaign* (New York: Oxford Univ. Press, 1969); Dan L. Thrapp, ed., *Dateline Fort Bowie* (Norman: Univ. of Oklahoma Press, 1979); Donald E. Worcester, *The Apaches, Eagles of the Southwest* (Norman: Univ. of Oklahoma Press, 1979); H. B. Wharfield, *Apache Indian Scouts* (El Cajon, Calif.: n.p., 1964).

28. Richard Hulbert Wilson was in the 8th Infantry for twenty-nine years, nineteen of which were on the frontier. He later served as PMS&T at Massachusetts Agricultural College at Amherst. *1990 Register of Graduates*; *AOG Report for 1937*.

29. In addition to Wilson, other classmates were Robert Emmet, James Maney, Ben Butler, Charles Bradley, and John Hegewald. Todd, pp. 31, 32.

30. Ibid., p. 49.

31. Similar to Wilson, John January Haden of Texas, son of a Confederate officer, was on his way to join the 8th Infantry in Arizona. After thirteen years on the frontier and four years as PMS&T at the University of Missouri, he was retired for disability and died a few years later. Heitman; *1990 Register of Graduates*; *AOG Report for 1903*, pp. 138–42.

32. Todd, pp. 57, 58.

33. Ibid., pp. 67–72.

34. Ibid., p. 34.

35. Ibid., p. 29.

36. San Antonio was the hub for several stagecoach companies including the San Antonio and Eagle Pass U.S. Mail Line. By late 1877 its stages departed daily for Fort Duncan, passing through stations ten to twenty-five miles apart at Rio Medio, Castroville, New Fountain, D'Hanis, Sabinal, Uvalde, Turkey Creek, Midway Station, and Fort Clark. Robert H. Thonhoff, *San Antonio Stage Lines, 1847–1881* (El Paso: Texas Western Press, 1971).

37. See Wooster, *Soldiers, Sutlers, and Settlers*, pp. 193–95.

38. Second Lt. Clayton S. Burbank had been commissioned in the 10th Infantry in 1867. Heitman; *1878 Army Register*.

CHAPTER 5

1. In 1700 the Spanish, to counter a perceived threat from further French colonization of Louisiana, established a mission a few miles south of what later became Fort Duncan. Within three years two other missions were located about a mile to two miles apart from it to form a triangle in the center of which a company of thirty soldiers was garrisoned. For the next several decades this outpost, called *Presidio de San Juan Bautista del Rio Grande*, served as the principal route of travel between Mexico and Texas. Paul Horgan, *Great River: The Rio Grande in North American History*, vol. 1 (New York: Rinehart, 1954), pp. 323–27.

2. *Outline Descriptions of the Posts in the Military Division of the Missouri* (Chicago: Mil. Div. of the Missouri, 1876; fac. ed., Bellevue, Nebr.: Old Army Press, 1969), pp. 203, 204; WPA, *Texas: Guide to the Lone Star State* (New York: Hastings, 1940), pp. 507, 508; Charles M. Robinson III, *Pioneer Forts of Texas* (Houston: Gulf, 1986), pp. 37–39; Miller, *Texas Forts*, p. 25.

3. Abner Doubleday, Class of 1838, is credited with popularizing baseball. He was a major general in the Civil War, and afterwards was colonel of the 24th Infantry. Heitman; Lydia Spencer Lane, *I Married a Soldier* (1892; reprint, Albuquerque: Horn & Wallace, 1964), p. 29.

4. P. H. Sheridan, *Personal Memoirs*, vol. 1 (New York: Webster, 1888), pp. 25–27.

5. Lane, *I Married a Soldier*, pp. 28, 29. In 1846 William B. Lane was commissioned in the Regiment of Mounted Riflemen, which became the 3d Cavalry in 1861.

Heitman, pp. 80, 143; *Act of August 3, 1861*. Fort Inge, near Uvalde, was used from 1849 until 1855, then intermittently until abandoned in 1869. Robert W. Frazer, *Forts of the West* (Norman: Univ. of Oklahoma Press, 1965), p. 152.

6. Teresa Viele, *Following the Drum: A Glimpse of Frontier Life* (1858; reprint, Austin: Steck-Vaughn, 1968), pp. 151, 152.

7. Ibid., pp. 140, 141.

8. Hutton, *Phil Sheridan and His Army,* p. 6.

9. See Frazer, *Forts of the West,* pp. 148, 149; Miller, *Texas Forts,* pp. 25, 26; Joseph H. and James R. Toulouse, *Pioneer Posts of Texas* (San Antonio: Naylor, 1936), pp. 89–91; Herbert M. Hart, *Pioneer Forts of the West* (Seattle: Superior, 1967), pp. 49–51; M. L. Crimmins, "Old Fort Duncan: a Frontier Post," *Frontier Times* (1937–1938), pp. 379–385; Ernest Wallace, ed., "History in West Texas," *West Texas Historical Association Yearbook* 47 (1971), p. 155; and William T. Field, "Fort Duncan and Old Eagle Pass," *Texas Military History* 6 (Summer 1967), pp. 160–71.

10. *ANJ,* August 10, 1867, p. 810.

11. Frances Anne Mullen Boyd, *Cavalry Life in Tent and Field* (1894; reprint, Lincoln: Univ. of Nebraska Press, 1982). See Susan Miles, "Fort Concho in 1877," *West Texas Historical Association Yearbook* (October 1959), pp. 29–49.

12. Boyd, *Cavalry Life in Tent and Field,* pp. 285, 286.

13. See Robert Wooster, "The Army and the Politics of Expansion: Texas and the Southwestern Borderlands, 1870–1886," *Southwestern Historical Quarterly* 93 (October 1989), pp. 151–67.

14. See Robert M. Utley, *Frontier Regulars, 1866–1891* (Bloomington: Univ. of Indiana Press, 1973), pp. 344–56; Hutton, *Phil Sheridan and His Army,* pp. 217–26; Charles M. Robinson III, *Bad Hand: A Biography of General Ranald S. Mackenzie* (Austin: State House Press, 1993), pp. 130–44; and Michael D. Pierce, *The Most Promising Young Officer: A Life of Ranald Slidell Mackenzie* (Norman: Univ. of Oklahoma Press, 1993), pp. 124–34. The communications between the principals (NARA, RG 94, AGO 1873) are reprinted in *The Museum Journal* 9 (1965), pp. 159–90, and 10 (1966), pp. 19–76 and 199–227 (Lubbock: West Texas Museum Association, 1967 and 1968). Also see Joseph H. Dorst, "Ranald Slidell Mackenzie," *Journal of the U.S. Cavalry Association* 10, no. 39 (December 1897), pp. 367–82; Joseph Mills Hanson, "Ranald Slidell Mackenzie," *Cavalry Journal* 43, no. 18 (January-February 1934), pp. 25–32; and Edward S. Wallace, "General Ranald Slidell Mackenzie: Indian Fighting Cavalryman," *Southwestern Historical Quarterly* 56 (June 1953), pp. 378–96.

15. William Rufus Shafter, the tough, athletic son of a Michigan frontiersman and abolishionist, taught school before entering the equivalent of a two year college in 1861. A few months later he was made a lieutenant in a Michigan regiment, then transferred to the 17th Colored Infantry. Later he became a brevet brigadier general and a Medal of Honor recipient. When the 41st Infantry was formed he became its lieutenant colonel, and in 1879 colonel of the 1st Infantry. The name "Pecos Bill" was acquired when he ordered a fifty-mile march to the Pecos in lieu of turning back from a scout. His achievements include exploring the Staked Plains and raiding into Mexico. Heitman; *1878 Army Register; Dictionary of American Biography,* vol. 9, pp. 15, 16; Paul H. Carlson, *"Pecos Bill": A Military Biography of William R. Shafter* (College Station: Texas A&M Press, 1989), passim; Robert M. Utley, "Pecos Bill on the Texas Frontier," *The American West* 6, no. 1 (January 1969), pp. 4–13, 61, 62.

16. Bullis enlisted in 1862 and later became a captain in a black infantry regiment. In 1867 he was appointed a Regular Army second lieutenant and from 1873 until 1882 commanded the Seminole Negro-Indian Scouts who were descendants of runaway slaves that had found refuge among the Seminoles in Florida before being removed to the Indian Territory in the late 1840s. One band left there and settled near Piedras Negras where many of the men were recruited. Heitman; Thrapp, *Encyclopedia of Frontier Biography*, vol. 1, pp. 189, 190; Dunlay, *Wolves for the Blue Soldiers,* passim; Williams, *Texas' Last Frontier,* passim; Scott Thybony, "Against All Odds, Black Seminoles Won Their Freedom," *Smithsonian* 22 (August 1991), pp. 90–101; Kenneth Wiggins Porter, "The Seminole Negro-Indian Scouts," *Southwestern Historical Quarterly* 55 (January 1952), pp. 364, 369; and Edward S. Wallace, "General John Lapham Bullis: Thunderbolt of the Texas Frontier," *Southwestern Historical Quarterly* 55 (July 1951), pp. 77–85.

17. *Outline Description of Posts,* p. 204.

18. Todd, p. 34.

19. Rev. Stat. of 1877, sec. 1136; GO 95, AGO, 1868; GO 60, AGO, 1870; GO 103, AGO, 1872. Because of the "frequent changes in stations of troops...officers [were] prohibited from expending any labor or money upon them...upon penalty of being held pecuniarily responsible." Also, unless Congress appropriated money and authorized citizen mechanics, all repairs and "wherever practical" all construction had to be done by soldiers. *1881 Regulations*, paras. 333 and 334; also see Erna Risch, *Quartermaster Support of the Army: A History of the Corps, 1775–1939* (Washington, D.C.: Office of the QMG, 1962), pp. 484–91; Knight, *Life and Manners,* pp. 112–27.

20. Risch, ibid., pp. 488, 489.

21. *Sherman Papers,* LC, Container 95, pp. 39, 40.

22. Todd, pp. 25, 26. After a year at the short-lived "new" Spotted Tail Agency on the Missouri River, Baxter's company moved to Fort Robinson where in midwinter it fought Dull Knife's Cheyennes. He resigned in 1881, became a wealthy cattleman, had a key role in the Johnson County War, and in 1886 briefly served as territorial governor of Wyoming. Heitman; *1990 Register of Graduates*; *1879 Army Register*; *AOG Report for 1930,* pp. 125, 126; Helena Huntington Smith, *War on the Powder River* (New York: McGraw-Hill, 1966), passim; Mari Sandoz, *The Cattlemen* (New York: Hastings, 1958), pp. 329–402.

23. Todd, pp. 101–3. Most officers were brutally caustic about their surroundings. For example, in 1877 Colonel Bradley wrote, "Omaha is a detestable place in a wet time, and not a very attractive place at any other time...." *Journal of Luther P. Bradley,* May 18, 1877, U.S. Army Military History Institute. Also see *ANJ,* December 7, 1875, p. 262. For a sample of unflattering views of Arizona see Robert M. Utley, "Arizona Vanquished," *The American West* 6 (November 1969), pp. 16–21.

24. William H. Rideing, "Life at a Frontier Post," *Appleton's Journal* 15 (April 29, 1876), pp. 564, 565; also see Martha Fleishman and Carol Joy Justice, *Bugs to Blizzards: An Army Wife at Fort D. A. Russell* (Cheyenne, Wyo.: Wigwam, 1974).

25. August 11, 1888, letter to the *Galveston News* from John Highland, who wrote that he had been with Sheridan when the remark was made. To make amends Sheridan explained that he liked Texas and even planned to send his wife and children to Galveston which was "a fine place...to have a drive." Note, *Southwestern Historical Quarterly* 45 (October 1941), pp. 197, 198; Wooster, *Soldiers, Sutlers, and Settlers,* p. 176.

26. April 14, 1882, letter, *Sherman Papers,* Container 95, LC, p. 307. Earlier in the century Manuel Armijo, three-time governor of New Mexico between 1827 and 1846, supposedly lamented, "Poor New Mexico. So far from Heaven but so close to Texas."

27. Lloyd Lewis, *Sherman: Fighting Prophet* (New York: Harcourt, Brace, 1932), p. 596.

28. Asst. Surgeon W. R. Steinmetz, "Fort Duncan, Texas," *Circular No. 8,* pp. 201–7; Crimmins, "Old Fort Duncan." For the impressions of the post in 1886 by the fourteen-year-old daughter of an officer recently assigned there, see Mary Leefe Laurence, *Daughter of the Regiment,* ed. Thomas T. Smith (Lincoln: Univ. of Nebraska Press, 1996), pp. 85–89.

29. Four officers were unmarried, and the wives of the other two remained in the East, which was not uncommon because of the costs, hardships, and absence of educational opportunities at western posts. Knight, *Life and Manners,* p. 193.

30. In 1862 Edwin J. Stivers entered the army as a fifer. The next year he was commissioned in the 17th U.S. Colored Infantry and later became a brevet major. In July 1866 he was appointed in the 40th Infantry. Mrs. Gasman was the wife of 2d Lt. Hans Jacob Gasman, who had been disenrolled from West Point in 1870 after one year there. In 1873 he was commissioned in the 10th Cavalry. During Bigelow's first few weeks at Duncan, Gasman was on scouting duties. Earlier in 1877 he also had been scouting when his wife gave birth to a child who died six days later, before he returned. Heitman; *1878 Army Register*; *ANJ,* October 4, 1879; Leckie, *The Buffalo Soldiers,* p. 163.

31. John K. Herr and Edward S. Wallace, *The Story of the U.S. Cavalry, 1775–1942* (Boston: Little, Brown, 1953), pp. 146, 147.

32. *ANJ*, February 2, 1877, p. 411.

CHAPTER 6

1. George W. Schofield, a Civil War brigadier general who received a commission in the 41st Infantry, was John M. Schofield's brother. He transferred to the 10th Cavalry in 1870. Heitman; *1878 Army Register*; James L. McDonough, *Schofield: Union General in the Civil War and Reconstruction* (Tallahassee: Florida State Univ. Press, 1972); Dan L. Thrapp, *The Conquest of Apacheria* (Norman: Univ. of Oklahoma Press, 1976), pp. 237ff.

2. Todd, p. 40. Crane erred because "it did not occur to (him) to visit the Adjutant General of the Department (before leaving San Antonio)," who would have informed him of the change of post.

3. Richard I. Dodge, "The Enlisted Soldier," *JMSI* 8 (1887), pp. 259–318, at 298. The nomadic lifestyle implicit in such prevailing wisdom was accepted by most officers and their families. One wife wrote that she could never "settle down to quiet, civilized, respectable life, and remain in the same place year after year.... We had never lived more than six months at any one post, and three or four in the same place gave us the feeling of old inhabitants. We made nine moves in eighteen months in New Mexico." Lane, *I Married a Soldier,* p. 190.

4. In addition to the "Long House" Fort Duncan had four other one-story buildings from 75 feet to 225 feet apart that housed the officers and their families. Two

adobe buildings with four rooms served as the commandant's quarters, while a 50-by-24-foot stone and adobe building divided into three rooms, and two stone buildings, one 50-by-30 feet, and the other 64-by-23 feet, were shared by two or more officers and their families. Each set of quarters had a kitchen and sink (outhouse) nearby. *Circular 8,* p. 203. A lieutenant was assigned one room, a captain two, a major or lieutenant colonel three, a colonel or brigadier general four, and other generals five; each room was supplied with one heating stove and, depending on the occupant's rank, received two to five cords of wood monthly from September through April. *1881 Regulations,* paras. 1840, 1863; GO 2 and GO 92, 1877. See William L. Brown III, *The Army Called It Home: Military Interiors in the 19th Century* (Gettysburg, Pa.: Thomas Publications, 1992) for a magnificent collection of photographs of officers' quarters, enlisted men's barracks, and other facilities at various posts.

5. Capt. Charles B. Byrne, 25th Infantry, had been appointed an assistant surgeon in 1868. He served as the army's deputy surgeon general in 1901. Morris C. Wessells of New Jersey, a lieutenant in the 24th Infantry, was later court-martialed for disobedience and public drunkenness in Laredo; because he was too intoxicated to understand the order, he was acquitted. He died in 1895, three weeks after resigning. Heitman; *1878 Army Register; GCMO 50, Dept. of Texas,* November 22, 1878; *ANJ,* December 21, 1878, p. 321.

6. The lady probably was Mrs. Cornelius W. Lawrence, who in 1879 under the name "L. A. Lawrence" published a book on spiritualism intriguingly titled *Do They Love Us Yet?* Bigelow did not expand on his somewhat caustic comment.

7. David Schooley, 25th Infantry, had been a Civil War captain who was commissioned in the 40th Infantry in 1866. Second Lt. Henry H. Landon, Class of 1872, was assigned to the 25th Infantry. Heitman; *1878 Army Register.*

8. At each post a sutler (a civilian who sold food, liquor, and merchandise) was appointed by the secretary of war for a three-year term. *Revised Regulations of 1861,* para. 211ff. The much-criticized system was abolished after Secretary W. W. Belknap resigned in 1876 to avoid impeachment for selling sutlerships for personal gain. Sutlers were succeeded by post traders who had to be recommended by the post's council of administration and approved by the commanding officer, but for years the terms were used interchangeably. *Act of July 24, 1876*; GO 70, AGO, 1876. See David Michael Delo, *Peddlers and Post Traders: The Army Sutler of the Frontier* (Salt Lake City: Univ. of Utah Press, 1992); Weigley, *History of the United States Army,* pp. 286, 287; Lewis, *Sherman: Fighting Prophet,* pp. 608, 622; Wooster, *Soldiers, Sutlers, and Settlers,* p. 77. In 1889 canteens were established, only to be superseded three years later by post exchanges. GO 10, AGO 1889; GO 11, AGO 1892.

9. *Act of July 15, 1870*; Rev. Stat. of 1878, sec. 1232. Despite circulars admonishing officers not to violate the prohibition, for many more years soldiers were hired to perform domestic labor. *ANJ,* September 10, 1881, p. 115.

10. See Appendix D; *1878 Army Register,* p. 258C.

11. Knight, *Life and Manners,* p. 128.

12. Don Rickey, Jr., *Forty Miles a Day on Beans and Hay* (Norman: Univ. of Oklahoma Press, 1963), passim; Summerhayes, *Vanished Arizona,* pp. 88, 89; Wooster, *Soldiers, Sutlers, and Settlers,* pp. 73, 74. Not all such relationships were harmonious. In 1881 Frances Roe ordered their "terrible tempered" striker from her house for using loud and abusive language; she later learned he previously had been acquitted of a

homicide. Frances Roe, *Army Letters from an Officer's Wife, 1871–1888* (1909; reprint, Lincoln: Univ. of Nebraska Press, 1981), pp. 285–88.

13. Captain Van de Wiele's career commenced as a corporal in 1861. He soon became a lieutenant and later a brevet major. In 1867 he was appointed a captain in the 10th Cavalry. Heitman; *1878 Army Register.*

14. Army directives required horses to be groomed from one-and-one-half to two hours daily, and stable call (normally in early morning and late afternoon) was tedium incarnate for cavalrymen. When the call was sounded, soldiers and officers donned white frocks and proceeded to the stables where the men would brush, currycomb, and tend to their mounts, then "stand to heel" for inspection. Other measures to assure the health of horses included examining their feet daily and stuffing them with wet clay or cow manure at least weekly, reshodding at least monthly, sponging nostrils with water and vinegar at least weekly, never wetting an animal when it was heated, and keeping the stables policed, free from smells, and well whitewashed. See *1881 Regulations,* paras. 297–316.

15. Border violations and pillaging had raged on both sides of the river for years. See H. Rpt. 395, 43d Cong., 1st sess. vol. 2 (1874), *Depredations on the Texas Frontier* (Serial 1624). In addition to livestock raids, the violations included an August 1877 attack by Mexicans on the Rio Grande City jail and release of two "notorious murderers," as well as an assault that October on San Elizario by about 300 Mexicans who "arrested" several citizens, including the judge. H. Exec. Doc. 13, 45th Cong., 1st sess., vol. 1 (1877), *Mexican Border Troubles* (Serial 1773).

16. The population of this highly productive river region was primarily Mexican and Indian, with whites constituting only a small fraction (probably less than 10 percent) of the 30,000 or so people living on the United States side. The posts most directly involved were, from south to north, Fort Brown, Ringgold Barracks, Fort McIntosh, and Fort Duncan (all on the river) as well as Fort Clark (inland some forty-plus miles northeast of Duncan). The river region above Duncan was so sparsely settled on both sides that incursions there, most of which were by Indians, seldom occurred since there was so little to steal. See H. Misc. Doc. 64 for 1878, passim.

17. The raids were not just by Indians. Some into Texas were by Mexicans (at times dressed as Indians) and some into Mexico were by "river outlaws" that included "cow-boys" who, having become unemployed as cattle business declined and ranches were fenced, would not "work" but instead took up marauding. Ibid. p. 119; see Horgan, *Great River,* vol. 2, pp. 853–67.

18. H. Misc. Doc. 64 for 1878, p. 241.

19. Ibid. The apprehensions of losing more territory to the United States might have been well founded. A leading periodical commented at length on the designs of a large, heterogeneous group to force hostilities with Mexico. Its members supposedly included owners of mining concessions and railroad franchises, ex-Confererate soldiers, contractors, Roman Catholic clergymen, politicians who thought a war might revive business and "quell the Communists," and claimants of all sorts. Within the last category, the experiences of a special commission appointed in 1873 to investigate cattle theft from Texas were cited. Among the claimants were twenty ranchers in one county who purportedly had stolen from them five times the entire number of cattle in the county, and sixty-five owners in eleven counties who claimed that their losses

were worth three-fourths of the value of all the cattle in the entire state. "The Mexican Border Grievances," *The Nation,* August 29, 1878, pp. 125, 126.

20. Testimony of Julius R. Tucker, a Brownsville banker and rancher, in H. Misc. Doc. 64 for 1878, pp. 236ff. John Salmon Ford, a doctor, editor, legislator, statesman, soldier, and Texas Ranger, is best remembered as "Rip" Ford, a name acquired during the Mexican War when he commenced his letters of condolence to the relatives of dead soldiers with the words, "Rest in Peace," which he later shortened to "R.I.P." as the number of messages surged. Harold B. Simpson, *Cry Comanche: The 2nd U.S. Cavalry in Texas, 1855–1861* (Hillsboro, Tex.: Hill Junior College Press, 1979), p. 108 n17.

21. H. Misc. Doc. 64 for 1878, p. 260.

22. Gen. Gerónimo Treviño commanded more than 2,000 Mexican troops on the Rio Grande; the soldiers at Piedras Negras were headed by General Falcón. They had to contend with not only "predatory" Indians and their Mexican sympathizers (largely French or Mexican deserters recruited by "cleaning out the prisons"), but also irregulars under the control of local strong men. Horgan, *Great River,* vol. 2, p. 854. H. Misc. Doc. 64 for 1878, pp. 77–114. José de la Cruz Porfirio Díaz, a hero of the French War and the 1876 overthrow of President de Tajada, was president from 1877 to 1880 and from 1884 until exiled in 1910. James A. Magner, *Men of Mexico* (Milwaukee: Bruce, 1943), pp. 440–82; James Creelman, *Diaz: Master of Mexico* (New York: D. Appleton, 1911).

23. H. Misc. Doc. 64 for 1878, p. 43.

24. Soon after Bigelow assumed command there were only forty men present for duty. Of the balance twelve were on extra duty, five sick, one on leave, and eight in arrest or confinement. *10th Cavalry Return for January 1878,* NARA, RG 391, M744, roll 96 (1873–1880).

25. Todd, p. 35.

26. Ibid.

27. WPA, *San Antonio,* p. 34.

28. Bushick, *Glamorous Days,* p. 243. In 1877 the governor of Texas reportedly published a list of 5,000 men "wanted in Texas by the law." Horgan, *Great River,* vol. 2, p. 854.

29. Ibid. With the passage of time, reports of violence in Texas during the period in question have become overblown, of course. A study of conditions around Fort Griffin showed, for example, that although "victimless" crimes (such as gambling, drinking, and prostitution) often were condoned, homicides were treated severely, and that the legal system generally performed well except "where the outcasts of society were concerned—African Americans, Jews, and Indians." Ty Cashion, "(Gun)smoke Gets in Your Eyes: a Revisionist Look at 'Violent' Fort Griffin," *Southwestern Historical Quarterly* 99 (July 1995), pp. 81–94.

30. Crane, *Experiences,* p. 70. John King Fisher, a notorious gunfighter and rustler who admitted seven homicides, "not counting Mexicans," operated out of Eagle Pass. In 1884 he and Ben Thompson were killed in a San Antonio saloon. Thrapp, *Encyclopedia of Frontier Biography,* vol. 1, p. 494; Odie Fisher, *King Fisher: His Life and Times* (Norman: Univ. of Oklahoma Press, 1966), passim; Paul Trachtman, *The Gunfighters* (New York: Time–Life, 1974), p. 179; James D. Horan, *The Authentic Wild West: The Gunfighters* (New York: Crown, 1976); and Bushick, *Glamorous Days,*

pp. 174-96. Although carrying firearms was customary, "people are polite to each other [and] you hardly ever hear of a street-fight, for if a man has a quarrel...he shoots it out and that ends the trouble." Testimony of Capt. Henry C. Corbin, 24th Infantry, H. Misc. Doc. 64 for 1878, p. 150. In a similar vein, a few days later Bigelow met Edgar S. Beacom, Class of 1873, whom he had known at West Point. Beacom was then collector of customs at Eagle Pass, an occupation "accompanied with some danger, one of his colleagues having been shot a short time ago by smugglers." Whether Beacom's death at age thirty-four was from natural causes or at the hands of smugglers is not known.

31. In 1874 only $75,000 a year (about $3 a soldier) was allotted for small arms ammunition. How the funds were used depended on the commander, and as early as 1869 General Ord ordered weekly target practice.

32. Albert G. Brackett, "Our Cavalry," *JMSI* 4 (1883), pp. 383–407. Colonel Brackett's paper was read before a meeting of the Military Service Institution attended by Sherman, Bigelow, and a dozen other members.

33. GO 95, 1877; *1881 Regulations*, paras. 481ff. In Sherman's view, "one who...has confidence in his musket is worth in a fight half a dozen dummies." Rpt. of General of the Army in H. Exec. Doc. 1, 48th Cong., 1st sess., vol. 1 (1883), *Report of the SecWar* (Serial 2182); *New York Times*, November 2, 1883. During the next several years various officers wrote about how to make best use of such practice. See Sedgwick Pratt, "Target Practice at a Fixed Target," *JMSI* 4 (1883), pp. 67–72, and James E. Brett, "Target Practice," *JMSI* 14 (1893), pp. 573–77.

34. Major Schofield had designed the ejector for this weapon. He was also noted for his miserly propensities that led one private to conclude that "the penny was his god." See Emil A. Bode, *A Dose of Frontier Soldiering*, ed. Thomas T. Smith (Lincoln: Univ. of Nebraska Press, 1994), pp. 40, 41.

35. The officer of the day's duties included being present at guard mount, inspecting the guard house, verifying the number of prisoners, enforcing police regulations, assuring cleanliness on the post, supervising fatigue parties, visiting guards during the day and at least once after midnight, and rendering reports to the commanding officer. *1881 Regulations*, paras. 352–55.

36. A couple of days later Bigelow noted that "the two parties that went after game...have returned. The Sergeant...only brought back two deer. I was too formal in receiving his report. Should have asked him what luck he had, how the game was, &c." Apparently he was beginning to realize that there was more to leading soldiers than affecting an unbending formality.

CHAPTER 7

1. William H. Givens of Kentucky, one of Company B's "old soldiers," had enlisted in the 10th Cavalry in 1869; he was a highly effective NCO who later distinguished himself in combat. See Epilogue.

2. Faro was the most widespread gambling game in the West, but monte (also called "Spanish monte" or "monte bank"), was quite popular, especially among Mexicans. There were several versions but commonly "layouts" of three or four cards were dealt to each player from a deck of forty cards, then the deck was turned over to expose the "gate" card. If it matched a layout card (or in some games was simply of the

same suit) on which bets had been made, the player won. Not only did the odds favor the dealer, but as larcenous gamblers increasingly manipulated decks to prevent a player from winning, the game was so discredited that the ancient term of "mountebank" was resurrected as a frontier synonym for swindler. After experienced gamblers abandoned the game and more timorous bettors commenced to play ("pike") it, a person wagering trivial amounts came to be known as a "piker." Robert K. DeArment, *Knights of the Green Cloth* (Norman: Univ. of Oklahoma Press, 1975), pp. 395–98; Peter Watts, *A Dictionary of the Old West* (New York: Promontory, 1987).

3. Before Bigelow arrived at Fort Duncan, Orleman had been placed on sick leave because of failing vision. His absence provided the opportunity for Bigelow to command the company.

4. AW 66 of 1874; Scott, p. 301; Brig. Gen. George B. Davis, *A Treatise on the Military Law of the United States* (New York: John Wiley & Sons, 1909) (hereafter Davis), pp. 66–68 and 483–85; *Regulations of 1895*, para. 936.

5. AWs 66, 68, and 70 of 1874. In 1895 the need for many pre-trial confinements was reduced significantly when "crimes" was interpreted to mean only "serious offenses."

6. Steinmetz, "Fort Duncan, Texas," p. 203.

7. *ANJ*, January 27, 1872, pp. 38; also see Capt. J. W. Pope, "Military Penology," *JMSI* 12 (July 1891), pp. 782–96.

8. *Act of March 3, 1873*, Rev. Stat. of 1878, sec. 1344–61. A board was appointed to plan and draft regulations for the prison, which was to be built at Rock Island, Illinois. GO 100, AGO, October 4, 1873. Congress later changed the location to Fort Leavenworth. *Act of May 21, 1874*, Rev. Stat. of 1878, sec. 1344.

9. See Wooster, *Soldiers, Sutlers, and Settlers*, passim.

10. The "commissary of subsistence" (commissary officer) was permitted to sell supplies to officers and enlisted men on credit. *1881 Regulations*, paras. 2199–225. However, complaints about both the quality and quantity of available food were common. See *ANJ*, August 24, 1867, p. 10; Emily Boynton O'Brisen, "Army Life at Fort Sedgwick, Colorado," *The Colorado Magazine* 6, no. 5 (September 29, 1929), p. 176; and Brackett, *Our Cavalry*, p. 387.

11. Wives' perspectives of social life can be found in Elizabeth Custer, *Boots and Saddles* (New York: Harper and Row, 1885); Frances Roe, *Army Letters from an Officer's Wife*; and Katherine Gibson Fougera, *With Custer's Cavalry* (1940; reprint, Lincoln: Univ. of Nebraska Press, 1986) as well as Knight, *Life and Manners*, pp. 110–62. Excellent secondary sources include Patricia Y. Stallard, *Glittering Misery: Dependents of the Indian Fighting Army* (San Rafael, Calif: Presidio Press, and Fort Collins, Colo.: Old Army Press, 1978), passim; and Wooster, *Soldiers, Sutlers, and Settlers*, pp. 163–81. Also see Sandra L. Myres, "Romance and Reality on the American Frontier: Views of Army Wives," *Western Historical Quarterly* 13 (October 1982), and "The Ladies of the Army—Views of Western Life," *The American Military on the Frontier*, Proceedings of the Seventh Military History Symposium, U.S. Air Force Academy, 1976.

12. Participatory entertainment was generally all that existed at frontier posts. Insofar as is known the first theatrical group was formed at Fort Towson, Indian Territory, in 1839. Its initial performance included a poetic address, a romantic Indian play, and a musical farce. Among the audience was a group of Choctaw Indians who

reportedly "exhibited the most intense excitement" on each appearance of an actress portraying a "young squaw." R. I. E., "Army Theatricals," *JMSI* 6 (1884), p. 111.

13. See Richard Dalzell Gamble, *Garrison Life at Frontier Military Posts, 1830–1860* (Ph.D. diss., Univ. of Oklahoma, 1956), pp. 182–99; Rickey, *Forty Miles a Day on Beans and Hay,* pp. 185–213. Laundresses were a routine part of a post's complement until 1878 when Congress prohibited them from accompanying troops. Their demise was gradual, however, as regimental commanders were permitted to retain those married to soldiers until their husbands' enlistments expired. *Act of June 18, 1878*; GO 37, AGO, 1878; *1881 Regulations,* para. 176. See Miller J. Stewart, "Army Laundresses: Ladies of the 'Soap Suds Row,'" *Nebraska History* 61 (Winter 1980), pp. 421–36.

14. Brackett, *Our Cavalry,* p. 390.

15. Steinmetz, "Fort Duncan, Texas," p. 205.

16. For example, Christmas 1873 at Fort Lyon involved a parade with "grotesque" costumes, field sports, and a masquerade ball for which the ladies prepared "an elegant supper." *ANJ,* January 10, 1874. Similarly, barracks at Fort Tularosa, New Mexico, were decorated with flags, cut evergreens, howitzers with wreaths, and a chandelier with "Merry Christmas to all" on it that revolved above the revelers. At midnight roasted pigs, turkeys, chickens, sweetmeats, and cakes were served. *ANJ,* January 24, 1875; see Knight, *Life and Manners,* pp. 155, 156.

17. See testimony of General Sherman, General Ord, and others in H. Misc. Doc. 64 for 1878, passim.

18. Joseph Bush, a Vermont volunteer veteran during the Civil War, was commissioned in the 22d Infantry in 1866 and transferred to the 25th Infantry in 1879. Heitman; *1880 Army Register.*

19. After Civil War service as a lieutenant and captain, John W. French received an "at large" appointment in the 40th Infantry when it was organized, then transferred to the 25th Infantry in 1869. Heitman; *1879 Army Register.*

20. Bigelow could have invoked AW 53, imposing a fine of one dollar for an officer or one-sixth of a dollar for an enlisted man for any profane oath, but the offense had long been ignored. John Gibbon, "Law in the Army," *JMSI* 1 (1880), pp. 438–48.

CHAPTER 8

1. See William Winthrop, *Military Law and Precedents* (Washington: GPO, 2d ed., 1920) (hereafter Winthrop), pp. 57–119.

2. AW 64–67, 89; Sec. 1, *Act of May 29, 1830*; Scott, pp. 278–96; Davis, pp. 13–25b; Winthrop, pp. 480–90.

3. A written "charge" identified the Article of War violated, followed by one or more "specifications" setting forth who, when, where, how, and (if a required element) why the crime was committed. See Winthrop, pp. 132ff, 1010–23.

4. If the accused was found guilty of an alleged offense but if a reasonable doubt existed as to some particular, the court still could convict if what remained amounted to a "lesser included" offense. Ibid. pp. 315ff, 380–82.

5. Several Articles of War prescribed the sentence to be imposed, in which event the court's function was merely ministerial. Most of these required dismissal of an

officer convicted of a crime such as conduct unbecoming an officer and a gentleman (AW 61), making a false return (AW 8), or being drunk on duty (AW 38). Ibid., p. 395.

6. See Winthrop, pp. 390–446.

7. Bigelow Papers, USMA Library, Box 5. AW 94; Davis, pp. 134, 135; Scott, p. 281.

8. McDowell's remark appears in Report of General of the Army in H. Exec. Doc. 1, 47th Cong., 2d sess., vol. 2 (1882), *Report of the SecWar* (Serial 2091); *Sherman Papers,* Container 95, p. 43. The law was repealed in 1901.

9. Stephen Vincent Benet, *Treatise on Military Law and the Practice of Courts-Martial* (New York: D. Van Norstrand, 1862).

10. If the limited sentencing power of a garrison or regimental courts-martial would prevent a "proper disposition" of a case it should have been referred to a general court. Winthrop, p. 485.

11. AW 74; GO 29, AGO, 1890; Winthrop, pp. 165–7, 483.

12. Clause 14, Article I. *Barron v. Mayor of Baltimore,* 7 Peters 243; *Pearson v. Yewdall,* 95 U.S. 294; Winthrop, p. 165; Frederick Bernays Wiener, "Courts-Martial and the Bill of Rights: The Original Practice I," 72 *Harv. L. Rev.* 1–49 (1958); see Walter T. Cox III, "The Army, the Courts, and the Constitution," *Mil. L. Rev.* 118 (Fall 1987), pp. 23–27.

13. Bigelow missed the point. The orders did no more than reflect the law with respect to joint or common trials.

14. This time Bigelow was correct. Regardless of a guilty plea courts-martial had a duty to receive and report such evidence as might provide a better understanding of the circumstances surrounding the offense, and hence what sentence would be appropriate. GO 23, AGO, 1830; GO 21, AGO, 1833; Winthrop, pp. 191 n80, and 278–80.

15. AW 70 and 78; Winthrop, pp. 125, 126, 156, 157; Scott, p. 301; *ANJ,* January 24, 1885, pp. 504–6.

16. The first judge advocate was appointed in 1797, but in 1802 the position was abolished. From 1812 until 1821 each army division had a chief legal officer, and for the next twenty-eight years each major command had a judge advocate (usually a line officer). In 1849 the Office of the Judge Advocate General was created, followed in 1864 by the Bureau of Military Justice. In the 1870s one brigadier general and four majors were authorized, and in 1884 the BMJ was replaced by an eight-officer department. *Records of the Office of the Judge Advocate General,* NARA, RG 153, M1105, roll 7; Heitman, vol. 2, pp. 596, 597; *Acts of June 23, 1874,* and *June 26, 1876*; Anon., "A History of the Judge Advocate General's Corps," *The Army Lawyer* (1975), pp. 72–74.

17. December 9, 1890, letter, *Sherman Papers,* LC, Container 91, no. 202. Although Sherman's father had been a judge, his foster father a lawyer, and his brother a senator, he had an aversion to lawyers. See April 5, 1878, letter, *Sherman Papers,* Container 99, pp. 212, 213. His pragmatic (if not serious) approach is shown in his laconic response to a commander who had an alcoholic forage master: "George is not reforming very fast. I guess the best thing for him will be a shanty some distance from the post where he may drink himself to death as soon as possible." March 20, 1883, endorsement, *Sherman Papers,* Container 100, p. 51.

18. Leading colleges then taught some law courses, but decades passed before law schools became the common avenue to legal practice. William R. Johnson, *Schooled Lawyers: A Study in the Clash of Professional Cultures* (New York: New York Univ. Press,

1978), passim. In frontier towns settlers often established their own tribunals to dispense justice. See Wayne Gard, *Frontier Justice* (Norman: Univ. of Oklahoma Press, 1949), pp. 254–89; Richard B. Burg, "Administration of Justice in the Denver People's Courts: 1859–1861," *Journal of the West* 7, no. 4 (October 1968), pp. 510–21.

19. William T. Sherman, "Military Law," *JMSI* 1 (1879 and 1880), pp. 129–32, 320–55, and 385–437, at 437. Also see Gibbon, "Law in the Army." Before returning to the army in 1861 Sherman had been admitted to the Kansas Bar, but gave up practice after being "pettifogged out of" his first trial. W. Fletcher Johnson, *Life of Wm. Tecumseh Sherman* (Chicago: Donohue, Henneberry, 1891), pp. 61, 63; Lloyd Lewis, *Sherman: Fighting Prophet* (New York: Harcourt, Brace, 1932), pp. 102–12; Robert G. Athearn, *William Tecumseh Sherman and the Settlement of the West* (Norman: Univ. of Oklahoma Press, 1956), p. xiii; *1990 Register of Graduates*.

20. Legal studies taught by the chaplain commenced at West Point in 1821. In 1874 a separate Law Department was created under a judge advocate who taught a year-long course that included constitutional, international, elementary, and military law. Section 2, *Act of April 14, 1818*; Regulations of the Military Academy, July 10, 1818; Griess and Luvaas, *The Centennial of the United States Military Academy*, pp. 234, 366–74; Keith L. Sellen, "The United States Military Academy Law Department, Yesterday and Today," *Federal Bar News and Journal* 37, no. 4 (May 1990), pp. 231–39.

21. William E. Birkheimer, "Abridgment of Military Law," *JMSI* 13 (1893), p. 684.

22. See Robert O. Rollman, "Of Crimes, Courts-Martial and Punishment," *Air Force JAG L. Rev.* 11, no. 2 (Spring 1969), pp. 212–22; Cox, "The Army, the Courts, and the Constitution," pp. 3–30; Winthrop, pp. 45–48; Davis, pp. 13–25b; and letter to Justice Field, *Sherman Papers*, LC, Container 91, p. 286.

23. Jan. 28, 1868, letter, *Sherman Papers*, LC, Container 90, pp. 22, 23.

24. Winthrop, pp. 444–46. The punishments included having ears cropped or heads shaved, carrying a log or loaded knapsack, "riding" a wooden horse, wearing a barrel "overcoat," being spread-eagled on a wagon wheel, or bucking and gagging. See John B. Billings, *Hardtack and Coffee: The Unwritten Story of Army Life* (1887; reprint, Williamstown, Mass.: Corner House, 1980), pp. 143–63; John DeMorgan, "Barbaric Military Punishments," *The Green Bag* 10 (1898), pp. 34–36; *ANJ*, May 4, 1867, p. 585; and Rickey, *Forty Miles a Day on Beans and Hay*, pp. 156–84.

25. Describing the last punishment, a spectator wrote that "Gradually the deep, red wales assumed a blackish color, and in short time crimson drops of blood rolled down the naked legs, filling his shoes, or were splatched [*sic*] over the clothes of the spectators. Toward the seventy-fifth stroke the flesh around the hips hung in shreds, as if rudely torn by an animal's claws. From the middle of the back to within six inches of the knees, the body was perfectly raw and black.... The man's screams were awful; he bounded from side to side, spasmodically upward, and hung as if lifeless on the cross." *ANJ*, July 6, 1867, p. 725.

26. Report of TJAG, 49th Cong., 1st sess., vol. 1 (1885), *Report of the SecWar*, pp. 339, 340 (Serial 2369).

27. All officers were subject to serve on courts-martial, although the secretary of war "decidedly disapproved" of chaplains as members. Letter, Army Hq. to Dept. of the Columbia, May 13, 1875; *ANJ*, July 3, 1875, p. 573.

28. Quoted in Jack D. Foner, *The United States Soldier between Two Wars: Army Life and Reforms, 1865–1898* (New York: Humanities Press, 1970), p. 36. The doctor went on to propose a solution worthy of Torquemada:

> I'd respectfully make suggestion,
> That small cases to decide,
> We select a stalwart African
> Armed with a stout cowhide.
>
> Let him agitate the prisoner
> Upon his back so bare,
> Should the misguided warrior
> To plead "not guilty" and "dare."
>
> Then will justice be out-meted
> With an unflinching hand.
> There'll be very few small cases,
> There'll be quiet thro' the land.

29. Major Schofield correctly stated the evidentiary rules concerning leading or immaterial questions and the general limitation on the scope of recross-examination.

30. See January 1, 1877, letter from Chaplain George T. Mullins, 25th Infantry, to Army AAG in *ANJ*, January 27, 1877, p. 395.

31. GO 6, Hqs. Fort Duncan, Texas, January 13, 1878.

32. Bigelow Papers, USMA Library, box 5, pp. 108–26, 131.

33. The answer caused Bigelow to complain that "the ignorance of colored soldiers is very trying to a recorder. Questions have to be put to them almost in monosyllables [and] their answers are in such bad english [*sic*] that it is sometimes almost impossible to punctuate them and very hard to get at their meaning."

34. Such conflicts were undesirable but not necessarily disqualifying, especially if they resulted from exigencies of the service (such as the small number of officers available), unless the officer was "strongly prejudiced for or against the accused." Winthrop, pp. 173, 174, 185, 186.

35. A hospital matron's position was thankless enough without the risk of being murdered. Compared to the pay of a private (thirteen to eighteen dollars a month), a matron received only ten dollars a month. (But then, female nurses in general hospitals earned only forty cents a day.) The lowest grade male hospital steward was paid twenty to twenty-five dollars monthly, and a steward first class thirty to thirty-five dollars. Rev. Stat. of 1878, sec. 1280–84; *1881 Army Register*, p. 258C.

36. *ANJ*, March 4, 1878, p. 621. *United States v. Maulsby*, NARA, RG 153, Case QQ 539 (1878). Captain Schooley was president and Lieutenant Wessells judge advocate of the court.

37. Second Lt. Charles Dodge, Jr., of the District of Columbia was an enlisted man from 1875 until 1878 when he was commissioned in the 24th Infantry. He died in 1898, by which time he had become a first lieutenant. Heitman.

38. Crane, *Experiences*, pp. 126–28.

CHAPTER 9

1. "Calling" was practiced well into the twentieth century before being gradually replaced by receptions. Ester Wier, *Army Social Customs* (Harrisburg, Pa.: Stackpole, 1958), pp. 1–8; Wooster, *Soldiers, Sutlers, and Settlers,* pp. 175–78.

2. During the Civil War Charles Crook Hood had been a captain in an Ohio regiment. In 1866 he was commissioned in the 41st Infantry. Heitman; *1878 Army Register.*

3. A "court of inquiry" was a board to recommend whether a court-martial was appropriate. An individual who thought he was unjustly suspected of a wrongdoing could request (but not demand) a hearing. AW 91 and 92 of 1806; AW 115–121 of 1874; Scott, pp. 220–23; Davis, pp. 294, 295; and Winthrop, pp. 516–33.

4. *Acts of July 7, 1838,* ch. 194; *March 3, 1849,* ch. 83; and *July 17, 1862,* ch. 200. Scott, pp. 216, 217.

5. Tenth Cavalry headquarters was at Fort Concho, 400 miles from Duncan; the 25th Infantry at Fort Davis, a distance of 650 miles; and the 24th Infantry at Fort Clark, 45 miles away.

6. Deoch Fulton, ed., *The Journal of Lieut. Sydenham* (New York: New York Public Library, 1940), p. 7.

7. Knight, *Life and Manners,* p. 183.

8. John P. Wisser, "Practical Instruction of Officers at Posts," *JMSI* 9 (1888), pp. 198–221.

9. See Coffman, *The Old Army,* pp. 276, 277; GO 80, AGO, October 5, 1891. The lyceum program was adopted from a German practice. See Eban Swift, "The Lyceum at Fort Agawam," *JMSI* 20 (1897), pp. 233–77. Not all officers thought that lyceums served the purposes intended. William E. Birkhimer, "Comment on Swift's Lyceum Article," *JMSI* 20 (1897), pp. 634, 635.

10. J. J. O'Connell, "Kriegspiel of Vinturnus," *JMSI* 4 (1883), pp. 418–22; and Swift, "The Lyceum at Fort Agawam," pp. 234ff.

11. Enlisted men received an allowance for clothing issued ("sold") to them from army supplies. In 1890 a recruit's handbook discloses that his allowance was $66.60 the first year, $31.75 the second year, and $30.66 the third year. The first year he expended $52.47 for clothing and equipment such as a helmet, a poncho, and blankets in addition to blouses (uniform coats) at $3.15 each, trousers at $1.82, and shoes at 81 cents a pair. Copy of N. Herschler, *The Soldier's Handbook* (Washington, D.C.: GPO, 1900), issued to Pvt. James S. Elliott, in USAFA Library collection.

12. See Risch, *Quartermaster Support of the Army,* pp. 453–514.

13. Despite the greater selections authorized, "size 4" was the largest coat and blouse stocked. Indicative of the small physical stature of most troops at that time, the percentages of sizes routinely sent to posts were 30 percent size 1 (the smallest), 45 percent size 2, 20 percent size 3, and 5 percent size 4. In 1884, for example, the standards for cavalry recruits were from five feet four to five feet ten inches and 165 pounds or less, while infantry and artillery could range from from five feet four inches to any height and from 120 to 190 pounds. *1881 Regulations,* paras. 2072–74; *ANJ,* January 26, 1884, p. 518.

14. Bigelow's Journal, August 28, 1878.

15. Report of Brig. Gen. Stanley in H. Exec. Doc. 1, 48th Cong., 2d sess. vol. 2 (1884), *Report of the SecWar,* p. 126 (Serial 2277).

16. See ibid., pp. 500–5; GO 76, AGO, 1879; *1881 Regulations,* para. 2777; also see S. A. Holabird, "Army Clothing," *JMSI* 2 (1882), pp. 355–87; Theo. A. Bingham, "Army Uniforms," *JMSI* 20 (1897); and "Army Uniforms," *Harper's Weekly,* May 4, 1895, p. 417; for changes in cavalry uniforms during this period see Douglas C. McChristian, *The U.S. Army in the West, 1870–1880* (Norman: Univ. of Oklahoma Press, 1995), passim; Sidney E. Whitman, *The Troopers: An Informal History of the Plains Cavalry, 1865–1890* (New York: Hastings House, 1962), pp. 190–203; and Randy Steffen, *The Horse Soldier, 1776–1943,* vol. 2 (Norman: Univ. of Oklahoma Press, 1978), passim. Also see Foner, *The United States Soldier between Two Wars,* pp. 19, 20.

17. Before trial NCOs were normally restricted to their quarters but privates were confined. Davis, pp. 66–68.

18. Officers were required to provide their own horses, but on the frontier a commander could permit a mounted officer to purchase a government horse at one-third more than the average cost of the lot from which it was selected, or at actual cost if that could be ascertained. *1881 Regulations*, paras. 1913, 1914.

19. General Falcón was the commander at Piedras Negras. The "grand ball" is described in *ANJ,* February 23, 1878, p. 453.

20. The commander of a black regiment in the Spanish-American War observed that all the soldiers in such regiments (most of which were raised in the South) were "men with a big proportion of white blood." R. L. Bullard, "The Negro Volunteer: Some Characteristics," *JSMI* 29 (1901), pp. 29–39 at 30, 31.

21. See James Ernest Conyers, *Selected Aspects of the Phenomenon of Negro Passing* (Ph.D. diss., Washington State Univ., 1962), p. 121, and Juanita Miller, "White Negroes," *Sociology and Social Research* 12 (May-June 1928), pp. 449–54. Dr. Conyers notes that "basic studies of Negro passing [were] practically non-existent," but the primary reasons might include obtaining economic, social, cultural, and recreational advantages, and in some cases marriage (especially prior to the mid-twentieth-century invalidation of miscegenation laws in all states).

22. Sgt. Thomas Shaw, 8th Cavalry, who received the Medal of Honor for heroism at Carrizo Canyon, New Mexico, in 1881, might have been added to Dillwood's list. Although a member of a white regiment, he is now listed among the African Americans recognized by that award. Senate Committee on Veterans' Affairs, *Medal of Honor Recipients, 1863–1978,* (Washington, D.C.: GPO, 1979); *Documents Relating to Blacks Awarded the Congressional Medal of Honor,* NARA, RG 94, M929, roll 2 (Indian Campaigns—U.S. Regular Army).

23. SO 20, Dept. of Texas, January 26, 1878; SO 7, Dist. of the Nueces, January 28, 1878; *ANJ,* February 9, 1878, p. 420.

24. If the suggestion implied that a military court should award monetary or other relief to victim, or that a commander order a debtor to pay a debt, Bigelow should have given the proposal more thought. The jurisdiction of courts-martial is solely criminal, and directing payment of a debt would be unlawful.

CHAPTER 10

1. June 1, 1877, letter from Secretary of War to the General of the Army; see GO 9, Dept. of Texas, May 4, 1878 (Appendix E).

2. SO 130, July 17, 1877, Dept. of Texas; *ANJ*, July 28, 1877, p. 811. See Clayton Williams, *Texas' Last Frontier* (College Station: Texas A&M Press, 1982), pp. 218–21.

3. In November 1877 Francis Rooney, a prominent cattleman near Fort Stockton, complained, "We have no protection of property.... The commanding officer...has no horses and few men [so] the Indians...have a free field." Williams, *Texas' Last Frontier*, p. 219. No relief was forthcoming, however, and during the ensuing three months several Apache raids and killings occurred nearby.

4. SO 20, January 26, 1878, Dept. of Texas; *ANJ*, February 9, 1878, p. 420. Other 10th Cavalry companies shifted northward included K (from Clark to Davis), M and F (Clark to Concho), and D (District of the Nueces to McKavett).

5. Army ambulances were four-wheeled, spring-supported vehicles used by officers and their families on cross-country moves. Rucker ambulances were assigned to each regiment, but many officers purchased the preferred Dougherty wagons, first made in the mid-1870s. They were usually painted blue and covered by canvas that rolled up on the sides and behind the driver. There were two longitudinal seats inside, and a mattress might be placed on the floorboards. Steffen, *The Horse Soldier 1776–1942*, vol. 2, pp. 79, 202–5; Bernard James Byrne, *A Frontier Army Surgeon* (New York: Exposition, 2d ed., 1935), p. 17; Knight, *Life and Manners*, pp. 45–47. On a march the position of each conveyance was generally based on rank. Lane, *I Married a Soldier*, p. 83.

6. On routine marches cavalry units normally traveled about twenty miles a day to avoid overworking their mounts. Knight, *Life and Manners*, p. 205.

7. Rev. Stat. of 1878, sec. 1146; *1881 Regulations*, sec. 1146. A ration was one day's subsistence for one man.

8. *Act of March 3, 1863;* Rev. Stat. of 1878, sec. 1233.

9. GO 117, AGO, December 20, 1877; Sen. Exec. Doc. 47, 45th Cong., 2d sess., vol. 2 (1878), *Company Cooks* (Serial 1781). Also see E. E. Hardin, "Army Messing," *JMSI* 6 (1885), pp. 274, 275; and Henry J. Reilly, "How Army Cooking Can Be Improved," *JMSI* 6 (1885), pp. 394–99.

10. Reilly, "How Army Cooking Can Be Improved," at 398, 399.

11. The infamous "northers" could wreak havoc with tents, wagons, and equipment. See Lane, *I Married a Soldier*, passim; and Elizabeth B. Custer, *Tenting on the Plains* (1887; reprint, Williamstown, Mass.: Corner House, 1973), pp. 115ff.

12. In 1861 Joseph Morgan Kelley, then sixteen, enlisted in a Pennsylvania regiment; four months later he became a first lieutenant. He was commissioned in the 38th Infantry in 1867, and in 1879 transferred to the 10th Cavalry. Heitman; *1879 Army Register*; Cashin, *Under Fire with the Tenth U.S. Cavalry*, p. 289.

13. Levi Pettibone Hunt, Class of 1870, a first lieutenant in the 10th Cavalry, served on the frontier for fifteen years. *1878 Army Register*; Heitman; *1990 Register of Graduates*.

14. On other than forced marches cavalry units alternated riding with walking. The habitual gait was at a walk, but if forage (not just grazing) was available limited trotting (about a mile in every hour) was permitted. *1881 Regulations*, para. 315.

15. Camp Hudson was named after Lt. Walter Hudson who had been killed in an 1850 skirmish with Indians. The camp had a brief role in providing emigrants with protection from Indians, and in 1859 it took part in the army's short-lived camel

experiment. Frazer, *Forts of the West,* p. 152; Odie B. Faulk, *The U.S. Camel Corps: An Army Experiment* (New York: Oxford Univ. Press, 1976).

16. Bigelow's first orderly, Pvt. Thomas Dillwood, was discharged on February 3 when his enlistment expired. The new orderly, Cpl. Robert Reinhart, was with Bigelow for several months before being replaced by Cpl. Steven Ford.

17. In 1872 several wagons, each drawn by ten mules, were attacked at Howards Well by Comanches and Kiowas. Eight teamsters were tied to wheels, soaked with kerosene, and set on fire, cremating six. A young woman was captured, her one-year-old infant's head smashed, and her mother lanced and scalped. As the wagons were still burning, Gen. Wesley Merritt and a detachment appeared. Lt. Frederick R. Vincent, 9th Cavalry, and some troops pursued and engaged the Indians. Vincent was killed. Williams, *Texas' Last Frontier,* pp. 154–57; Shipman, *Taming the Big Bend,* p. 45.

18. The now-antiquated word "riffles" was used to refer to any of the rapids on the Pecos. A few miles above the Great Falls another riffles was the site of a system that diverted water from the Pecos to irrigate nearby crops raised mainly by Hispanic farmers. Williams, *Texas' Last Frontier,* p. 211.

19. This was not, of course, the historic site of Kit Carson's 1864 battle with Comanches and the 1874 engagement between buffalo hunters and Indians led by Quanah Parker. That Adobe Walls is a few hundred miles away on the Canadian River in the northern part of the Texas Panhandle.

CHAPTER 11

1. See Carlysle Raht, *The Romance of Davis Mountains and Big Bend Country* (El Paso: Rahtbooks, 1919), pp. 33ff.

2. WPA, *Texas,* pp. 641, 642; Robinson, *Pioneer Forts of Texas,* pp. 51, 52; Miller, *Texas Forts,* pp. 102–5; see Williams, *Texas' Last Frontier,* for a history of Fort Stockton.

3. As the "only [tree] within a distance of 45 miles," this tenacious survivor was known as "Lone Tree." Sandra L. Myres, ed., "A Woman's View of the Texas Frontier, 1874," *Southwestern Historical Quarterly* (July 1982), pp. 49–80, at 75.

4. Assistant Surgeon P. J. A. Cleary and Acting Assistant Surgeon E. Alexander, "Fort Stockton, Texas," *Circular no. 8,* pp. 240–44.

5. See *Outline Description of Posts,* pp. 194, 195. If suitable public land was available, regulations required vegetables to be grown for the command. Seeds and agricultural implements were purchased with company or post funds, and surplus crops could be sold and the proceeds credited to such funds. *1881 Regulations,* paras. 571–75; GO 18, 1868.

6. That May a forage master and a mason also were hired; each was paid sixty dollars a month.

7. After three years at King's (Columbia) College, Matthew March Blunt was appointed to West Point, from which he graduated in 1853 and where he later taught mathematics. During the Civil War he was wounded and received three brevet promotions. Heitman; *1879 Army Register; 1990 Register of Graduates.*

8. David Van Valzah of Illinois was commanding officer of D Company. After serving as a Civil War captain, he was in the 30th Infantry until transferring to the 25th in 1871. Charles Robe, a New York volunteer officer in the Civil War, received a Regular Army commission in 1866; four years later he transferred to the 25th Infantry,

in which he commanded C Company. Daniel Hart, commanding officer of F Company, was a former lieutenant colonel in the 7th New Jersey Infantry who became a first lieutenant in the 40th Infantry when that regiment was formed. Benjamin Pope, a New York physician, had been an assistant surgeon during the final year of the Civil War, after which he served in various army medical positions for thirty-five years. In 1867 Owen Sweet, a former captain in a New York volunteer regiment, joined the 40th (later 25th) Infantry, in which he remained for thirty years. Henry Ritzius (Company F), a native of Prussia who had been in a New York volunteer regiment as a major, was appointed in the 39th (later 25th) Infantry in 1867. Second Lt. Harry Reade was a Kansan first commissioned in 1872. Heitman, vols. 1 and 2; *1879 Army Register; Fort Stockton Post Return for February 1878,* NARA, RG 94, M617, roll 1230 (Fort Stockton, January 1875-July 1880).

9. The assigned but absent officers were 1st Lieutenants H. Baxter Quimby, Frederick A. Kendall, and Louis Orleman, who was the 1st lieutenant of Bigelow's company. *Fort Stockton Post Return for February 1878.*

10. Bigelow refers to the regulation and custom which entitled a newly arrived officer to the quarters occupied by any officer junior to him in rank. *Army Regulations of 1863,* para. 1076.

11. M. F. Corbett was an early settler at Stockton where until May 1876 he and Joe Friedlander had been the post traders. According to Clayton Williams, the descendant of a Pecos County pioneer, they were replaced after Maj. George Schofield, then post commanding officer, complained about the exorbitant prices they charged. Williams, *Texas' Last Frontier,* p. 202.

12. Fort Stockton's garden was on the far side of Comanche Creek, about three miles from the post. It was divided into four tracts, one for each company, that were tended by soldiers. Pvt. Edward Taylor of B Company, who presumably had some farm experience, was on detached service as the "post gardener." *10th Cavalry Returns for 1878 and 1879,* NARA, RG 391, M744, roll 96.

13. Even into the mid-1900s cadets were instructed that when reporting to a post they should call on the commander during specified hours, engage in polite conversation for fifteen minutes or so, and when departing unobtrusively drop a calling card on a tray invariably located on a table near the door.

14. Glenn's condition elicited another comment a few days later when Bigelow wrote, "Glenn's hands being very shaky at dinner time he took thirty grains of bromide to quiet his nerves."

15. SO 48, Dept. of Texas, March 5, 1878; *Post Return for April 1878.*

16. *ANJ,* May 11, 1878, p. 640.

17. Dept. of Texas, SO 48, March 5; SO 133, June 25; and SO 273, December 28, 1878. For example, when Pvt. James Harris, 25th Infantry, was hauled before a court charged with being drunk on duty and disobeying an order, Bigelow established that the accused was drunkenly lolling about Joe Friedlander's store when he should have been at work, which cost him five dollars and five days in the guardhouse. Bigelow Papers, USMA Library, box 5.

18. SO 28, Dept. of Texas, February 6, 1878; *ANJ,* February 16, 1878, p. 437.

19. The charges alleged using reproachful or provoking speeches or gestures toward him in violation of AW 25, and degrading and humiliating him in the presence of subordinates.

20. Challenges to duels (personal combat with deadly weapons to satisfy wounded honor), which had been prohibited at least as early as the 1688 Articles of War of James II, were incorporated into the first American articles in 1775. In the eighteenth and early nineteenth centuries some English army officers regarded dueling as an "indispensable custom." Although never as widespread in the American army, duels were not unknown, and even involved such luminaries as Horatio Gates and Sam Houston. After the Civil War, though, the concept that wounded honor could be cured only by killing the offender was regarded as anachronistic by most people. One of the last cases was in 1879 after Capt. Phillip L. Lee of the 10th Cavalry challenged a Lieutenant Whitall to a duel "with and against him" at Fort Sill. Lee was acquitted of the challenge but convicted of a battery by repeatedly striking Whitall on the head with a walking cane. *United States v. Lee,* GCMO 22, AGO, April 10, 1879; also see Davis, pp. 394–98 and Winthrop, pp. 590–600. For an account of dueling in this country, see Hamilton Cochran, *Noted American Duels and Hostile Encounters* (Philadelphia: Chilton Books, 1963).

21. SO 78, Dept. of Texas, April 11, 1878; *Post Return for April 1878.*

22. Robert Utley accurately described the practice of resorting to charges "as a means of pursuing personal controversies" as a misuse of courts-martial. Robert M. Utley, *Frontier Regulars, 1866–1891* (New York: Macmillan Publishing, 1973), p. 85.

23. See *ANJ,* March 29 through July 5, 1879, pp. 583–874, passim. Also see Marvin E. Kroeker, *Great Plains Command* (Norman: Univ. of Oklahoma Press, 1976), pp. 153–66.

24. Letter to Gen. D. S. Stanley, March 12, 1879, *Sherman Papers,* Container 91, p. 127.

25. At Shiloh Stanley commanded a corps in which Hazen headed a brigade. On the battle's second day Hazen became separated from his command for several hours. Stanley later said that Hazen had "skulked...and fled" away. Despite credible evidence to the contrary, the truth or falsity of such "fighting words" was never resolved by a court. *New York Times,* March 14, 1879, p. 8. See Kroeker, *Great Plains Command,* pp. 143–52.

26. *ANJ,* May 3, 1879, p. 702. In 1877 Stanley wrote Hazen, threatening to use his "disgraceful conduct at Shiloh" and testimony in the Belknap hearing to "stop [his] career as an imposter." Copies were sent to the *New York Times* and a St. Paul newspaper. Hazen, denying the accusations, based his charges on the letter and its publication "with intent to injure, defame, and degrade him." *ANJ,* April 19, 1879, pp. 654–56.

27. GCMO 35, AGO, June 18, 1879.

28. *ANJ,* 28 June 1879, p. 852.

29. Letter to Gen. John Gibbon, May 31, 1879, *Sherman Papers,* Container 91, p. 190.

30. The son of presumed Francophiles from Vermont, McLaughlen enlisted in the 2d Dragoons in 1850. In 1861 he became a lieutenant and four brevet promotions later was a brigadier general. He was appointed a major in the 10th Cavalry in 1867. Heitman*; 1879 Army Register*; *10th Cavalry Returns for June and July 1878.*

31. *Post Return for April 1878*; SO 762, AGO, April 6, 1878.

32. Benjamin Logan Baldridge, a United Presbyterian clergyman, entered the army at an advanced age in 1876 and retired as a captain in 1885 after only nine years of active duty. Heitman; *1879 Army Register.*

33. Andrew Geddes, a Canadian, enlisted in 1861, was later commissioned, and in 1865 became a lieutenant colonel. In 1867 he was appointed a second lieutenant in the 40th Infantry. Heitman; *1879 Army Register.*

34. *Post Return for February 1879.*

35. SO 100, Dept. of Texas, May 11, 1878. William Henry Beck enlisted in 1861 and soon became a lieutenant, but for unknown reasons resigned. In 1867 he was commissioned in the 10th Cavalry in which he served for twenty-two years (see Epilogue). Heitman; *1879 Army Register;* Cashin, *Under Fire,* p. 294.

36. SO 115, Dept. of Texas, June 3, 1878; *Post Return for June 1878.* At his first French recitation at West Point, Mason Marion Maxon of Wisconsin acquired a lifelong sobriquet by pronouncing *aux bijoux* as "oucks bijoucks." Perhaps unsurprisingly, he graduated last in the thirty-nine-member Class of 1869. *1990 Register of Graduates; AOG Report for 1935.* William T. Corbusier, *Verde to San Carlos* (Tucson: Dale Stuart King, 1968), p. 215.

37. *Act of April 23, 1878*; *ANJ,* June 12, 1880, p. 916, and July 9, 1881, pp. 1025, 1030; Sen. Exec. Doc. 52, 45th Cong., 2d sess., vol. 2 (1878), *SecWar Transmittal of Grierson's Letter* (Serial 1781). Armes's first four trials were in 1865 (RG 153, NARA, M1105, roll 7, Case MM2180), two in 1868 (OO2819 and 003427), and one in 1869 (PP654). He was convicted in the first but restored to duty, acquitted in the next two, and in the fourth the charges were withdrawn.

CHAPTER 12

1. Stevens Thomson Norvell had been an enlisted man from 1858 until 1863 when he became a second lieutenant. He transferred to the 10th Cavalry in 1870. Heitman; *1879 Army Register.*

2. *ANJ,* July 26, 1879, p. 929.

3. *ANJ,* March 6, 1879, p. 547.

4. *Bigelow Journal,* August 18, 1878.

5. See generally *Post Returns for April through August 1878.*

6. *Post Return for April 1878*; SO 30, Hq. Fort Stockton, April 15, 1878; *Roster of Non-commissioned Officers of the Tenth U.S. Cavalry with Reminiscences* (1897; reprint, Bryan, TX: J. M. Carroll, 1983), p. 41, 42. Escondido Station was a stage stop twenty-three miles east of Stockton. Williams, *Texas' Last Frontier,* pp. 222, 223.

7. *Post Return for May 1878.*

8. GO 9, Dept. of Texas, May 4, 1878 (see Appendix E); Wooster, "The Army and the Politics of Expansion," pp. 157–59.

9. Ord's directive cited the secretary's letter of June 1, 1877, to General Sherman, stating that the help of Mexican authorities to suppress raids from their territory should be sought, but if they continued to neglect their duties, United States troops would perform them, even if doing so required "occasionally" crossing the border in pursuit of marauders. When the order was rescinded in February 1880, the relations with Mexico improved. See Bruce J. Dinges, "The Victorio Campaign of 1880: Cooperation and Conflict on the United States-Mexico Border," *New Mexico Historical Review* 62 (January 1987).

10. Glass, *History of the Tenth Cavalry,* pp. 96–103.

11. *Post Returns for May through September 1878.*

12. See Frederick Whittaker, *A Complete Life of General George A. Custer*, vol. 2 (1876; reprint, Lincoln: Univ. of Nebraska Press, 1993), pp. 618–24. In his introduction to the reprint, Robert Utley observed that "In the lavish hyperbole of the dime novels and penny dreadfuls in which he specialized, Whittaker created a demigod."

13. Charles Delavan Viele of New York was an infantry lieutenant in the Civil War. In 1870 he transferred to the 10th Cavalry. Insofar as could be determined, he was not related to Egbert L. Vielé, Class of 1847, whose wife, Teresa, wrote *Following the Drum*. Egbert served in Texas before the Civil War, resigned in 1852, was a brigadier general of volunteers, resigned again in 1863, later divorced Teresa, then held several positions including one term as a congressman. Heitman; *1879 Army Register;* foreword by Sandra L. Myres to reprint of *Following the Drum.*

CHAPTER 13

1. Army records often misspell the name as Peña Blanco (white rock). In the late 1870s it was an outpost from which cavalry units scouted. Renamed Peña Colorado (red rock) in 1879 and eventually Fort Peña, it became an active post until abandoned in 1893. Nothing now remains but a plaque about four miles from Marathon, Texas. Miller, *Texas Forts,* pp. 161, 162; Herbert M. Hart, *Old Forts of the Southwest* (Seattle: Superior, 1964), p. 189.

2. See Monnett, *The Battle of Beecher Island,* passim.

3. The often-raw frontier whiskey was labeled or referred to by various names including, seductively, "Moral Suasion." The brand usually found at post traders' stores, however, apparently was known as "Forty Rod." Summerhayes, *Vanished Arizona,* p. 201.

4. Even nonluminaries such as Lt. "Oucks Bijoucks" Maxon, who as a cadet had been less than fluent in French, had a small spring east of the present town of Marathon named "Maxon" in his honor. Mrs. O. L. Shipman, *Taming the Big Bend* (Marfa, Texas: Mrs. O. L. Shipman, 1926).

5. *Post Return for November 1878. 10th Cavalry Organizational Returns for November and December 1878,* NARA, RG 391, M744, roll 96.

6. Robert G. Smither, AAAG of the 10th Cavalry at Concho, had been an enlisted man and lieutenant during the Civil War. After mustering out he was appointed a lieutenant in the 10th Cavalry. Heitman; *1879 Army Register.* See Armes, *Ups and Downs,* pp. 455–61.

7. *ANJ,* December 14, 1878, p. 304; SO 255, Dept. of Texas, December 3, 1878.

8. A Civil War captain, Thomas Coverly Lebo was commissioned in the 10th Cavalry. He was once convicted of striking a soldier with his sabre during an inspection, but the court "attached no criminality thereto," believing he did not intend to inflict punishment. *GCMO 23, Dept. of Arizona, 1891; ANJ,* November 14, 1891, p. 199; Heitman; *1879 Army Register.*

CHAPTER 14

1. SO 245 (November 19, 1878), and SO's 3, 7, 14, and 15 (January 6, 10, 21, 1878), Dept. of Texas. The specifications alleged unbecoming conduct by unjustifiably marching troops on foot, abusing Private Mack, cursing Dr. Price, creating the distur-

bance at Corbett's store, and carousing with teamsters. Beck was also charged with three offenses of drunk on duty and two of prejudicial conduct. GCMO 34, AGO, May 30, 1879.

2. In addition to Bigelow, the witnesses were Dr. Price, McMartin, and seven soldiers (Sergeants Jacob Young and William Givens, and Privates Samuel Ford, Albert Fulsome, Simon Turner, James Watkins, and George Young). *Post Return for December 1878.*

3. Between January 3 and February 21 Bigelow either neglected his journal or, except for unrelated comments on February 5 and 16, any entries he might have made have been lost or destroyed.

4. Clous, a native of Germany, had been an enlisted man who received a commission in 1862. In 1867 he was appointed a captain in the 38th Infantry which became part of the 24th in 1869. Although he was not then a lawyer, his experience and effectiveness as a prosecutor resulted in his serving as the judge advocate in most officer cases tried in Texas, leaving little time for troop duty. *1878 Army Register*; Heitman.

5. Croquet was immensely popular in Western Europe and the United States, in part because it enabled Victorian women to "exercise outdoors and compete equally with men." By the 1890s, however, the game became associated with "gambling, drinking and philandering" to such an extent that clergymen banned it in Boston. See Richard Wolkomir, "With Mallets and Forethought, Croquet Is Back," *Smithsonian* 23, no. 7 (October 1992), pp. 102–11. Bigelow never disclosed the reason for his aversion.

6. Maj. John Moore, who first entered the army in 1853, was the chief surgeon for the Department of Texas. See Epilogue.

7. The reference is to the wife of George W. Brackenridge, a leading citizen of San Antonio who later donated land for Brackenridge Park and San Pedro Park; his home is now the Incarnate Word College.

8. William T. Howard, an 1876 graduate of West Point, was in an artillery battery in San Antonio. From 1879 until 1881 he served as aide-de-camp to General Ord and later to General Augur (see Epilogue). Heitman; *1879 Army Register.*

9. As the principal site for concerts, operas, balls, and other entertainment, Old Casino Hall, built in 1857, was San Antonio's "temple of culture." Although membership was largely restricted to those who spoke German, privileges were extended to army officers, who included Robert E. Lee and U. S. Grant. Ramsdell, *San Antonio,* pp. 84, 158–61.

10. Presumably the Miss Mackenzie mentioned was Ranald Mackenzie's unmarried sister, Harriett, who was then in her early thirties. She and her mother, both of whom later lived with Mackenzie in Santa Fe and San Antonio, were visiting Maj. Benjamin Card and his wife in 1879. *Bigelow Journal*, February 29, 1879; Pierce, *The Most Promising Young Officer*, pp. 219, 266 n42. After two brevets and a few months as a lieutenant colonel of Civil War volunteers, George Lippitt Andrews (not to be confused with George Leonard Andrews, professor of French at West Point from 1871 until 1892) became a major in the 17th Infantry. He commanded the 25th Infantry from 1870 until 1892. Heitman; *1879 Army Register.*

11. SO 44, Dept. of Texas, March 5, 1879; *ANJ,* March 15, 1879, p. 564.

12. Col. Henry Boynton Clitz (a brevet brigadier in the Civil War) was an 1845 graduate of West Point. In 1879 he was commanding officer of the 10th Infantry with headquarters at Fort McKavett. Heitman; *1990 Register of Graduates.*

13. SO 56, Dept. of Texas, March 19, 1879; SO 67, Dept. of Texas, April 1, 1879; *ANJ,* March 29, 1879, p. 600, and April 12, 1879, p. 632; GCMO 34, AGO, May 30, 1879.

14. Peter D. Olch, "Medicine in the Indian Fighting Army," *Journal of the West* 21 (July 1982), p. 37. On medical problems in the pre–Civil War Frontier Army, see James O. Breeden, "Health in Early Texas: The Military Frontier," *Southwestern Historical Quarterly* 80 (April 1977), pp. 357–98.

15. *1881 Regulations,* para. 195; GO 94, AGO, 1873.

16. Samuel L. S. Smith was Fort Concho's acting assistant surgeon. In 1878 at age thirty he moved from Louisville, Kentucky, to San Angelo, where he remained for forty-seven years as a practicing physician after his army contract ended in 1881. August 2, 1993, letter from John Neilson, historian/archivist, Fort Concho National Historic Landmark, to the author; J. Evetts Haley, *Fort Concho and the Texas Frontier* (San Angelo, Tex.: Standard-Times, 1952), pp. 321ff.

CHAPTER 15

1. Bigelow's refusal reflected the values of a society that eschewed unspeakable (let alone unprintable) conduct. For example, the *Army and Navy Journal* considered the behavior "to be of such a vulgar character as to be unfit for publication." *ANJ,* November 29, 1879, p. 333. And although GCMOs, which were distributed throughout the army, routinely set forth the specifications, here they were completely omitted. GCMO 66, AGO, December 4, 1879.

2. By 1878 the desertion rate, which exceeded 30 percent annually in the early 1870s, tapered off to less than 10 percent. From 1873 through mid-1878 the desertions were 7,271, 4,606, 2,521, 1,844, 2,516 and 1,678. H. Exec. Doc. 1, 45th Cong., 3d sess., vol. 1 (1878), *Report of the SecWar,* p. 1 (Serial 1843); *ANJ,* December 7, 1878, p. 285. Such losses decreased effectiveness as inexperienced men had to be recruited and trained to replace those who had sought greener pastures on the other side of the hill. H. Exec. Doc. 1, 51st Cong., 1st sess., vol. 2 (1889), *Report of the SecWar,* p. 64 (Serial 2715); see Foner, *The United States Soldier between Two Wars,* pp. 222–24 and passim; also see Rickey, *Forty Miles a Day,* pp. 143–55.

3. Letters to the *ANJ* often speculated on the reasons for desertion, and articles on the same subject appeared in the *JMSI.* Numerous remedies were proposed, but without fundamental improvements in soldiers' lives nothing met with much success. GO 102, War Dept., October 10, 1873; *ANJ,* January 5, 1878, p. 339. See William D. McAnaney, "Desertion in the United States Army," *JMSI* 10 (1889). Sheridan believed that many desertions resulted from the opportunties in mining, railroad, cattle, and agriculture, which induced young men "wanting to better their condition...and not having money enough to reach this Eldorado" to enlist. H. Exec. Doc. 1, 48th Cong., 1st sess., vol. 1 (1883), *Rpt. of the SecWar,* p. 105 (Serial 2182); *New York Times,* November 15, 1883, p. 3. General Stanley thought that desertions in Texas were caused mainly by the thick clothing worn in summer and the lack of variety in the diet. H. Exec. Doc. 1, 48th Cong., 2d sess., vol. 2 (1884), p. 126 (Serial 2277).

4. See McAnaney, "Desertion in the United States Army"; also see Leckie, *The Buffalo Soldiers,* passim. In his journal entry for February 26, 1878, Bigelow wrote, "Major Hart told me...that during the year 1877, the number of white men in this dept tried by Court Martial was 178 to 118 blacks, although there were about twice as many colored troops...as there were white."

5. McAnaney, "Desertion in the United States Army," pp. 464, 465.

6. Fowler, *The Black Infantry in the West,* p. 78 and passim.

7. January 1, 1877, letter from Chaplain George T. Mullins to Army AAG, *ANJ,* January 27, 1877, p. 395.

8. Private citizens and state law enforcement officers received awards (then thirty dollars but later reduced to ten dollars) for arresting and detaining deserters, which induced some people to become bounty hunters. *1881 Regulations,* para. 214; *Act of August 6, 1894.*

9. The first desertions were in 1867 when three soldiers left Fort Leavenworth, and the last in 1878 when Peter Morris disappeared as the company marched to Fort Stockton. Only nine had been apprehended, indicating that blacks were as able as whites to vanish with little risk of being caught.

10. *Kurtz v. Moffatt,* 115 U.S. 487 (1885). In 1890, though, Congress authorized nonfederal officers to capture deserters. *Act of October 1, 1890.*

11. To reassure himself Bigelow consulted McClellan's report on European armies. He learned that saddles were kept in stables by Russians, in quarters by Prussians, in lofts by the French, and in hallways by Austrians. But Russia, he rationalized, had the poorest cavalry in Europe.

12. Armes, *Ups and Downs,* pp. 412, 469. Believing that numerous officers were conspiring to force him out of the army (which might have been true, but for understandable reasons), Armes characterized those he suspected with labels such as "the old fossil" (Col. Thomas Neill, 8th Cavalry), "a spy" (Lieutenant Sweet), and a "drunk" (Col. David Stanley, 22d Infantry). He also thought that those who convicted him in 1870 were "a picked court of Army loafers," while those who acquitted him in 1868 were "honorable and just men," and that officers who ordered him before a medical board in 1881 on a "malicious charge questioning [his] sanity" were his persecutors. Armes, *Ups and Downs,* passim; SO 8, War Dept., January 12, 1881; *ANJ,* January 15, 1881, p. 475.

13. *Circular No. 8,* pp. 240–44.

14. The cemetery was located one mile north of the post. *Circular No. 8,* p. 242.

15. Dannels was the young soldier from Macon, Georgia, who once irritated Bigelow by awkwardly saluting with his left hand.

16. The only information relating to the cause of death is that Dannels was suffering from acute bronchitis.

17. By law, a post chaplain had a duty to provide enlisted men with instruction in "the common English branches of education." *Act of July 28, 1866*; Rev. Stat. of 1878, sec. 1124. When provided by a competent and conscientious instructor, the value of this ancillary service could be impressive. For example, General Ord commended Chaplain George Mullins, 25th Infantry, for the "admirable results" he achieved at Fort Davis where "eighty enlisted men who twelve months ago did not even know the alphabet, now read and write." Letter from General Ord, *ANJ,* September 9, 1877, p. 74; also see *ANJ,* January 27, 1877, p. 395. The first African

American chaplain was Henry Plummer, a former slave who served in the Union Navy during the Civil War. Frederick Douglass helped him obtain an appointment to the 9th Cavalry in 1884. Two years later Allen Allensworth, also an ex-slave and navy veteran, became the 24th Infantry's chaplain. He introduced then-innovative teaching techniques, substituting praise for intimidation, and inspired large numbers of illiterate black troops to read and write. See Miller J. Stewart, "A Touch of Civilization: Culture and Education in the Frontier Army," *Nebraska History* 65 (Summer 1984), pp. 257–82.

18. *1881 Regulations,* paras. 1121–24, 2598, 2675; see David H. Stratton, "The Army and the Gospel in the West," *Western Humanities Review* 8, no. 3 (Summer 1954), pp. 247–62, passim. In 1880 chaplains were authorized to wear a black velvet shoulder strap with a shepherd's crook of frosted silver in the center.

19. Letter, SecWar to CG, Dept. of the Columbia, May 13, 1875; *ANJ,* July 3, 1875, p. 753. The Judge Advocate General, *Digest of Opinions* (1895), p. 94; Davis, p. 24.

20. *New York Times,* April 7, 1876, p. 5.

21. McAnaney, "Desertion in the United States Army," p. 459.

22. Stratton, "The Army and the Gospel," p. 251.

23. Ibid., pp. 251, 252, quoting from a July 26, 1882, letter to Orville J. Nave.

24. Vielé, *Following the Drum,* p. 161.

25. Ibid., p. 163.

26. Ibid., pp. 161, 162.

27. H. Baxter Quimby, a Civil War sergeant and lieutenant, was assigned to F Company but absent on sick leave for a year. He died four years later. Heitman; *1879 Army Register.* Joseph Friedlander, a Prussian native who settled at Stockton in 1868, supplied fuel and foodstuffs to most of the forts in West Texas. He had been post trader, operating from a building near the southwest corner of the parade ground, until his license was revoked in 1876. The business was taken over by Frederick W. Young, another Prussian, who constructed a still-existing building where the San Antonio-El Paso road crossed Comanche Creek. Friedlander later reopened his store, which he operated until the fort was abandoned in 1886. Raht, *The Romance of Davis Mountains,* p. 175; Williams, *Texas' Last Frontier,* p. 202. Letter to the author from Richard T. Roome, historian at Historic Fort Stockton. There were three Edgar brothers. This one might have been John who became the Pecos County sheriff.

28. Each company provided a mess for its men. The quartermaster sergeant procured most of the rations, but company commanders generally tried to obtain better foodstuffs for their troops.

29. At least bimonthly each post commander had to convene a "Council of Administration" of the three next highest-ranking officers. Its principal duties were to investigate and recommend action if any funds were lost, prescribe the kinds and quantities of goods the post trader would stock and the prices he charged, fix the laundresses' fees, and make regulations for the post schools. *1881 Regulations,* paras. 517–23; GO 24, 1878.

30. Herman Koehler owned and operated a general merchandise store located on the shore of Comanche Springs.

31. Because larceny requires stolen property to have some value, the amount of which determines the punishment authorized, more than a "technical" rule was involved. Winthrop, pp. 685–87.

32. SO 87, April 25, 1879, Hq., Dept. of Texas.

33. A brief account of the issues and evidence in the case, which required almost 750 handwritten pages to transcribe, appears in Stallard, *Glittering Misery,* pp. 117–21.

34. SO 48, March 10, 1879, Dept. of Texas; *ANJ,* March 22, 1979; SO 7, April 7, 1879, War Dept.; *ANJ,* April 12, 1879, p. 633.

35. GCMO 66, AGO, December 4, 1879.

36. SO 87, Dept. of Texas, April 25, 1879.

37. Officers were housed in seven one-story adobe buildings. Most contained two sets of quarters separated by a wall extending from front to back. All had shingled roofs, porches, wooden floors, and plastered and whitewashed interior walls. Each room was fifteen by eighteen feet and fourteen feet high, and heated by a fireplace. There were no inside water closets nor bathrooms, but kitchens and sinks (outhouses) were behind the quarters, and each morning a water wagon came around to fill barrels. *Circular No. 8,* p. 241.

CHAPTER 16

1. Hord's Hotel, on Main Plaza at Dolorosa Street, became the Southern Hotel. Mary A. Maverick, *Memoirs of Mary A. Maverick,* ed. Rena Maverick Green (1921; reprint, Lincoln: Univ. of Nebraska Press, 1989), p. 108; WPA, *San Antonio,* p. 53.

2. Second Lt. William T. Howard, with whom Bigelow spent much time when in San Antonio for Beck's trial, had a room in Mrs. Napier's house west of Travis Park. Vinton Lee James, *Frontier and Pioneer Recollections of Early Days in San Antonio and West Texas* (San Antonio: Artes Gráficas, 1938), p. 54.

3. SO 87, Dept. of Texas, April 25, 1879. Sweitzer, Class of 1853, was with the 8th Cavalry at Ringgold Barracks. During the Civil War he was breveted repeatedly for gallant service and became a brigadier general. Appointed a major in the 2d Cavalry in 1866, he served on the frontier for twenty-one years. Heitman; *1879 Army Register.* Other members were Maj. William R. Price, 8th Cavalry; Maj. A. E. Bates, Pay Dept.; Capt. John H. Patterson, 20th Infantry; Capt. John C. Gilmore, 24th Infantry; 1st Lt. Jonathan D. Stevenson, 8th Cavalry; and Asst. Surgeon Harvey E. Brown.

4. Some of the books Bigelow read included Motley's *History of John of Barneveldt;* Scott's *Waverly;* Hamley's *Battle of Rossbach, The Tactics of the Three Arms,* and *The Battle of Woerth;* Comte de Paris's account of Civil War military operations; Holland's *Lessons in Life* and *Gold Foil; Charles the Fifth; The Life of Henry V;* the three-volume *History of Charles the Bold;* and several of Shakespeare's plays.

5. Until the Quadrangle (Fort Sam Houston) was occupied starting in 1879, headquarters were in leased facilities, then a building on Houston Street north of Alamo Plaza which became the Maverick Hotel. William Corner, *San Antonio de Bexar* (San Antonio: Bainbridge & Corner, 1890), p. 5.

6. Mrs. Sappington's boarding house (at Navarro and Houston Streets) enjoyed "a first class reputation for the excellent table that is kept and the attention paid to the general comfort." James, *Frontier and Pioneer Recollections,* p. 44; Corner, *San Antonio de Bexar,* p. 4.

7. Miss Grimshaw, a niece of Mrs. Marucheaux, resided with that family on North St. Mary's Street opposite St. Mary's Church. James, *Frontier and Pioneer Recollections,* p. 44.

8. Construction of St. Mark's Church, north of Travis Park and not far from the Alamo, commenced in 1859 and was completed in 1875. Robert E. Lee had been among its parishioners. WPA, *San Antonio,* p.83; Ramsdell, *San Antonio,* pp. 231–34.

9. St. Mary's Church, built in 1855 near John Twohig's house, was a ten-to-fifteen-minute walk from the Menger. Its congregation was mainly Irish and other English-speaking people. WPA, *San Antonio,* p. 71; Ramsdell, *San Antonio,* pp. 225, 226.

10. The original structure at Fort Sam Houston, built between 1876 and 1879 on land donated to induce the army to locate headquarters there, was used as a quartermaster depot. Eldon Cagle, Jr., *Quadrangle: The History of Fort Sam Houston* (Austin: Eakin, 1985), passim; Corner, *San Antonio de Bexar,* pp. 25–30. Creedmore, Long Island, had been the National Rifle Association's site of annual small-arms matches since 1873. Selection for an army team provided troops an opportunity to earn prizes of up to $260. Captain Livermore was one of the army's best marksmen and coaches. See *ANJ,* August 31, 1878, pp. 60, 61; Rickey, *Forty Miles a Day,* pp. 103–5.

11. The first known Protestant ceremony in San Antonio was in 1844 when John McCullough, a Presbyterian, held services. In 1846 he built a church on Commerce Street from which he used his pulpit to rebuke gamblers and rowdy elements and to urge formation of a Vigilance Committee. After being subjected to verbal and physical abuse, including target practice with handguns, by the lowlifes he tried to reform, he left town in 1849. In 1865 a new Presbyterian church was completed a few blocks north of the Alamo; this probably was where Bigelow went. James, *Frontier and Pioneer Recollections,* pp. 30, 137; Ramsdell, *San Antonio,* pp. 228, 229.

12. William H. W. James, fourth from bottom in his 1872 class, was adjutant of the 24th Infantry in which he served for thirty-one years. Heitman; *1879 Army Register; 1990 Register of Graduates.*

13. Alexander Rodgers, a member of the 4th Cavalry, was two years ahead of Bigelow at West Point. He was the son of Adm. C. R. P. Rodgers and a cousin of Ranald Mackenzie. From 1882 until Mackenzie was retired for disability in 1884, he served as his aide-de-camp. Heitman; *1879 Army Register; 1990 Register of Graduates;* see Robinson, *Bad Hand,* pp. 319, 320; Pierce, *The Most Promising Young Officer,* p. 222.

14. The Marucheaux had resided in San Antonio for several years. The whereabouts of Miss Grimshaw's parents, if then living, could not be determined. James, *Frontier and Pioneer Recollections,* p. 44; Bushick, *Glamorous Days,* pp. 21, 22; WPA, *San Antonio,* p. 25.

15. WPA, *San Antonio,* p. 35.

16. First Lt. Edwin Styles Curtis was an enlisted man until he was appointed to West Point, from which he graduated in 1867. In 1878 he was in San Antonio with the artillery. Heitman; *1878 Army Register; 1990 Register of Graduates.*

17. In cadet slang "spoons" meant sweethearts, "spoony man" a ladies' man, "spoony letter" a love letter, and "to get excessively spoony" falling in love. "Spoony" also implied foppish dress and appearance. *ANJ,* February 23, 1878, p. 453.

18. Benjamin C. Card, a wartime brigadier general, was a major and department quartermaster. Heitman; *1879 Army Register.*

19. *ANJ,* May 24, 1879; SO 150, AGO, June 26, 1879; GO 8, Dept. of Texas, June 28, 1879; SO 114, AGO, July 30, 1879.

20. Not only had Kelley enlisted while still a boy, but he became a second lieutenant before he was seventeen and ended the war as a twenty-year-old captain. Heitman; Cashin, *Under Fire,* p. 289.

21. Private Young was the miscreant who at Fort Duncan had bashed Saddler Jones in the face with a spade.

22. Company L, 10th Cavalry, accompanied by Dr. Price, had been on detached field service at Camp Santa Rosa, north of Stockton, since March. SO 1, Dist. of the Pecos, March 1, 1879. The "antagonism" led Esterly and Price to report questionable conduct by Armes, and his assertion that they connived to "fix up a set of false charges." After investigation of the allegations, Armes was relieved of command, arrested (no. 21), and charged with mistreating enlisted men and trying to coerce two soldiers to make a false sworn statement. That October a court-martial (his eighth) convicted him. See Epilogue.

23. During the Civil War, Abram Epperson Wood was an enlisted man and lieutenant. In 1868 he was appointed to West Point, and afterwards served in the frontier cavalry for thirteen years, earning a brevet promotion for his performances against Indians in 1878. Heitman; *1879 Army Register; 1990 Register of Graduates.*

24. A major San Antonio event in 1878 was the inauguration of mule-drawn cars on tracks between Alamo Plaza and San Pedro Springs. WPA, *San Antonio,* p. 35.

25. Bigelow shows signs of prescience concerning smoking. A few years later 1st Lt. Adolphus W. Greely, 5th Cavalry, the leader of an ill-fated polar expedition, reported that all but one of the nineteen men who died had smoked tobacco, but all seven survivors were non-smokers. *ANJ,* November 22, 1884, p. 327.

26. Andrews, Class of 1876, of Company I, 25th Infantry, was the son of that regiment's commander. Heitman; *1879 Army Register; 1990 Register of Graduates.*

27. Lieutenant Andrews's comments contrast with the attitude of his father, Colonel Andrews, who (similar to Colonel Grierson) was protective of black troops and "particularly sensitive of any evidence of prejudice" against them. See Fowler, *The Black Infantry in the West,* pp. 129, 130.

28. Annie Laura James, then eighteen, was a daughter of John James who became wealthy through real estate purchases that included Comanche Springs (Fort Stockton) and the site of Fort Davis. James, *Frontier and Pioneer Recollections,* pp. 23–29.

29. Henry Dana Borup of Wisconsin, Class of 1876, was a member of the 2d Artillery in San Antonio. Heitman; *1879 Army Register; 1990 Register of Graduates.*

30. Samuel Howard Loder was in D Company, 7th Infantry, at Fort Benton. Little is known of the reasons for his suicide. The *ANJ* merely stated that he shot himself in the head while sitting in his tent, and that he had recently distinguished himself at Judith Basin. Heitman; *1879 Army Register; 1990 Register of Graduates; ANJ,* July 12, 1879, p. 884, and July 19, 1879, p. 904.

CHAPTER 17

1. The examining physicians included John Moore (Minnie's father) and M. K. Taylor (the department's new surgeon).

2. Understanding of the causes and cures of dysentery, long the scourge of armies, came too late to help Safford. See Olch, "Medicine in the Indian Fighting Army, 1866–1890"; *Circular No. 8.*

3. *Chillicothe (Ohio) Register,* week of July 28, 1879.

4. Ramsdell, *San Antonio,* passim; WPA, *Texas,* passim; see Bushick, *Glamorous Days,* pp. 57–59.

5. In contrast to the image of frontier barrooms as "brawlrooms," service in German establishments often was provided by a barmaid who might knit or sew when not busy. And instead of fights and vulgarity, musicians might provide entertainment.

6. The Turner-Halle was a gymnastics (athletic) club next to the Menger Hotel, which acquired it in 1875 for expansion.

7. Elizabeth Land and Carroll Glines, *Complete Guide for the Serviceman's Wife* (Boston: Houghton Mifflin, 1956), p. 326.

8. SO 164, Hq. Dept. of Texas, August 4, 1879. John Henry Patterson, 20th Infantry, a member of the Geddes court-martial, received the Medal of Honor for gallantry in the Civil War. Heitman; *1879 Army Register.* The purpose of a board of survey was to determine whether an officer should be held pecuniarily liable for lost or damaged government property.

9. John Withers, Class of 1849, was a captain at the outbreak of the Civil War. He resigned to become a lieutenant colonel in the Confederate Army. Heitman; *1990 Register of Graduates.*

10. After entering the army as a captain in 1812, David Emanuel Twiggs of Georgia participated in the storming of Monterrey, and in 1861 commanded the Department of Texas. As hostilities became imminent he asked to be relieved, but before his successor arrived he surrendered all arms, munitions, and posts. He was dismissed from the army but became a Confederate major general before dying a year and a half later. See Robert M. Utley, *Frontiersmen in Blue* (Lincoln: Univ. of Nebraska Press, 1967), passim; Ray C. Colton, *The Civil War in the Western Territories* (Norman: Univ. of Oklahoma Press, 1959), pp. 1–12; and Douglas Southall Freeman, *Lee's Lieutenants,* vol. 1 (New York: Charles Scribner's Sons, 1946), p. 709.

11. William Alexis Thompson, called "Hurricane Bill," was an enlisted man in the Civil War. Commissioned in 1867, he served on the frontier until 1897, receiving a brevet promotion after an 1874 Indian skirmish. Heitman; *1879 Army Register.*

12. George W. Bradley of the Quartermaster's Department, a Civil War colonel, became a captain in the Regular Army in 1865.During Bigelow's stay in San Antonio he headed the depot. Heitman; *1879 Army Register.*

13. John Twohig, an Irishman, was a prominent San Antonio merchant and banker who in 1842 destroyed his store and the munitions it contained to prevent General Vásquez from retaking the town. He was the primary founder of Eagle Pass, and as a seemingly avaricious banker or unreconstructed Confederate, or both, demanded unreasonably high rent for use of the Fort Duncan site after the Civil War. His house still stands on the San Antonio River. Ramsdell, *San Antonio,* pp. 25, 33, 180, 183.

14. H. Rpt. 240, 44th Cong., 1st sess., vol. 1 (1876), *Transfer of the Indian Bureau* (Serial 1708). H. Rpt. 241, 45th Cong., 2d sess., vol. 1 (1878), *Transfer of the Indian Bureau* (Serial 1822). See Wooster, *The Military and United States Indian Policy, 1865–1903,* passim; Francis Paul Prucha, *American Indian Policy in Crisis: Christian*

Reformers and the Indian, 1865–1900 (Norman: Univ. of Oklahoma Press, 1976), passim; and Utley, *Frontier Regulars*, pp. 112, 113, 136–39, 188–92.

15. Charles M. Terrell, paymaster for the Department of Texas, had been in volunteer regiments from 1862 until 1867 when he was commissioned in the Regular Army. Heitman; *1879 Army Register.*

16. SO 176, Dept. of Texas, August 19, 1879; *ANJ*, August 30, 1879, p. 56.

17. First Lt. Jonathan D. Stevenson, F Company, 8th Cavalry, at Fort McIntosh, also was a member of the Geddes court-martial. An enlisted man and lieutenant during the Civil War, he became a second lieutenant in the 8th Cavalry in 1866. He died in 1882. Heitman; *1879 Army Register.*

18. Articles 104 et seq., AWs of 1874; Winthrop, pp. 478, 479. If an accused officer was acquitted, the appropriate commander could (and often did) release him from arrest and restore him to duty. And to avoid keeping an accused too long in ignorance of the results of trial, he could be notified as soon as reasonably practicable. Otherwise, though, the results were not promulgated until after the final reviewer (the president if dismissal had been adjudged) had taken action.

19. GCMO 66, AGO, December 4, 1879. Under British and earlier American military law, "dismissal" and "cashiering" were distinct sentences. Both represented dishonorable separation of an officer, but someone "cashiered" was also disqualified from ever holding any military office. By the 1870s the terms had become synonymous, with "cashiered" rarely used. The seeming redundancy here probably reflected the court's disgust with the accused. Winthrop, pp. 406–8.

CHAPTER 18

1. James Pratt, 25th Infantry (not to be confused with Richard Pratt), had been a Civil War captain in a black infantry regiment; in 1866 he was commissioned in the 41st Infantry. Heitman; *1879 Army Register*. Richard Pratt, an initial member of the 10th Cavalry cadre, is best known for his work with the Indian Industrial School at Carlisle Barracks. In 1871 he preferred numerous court-martial charges against Grierson, who then arrested Pratt and preferred charges against him. See Richard Henry Pratt, *Battlefield and Classroom: Four Decades with the American Indian, 1867–1904,* ed. Robert M. Utley (New Haven: Yale Univ. Press, 1964); Frank M. Temple, "Discipline and Turmoil in the Tenth U.S. Cavalry," *West Texas Historical Association Yearbook,* pp. 103–117; letter from John Neilson, Fort Concho, to author, August 13, 1993. Cyrus Nutt Gray, 25th Infantry, a Civil War lieutenant, was appointed a lieutenant in the 39th Infantry in 1867. Twenty years later he was dismissed for being drunk on duty at Fort Meade and in Sturgis. Heitman; *1879 Army Register;* GCMO 14, AGO, August 24, 1887; *ANJ,* September 8, 1887, p. 103.

2. Anson Mills was appointed a cadet in 1855, but departed West Point two years later and became a surveyor in West Texas. When El Paso conducted a referendum on seccession, only Mills and one other person voted against it. In 1861 he was appointed a first lieutenant, and later he received three brevet promotions. In 1871 he transferred to the 9th Cavalry. Five years later he took part in the Rosebud and Slim Buttes battles. In 1878 he became a major in the 10th Cavalry. Heitman; *1879 Army Register; 1990 Register of Graduates;* Altshuler, *Cavalry Yellow and Infantry Blue,* pp. 231, 232.

3. The condition of the barracks should not have surprised Bigelow, who did not think highly of Grierson as a disciplinarian. McChristian, ed., *Garrison Tangles,* p. 50 n34; see Leckie and Leckie, *Unlikely Warriors,* passim.

4. Alexander S. B. Keyes, D Company, enlisted during the Civil War and later became a lieutenant. In 1877 he had been tried but acquitted for a "want of energy" on a scout and "laxity of discipline" by allowing his men to make noises that warned the Indians of their presence. *ANJ,* August 25, 1877, p. 36.

5. Wallace Tear, a Civil War sergeant and lieutenant, was a 25th Infantry lieutenant. Heitman; *1879 Army Register.*

6. SO 60, Hq. Ft. Stockton, July 27, 1879.

7. See Steffen, *The Horse Soldier,* vol. 2, pp. 103ff.

8. Soldiers could voluntarily deposit a portion of their pay that would earn 4 percent interest a year that they received on discharge. Rev. Stat. of 1878, sec. 1306.

9. Some of his wards reportedly regarded Russell as "an old woman who did not know the Apaches and was afraid of them." Joseph A. Stout, Jr., *Apache Lightning* (New York: Oxford Univ. Press, 1974), pp. 91, 148–50, 168, 169.

10. Glass, *The History of the 10th Cavalry, 1806–1921,* p. 100; telegram from Ord to SecWar, August 29, 1879; *ANJ,* September 20, 1879, p. 118; Williams, *Texas' Last Frontier,* pp. 231, 232.

11. The promotions of lieutenants were normally based on seniority, and a "file" is the position held by a person on a list. Of 118 cavalry second lieutenants Bigelow was 90th, Gasman 38th, and Safford 89th. *1879 Army Register.*

12. Brevet Col. William Mackey Wherry's *The Command of the Army* (n.p., 1879) is an obscure, eleven-page pamphlet. Wherry had been General Schofield's aide from 1862 to 1866 and from 1867 to 1885. *Who Was Who in America,* vol. 1, p. 1330.

13. Hayes, a graduate of Kenyon College and Harvard Law School, was an Ohio lawyer from 1845 until commissioned as a major in a volunteer regiment in 1861. He became a major general of U.S. Volunteers in 1865, then served one term in Congress. McCrary, also a lawyer, was an Iowa state legislator during the Civil War, and a congressman from 1869 to 1877 when appointed secretary of war. *Who Was Who in America, Historical Volume 1607–1896* (Chicago: Marquis, 1967), pp. 311, 415.

14. See Samuel P. Huntington, *The Soldier and the State: The Theory and Politics of Civil-Military Relations* (Cambridge: Belknap Press of Harvard Univ. Press, 1957), pp. 80–97 and 163–92. Among the principal constitutional provisions relating to the army are the powers granted Congress in Article I to declare war (Sec. 8), raise and support armies (Sec. 12), and make rules for the government and regulation of the land and naval forces (Sec. 14). Article II designates the president as commander in chief of the army and navy, and authorizes him to appoint officers by and with the advice and consent of the Senate (Sec. 2).

15. Although George Washington muddled through the Revolution with only the barest semblance of a staff, in 1798 he vigorously urged creation of a general staff. It was not until the 1812–1821 period, though, that several staff departments were organized. Their nature and numbers changed over time, but by the late 1800s there were departments of the Adjutant General, the Inspector General, the Judge Advocate General, Subsistence, Medical, Pay, and Ordnance, as well as the Signal Corps, the

Corps of Engineers, and a few minor bureaus. AGO, *Legislative History of the General Staff of the Army, 1775 to 1901* (Washington: GPO, 1901), pp. 4, 5, and passim.

16. Ibid., p. 188.

17. Stat. at Large, vol. 14, pp. 485ff. The Command Act required that all "orders and instructions relating to military operations issued by the President or Secretary of War shall be issued through the General of the army." In signing the Appropriations Act with reservations, Johnson protested that he would be deprived of command of the army by the provision cited. Weigley, *History of the United States Army*, pp. 260, 261.

18. Utley, *Frontier Regulars*, pp. 63, 64.

19. Belknap, an 1853 Princeton graduate, was commissioned in an Iowa Infantry regiment in 1861. Although Sherman had recommended him for promotion to brigadier general, Belknap apparently harbored a deep enmity toward him and, as described by Russell Weigley, "took to tormenting Sherman seemingly with no purpose but to make life miserable for him, allying himself with...[Congressman] John Logan...who was suspicious of all professional soldiers." Belknap, like Logan, undoubtedly resented Sherman's bluntness when he wrote that in the Atlanta Campaign he did not select Logan for a key command position because he "needed commanders who were...soldiers, men who would obey orders and execute them promptly.... I regarded both Generals Logan and Blair as 'volunteers,' that looked to personal fame and glory as auxiliary and secondary to their political ambition, and not as professional soldiers." *Who Was Who in America, Historical Volume 1607–1896*, p. 118; Russell F. Weigley, *History of the United States Army* (New York: Macmillan Co., 1967), p. 286; Sherman, *Memoirs of General William T. Sherman*, vol. 2 (New York: D. Appleton and Co., 1876) pp. 86, 95.

20. After Sherman, Sheridan was commanding general until his death in 1888. He was followed by John M. Schofield, who believed that under the Constitution a commanding general could never be more than a "chief of staff." Hence, he relinquished "command" to the secretary, but continued to provide military advice to him. This arrangement worked satisfactorily until 1895 when Nelson Miles became commanding general. As "perhaps the least qualified man" to ever serve in that position, he and the staff chiefs continually thwarted efforts to achieve a workable solution. But a week after Miles retired in 1903, the Chief of Staff Act, conceived and advocated by Secretary Elihu Root, became effective. See Weigley, *History of the United States Army*, pp. 289, 290; Huntington, *The Soldier and the State*, pp. 251–54, 297–301.

21. One hundred rations then included fifty rations of beans (seven and one half pounds) and fifty rations of rice (five pounds), but the rice ration could be commuted to beans. *1881 Regulations*, para. 2174; *1863 Regulations*, para. 1217.

22. Bigelow wrote to Colonel Blunt that "[Rice] is not as nourishing nor as palatable as beans and is only wasted by being issued, as the men will not eat it."

23. In seeking a route between Fort Smith and Santa Fe in 1850, Captain Marcy crossed the White Sand Hills from southwest to northeast. He found good water in "the very last place on earth where one would ever think of looking for it." Three months later Lt. Nathaniel Michler, following Marcy's route in the opposite direction, also was impressed with the quantity and quality of water available, and in 1854 Capt. John Pope traversed the same trail. Sen. Exec. Doc. 64, 31st Cong., 1st sess., vol. 14 (1850), *Report of Captain Marcy*, pp. 169–227, and *Report of Lieutenant Michler*, pp. 29–39

(Serial 562); Grant Foreman, *Marcy and the Gold Seekers* (Norman: Univ. of Oklahoma Press, 1939), pp. 359, 360.

24. See Chapter 3 for General Sherman's views on the differences between white and black soldiers in tolerating heat, and the results of later physiological studies.

25. The guide was a deputy sheriff and rancher in Pecos County.

26. Emigrant (or Emigrants') Crossing was about forty miles south of New Mexico and thirty miles southwest by west of the southern part of the White Sand Hills. Emigrants used it in traveling to California by way of the Marcy-Michler-Pope trail (Emigrant Road), which connected with the Southern Overland Mail Route a few miles below the river near the present town of Pecos.

CHAPTER 19

1. Matthias W. Day was commissioned in the 10th Cavalry but soon transferred to the 9th. Earlier in 1879 he surprised some Mescaleros in the Cornudas Mountains, impulsively led a charge up a hill, and captured all their livestock and supplies. Heitman; *1990 Register of Graduates*; *AOG Report for 1932*, pp. 104–7. The other members of the 9th were John Guilfoyle, Charles Bradley, and Ben Butler.

2. Soon after Flipper, who was assigned to Company A, reported to Fort Sill in January 1878, the president of Texas A&M asked the secretary of war to detail him to the ROTC there. The request was denied because Texas A&M already had a PMS&T. He also served briefly at Fort Concho and then longer at Fort Davis. His friendship with the Irish sister of his company commander's wife might have led to resentment among some junior officers and others, such as the "lady" who wrote northern newspapers to criticize his commander, Capt. Nicholas Nolan, and his family for "recognizing and entertaining" Flipper. Nolan replied that he had "found him to be all that West Point turns out." Heitman; *1990 Register of Graduates*; NARA, RG 153, T1027, *Records Relating to the Army Career of Henry Ossian Flipper, 1873–1882*; *ANJ*, October 11, 1879, p. 176. See Epilogue.

3. Maney, Gatewood, and Blocksom all had key roles in the Battle of Hembrillo Canyon and other engagements during the campaign. Heitman; *1879 Army Register*; *1990 Register of Graduates*; see *AOG Reports for 1921*, pp. 88–90, and *for 1932*, pp. 99–103.

4. See Thomas E. Mails, *The People Called Apache* (New York: Promontory, 1981), passim.

5. John Upton Terrell, *Apache Chronicle* (New York: World Publishing, 1972), p. 338.

6. The Victorio Campaign is analyzed in several works including Dan L. Thrapp, *Victorio and the Mimbres Apaches* (Norman: Univ. of Oklahoma Press, 1974) and *The Conquest of Apacheria*; Worcester, *The Apaches: Eagles of the Southwest*; C. L. Sonnichsen, *The Mescalero Apaches* (Norman: Univ. of Oklahoma Press, 2d ed., 1973); Utley, *Frontier Regulars*, pp. 344–68; Ralph H. Ogle, *Federal Control of Western Apaches, 1848–1886* (Albuquerque: Univ. of New Mexico Press, 1970); Stout, *Apache Lightning*; Eve Ball, *In the Days of Victorio* (Tucson: Univ. of Arizona Press, 1970); David Roberts, *Once They Moved Like the Wind* (New York: Simon and Schuster, 1993); John P. Clum, "Apache Misrule: A Bungling Agent Sets the Military Arm in Motion," *New Mexico Historical Review* 5, nos. 2 and 3 (1930), pp. 138–53 and 221–29, and "The Apaches," 3, no. 2

(April 1929), pp. 107–27; and Ralph H. Ogle, "The Apaches and the Government, 1870s," *New Mexico Historical Review* 33, no. 2 (April 1958), pp. 81–102.

7. Annual Report for 1885, quoted in John J. Bourke, *On the Border with Crook* (1891; reprint, Lincoln: Univ. of Nebraska Press), p. 464.

8. Brig. Gen. George Crook, "The Apache Problem," *JMSI* 7 (1886), pp. 257–69, at 260–62.

9. A subcamp of Fort Craig was established at Ojo Caliente in 1859, and in 1874 a reservation of the same name was created with headquarters at the camp. Frazer, *Forts of the West,* pp. 101, 102; Thrapp, *Victorio and the Mimbres Apache,* passim.

10. Hatch to AAG, Dept. of the Missouri, September 8, 1879; *ANJ,* September 27, 1879, p. 137.

11. *ANJ,* September 13, 1879, p. 97; September 6, 1879, dispatch from Captain Hooker to Colonel Hatch, *ANJ,* September 27, 1879, p. 137; September 18, 1879, telegram from AAG, 9th Cavalry, to AAG, 3d Cavalry; see Thrapp, *Victorio and the Mimbres Apaches,* pp. 237ff; Utley, *Frontier Regulars,* pp. 344–68; Stout, *Apache Lightning,* p. 92.

12. Lt. C. B. Gatewood, "Campaigning against Victorio in 1879," *The Great Divide* (April 1894), pp. 102–4; see Thrapp, *The Conquest of Apacheria,* pp. 184–89, and *Victorio and the Mimbres Apaches,* pp. 241ff; and Stout, *Apache Lightning,* pp. 96–100.

13. See Thrapp, *Victorio and the Mimbres Apaches,* pp. 218–51.

14. Letter from an "anonymous observer" in Silver City, New Mexico. *ANJ,* April 3, 1880, pp. 704, 705.

15. During investigations the commissioner of Indian affairs, Ezra A. Hayt, was accused of failing to pay money due the Utes under a treaty. The Indian Bureau also was criticized for leaving supplies to rot at Rawlins instead of transporting and issuing them, and for appointing Meeker, "a man having no tact in the management of Indians." *ANJ,* January 31, 1880, p. 516. The best accounts of the battle are in H. Misc. Doc. 38, 46th Cong., 2d sess., vol. 4, *The Ute Indian Outbreak* (1880), pp. 62–71 (Serial 1931); the 1879 *"Ute Campaign"* series of articles in *ANJ,* October 8 and 25, pp. 196–98 and 217–19, and November 1, 8, and 15, pp. 237, 238, 257, and 277, 278; and Wesley Merritt, "Three Indian Campaigns," *Harper's New Monthly Magazine* (April 1890), pp. 720–37. Also see Elmer R. Burkey, "The Thornburgh Battle with the Utes on Milk Creek," *The Colorado Magazine* 12, no. 1 (January 1936), pp. 90–110; Utley, *Frontier Regulars,* pp. 335–38; Marshall Sprague, *Massacre: The Tragedy at White River* (Boston: Little, Brown, 1957); Wilson Rockwell, *The Utes: A Forgotten People* (Denver: Sage, 1956); and Marshall D. Moody, "The Meeker Massacre," *The Colorado Magazine* 30, no. 1 (January 1953).

16. In 1862 "Tip" Thornburgh, then eighteen, enlisted. He soon became a sergeant major and in 1863 was appointed to West Point. After graduation he advanced rapidly to major and paymaster, then transferred to the 4th Infantry in 1878. Heitman; *1879 Army Register; 1990 Register of Graduates; ANJ,* October 4, 1879, p. 162.

17. James V. S. Paddock of Illinois, thirty-fourth in the Class of 1877, was with the 5th Cavalry from 1877 until 1885. His multiple wounds resulted in his disability retirement in 1891. *AOG Report for 1908,* pp. 124, 125. Samuel Austin Cherry was the second lieutenant of F Company, 5th Cavalry. His career ended abruptly with his murder less than two years later. See Epilogue; Heitman; *Register of Graduates.*

18. Meeker, an eccentric poet and agricultural editor for Horace Greeley's *New York Tribune,* was a proponent of social experimentation. After Greeley's suicide following his defeat for president by Grant in 1872, Meeker's efforts to establish a utopian "colony" at Greeley, Colorado, flopped financially. He then obtained an appointment as an Indian agent in which capacity he was even less effective, for although honest he lacked sound judgment and temperamental stability. See Prucha, *American Indian Policy in Crisis,* passim; James F. Willard, *The Union Colony at Greeley, Colorado, 1869–1870* (Boulder: W. F. Robinson, 1918); Sprague, *Massacre,* passim; and Rockwell, *The Utes,* passim.

19. See H. Misc. Doc. 38 for 1880, pp. 62–71 (Serial 1931).

20. Francis Safford Dodge, a Civil War veteran, was appointed a second lieutenant in the 9th Cavalry in 1866. The Medal of Honor was awarded him for gallantry at Milk Creek. Heitman.

21. *ANJ,* October 25, 1879, p. 226.

22. Ibid.

23. Sen. Comm. on Veterans' Affairs, *Medal of Honor Recipients, 1863–1978*; Irvin H. Lee, *Negro Medal of Honor Men* (New York: Dodd, Mead, 1967), pp. 67–71; NARA, RG 94, M929; Preston E. Amos, *Above and Beyond in the West: Black Medal of Honor Winners, 1870–1890* (Washington, D. C.: Potomac Corral, The Westerners, 1974), pp. 14–17. What today would be considered demeaning references to racial and ethnic groups were then common. For example, Irishmen were routinely called "paddies," "micks," or "Patlanders," Germans were known as "dutchies," and Mexicans as "greasers." Some of the names for African Americans were slurs, but there is little doubt that the soldiers quoted did not use them in a derogatory sense.

24. From 1870 when Emanuel Stance received the nation's highest recogition for gallantry until 1890 when William O. Wilson was cited for bravery at Wounded Knee, a total of thirteen black soldiers were similarly acclaimed. Six (Thomas Boyne, John Denny, George Jordan, Augustus Walley, Moses Williams, and Brent Woods) were singled out during the Victorio Campaign; another (Clinton Greaves) for his hand-to-hand fight with Indians in the Florida Mountains in 1877; and William McBryar for his bravery against Apaches in 1890. And in 1889 Benjamin Brown and Isaiah Mays prevented stagecoach robbers from seizing a payroll from a paymaster named Wham. In addition, Sgt. Thomas Shaw, 4th Cavalry, who apparently "crossed over" to a white regiment, was awarded the Medal of Honor for his 1881 performance in Carrizo Canyon, New Mexico, and four Seminole Negro-Indian Scouts (Pompay Factor, Adam Paine, Isaac Paine, and John Ward) were also decorated for charging a party of twenty-five hostile Indians. Sen. Comm. on Veterans' Affairs, *Medal of Honor Recipients, 1863–1978*; Lee, *Negro Medal of Honor Men,* passim; Records of the Adjutant General's Office. NARA, RG 94, M929 (*Documents Relating to the Military and Naval Service of Blacks Awarded the Congressional Medal of Honor*), roll 2 (Indian Campaigns).

25. Capt. J. Scott Payne, Class of 1866, received a brevet promotion to major for his action at Milk Creek. *ANJ,* October 11, 1879, p. 177; Heitman; *Register of Graduates.*

26. *ANJ,* October 11, 1879, p. 177, and October 18, 1879, p. 196; also see Merritt, "Three Indian Campaigns," pp. 732–37; Rockwell, *The Utes,* p. 133; Sprague, *Massacre,* p. 228; and Moody, "The Meeker Massacre," p. 101.

27. Twenty-three Utes were killed the first day and fourteen others later. Wilcomb E. Washburn, *The American Indian and the United States,* vol. 1 (New York: Random House, 1973), p. 271.

28. SO, War Dept., November 22, 1879; *ANJ,* November 29, 1879, p. 320; SO 245, Dept. of Texas, November 19, 1879; *1881 Army Register,* p. 260. Company B's new commander was 2d Lt. Thaddeus Winfield Jones, Class of 1872, the most senior second lieutenant in the regiment. Heitman; *1879 Army Register; 1990 Register of Graduates.*

29. Fort Stockton *Post Return,* November 1879.

30. *1881 Army Register,* p. 260; *1990 Register of Graduates; AOG Report for 1936,* pp. 103, 104; Cullum, *Biographical Register,* vols. 3–5.

EPILOGUE

1. SO 167, Div. of the Missouri, September 16, 1878; *ANJ,* September 28, 1878, p. 116; GCMO 74, *ANJ,* December 13, 1879, p. 360; McChristian, *Garrison Tangles,* p. 52 n35.

2. *1990 Register of Graduates; AOG Report for 1900,* pp. 88–92.

3. *Handbook of International Law* (St. Paul: West, 1895), and *Rules of Land Warfare* (Washington, D.C.: General Staff, 1914).

4. A "water cure" involved forcing water down the throat of a person until he provided whatever information was desired. Under political and antiwar pressure, Theodore Roosevelt ordered the courts-martial of Glenn and Brig. Gen. Jacob Smith. In his first trial Glenn was fined fifty dollars and suspended for one month; in the second he was acquitted. Evidence established that Smith and other superiors encouraged reprisals against natives who engaged in barbarities such as piercing captured troops with sticks and roasting them alive by slow rotation over a fire. Moreover, because the natives were not lawful combatants, they did not qualify for treatment as prisoners of war. See William Thaddeus Sexton, *Soldiers in the Sun: An Adventure in Imperialism* (Freeport, NY: Books for Libraries, 1939), pp. 268–74; Daniel B. Schirmer, *Republic or Empire: American Resistance to the Philippine War* (Cambridge, Mass.: Schenkman, 1972), pp. 225–40; Brian McAllister Linn, *The U.S. Army and Counterinsurgency in the Philippine War* (Chapel Hill: Univ. of North Carolina Press, 1989), pp. 26, 27; and *ANJ,* April 26 to February 21, 1903, passim.

5. *1990 Register of Graduates; AOG Report for 1928,* pp. 67–70; *Who Was Who in America,* vol. 1 (Chicago: Marquis, 1943), p. 461.

6. Heitman; *1990 Register of Graduates*; GCMO 48, AGO, July 2, 1894; *ANJ,* July 14, 1895, p. 803.

7. *United States v. Beck,* NARA, RG 153, QQ 1107 (1879); Altshuler, *Cavalry Yellow and Infantry Blue,* pp. 271, 272.

8. Heitman; *1990 Register of Graduates; AOG Report for 1920; United States v. Read,* NARA, RG 153, M1105, roll 7, Case QQ 1482 (1879); GCMO 64, AGO, November 29, 1879, and GCMO 57, AGO, November 8, 1880; *ANJ,* December 13, 1879, p. 360, and November 20, 1880, p. 308.

9. Heitman; *1879 Army Register*; Altshuler, *Cavalry Yellow and Infantry Blue,* pp. 225, 226.

10. *AOG Report for 1908,* pp. 101–3.

11. In 1879 Armes was convicted of prejudicial conduct for mistreating soldiers, and of unbecoming conduct for attempting to coerce two men to falsely swear to a statement. His dismissal was commuted. *United States v. Armes,* NARA, RG 153, M1105, roll 7, Case QQ 1658 (1879); GCMO 36, AGO, May 27, 1880; *ANJ,* June 12, 1880, p. 916. Then in July 1880 Armes was found guilty of disobeying an order from Blunt. His dismissal was again mitigated, suggesting impressive political clout. *United States v. Armes,* NARA, RG 153, M1105, roll 7, Case QQ 1969 (1880); GCMO 42, AGO, July 1, 1881; *ANJ,* July 9, 1881, p. 1025.

12. Armes continued to demand reinstatement and promotion to major. *ANJ,* November 24, 1883, p. 331. For an excellent and fascinating account of the career of this troubled officer, see Bruce J. Dinges, "The Irrepressible Captain Armes," *Journal of the West* (April 1993), pp. 38–52.

13. *United States v. Geddes,* NARA, RG 153, QQ 2023 (1879). GCMO 64, AGO, December 4, 1880; *ANJ,* December 18, 1880, p. 389, and December 11, 1880, p. 369.

14. Letters, Sherman to Terry, July 20 and December 4, 1880, Sherman Papers, Container 91, nos. 319 and 381, 1880.

15. SO 125, AGO, May 27, 1879; *ANJ,* May 31, 1879, p. 764; SO, War Dept., November 18, 1879.

16. See Thrapp, *Victorio and the Mimbres Apaches,* pp. 248–51.

17. *ANJ,* May 12, 1880, p. 217.

18. After resigning in 1883 because of his wife's health, Esterly was a school superintendent in Kansas and El Paso, then president of Los Angeles Baptist College before moving to Berkeley. His son, born at Fort Stockton in 1879, became a leading zoologist, marine biologist, and author. *1990 Register of Graduates; AOG Report for 1921,* pp. 158, 159; *ANJ,* May 12, 1880, p. 217; *Who Was Who in America,* vol. 1, p. 376.

19. Douglas C. McChristian, "Grierson's Fight at Tinaja de las Palmas: An Episode in the Victorio Campaign," *Red River Valley Historical Rev.* (Winter 1982), pp. 45–63; Thrapp, *Victorio and the Mimbres Apaches,* pp. 275–92; Donald R. McClung, "Second Lieutenant Henry O. Flipper: A Negro Officer on the West Texas Frontier," *West Texas Historical Association Yearbook* 47 (1971). The tactics of stationing infantry troops at major water holes and using cavalry to pursue marauders were less than successful until Grierson, with Ord's concurrence, decided to forego the usually futile and exhausting chases in favor of concentrating forces at springs and river crossings to intercept their adversaries. William H. and Shirley A. Leckie, *Unlikely Warriors,* pp. 250ff; see Dinges, "The Victorio Campaign of 1880," pp. 81–94 passim.

20. See Thrapp, *The Conquest of Apacheria,* pp. 240–45. McDonald resigned in 1888 to become a farmer and hotel keeper. Heitman; *1990 Register of Graduates; AOG Report for 1919,* p. 35.

21. Wilber Elliott Wilder, 4th Cavalry, was on the frontier for eighteen years before participating in the Philippine Insurrection, Mexican Punitive Expedition, and World War I as a brigadier general. Heitman; *1990 Register of Graduates;* Sen. Comm. on Veterans' Affairs, *Medal of Honor Recipients, 1863–1978.*

22. In 1861 Nelson Appleton Miles, a twenty-two-year-old Boston store clerk, became a lieutenant in a Massachusetts Infantry company he organized and outfitted with funds from his family, hence in a sense "buying" a company, which was not unprecedented. The next year he joined a New York regiment in which he became a brevet colonel. He was wounded four times and received the Medal of Honor for gal-

lantry. His unquestioned bravery and performance earned him a brigadier general's star in 1864, and the next year he became a major general. After the war he was commissioned as colonel of the 40th Infantry, one of the six new "colored" regiments. From the outset of his military career, when he had to settle for the rank of first lieutenant instead of a captaincy, he seemed consumed to the point of obsession with obtaining higher and higher positions. He was not alone in using whatever political or other influence he could muster to further his career, but at times his inordinate efforts earned him the enmity of many army officers and others. Heitman; for a superb analysis of this complex and controversial officer, see Robert Wooster, *Nelson A. Miles and the Twilight of the Frontier Army* (Lincoln: Univ. of Nebraska Press, 1993), passim; also see Nelson A. Miles, *Personal Recollections and Observations* (1896; reprint, New York: Da Capo, 1969), passim; and Virginia W. Johnson, *The Unregimented General* (Cambridge, Mass.: Riverside, 1962), passim. Sherman thought "General Miles is too apt to mistake the dictates of his personal ambition for wisdom." Letter to Sheridan, July 19, 1879, *Sherman Papers*, LC, Container 91, p. 239. Another officer found him "restless and ambitious, after 'glory' all the time not caring how much it costs others in life or property." Letter, Maj. Alfred Hough to his wife, June 11, 1877, *Hough Papers*, Western History Dept., Univ. of Colorado. Also see Col. H. B. Wharfield, *With Scouts and Cavalry at Fort Apache*, ed. John A. Carroll (Tucson: Arizona Pioneers' Historical Soc., 1965), p. 40; and Davis, *The Truth about Geronimo*, pp. 235, 236 and passim.

23. *AOG Report for 1896*, pp. 169–71; Hutton, *Phil Sheridan and His Army*, pp. 156, 157; Altshuler, *Cavalry Yellow and Infantry Blue*, pp. 138, 139; Davis, *The Truth about Geronimo*, pp. 233–35 and passim.

24. *AOG Report for 1932*, pp. 100–3.

25. Ibid., pp. 105–7; *1990 Register of Graduates.*

26. *1990 Register of Graduates; AOG Report for 1938*, pp. 106–12.

27. GCMO 58, AGO, October 17, 1881; *ANJ*, October 22, 1881, p. 248, and November 15, 1884, p. 302.

28. Hedberg, a Swedish immigrant, enlisted in 1862 and was commissioned two years later. He was cashiered in 1873 but reappointed in 1889. Heitman.

29. Maney wrote, "Your cowardly action in attempting to use your pistol when your want of courage made your threat to use it but the empty boast of a cur incensed me to the degree of determining to kill you.... Cooling thought points out how degrading that would be and you are spared. My advice to you is not to provoke me again."

30. *United States v. Maney*, 61 Fed. 140 (U.S. Cir. Ct., 1894). Neither the Supreme Court nor any federal tribunal then had appellate jurisdiction or authority to interfere with a court-martial. *Wales v. Whitney*, 158 U.S. 109; Winthrop, pp. 50, 51. The defense argued that in peacetime courts-martial did not have jurisdiction over offenses such as murder. AW 58 of 1874; Winthrop, pp. 666–71. Although correct, the offense alleged was not homicide but "conduct prejudicial to good order and discipline." Ex parte Mason, 105 U.S. 609; Winthrop, p. 94 n65.

31. GO 28, AGO, 1894; Winthrop, p. 674 n59.

32. Barber had been a lawyer before enlisting in the 10th Vermont Infantry in 1862. He became a lieutenant and in 1864 was breveted as a major, then commissioned in the 16th Infantry in 1866. Clous and he were skilled advocates who presented impressive cases. Shafter and Wilhelmi were among the government wit-

nesses, while those for the defense included McLaughlen, Charles Viele, and several businessmen. The proceedings commenced on September 17, but Flipper was granted a continuance until November 1; the case lasted from then until December 8.

33. *United States v. Flipper,* NARA, RG 153, Case QQ2951, T1027, Record of Trial, p. 67.

34. In earlier times in England a defendant could not testify because of his interest in the outcome of the case. And courts-martial in nineteenth-century Europe still pursued the inquisitorial form of examination, compelling an accused to testify. In the United States, though, under the Act of March 16, 1878, at a court-martial an accused could testify if he so requested, but his failure to do so did not create any presumption against him. Winthrop, pp. 335ff; Davis, p. 312.

35. See *United States v. Flipper,* Record of Trial, p. 577. Shafter, a "harsh disciplinarian" who "drank heartily, gambled earnestly, ate plentifully, and cursed incessantly," was regarded by some as abusive and gruff. Utley, *Frontier Regulars,* p. 350. Carlson, *"Pecos Bill,"* pp. xi, 73. But Charles Crane thought he was "a most energetic and efficient officer...[and] an excellent post commander." Crane, *Experiences,* p. 64. In his statement, Flipper referred to him as a "severe, stern man" whom he hoped to "avoid giving...any knowledge of [his] embarrassment." Record of Trial, p. 506. And in an impassioned closing argument, Capt. Barber related Flipper's rise from slavery to become the "only one of his people" to graduate from West Point. He then asked the court, "By what standard will you measure him? By that of your race or his?... [By] his success...or by an error to which he was moved by carelessness...and the dread of a harsh master?" Record of Trial, p. 577.

36. The guilty finding of "conduct unbecoming an officer and gentleman" required a sentence of dismissal, which only the president could disapprove or commute. AW 61 and 106 of 1874; Winthrop, pp. 710–20; Davis, pp. 544–52. Court members could recommend clemency, but in Flipper's case none did.

37. HR 9849, 56th Cong., 1st sess., introduced in 1898, was the first of several bills unsuccessfully asserting that prejudicial errors tainted the findings and sentence. See NARA, RG 153, T1027, *Records Relating to the Army Career of Henry Ossian Flipper, 1873–1882.* In his brief accompanying HR 9849, Flipper argued that the findings should have been guilty of lying to Shafter on August 10 about having transmitted the funds, not guilty of misrepresentation by showing him the $1,440 check because it was never presented for payment, and guilty "without criminality" of making the three false reports. He also contended that he was only guilty of "prejudicial conduct" (which did not require dismissal) instead of "unbecoming conduct."

38. As a former prosecutor as well as defense counsel in courts-martial, trial judge, appellate defense counsel, and military court of review judge, the author believes that the transcript clearly establishes that Flipper was guilty of making false official statements, and that there is no merit in any of the alleged errors. The acquittal of embezzlement and the subsequent reimbursement of the funds missing are irrelevant, of course, to whether Flipper made the false statements. Among other arguments at times advanced is that some officers at Davis were racially prejudiced, but even if bigotry did exist, he alone was responsible for his acts. Suggestions have also been made that poor record keeping was not uncommon, and if Flipper were white his derelictions probably would have been ignored. If true (and the author is not aware of any supporting evidence), lying about official matters, not deficient record keeping, was

the gravamen of the crimes, and the army cannot tolerate a lack of veracity in an officer. GCMO 39, AGO, June 14, 1882; the 613-page transcript is in NARA, RG 153, QQ 2952, boxes 2032 and 2033 (1882), and also in T1027.

39. The BCMR, an administrative body, may change the type of discharge, but not the findings of a court-martial, which the BCMR's decision specifically recognized. *Baxter v. Clayton,* 652 F.2d 181 (D.C. Cir., 1981); *OpJAGAF 1980/20,* March 14, 1980; *OpJAGAF 1988/34,* May 23, 1988; 10 USC 876.

40. Much has been written about this remarkable young man, but most of it demonstrates little understanding of criminal or military law. Anyone interested in pursuing the issues might start with Flipper, *The Colored Cadet at West Point,* ed. Theodore D. Harris; *Negro Frontiersman: The Western Memoirs of Henry O. Flipper* (El Paso: Texas Western College Press, 1963); McClung, "Second Lieutenant Henry O. Flipper"; Ezra J. Wanner, "A Black Man in the Long Gray Line," *American History Illustrated* 6 (January 1970); Bruce J. Dinges, "The Court-Martial of Lieutenant Henry O. Flipper," *The American West* 9 (January 1972); and Carlson, *"Pecos Bill,"* pp. 122–27. For a thorough, judicial-like analysis see Barry C. Johnson, *Flipper's Dismissal: The Ruin of Lt. Henry O. Flipper, U.S.A., First Coloured Graduate of West Point* (London: n.p., 1980).

41. Fort Niobrara was on the Niobrara River near the present town of Valentine in north-central Nebraska, a dozen miles below the South Dakota border and about 140 miles east of Chadron. Frazer, *Forts of the West,* p. 89.

42. *ANJ,* May 21, 1881, p. 869.

43. Amos, *Above and Beyond in the West,* pp. 14–17; Shubert, *On the Trail of the Buffalo Soldier,* pp. 232, 233.

44. *ANJ,* July 31, 1880, p. 1062.

45. See Utley, *Frontier Regulars,* pp. 355, 356, and 366 n26. The brigadiers were Pope, Howard, Terry, Ord, Augur, and Crook.

46. Cresap, *Appomattox Commander,* p. 353. See Wooster, *Nelson A. Miles and the Twilight of the Frontier Army,* pp. 129ff. Perhaps to partially compensate for the politically motivated action, the following year Ord was advanced in retirement to his brevet rank of major general. Sen. Rpt. 740, 46th Cong., 3d sess. vol. 1 (1881), *Relief of General Ord* (Serial 1948); SO 112,. para. 9, AGO, January 5, 1881.

47. Letter, Surg. Smith to AAG, Dept. of Texas, December 19, 1883; Telegram, AAG, Dept. of Texas, to AAG, Chicago, December 19, 1883; and AAG, Dept. of Texas, to AG, Washington, D.C., December 22, 1883; *Mackenzie Papers,* NARA, RG 94.

48. SO 52, AGO, March 3, 1883; *Proceedings of the Army Retiring Board,* March 5, 1883, ibid. Mackenzie's condition was ascribed to "wounds received and exposure." However, "general paresis" was also called "brain syphilis," and no autopsy was conducted. See Robinson, *Bad Hand,* pp. 332–38.

49. The precise cause of Mackenzie's death is unknown, but suicide, which his sister might have been reluctant to disclose, cannot be ruled out.

50. *AOG Report for 1889,* pp. 56, 57.

51. The Rendezvous at 174 Hudson Street was where recruits were enlisted and assembled. *ANJ,* November 1, 1879, p. 235.

52. Wharfield, *With Scouts and Cavalry at Fort Apache,* pp. 46, 47. In his memoirs Miles quibbled, "I left Fort Bowie...at the same time as the Indians, and accordingly did not receive a telegram concerning their disposition...[until] the afternoon of that day." Miles, *Personal Recollections,* p. 528.

53. *ANJ*, May 5, 1883, p. 900.

54. The articles are compiled in John Bigelow, Jr., *On the Bloody Trail of Geronimo* (Los Angeles: Westernlore, 1958). When they were students, Remington, then a struggling artist, and Poultney, later editor of *Outing* (the nation's first sports magazine), had worked together on the *Yale Courant*, which Poultney edited. He persuaded Remington to submit a sketch that became the artist's first published work. Remington dropped out of college after the fall semester of his sophomore year because of his father's fatal illness. Nevertheless, he and Poultney became lifelong friends and frequent correspondents. Allen P. Splete and Marilyn D. Splete, *Frederic Remington—Selected Letters* (New York: Abbeville, 1988), passim.

55. Based on information provided by Remington, Poultney Bigelow wrote that Roosevelt was never on San Juan Hill nor even on horseback, despite the artist's painting depicting him spurring his horse toward Spanish lines while swinging a sabre. Moreover, he added that Roosevelt, planning to run for governor of New York that fall and seeking publicity, was "merely a hindrance" and "useless" as a soldier. Bigelow, *Seventy Summers*, pp. 283, 284.

56. See John Bigelow, Jr., *Reminiscences of the Santiago Campaign* (New York: Harper, 1899); Richard Harding Davis, *The Cuban and Porto Rican Campaigns* (New York: Charles Scribner's Sons, 1898); Herbert H. Sargent, *The Campaign of Santiago de Cuba* (Chicago: A. C. McClurg, 1907); Vincent J. Esposito, ed., *The West Point Atlas of American Wars*, vol. 1 (New York: Praeger Publishers, 1959), pp. 155–58; and Cashin, *Under Fire*.

57. Jules Garesche Ord enlisted in 1887 and became a lieutenant in the 6th Infantry three years later. Heitman.

58. Cashin, *Under Fire*, p. 268.

59. Bigelow, *Reminiscences*, p. 132.

60. Ibid., pp. 209, 210. At San Juan 142 American officers and soldiers were killed and 1,014 wounded. Heitman, vol. 2, p. 291.

61. Pershing, first captain and thirtieth in the seventy-seven-member Class of 1886, was on frontier duty until 1891 when he became PMS&T at the University of Nebraska. In 1895 he commanded a 10th Cavalry troop at Fort Assinniboine, from which he was transferred to Washington in late 1896 as aide for Nelson Miles. A year later he became an intensely disliked tactical officer at West Point where the cadets privately called him "Nigger Jack." Thereafter he was known as "Black Jack." He rejoined the 10th Cavalry in May 1898 and served with distinction in Cuba. *1990 Register of Graduates*; Richard O'Connor, *Black Jack Pershing* (Garden City, N.Y.: Doubleday, 1961), pp. 42ff.

62. Cashin, *Under Fire*, pp. 209, 210. During his frontier service with the 10th Cavalry, Pershing developed the highest confidence in and respect for black troops, which was cemented by their performance in Cuba. See Frank E. Vandiver, *Black Jack: The Life and Times of John J. Pershing*, vol. 1 (College Station: Texas A&M Press, 1977), pp. 47–104, 136–51, 176–312 passim.

63. Bigelow, *Reminiscences*, p. 37. See "The Negro as Soldier and Officer," *JSMI* 29 (1901), p. 286.

64. Ibid., pp. 275, 276. Most of the verses are short on skill but long on poignancy. Reflecting a common impression of blacks at the turn of the century, one commences:

We used to think the Negro didn't
count for very much—
Light fingered in the melon patch
and chicken yard, and such;
Much mixed in point of morals and
absurd in point of dress,
The butt of droll cartoonists and the
target of the press;
But we've got to reconstruct our
views on color, more or less,
Now we know about the Tenth at Las
Guasimas!

65. Cashin, *Under Fire*, pp. 335–61.

66. In addition to the associations dating back to Bigelow's time in B Company, he and Sergeant Givens were together again from 1884 to 1887 in K Troop at Forts Davis and Grant, from which they pursued Geronimo over hundreds of miles, and later they served with D Troop in northern Montana at Fort Assinniboine. Such assignments are most unlikely to have been coincidental, but instead reflect mutual respect and the desire of each to be in the same organization. Ibid., pp. 166–72; Theophilus G. Steward, *The Colored Regulars in the United States Army* (1904; reprint, New York; Arno, 1969), pp. 245–50; Shubert, *On the Trail of the Buffalo Soldier*, pp. 164, 165; also see Bigelow, *Reminiscences*, passim.

67. Among Bigelow's obscure but impressive works are *Mars-Le-Tour and Gravelotte; The Campaign at Chancellorsville; American Policy; World Peace;* and *Breaches of Anglo-American Treaties.* His *Principles of Strategy* (1894; reprint, New York: Greenwood, 1968) drew the most acclaim.

68. Cullum, *Biographical Register*, vol. 3, p. 285; vol. 4, p. 287; vol. 5, p. 263; *AOG Report for 1936*, pp. 103, 104; Heitman; *1990 Register of Graduates*; *New York Times*, March 1, 1936, p. 10.

69. In 1883 Sherman reported that the Indians "had been substantially eliminated from the problems of the army, although there may be sporadic and temporary alarms," which he credited to the army, the immigration of industrious farmers and miners, and the railroads that had gone "forward with the picket line." *New York Times*, November 2, 1883, p. 3.

70. For an analysis of the remarkable progress that the army has made, especially over the past two decades, see Charles C. Moskos and John Sibley Butler, *All That We Can Be: Black Leadership and Racial Integration the Army Way* (New York: Basic Books, 1996).

71. For discussions of the advanced military schools and the growth of military professionalism, see Huntington, *The Soldier and the State*, pp. 237–44, and Weigley, *History of the United States Army*, pp. 273–87, 326.

72. Sherman estimated that 90 percent of all general courts-martial of soldiers were for "simple disorders, which in civil life are punished by a magistrate without a jury." Report of the General of the Army in H. Exec. Doc. 1, 47th Cong., 2d sess., vol. 2 (1882), *Report of the SecWar*, p. 6 (Serial 2091); *New York Times*, November 8, 1882, p. 3. To handle such minor offenses, the *Act of October 1, 1890*, chap. 1259, sec. 1, created summary courts-martial (one officer who served as judge, jury, and counsel), which

had the same jurisdiction as a garrison court. Unnecessary pretrial confinement was prohibited, and an accused had to be brought before the court within twenty-four hours after arrest. If he preferred, his case would be heard by a garrison court. See Winthrop, pp. 493–97.

73. The 1920 Articles of War included a prosecutor and a defense counsel for special courts-martial (which could impose sentences of six months), and permitted an accused to select his counsel. Also, a table was promulgated setting forth the maximum punishments for most offenses. Additionally, commanders could impose limited types of "disciplinary punishments" without trial. *MCM, U.S. Army, 1928* (Washington, D.C.: GPO, 1943), passim. The UCMJ (an act of Congress) or the MCM (an executive order) provides for lawyers as counsel in both general and special courts. Art. 27, UCMJ; *MCM, U.S. 1951,* pp. 9–12; *MCM, U.S. 1984,* pp. II–48, II–49. Each armed force now has an independent judiciary and defense system. See Cox, "The Army, the Courts, and the Constitution," p. 19 n89.

74. F. Lee Bailey, *For the Defense* (New York: Atheneum, 1975). As examples of early advancements in military justice, long before state courts furnished counsel in noncapital cases [*Gideon v. Wainwright,* 372 U.S. 335, 83 S. Ct. 792, 9 L. ed. 2d 799 (1963)], courts-martial defendants received such assistance, and years before civilians were told of their Fifth Amendment rights [*Miranda v. Arizona,* 384 U.S. 436, 86 S. Ct. 1602, 16 L. ed. 2d 694 (1966)], military investigators routinely recited the now-familiar "you have the right to remain silent" litany before questioning any suspect (Art. 31, UCMJ; see MCM, 1951, p. 496).

75. John Bigelow, "Obituary of Robert D. Read, Class of 1877," *Report of the AOG for 1920,* p. 103.

Bibliography

The principal source for this book is the *Personal and Private Journal* of Second Lieutenant John Bigelow, Jr., from October 16, 1877, to February 18, 1878, and from February 5, 1879, to November 14, 1879, in the Manuscript Collections of the U.S. Military Academy Library at West Point, New York, and unbound journal entries and letters home from February 20, 1878, to January 3, 1879, in the Schaffer Library of Union College, Schenectady, New York. To augment and help explain his observations and comments, relevant entries from post returns, organization returns, and other government records and documents have been used, as well as various books, articles, periodicals, manuscripts, and the memoirs, letters, and reports of classmates and other contemporaries. These include:

GOVERNMENT DOCUMENTS AND PUBLICATIONS

Annual Report of the [USMA] *Board of Visitors for the Year 1877.* Washington: GPO, 1877.

Congress of the United States. Acts, Statutes at Large, and United States Code titles and sections.

———. Senate executive documents, miscellaneous documents, and reports.

———. House executive documents, miscellaneous documents, and reports.

———. *Congressional Globe.*

———. *Congressional Record.*

Honeywell, Roy J. *Chaplains of the United States Army.* Washington, D.C.: Dept. of the Army, 1958.

Manual for Courts-Martial, U.S. Army, 1928, Executive Order 4773. Washington, D.C.: GPO, 1943.

Manual for Courts-Martial, United States, 1951, Executive Order 10214. Washington, D.C., 1951.

Manual for Courts-Martial, United States, 1969, Executive Order 11476. Washington, D.C.: GPO, 1969.

Manual for Courts-Martial, United States, 1984, Executive Order 12473. Washington, D.C.: GPO, 1984.

Mackenzie Papers. National Archives and Records Administration, Record Group 94.

Reports of the Secretary of War. Washington, D.C.

Revised Statutes of the United States.

Roster of Non-commissioned Officers of the Tenth U.S. Cavalry, with Regimental Reminiscences. Bryan, Tex.: J. M. Carroll, 1983 reprint of 1897 publication.

Senate Subcommittee on Veterans' Affairs, *Medal of Honor Recipients, 1863–1978.* Washington, D.C.: GPO, 1979.

Sherman, Gen. William Tecumseh. *Papers, General Correspondence and Letterbooks, 1866–1891.* Library of Congress.

Supreme Court of the United States, United States Circuit Courts, and United States District Courts.

United States Air Force, Office of Air Force History. *The American Military on the Frontier.* Proceedings of the 7th Military History Symposium, U.S. Air Force Academy. Edited by James P. Tate. Washington, D.C., 1978.

United States Army, Adjutant General's Office. *Army Officers' Schools: Description of Current Educational and Training Systems.* Washington, D.C.: Dept. of the Army, 1966.

———. Baker, Paul T. "Theoretical Model for Desert Heat Tolerance" (Report EP-98) and "American Negro-White Differences in Heat Toleration" (Report EP-75), Environmental Protection Research Division, QM Research & Engineering Center. Natick, Mass., 1958.

———. Corps of Cadets. *The Cadet Honor Code and System.* West Point. N.Y.: USMA., 1967.

———. Department of Texas. General Orders, Special Orders, and General Court-Martial Orders. San Antonio.

———. Division of the Missouri. General Orders, Special Orders, and General Court-Martial Orders. Chicago.

———. General Court-Martial Orders. Washington, D.C.

———. General Orders and Special Orders. Washington, D.C.

———. Hershler, N. *The Soldier's Handbook.* Washington, D.C., 1900.

———. *Legislative History of the General Staff of the Army, 1775 to 1901.* Washington, D.C.: GPO, 1901.

———. NARA, Record Group 94, Microcopy 617 (Post Returns, 1800–1966).

———. NARA, Record Group 94, Microcopy M929 (Documents Relating to the Military and Naval Service of Blacks Awarded the Congressional Medal of Honor from the Civil War to the Spanish-American War), Roll 2 (Indian Campaigns—U.S. Regular Army).

———. NARA, Record Group 153, T1027 (Records Relating to the Army Career of Henry Ossian Flipper, 1873–1882).

———. NARA, Record Group 153, Microcopy 1105 (Registers of the Records of the Proceedings of the U.S. Army General Courts-Martial, 1809–1890), Roll 7, 1869–1883.

———. NARA, Record Group 391, Microcopy 744 (Records from Regular Army Cavalry Regiments, 1833–1916), Rolls 95 and 96, 10th Cavalry, 1866–1872 and 1873–1880.

———. Office of the Judge Advocate General. Digest of Opinions of The Judge Advocate General.

———. *Official Army Registers.* Washington, D.C.: AGO, 1876 through 1891.

———. *Official Registers of the Officers and Cadets of the U.S. Military Academy.* West Point, N.Y., 1874, 1875, 1876, and 1877.

———. *Outline Descriptions of the Posts in the Military Division of the Missouri, Commanded by Lieutenant General P. H. Sheridan.* Chicago: Military Division of the Missouri, 1876. Facsimile edition Bellevue, Nebr.: Old Army Press, 1969.

———. *Regulations of the Army of the United States and General Orders in Force on the 17th of February, 1881.* Washington, D.C.: GPO, 1881.

———. *Regulations of the Military Academy, July 10, 1818.*

———. *Revised Regulations for the Army of the United States, 1861.* Philadelphia: J. B. Lippincott, 1862.

———. *Revised Regulations for the Army of the United States, 1889.* Washington: GPO, 1889.

———. Risch, Erna. *Quartermaster Support of the Army: A History of the Corps, 1775–1939.* Washington, D.C.: Office of the Quartermaster General, 1962.

———. Slonaker, John. *The U.S. Army and the Negro.* Special Bibliography 2, U.S. Army Military History Research Collection. Carlisle Barracks, Pa.: 1971.

———. Stubbs, Mary Lee, and Stanley Russell Connor. *Armor-Cavalry, Part I: Regular Army and Army Reserve.* Washington, D.C.: GPO, 1969.

———. Surgeon General's Office. *Circular No. 8: A Report on the Hygiene of the United States Army with Descriptions of Military Posts.* Washington, D.C.: GPO, 1875.

United States v. First Lieutenant William H. Beck. General Court-Martial Order 34, AGO, May 30, 1879. NARA, Record Group 153, Case QQ1107 (1879).

United States v. Lieutenant Colonel George A. Custer. General Court-Martial Order 93, AGO, Nov. 20, 1867. NARA, Record Group 153, T1103 (1867).

United States v. Second Lieutenant Henry O. Flipper. General Court-Martial Order 39, AGO, June 14, 1882. NARA, Record Group 153, Case QQ2952, boxes 2032 and 2033, T1027 (1882).

United States v. Captain Andrew Geddes. General Court-Martial Order 66, AGO, Dec. 4, 1879. NARA, Record Group 153, Case QQ1387 (1879), and General Court-Martial Order 64, AGO, Dec. 4, 1880, Case QQ2020 (1880).

United States Court of Military Appeals and Courts of Military Review.

Utley, Robert M. *Fort Davis.* Washington, D.C.: National Park Service Historical Handbook No. 36, 1965.

Winthrop, Col. William. *Military Law and Precedents,* War Dept. Doc. 1001. Washington: AGO, 1886, 2d ed. 1920.

BOOKS

Adolph, E. F., & Associates. *Physiology of Man in the Desert.* New York: Interscience Publishers, 1947.

Altshuyler, Constance Wynn. *Cavalry Yellow and Infantry Blue: Army Officers in Arizona between 1851 and 1886.* Tucson: Arizona Historical Society, 1991.

Ambrose, Stephen E. *Duty, Honor, Country: A History of West Point.* Baltimore: Johns Hopkins Press, 1966.

Amos, Preston E. *Above and Beyond in the West: Black Medal of Honor Winners, 1870–1890.* Washington D.C.: Potomac Corral, The Westerners, 1974.

Armes, Col. George A. *Ups and Downs of an Army Officer.* Washington, D.C.: n.p., 1900.

Association of Graduates of the United States Military Academy. *Annual Reports.* Vols. 63–72. Newburgh, N.Y.: Moore Printing, 1932–1941 (when replaced by *Assembly,* the magazine of the AOG). Vol. 62, Crawfordsville, Ind.: Lakeside Press, 1931; Vols. 1–61, Saginaw, Mich.: Seamann & Peters, and other publishers, 1870–1930.

———. *Registers of Graduates and Former Cadets.*

Athearn, Robert G. *William Tecumseh Sherman and the Settlement of the West.* Norman: University of Oklahoma Press, 1956.

Bailey, F. Lee. *For the Defense.* New York: Atheneum, 1975.

Ball, Eve. *In the Days of Victorio.* Tucson: University of Arizona Press, 1970.

Barnard, Harry. *Rutherford B. Hayes and His America.* New York: Bobbs-Merrill, 1954.

Benet, Stephen Vincent. *A Treatise on the Military Law and the Practice of Courts-Martial.* New York: Van Nostrand, 1862.

Bigelow, John, Jr. *On the Bloody Trail of Geronimo.* Reprinted from articles in *Outing* magazine (March 1886-April 1887). Edited by Arthur Woodward. Los Angeles: Westernlore, 1958.

———. *Garrison Tangles in the Friendless Tenth.* Edited by Douglas C. McChristian. Bryan, Tex.: J. M. Carroll Co., 1985.

———. *Reminiscences of the Santiago Campaign.* New York: Harper & Brothers, 1899.

Bigelow, John, Sr. *Retrospections of an Active Life.* 3 vols. New York: Baker and Taylor, 1909.

Bigelow, Poultney. *Seventy Summers.* 2 vols. New York: Longmans, Green, 1925.

Billings, John B. *Hardtack and Coffee: The Unwritten Story of Army Life.* 1887. Reprint, Williamstown, Mass.: Corner House, 1980.

Black, Lowell D., and Sara H. Black. *An Officer and a Gentleman: The Military Career of Lieutenant Henry O. Flipper.* Dayton: Lora, 1985.

Bourke, John J. *On the Border with Crook.* 1891. Reprint, Lincoln: University of Nebraska Press, 1971.

Bode, Emil A. *A Dose of Frontier Soldiering.* Edited by Thomas T. Smith. Lincoln: University of Nebraska Press, 1994.

Boyd, Frances Anne Mullen. *Cavalry Life in Tent and Field.* 1894. Reprint, Lincoln: University of Nebraska Press, 1982.

Brown, William L. III. *The Army Called It Home: Military Interiors of the 19th Century.* Gettysburg, Pa.: Thomas, 1992.

Bushick, Frank H. *Glamorous Days.* San Antonio: Naylor, 1934.

Byrne, Bernard James. *A Frontier Army Surgeon.* 2d ed. New York: Exposition, 1935.

Cagle, Eldon, Jr. *Quadrangle: The History of Fort Sam Houston.* Austin: Eakin, 1985.

Carlson, Paul H. *"Pecos Bill": A Military Biography of William R. Shafter.* College Station: Texas A&M Press, 1989.

Carroll, John M. *The Black Military Experience in the American West.* New York: Liveright, 1971.

———, comp. *Buffalo Soldiers West.* Fort Collins, Colo.: Old Army Press, 1971.

Cashin, Herschel V. *Under Fire with the Tenth U.S. Cavalry.* 1889. Reprint, New York: Arno Press, 1969.

Catton, Bruce. *Never Call Retreat.* Garden City, N.Y.: Doubleday, 1965.

Cochran, Hamilton. *Noted American Duels and Hostile Encounters.* Philadelphia: Chilton, 1963.

Coffman, Edward M. *The Old Army: A Portrait of the Army in Peacetime, 1784–1898*. New York: Oxford University Press, 1986.

Colton, Ray C. *The Civil War in the Western Territories*. Norman: University of Oklahoma Press, 1959.

Corbusier, William T. *Verde to San Carlos*. Tucson: Dale Stuart King, 1968.

Corner, William. *San Antonio de Bexar*. San Antonio: Bainbridge & Corner, 1890.

Cornish, Dudley Taylor. *The Sable Arm: Negro Troops in the Union Army, 1861–1865*. New York: Longmans, Green, 1956.

Cox, Harvey G. *Military Chaplains*. New York: American Report, 1973.

Cox, Kurt Hamilton, and John P. Langellier. *Longknives: The U.S. Cavalry and Other Mounted Forces, 1845–1942*. Mechanicsburg, Pa.: Stackpole, 1996.

Crane, Charles Judson. *The Experiences of a Colonel of Infantry*. New York: Knickerbocker, 1923.

Creelman, James. *Diaz: Master of Mexico*. New York: D. Appleton, 1911.

Cresap, Bernarr. *Appomattox Commander: The Story of General E. O. C. Ord*. London: Tantivy, 1981.

Crook, George. *General George Crook: His Autobiography*. Edited by Martin F. Schmitt. Norman: University of Oklahoma Press, 1960.

Cruse, Brig. Gen. Thomas. *Apache Days and After*. Edited by Eugene Cunningham. Lincoln: University of Nebraska Press, 1987.

Cullum, George W. *Biographical Register of the Officers and Graduates of the U.S. Military Academy, 1802–1891*. 3d ed. Vols. 1–4. New York and Boston: Houghton Mifflin and Riverside, 1891. Supplement to vol. 4 (1890–1900), vol. 5 (1900–1910), vols. 6A and 6B (1910–1920), vol. 7 (1920–1930), vol. 8 (1930–1940), and vol. 9 (1940–1950), by various publishers.

Custer, Elizabeth B. *Boots and Saddles*. New York: Harper and Row, 1885.

———. *Tenting on the Plains*. 1887. Reprint, Williamstown, Mass.: Corner House, 1973.

Davis, Britton. *The Truth about Geronimo*. 1929. Reprint, Lincoln: University of Nebraska Press, 1976.

Davis, Brig. Gen. George B. *A Treatise on the Military Law of the United States*. New York: John Wiley & Sons, 1909.

Davis, Richard Harding. *The Cuban and Porto Rican Campaigns*. New York: Charles Scribner's Sons, 1898.

DeArment, Robert K. *Knights of the Green Cloth*. Norman: University of Oklahoma Press, 1975.

Delo, David Michael. *Peddlers and Post Traders: The Army Sutler on the Frontier*. Salt Lake City: University of Utah Press, 1992.

Downey, Fairfax. *The Buffalo Soldiers in the Indian Wars*. New York: McGraw-Hill, 1969.

Dunlay, Thomas W. *Wolves for the Blue Soldiers*. Lincoln: University of Nebraska Press, 1982.

Dupuy, R. Ernest. *Where They Have Trod: The West Point Tradition in American Life*. New York: Stokes, 1940.

Eckenrode, H. J. *Rutherford B. Hayes: Statesman of Reunion*. Port Washington, N.Y.: Kennikat, 1930.

Eliot, George Fielding. *Sylvanus Thayer of West Point*. New York: Julian Messner, 1959.

Esposito, Vincent J., ed. *The West Point Atlas of American Wars*. 2 vols. New York: Praeger, 1959.

Faulk, Odie B. *The Geronimo Campaign*. New York: Oxford University Press, 1969.

———. *The U.S. Camel Corps: An Army Experiment*. New York: Oxford University Press, 1976.

Fisher, Odie C. *King Fisher: His Life and Times*. Norman: University of Oklahoma Press, 1966.

Fleishman, Martha, and Carol Joy Justice. *Bugs to Blizzards: An Army Wife at Fort D. A. Russell*. Cheyenne, Wyo.: Wigwam, 1974.

Fleming, Thomas J. *West Point: The Men and Times of the United States Military Academy*. New York: William Morrow, 1969.

Flipper, Henry Ossian. *The Colored Cadet at West Point*. 1878. Reprint, New York: Johnson Reprint, 1968.

Foner, Jack D. *The United States Soldier between Two Wars: Army Life and Reform*. New York: Humanities, 1970.

Foreman, Grant. *Marcy and the Gold Seekers*. Norman: University of Oklahoma Press, 1939.

Forman, Sidney. *West Point: A History of the United States Military Academy*. New York: Columbia University, 1950.

Fougera, Katherine Gibson. *With Custer's Cavalry*. 1940. Reprint, Lincoln: University of Nebraska Press, 1986.

Fowler, Arlen L. *The Black Infantry in the West, 1869–1891*. Westport, Conn.: Greenwood, 1971.

Frazer, Robert W. *Forts of the West*. Norman: University of Oklahoma Press, 1965.

Freeman, Douglas Southall. *Lee's Lieutenants*. 3 vols. New York: Charles Scribner's Sons, 1946.

Friederich, Rudolf J. *Medal of Honor Citation Supplements*. Edited by Philip M. Weber. Chicago: Orders and Medals Society of America, Monograph No. 2, 1968.

Fulton, Deoch, ed. *The Journal of Lieut. Sydenham: 1889, 1890*. New York: New York Public Library, 1940.

Gard, Wayne. *Frontier Justice*. Norman: University of Oklahoma Press, 1949.

Glass, Maj. E. L. N. *The History of the Tenth Cavalry*. Tucson: Acme Printing Co., 1921. Micropublished in *Western Americana: Frontier History of the Trans-Mississippi West, 1550–1900*. New Haven: Research Publications, 1975.

Glatthaar, Joseph T. *Forged in Battle: The Civil War Alliance of Black Soldiers and White Officers*. New York: Free Press, 1990.

Grant, U. S. *Personal Memoirs*. 2 vols. New York: Charles L. Webster, 1886.

Greely, Adolphus W. *Reminiscences of Adventure and Service*. New York: Charles Scribner's Sons, 1927.

Griess, Thomas E., and Jay Luvaas, eds. *The Centennial of the United States Military Academy, 1802–1902*. 2 vols. 1904. Reprint, New York: Greenwood, 1969.

Grinnell, George Bird. *The Fighting Cheyennes*. 1915. Reprint, Norman: University of Oklahoma Press, 1956.

Guerra, Mary Ann Noonan. *The Alamo*. San Antonio: Alamo, 1983.

Haley, J. Evetts. *Fort Concho and the Texas Frontier*. San Angelo, Tex.: Standard-Times, 1952.

Hargrove, Hondon B. *Black Union Soldiers in the Civil War.* Jefferson, N.C.: McFarland, 1988.

Harris, Theodore D., ed. *Negro Frontiersman: The Western Memoirs of Henry O. Flipper.* El Paso: Texas Western College Press, 1963.

Hart, Herbert M. *Pioneer Forts of the West.* Seattle: Superior, 1967.

———. *Old Forts of the Southwest.* New York: Bonanza, 1964.

Heitman, Francis B. *Historical Register and Dictionary of the United States Army.* 2 vols. Washington: GPO, 1903.

Herr, Maj. Gen. John K., and Edward S. Wallace. *The Story of the U.S. Cavalry, 1775–1942.* Boston: Little, Brown, 1953.

Horan, James D. *The Authentic Wild West: The Gunfighters.* New York: Crown, 1976.

Horgan, Paul. *Great River: The Rio Grande.* 2 vols. New York: Rinehart, 1954.

Howe, M. A. DeWolfe. *Home Letters of General Sherman.* New York: Charles Scribner's Sons, 1909.

Huntington, Samuel P. *The Soldier and the State: The Theory and Politics of Civil-Military Relations.* Cambridge: Belknap Press of Harvard University Press, 1957.

Hutton, Paul Andrew. *Phil Sheridan and His Army.* Lincoln: University of Nebraska Press, 1985.

———, ed. *Soldiers West.* Lincoln: University of Nebraska Press, 1987.

James, Vinton Lee. *Frontier and Pioneer Recollections of Early Days in San Antonio.* San Antonio: Artes Gráficas, 1938.

Janowitz, Morris. *The Professional Soldier.* New York: Free Press, 1960.

Johnson, Barry C. *Flipper's Dismissal: The Ruin of Lt. Henry O. Flipper, U.S.A., First Coloured Graduate of West Point.* London: n.p., 1980.

Johnson, Virginia Weisel. *The Unregimented General: A Biography of Nelson A. Miles.* Cambridge, Mass.: Riverside Press, 1962.

Johnson, W. Fletcher. *Life of Wm. Tecumseh Sherman.* Chicago: Donohue, Henneberry, 1891.

Johnson, William R. *Schooled Lawyers: A Study in the Clash of Professional Cultures.* New York: New York University, 1978.

Karsten, Peter, ed. *The Military in America from Colonial Times until the Present.* New York: Free Press, 1980.

Knight, Oliver. *Life and Manners in the Frontier Army.* Norman: University of Oklahoma Press, 1978.

Kroeker, Marvin E. *Great Plains Command: William B. Hazen in the Frontier West.* Norman: University of Oklahoma Press, 1976.

Land, Elizabeth, and Carroll V. Glines, Jr. *The Complete Guide for the Serviceman's Wife.* Boston: Houghton Mifflin, 1956.

Lane, Lydia Spencer. *I Married a Soldier.* 1893. Reprint, Albuquerque: Horn & Wallace, 1964.

Laurence, Mary Leefe. *Daughter of the Regiment: Memoirs of a Childhood in the Frontier Army, 1878–1898.* Edited by Thomas T. Smith. Lincoln: University of Nebraska Press, 1996.

Leckie, Shirley A. *The Colonel's Lady on the Western Frontier: The Correspondence of Alice Kirk Grierson.* Lincoln: University of Nebraska Press, 1989.

Leckie, William H. *The Buffalo Soldiers: A Narrative of the Negro Cavalry in the West.* Norman: University of Oklahoma Press, 1967.

Leckie, William H., and Shirley A. Leckie. *Unlikely Warriors: General Benjamin H. Grierson and His Family.* Norman: University of Oklahoma Press, 1984.

Lee, Irvin H. *Negro Medal of Honor Men.* New York: Dodd, Mead, 1967.

Lewis, Lloyd. *Sherman: Fighting Prophet.* New York: Harcourt, Brace, 1932.

Linn, Brian McAllister. *The U.S. Army and Counterinsurgency in the Philippine War, 1899–1902.* Chapel Hill: University of North Carolina Press, 1989.

Mails, Thomas E. *The People Called Apache.* 1974. Reprint, New York: Promontory, 1981.

Malone, Dumas, ed. *Dictionary of American Biography.* 20 vols. New York: Scribner's Sons, 1933.

Manger, James A. *Men of Mexico.* Milwaukee: Bruce, 1943.

Mansell, *The National Union Catalog of Pre-1956 Imprints.* London: Mansell, 1977.

Marcy, Randolph B. *The Prairie Traveler.* New York: Harper and Brothers, 1859.

Masland, John W., and Laurence I. Radway. *Soldiers and Scholars: Military Education and National Policy.* Princeton: Princeton University Press, 1957.

Maverick, Mary A. *Memoirs of Mary A. Maverick.* Edited by Rena Maverick. 1921. Reprint, Lincoln: University of Nebraska Press, 1989.

McChristian, Douglas C., ed. *Garrison Tangles in the Friendless Tenth* (Journal of John Bigelow, Jr., from November 1884 to May 1885). Bryan, Tex.: J. M. Carroll Co., 1985.

———. *The U.S. Army in the West, 1870–1888.* Norman: University of Oklahoma Press, 1995.

McDonough, James L. *Schofield: Union General in the Civil War and Reconstruction.* Tallahassee: Florida State University Press, 1972.

Miles, Nelson A. *Personal Recollections and Observations of General Nelson A. Miles.* 1896. Reprint, New York: Da Capo, 1969.

Miller, Ray. *Texas Forts.* Austin: Capital, 1986.

Monnett, John H. *The Battle of Beecher Island and the Indian War of 1867–1869.* Niwot, Colo.: University Press of Colorado, 1992.

Morrison, James L., Jr. *"The Best School in the World": West Point, the Pre-Civil War Years, 1833–1866.* Kent, Ohio: Kent University Press, 1986.

Moskos, Charles C., and John Sibley Butler. *All That We Can Be: Black Leadership and Racial Integration the Army Way.* New York: Basic Books, 1996.

Muller, William G. *The Twenty-Fourth Infantry, Past and Present.* Fort Collins, Colo.: Old Army Press, 1972.

Nankivell, John N. *The History of the Twenty-Fifth United States Infantry, 1869–1926.* Fort Collins, Colo.: Old Army Press, 1972.

Nye, Colonel W. S. *Carbine and Lance: The Story of Old Fort Sill.* Norman: University of Oklahoma Press, 1969.

O'Connor, Richard. *Black Jack Pershing.* Garden City, N.Y.: Doubleday, 1961.

Ogle, Ralph Hendrick. *Federal Control of the Western Apaches, 1848–1886.* Albuquerque: University of New Mexico, 1970.

Ord, Edward O. C. *The City of Angels and the City of Saints.* Edited by Neal Harlow. San Marino, Calif.: Huntington Library, 1978.

Pappas, George S. *To the Point: the United States Military Academy, 1802–1902.* Westport, Conn.: Praeger Press, 1993.

Pierce, Michael D. *The Most Promising Young Officer: A Life of Ranald Slidell Mackenzie.* Norman: University of Oklahoma Press, 1993.

Pinkerton, Allan. *Mass Violence in America: Strikers, Communists, Tramps and Detectives.* 1878. Reprint, New York: Arno Press, 1969.

Porter, Joseph C. *Paper Medicine Man: John Gregory Bourke and His American West.* Norman: University of Oklahoma Press, 1986.

Powell, William H. *List of Officers of the Army of the United States from 1779 to 1900.* New York: L. R. Hamersly, 1900.

Pratt, Richard Henry. *Battlefield and Classroom: Four Decades with the American Indian, 1867-1904.* Edited by Robert M. Utley. New Haven, Conn.: Yale University Press, 1964.

Prescott, William H. *The Conquest of Mexico.* 3 vols. Philadelphia: J. B. Lippincott, 1843; revised 1883.

Prucha, Francis Paul. *American Indian Policy in Crisis: Christian Reformers and the Indian, 1865–1900.* Norman: University of Oklahoma Press, 1976.

Raht, Carlysle Graham. *The Romance of Davis Mountains and Big Bend Country.* El Paso: Rahtbooks, 1919.

Ramsdell, Charles. *San Antonio: A Historical and Pictorial Guide.* Austin: University of Texas Press, 1968.

Register of Graduates and Former Cadets. USMA, West Point: AOG, 1990 and earlier years.

Rickey, Don, Jr. *Forty Miles a Day on Beans and Hay.* Norman: University of Oklahoma Press, 1963.

Roberts, David. *Once They Moved Like the Wind.* New York: Simon and Schuster, 1993.

Robinson, Charles M. III. *Pioneer Forts of Texas.* Houston: Gulf, 1986.

———. *Bad Hand: A Biography of General Ranald S. Mackenzie.* Austin: State House Press, 1993.

Rockwell, Wilson. *The Utes: A Forgotten People.* Denver: Sage, 1956.

Rodenbough, Theophilus F., and William L. Haskin, eds. *The Army of the United States: Historical Sketches of Staff and Line.* New York: Maynard, Merrill, 1896.

Roe, Frances. *Army Letters from an Officer's Wife.* 1909. Reprint, Lincoln: University of Nebraska Press, 1981.

Sandoz, Mari. *The Cattlemen.* New York: Hastings House, 1958.

Sargent, Herbert H. *The Campaign of Santiago de Cuba.* Chicago: A. C. McClurg, 1907.

Schirmer, Daniel B. *Republic or Empire: American Resistance to the Philippine War.* Cambridge, Mass.: Schenkman, 1972.

Schubert, Frank N., ed. *On the Trail of the Buffalo Soldier.* Wilmington, Del.: Scholarly Resources, 1995.

Scobee, Barry. *Fort Davis, Texas, 1583–1960.* El Paso: Hill Printing, 1963.

Scott, Robert N. *An Analytical Digest of the Military Laws of the United States.* Philadelphia: J. B. Lippincott, 1873.

Sexton, William Thaddeus. *Soldiers in the Sun: An Adventure in Imperialism.* Freeport, N.Y.: Books for Libraries, 1939.

Sheridan, P. H. *Personal Memoirs.* 2 vols. New York: Charles L. Webster, 1888.

Sherman, William T. *Memoirs of General William T. Sherman.* 2 vols. New York: D. Appleton and Co., 1876.

Shipman, Mrs. O. L. *Taming the Big Bend: A History of the Extreme Western Portion of Texas from Fort Clark to El Paso.* Marfa, Tex.: Mrs.O. L. Shipman, 1926.

Simpson, Harold B. *Cry Comanche: The 2nd U.S. Cavalry in Texas, 1855–1861.* Hillsboro, Tex.: Hill Junior College Press, 1979.

Simpson, Jeffrey. *Officers and Gentlemen.* Tarrytown, N.Y.: Sleepy Hollow, 1982.

Smith, Helena Huntington. *War on the Powder River.* New York: McGraw-Hill, 1966.

Smith, Page. *Trial by Fire.* Vol. 5. New York: McGraw-Hill, 1982.

Sonnichsen, C. L. *The Mescalero Apaches.* Norman: University of Oklahoma Press, 1958.

Splete, Allen P., and Marilyn D. Splete. *Frederick Remington—Selected Letters.* New York: Abbeville Press, 1988.

Sprague, Marshall. *Massacre: The Tragedy at White River.* Boston: Little, Brown, 1957.

Stallard, Patricia Y. *Glittering Misery: Dependents of the Indian Fighting Army.* Fort Collins, Colo.: Old Army Press, 1978.

Stampp, Kenneth M. *The Peculiar Institution: Slavery in the Ante-Bellum South.* New York: Alfred A. Knopf, 1956.

Steffen, Randy. *The Horse Soldier, 1776–1942.* Vol. 2. Norman: University of Oklahoma Press, 1978.

Steward, Chaplain T. G. *The Colored Regulars in the United States Army.* 1904. Reprint, New York: Arno Press, 1969.

Stouffer, Samuel A., et al. *The American Soldier.* Vol. 1. Princeton: Princeton University Press, 1949.

Stout, Joseph A., Jr. *Apache Lightning: The Last Great Battles of the Ojo Calientes.* New York: Oxford University Press, 1974.

Strahorn, Carrie Adell. *Fifteen Thousand Miles by Stage.* 2 vols. 1911. Reprint, Lincoln: University of Nebraska Press, 1988.

Summerhayes, Martha. *Vanished Arizona: Recollections of the Army Life of a New England Woman.* Glorieta, N.Mex.: Rio Grande, 1970.

Tate, James P., ed. *The American Military on the Frontier.* 7th Military History Symposium, U.S. Air Force Academy. Washington, D.C.: Office of Air Force History, 1978.

Terrell, John Upton. *Apache Chronicle.* New York: World, 1972.

Thonhoff, Robert H. *San Antonio Stage Lines, 1847–1881.* El Paso: Texas Western Press, 1971.

Thrapp, Dan L. *Encyclopedia of Frontier Biography.* 3 vols. Glendale, Calif.: Arthur H. Clark, 1988.

———. *The Conquest of Apacheria.* Norman: University of Oklahoma Press, 1967.

———. *Dateline Fort Bowie: Charles Fletcher Lummis Reports on the Apache War.* Norman: University of Oklahoma Press, 1979.

———. *Victorio and the Mimbres Apaches.* Norman: University of Oklahoma Press, 1974.

Todd, Albert. *The Class of '77 at the United States Military Academy.* Cambridge, Mass.: Riverside, 1878.

Toulouse, Joseph H., and James R. Toulouse. *Pioneer Posts of Texas.* San Antonio: Naylor, 1936.

Trachtman, Paul. *The Gunfighters.* New York: Time-Life, 1974.

Utley, Robert M. *Cavalier in Buckskin.* Norman: University of Oklahoma Press, 1988.

———. *Frontier Regulars, 1866–1891.* Bloomington: University of Indiana Press, 1973.

———. *Frontiersmen in Blue.* Lincoln: University of Nebraska Press, 1967.

Vandiver, Frank E. *Black Jack: The Life and Times of John J. Pershing.* College Station: Texas A&M Press, 1977.

Vielé, Teresa Griffin. *Following the Drum: A Glimpse of Frontier Life.* 1858. Reprint, Austin: Steck-Vaughn, 1969.

Wallace, Ernest, ed. "Ranald S. Mackenzie's Official Correspondence Relating to Texas, 1871–1873." *The Museum Journal.* Vols. 9 (1965) and 10 (1966). Lubbock: Texas Technological College.

Warner, Ezra J. *Generals in Blue.* Baton Rouge: Louisiana State University Press, 1964.

Washburn, Wilcomb E. *The American Indian and the United States: A Documentary History.* Vol. 1. New York: Random House, 1973.

Watts, Peter. *A Dictionary of the Old West.* New York: Promontory, 1987.

Weigley, Russell F. *History of the United States Army.* New York: Macmillan, 1967.

Wharfield, H. B. *Apache Indian Scouts.* El Cajon, Calif.: n.p., 1964.

———. *With Scouts and Cavalry at Fort Apache.* Edited by John A. Carroll. Tucson: Arizona Pioneers' Historical Society, 1965.

Whitman, Sidney E. *The Troopers: An Informal History of the Plains Cavalry, 1865-1890.* New York: Hastings House, 1962.

Whittaker, Frederick. *A Complete Life of General George A. Custer.* Vol. 2. 1876, Reprint, Lincoln: University of Nebraska Press, 1993.

Who Was Who in America. Chicago: A. N. Marquis Co., 1943.

Wier, Ester. *Army Social Customs.* Harrisburg, Pa.: Stackpole, 1958.

Willard, James F. *The Union Colony at Greeley, Colorado, 1869–1870.* Boulder, Colo.: W. F. Robinson, 1918.

Williams, Clayton W. *Texas' Last Frontier: Fort Stockton and the Trans-Pecos, 1861–1895.* Edited by Ernest Wallace. College Station: Texas A&M Press, 1982.

Williams, T. Harry. *The History of American Wars from 1745 to 1918.* New York: Alfred A. Knopf, 1985.

Winther, Oscar Osburn. *The Transportation Frontier: Trans-Mississippi West, 1865–1890.* 1964. Reprint, Albuquerque: University of New Mexico Press, 1974.

Woodward, C. Vann. *Reunion and Reaction: The Compromise of 1877 and the End of Reconstruction.* Boston: Little, Brown, 1951.

Wooster, Robert. *Nelson A. Miles and the Twilight of the Frontier Army.* Lincoln: University of Nebraska Press, 1993.

———. *The Military and United States Indian Policy, 1865–1903.* Lincoln: University of Nebraska Press, 1988.

———. *Soldiers, Sutlers, and Settlers: Garrison Life on the Texas Frontier.* College Station: Texas A&M Press, 1987.

Worcester, Donald E. *Apaches, Eagles of the Southwest.* Norman: University of Oklahoma Press, 1979.

Works Progress Administration Writers' Program. *San Antonio: A History and Guide.* San Antonio: Clegg, 1941.

———. *Texas: Guide to the Lone Star State.* New York: Hastings House, 1940.

ARTICLES, PERIODICALS, MONOGRAPHS, AND OTHER MANUSCRIPTS

Andrews, Lt. George. "The 25th Regiment of Infantry." *Journal of the Military Service Institution* 13 (1892).

Andrews, George L. "West Point and the Colored Cadets." *The International Review* 9 (November 1880).

Army and Navy Journal, Washington, D.C.
Assembly, Association of Graduates, USMA.
Bateman, C. C. "The Army Chaplain: His Work and Worth." *Journal of the Military Service Institution* 36 (1905).
Bigelow, Lt. John, Jr. "The Tenth Regiment of Cavalry." *Journal of the Military Service Institution* 13 (1892).
———. "The Moral Training of the Soldier." *Journal of the Military Service Institution* 32 (1903).
Bingham, Theo. A. "Army Uniforms." *Journal of the Military Service Institution* 20 (1897).
Birkhimer, William E. "Abridgment of Military Law." *Journal of the Military Service Institution* 13 (1893).
———. "Comment on Swift's Lyceum Article." *Journal of the Military Service Institution* 20 (1897).
Bourke, Lt. John G. Diaries. Manuscript Collections, U.S. Military Academy.
Brackett, Col. Albert G. "Our Cavalry: Its Duties, Hardships, and Necessities at Our Frontier Posts." *Journal of the Military Service Institution* 4 (1883).
Bradley, Lt. Col. Luther P. Personal Journals, 1866–1910. 10 boxes. U.S. Army Military History Institute, Carlisle Barracks, Pa.
Breeden, James O. "Health in Early Texas: The Military Frontier." *Southwestern Historical Quarterly* 80 (April 1977).
Browne, Mark D. "The Negro in the Indian Wars." *Negro History Bulletin* 14 (March 1951).
Bullard, R. L. "The Negro Volunteer: Some Characteristics." *Journal of the Military Service Institution* 29 (1901).
Burg, Richard B. "Administration of Justice in the Denver People's Courts: 1859–1861." *Journal of the West* 7 (October 1968).
Burkey, Elmer R. "The Thornburgh Battle with the Utes on Milk Creek." *The Colorado Magazine* 12 (January 1936).
Carlson, Paul H. "William R. Shafter Commanding Black Troops." *West Texas Historical Association Yearbook* 50 (1974).
Carroll, John M. "Lieutenant Henry Ossian Flipper." In *The Black Military Experience in the American West.* New York: Livermore, 1971.
Cashion, Ty. "(Gun)smoke Gets in Your Eyes." *Southwestern Historical Quarterly* 99 (July 1995).
Cass, Ed. "Sylvanus Thayer 1817–1833: A Personal Glimpse." *Assembly* 40, no. 4 (March 1982).
Cleary, P. J. A., and E. Alexander. "Fort Stockton, Texas." In *Circular No. 8,* Surgeon General's Office (1875).
Clum, John P. "The Apaches." *New Mexico Historical Review* 4 (1929).
———. "Apache Misrule: A Bungling Agent Sets the Military Arm in Motion." *New Mexico Historical Review* 5 (1930).
Conyers, James Ernest. "Selected Aspects of the Phenomenon of Negro Passing." Ph.D. diss., Washington State University, 1962.
Cox, Walter T. III. "The Army, the Courts, and the Constitution: The Evolution of Military Justice." *Military Law Review* (Fall 1987).
Crimmins, Col. M. L. "Old Fort Duncan: a Frontier Post." *Frontier Times* (1937–1938).

Crook, Brig. Gen. George. Papers. U.S. Army Military History Institute, Carlisle Barracks, Pa.

———. "The Apache Problem." *Journal of the Military Service Institution* 7 (1886).

DeMorgan, John. "Barbaric Military Punishments." *The Green Bag* 10 (1898).

Dinges, Bruce J. "The Irrepressible Captain Armes: Politics and Justice in the Indian-Fighting Army." *Journal of the West* 32 (April 1993).

———. "Benjamin Grierson." In *Soldiers West*, edited by Paul Andrew Hutton. Lincoln: University of Nebraska Press, 1987.

———. "The Victorio Campaign of 1880: Cooperation and Conflict on the United States-Mexico Border." *New Mexico Historical Review* 62 (January 1987).

———. "Scandal in the Tenth Cavalry: A Fort Sill Case History, 1874." *Arizona and the West* 28 (Summer 1986).

———. "The Court-Martial of Lieutenant Henry O. Flipper." *The American West* 9 (January 1972).

Dixon, James W. "Across the Plains with General Hancock." *Journal of the Military Service Institution* 7 (March 1886).

Dodge, Richard I. "The Enlisted Soldier." *Journal of the Military Service Institution* 8 (1887).

———. "Comment on McAnaney's Desertion Article." *Journal of the Military Service Institution* 11 (1890).

Dorst, Joseph H. "Ranald Slidell Mackenzie." *Journal of the United States Cavalry Association* 10, no. 39 (December 1897).

Ferguson, S. W. "West Point before the War." *Assembly* 43, no. 3 (December 1954).

Field, William T. "Fort Duncan and Old Eagle Pass." *Texas Military History* 6 (Summer 1967).

Foner, Jack D. "The Socializing Role of the Military." In *The American Military on the Frontier*. Proceedings of the 7th Military History Symposium, U.S. Air Force Academy, 1976.

Gamble, Richard Dalzell. "Garrison Life at Frontier Military Posts, 1830–1860." Ph.D. diss., University of Oklahoma, 1956.

Gatewood, Charles B. "Campaigning against Victorio in 1879." *The Great Divide* (April 1894).

Gibbon, John. "Law in the Army." *Journal of the Military Service Institution* 1 (1880).

Graham, Stanley S. "Life of the Enlisted Soldier on the Western Frontier, 1815–1845." Ph.D. diss., North Texas State University, 1972.

Hanson, Joseph Mills. "Ranald Slidell Mackenzie." *The Cavalry Journal* 43 (January-February 1934).

Hardin, E. E. "Army Messing." *Journal of the Military Service Institution* 6 (1885).

"A History of the Judge Advocate General's Corps." *The Army Lawyer* (1975).

Holabird, S. A. "Army Clothing." *Journal of the Military Service Institution* 2 (1882).

Holden, Edward S. "Training of Cadets for the U.S. Army." *Journal of the Military Service Institution* 34 (1904).

Hough, Maj. Alfred. Papers. Western History Department, University of Colorado (Boulder).

Hovey, H. W. "The 24th Regiment of Infantry." *Journal of the Military Service Institution* 15 (1894).

Hutchinson, Grote. "The 9th Regiment of Cavalry." *Journal of the Military Service Institution* 16 (1895).

Larremore, Wilbur. "American Courts-Martial." *The North American Review* 177 (October 1903).

Lenti, John Michael. "The Black in Gray—Can West Point Attract the Black." Master's thesis, Army Command and General Staff College, 1972.

Leonard, Thomas C. "Red, White, and the Army Blue." In *The Military in America*, edited by Peter Karsten. New York: Free Press, 1980.

McAnaney, William D. "Desertion in the United States Army." *Journal of the Military Service Institution* 10 (1889).

McChristian, Douglas C. "Grierson's Fight at Tenaja de las Palmas." *Red River Valley Historical Review* (Winter 1982).

McClung, Donald R. "Second Lieutenant Henry O. Flipper: A Negro Officer on the West Texas Frontier." *West Texas Historical Association Yearbook* 47 (1971).

———. "Henry O. Flipper: First Negro Officer in the United States Army." Master's thesis, East Texas State University, 1970.

Menger Hotel. "The Grand Lady of the Plaza: A History of the Menger Hotel." N.p., n.d.

Merritt, Wesley. "Three Indian Campaigns." *Harper's New Monthly Magazine* 80 (April 1890).

Michie, P. S. "Education in Its Relation to the Military Profession." *Journal of the Military Service Institution* 1 (1880).

Miles, Susan. "Fort Concho in 1877." *West Texas Historical Association Yearbook* 35 (October 1959).

Miller, Juanita. "White Negroes." *Sociology and Social Research* 12 (May-June 1928).

Moody, Marshall D. "The Meeker Massacre." *The Colorado Magazine* 30 (January 1953).

Myres, Sandra L. "Romance and Reality on the American Frontier: Views of Army Wives." *Western Historical Quarterly* 13 (October 1982).

———. "A Woman's View of the Texas Frontier, 1874: The Diary of Emily K. Andrews." *Southwestern Historical Quarterly* 86 (July 1982).

———. "The Ladies of the Army—Views of Western Life." In *The American Military on the Frontier.* Proceedings of the 7th Military History Symposium, U.S. Air Force Academy (1976).

The Nation.

New York Post. "The Negro as Soldier and Officer." *Journal of the Military Service Institution* 29 (1901).

New York Times.

O'Brisen, Emily Boynton. "Army Life at Fort Sedgwick, Colorado." *The Colorado Magazine* 6 (September 29, 1929).

O'Connell, J. J. "Kriegspiel of Vinturnus." *Journal of the Military Service Institution* 4 (1883).

Ogle, Ralph H. "The Apaches and the Government, 1870's." *New Mexico Historical Review* 33 (April 1958).

Olch, Peter D. "Medicine in the Indian-Fighting Army, 1866–1890." *Journal of the West* 21 (July 1982).

Otis, Elwell S. "The Army in Connection with the Labor Riots of 1877." *Journal of the Military Service Institution* 6 (1885).

Pettit, James S. "The Proper Military Instruction for Our Officers." *Journal of the Military Service Institution* 20 (1897).
Pope, J. W. "Military Penology." *Journal of the Military Service Institution* 12 (1891).
———. "Desertion." *Journal of the Military Service Institution* 37 (1905).
Porter, Kenneth W. "The Seminole Negro-Indian Scouts, 1870–1881." *Southwestern Historical Quarterly* 55 (January 1952).
R. E. I. "Army Theatricals." *Journal of the Military Service Institution* 6 (1884).
Reilly, Henry J. "How Army Cooking Can Be Improved." *Journal of the Military Service Institution* 6 (1885).
Rideing, William H. "Life at a Frontier Post." *Appleton's Journal* 15 (April 29, 1876).
Rollman, Robert O. "Of Crimes, Courts-Martial, and Punishment—A Short History of Military Justice." *Air Force Law Review* 11 (Spring 1969).
Sellen, Keith L. "The United States Military Academy Law Department, Yesterday and Today: Purpose, Challenge, Reward." *Federal Bar News and Journal* 37 (May 1990).
Shafter, William R. "Shafter's Explorations in Western Texas, 1875." *West Texas Historical Association Yearbook* 9 (October 1933).
Sheridan, P. H. "Hell and Texas." *Southwestern Historical Quarterly* 45 (October 1945).
Sherman, William T. "Military Law." *Journal of the Military Service Institution* 1 (1879 and 1880).
Spofford, Harriet. "San Antonio de Bexar." *Harper's New Monthly Magazine* 55 (June to November 1877).
Steele, Matthew F. "Some Notes on the Clothing and Equipment of the Soldier for Service in the Tropics." *Journal of the Military Service Institution* 29 (1901).
Steinmetz, W. R. "Fort Duncan, Texas." In *Circular No. 8*, Surgeon General's Office (1875).
Stewart, Miller J. "A Touch of Civilization: Culture and Education in the Frontier Army." *Nebraska History* 65 (Summer 1984).
———. "Army Laundresses: Ladies of the 'Soap Suds Row.'" *Nebraska History* 61 (Winter 1980).
Stratton, David H. "The Army and the Gospel in the West." *The Western Humanities Review* 8 (Summer 1954).
Streett, William B. "West Point and the Rise of American Science in the 19th Century." *Assembly* 55, no. 2 (November/December 1996).
Swift, Eban. "The Lyceum at Fort Agawam." *Journal of the Military Service Institution* 20 (1897).
Swift, Henry. "Drunkenness in the Army." *Journal of the Military Service Institution* 30 (1901).
Temple, Frank M. "Discipline and Turmoil in the Tenth U.S. Cavalry." *West Texas Historical Association Yearbook* 43 (1982).
Thompson, Edwin N. "The Negro Soldiers on the Frontier: A Fort Davis Case Study." *Journal of the West* (April 1968).
Thybony, Scott. "Against All Odds, Black Seminoles Won Their Freedom." *Smithsonian* 22 (August 1991).
Utley, Robert M. "Pecos Bill on the Texas Frontier." *The American West* 6 (January 1969).
———. "Arizona Vanquished." *The American West* 6 (November 1969).

Walker, Henry P. "The Enlisted Soldier on the Frontier." In *The American Military on the Frontier.* Proceedings of the 7th Military History Symposium, U.S. Air Force Academy (1976).

Wallace, Edward S. "General John Lapham Bullis: Thunderbolt of the Texas Frontier." *Southwestern Historical Quarterly* 55 (July 1953).

Wallace, Ernest, ed. "History in West Texas." *West Texas Historical Association Yearbook* 47 (1971).

———. "General Ranald Slidell Mackenzie: Indian Fighting Cavalryman." *Southwestern Historical Quarterly* 56 (June 1953).

Wanner, Ezra J. "A Black Man in the Long Gray Line." *American History Illustrated* 6 (January 1970).

Wherry, William M. "The Command of the Army." N.p. Pamphlet, 1879.

White, Lonnie J. "The Hancock and Custer Expeditions of 1867." *Journal of the West* (July 1966).

Wiener, Frederick Bernays. "Courts-Martial and the Bill of Rights: The Original Practice." *Harvard Law Review* 72 (1958).

———. "Service without Pay." *The Infantry Journal* 58, no. 2 (February 1946).

Wisser, John P. "Practical Instruction of Officers at Posts." *Journal of the Military Service Institution* 9 (1888).

Wolkomir, Richard. "With Mallets and Forethought, Croquet Is Back." *Smithsonian* 23 (October 1992).

Wooster, Robert. "The Army and the Politics of Expansion: Texas and the Southwestern Borderlands, 1870–1886." *Southwestern Historical Quarterly* 93 (October 1989).

Index

Numbers in *italics* refer to photographs, maps, or drawings